Deutsche Gesellschaft
für Auswärtige Politik e.V.

The German Council on Foreign Relations (DGAP e. V.) is Germany's national foreign policy network. As an independent, non-partisan, and non-profit organization, we actively participate in the political decision-making process and promote the understanding of German foreign policy and international relations. The aims of the Council are to contribute to international cooperation and understanding, to inform the public about questions on global politics, and to strengthen the foreign policy community in Germany.

For these purposes the DGAP offers foreign policy makers and experts a platform for discussion in Germany. The DGAP operates a research institute and the only public library in Germany specializing on foreign affairs and publishes the monthly journal *Internationale Politik*, studies, analyses, and comments. All opinions expressed in its publications are those of the authors.

Research Institute of the DGAP e. V. | Rauchstraße 17/18 | 10787 Berlin | Germany
phone: +49 (0)30 25 42 31-0 | fax: +49 (0)30 25 42 31-16 | info@dgap.org | www.dgap.org

Cornelius Adebahr

Learning and Change in European Foreign Policy

The Case of the EU Special Representatives

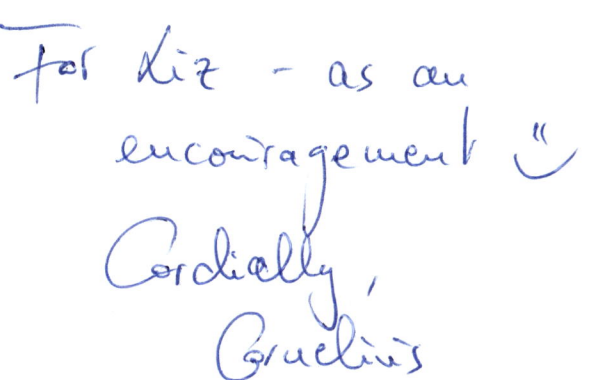

For Liz – as an
encouragement :).
Cordially,
Cornelius

This dissertation and its publication received generous funding from the Volkswagen Foundation under the "European Foreign and Security Policy Studies" Programme of Volkswagen Foundation, Compagnia di San Paolo, and Riksbankens Jubileums-fond.

Image on the cover page:
Geographical Reach of EUSR Mandates. World map showing the EU's 27 member states in dark blue and the areas covered by an EUSR in different blue and grey tones; © Johannes Bister and Simon Burkhardt 2009

DGAP-Schriften zur Internationalen Politik

Die Deutsche Nationalbibliothek verzeichnet diese Publikation in der Deutschen Nationalbibliografie; detaillierte bibliografische Daten sind im Internet über http://www.d-nb.de abrufbar.

Die Deutsche Nationalbibliothek lists this publication in the Deutsche Nationalbibliografie; detailed bibliographic data is available in the Internet at http://www.d-nb.de .

ISBN 978-3-8329-4721-7

Zugl.: Berlin, Freie Universität, Diss., 2008

1. Auflage 2009
© Nomos Verlagsgesellschaft, Baden-Baden 2009. Printed in Germany. Alle Rechte, auch die des Nachdrucks von Auszügen, der fotomechanischen Wiedergabe und der Übersetzung, vorbehalten. Gedruckt auf alterungsbeständigem Papier.

To my Family

Contents

Chapter 6: Institutional and Policy Change based on Organizational Learning

Acknowledgements

Academic research is a collaborative exercise; a study about a collective cognitive process such as learning even more so. Thus I owe great thanks to the many people that supported me in the process of writing this dissertation.

First of all, I thank Prof. Dr. Eberhard Sandschneider for accepting to supervise this research and for offering me such an inspiring working environment at the Research Institute of the German Council on Foreign Relations in Berlin. He was always approachable when I needed support or advice. I would also like to thank Prof. Dr. Michael Zürn for co-supervising my work despite his many other pressing needs.

Over the years, I was glad to receive, through feedback from presentations and conversations, precious stimuli and encouragement from fellow researchers: at the 2006 Graduate Student Conference of the BMW Center for German and European Studies of the Edmund A. Walsh School of Foreign Service at Georgetown University; at the 2006 Triennial Congress of the German Association for Political Science, with special thanks to Klaus-Dieter Wolf for his helpful comments on the draft contribution to the congress publication; at the 2007 Workshop on Learning and its application to EU foreign and security policy, organized by the Centre for the Study of International Governance of Loughborough University; at the 2007 Conference of the Standing Group on International Relations as well as the 2008 Joint Sessions of the European Consortium for Political Research with special thanks to Rafael Biermann, Richard Whitman and Stefan Wolff; and at the 2008 GARNET Conference "The EU in International Affairs."

In particular, I am grateful for the friendly support and useful advice from colleagues and fellow students from the European Foreign and Security Policy Studies Program (special thanks representatively to Stephanie Hofmann, Ana Juncos, and Alessandro Rotta); from the Research Institute as well as Library and Documentation Centre of the German Council on Foreign Relations (special thanks representatively to Henning Riecke, Simon Koschut, Tilmann Chladek, Martin Koopmann, and Verena Schrader); from the European Policy Centre (special thanks representatively to Antonio Missiroli); from the London School of Economics' IR department (special thanks representatively to Karen E. Smith and Ulrich Sedelmeier), and from Giovanni Grevi and Roy Ginsberg.

Research on the EU Special Representatives would not have been possible without the more than 50 individuals who, in personal conversations, shared with me their time and insights. In particular, I would like to thank the EUSRs in office Erwan Fouéré, Kalman Miszei, Pierre Morel, Marc Otte, Peter Semneby, Roeland van de Geer, and Francesc Vendrell for finding a slot in their busy schedules to give support to academic research, as well as Cesira d'Aniello, Tania von Uslar, and Thomas Schieb for their exceptional succor.

The Volkswagen Foundation generously granted financial support for this project. Special thanks go to Alfred Schmidt for his affable support as well as to the Compagnia di San Paolo and the Riksbankens Jubileumsfond for providing a stimulating research program.

My heartfelt thanks are owed to the friends and family who supported my dissertation and at the same time reminded me of worldly delights. I am grateful to Simon Burkhardt and Johannes Bister for their vivid illustrations of where the EUSRs actually work. I would like to especially thank Susan Dortants, Katja Patzwald, Beate Satory, Ursula Schröder, and Karen and Jost Brökelmann for helping to improve the clarity of argument and the study's appearance by painstakingly reading, commenting, and editing it. Needless—though appropriate—to say that solely I am responsible for the remaining errors and omissions in this book.

Finally, Maria—thank you for being with me.

Berlin, 21 March 2009   *Cornelius Adebahr*

There is nothing more difficult to take in hand,
more perilous to conduct, or more uncertain in its success,
than to take the lead in the introduction of a new order of things.

Inscription from the tomb of Niccolò Machiavelli,
Special Envoy of the Republic of Florence (1499–1512)

Introduction and Main Argument

Two observations marked the outset of this study: European politicians like to explain the rise of the European Union (EU) as a foreign policy actor after the end of the Cold War by alluding to profound 'learning experiences', in particular to learning from the EU's failure in the Balkans in the 1990s.[1] At the same time, the academic debate in political science and its subfield International Relations (IR) widely disregards the possibility of learning not only in, but also of organizations. Instead, much of the research trying to explain the development of European foreign policy[2] is directed at external events or crises that changed the international or regional order, or to significant transformations in major member states that trigger change at the EU level.[3]

This study makes an attempt to treat the notion of learning analytically and investigates the possibilities of whether and how organizations may learn: Can they learn from their own or others' experience? If so, what are the mechanisms and conditions of such organizational learning (OL)? As a case to provide potential answers to these questions, the study focuses on the evolving role of Special Representatives (or Envoys) in the EU's foreign policy. Only once an analytical framework to answer these questions has been established and tested on a number of cases within European foreign policy, the

---

1   A speech by Javier Solana, the EU's High Representative for CFSP, given in 2005, is exemplary, as he says: "Finally, there is a lesson for European foreign policy. There is no point denying that the war in Bosnia and Herzegovina was a dismal low for Europe. But look where we are today. We are united around a single, comprehensive strategy for the region. The Western Balkans are now one of the success stories in EU foreign policy. [...] Indeed, this points to one of Europe's key strengths. After every setback, we re-group, learn the lessons and emerge stronger" (Solana 2005a, 4-5); similarly on Bosnia and Herzegovina, see Bildt 1997.

2   European foreign policy encompasses both the intergovernmental Common Foreign and Security Policy (CFSP), the External Relations of the Community (Relex) and the European elements of national foreign policy of the Member states (White 2001, 39). For reasons of capacity, this study will limit itself to the first two areas.

3   The latter explanation (i.e. by internal developments) usually builds on the shift in British and French security policy in 1998, publicly declared at a bilateral summit in Saint Malo that was followed by the creation of ESDP (Biscop 1999; Howorth 2000 and 2005b). Others focus on processes of inter-state bargaining (Moravcsik 1993) or Europeanization (Tonra 2001). With regard to the former explanation (i.e. by external shocks), the most prominent cases usually mentioned are the demise of communism in 1989/91, the wars in Bosnia and Herzegovina (1992–95) and Kosovo (1998–99), the terrorist attacks in the United States of 2001, and the intra-EU dispute about the American-led intervention in Iraq in 2003 (Allen/Smith 1998b, 54; Nuttall 2000, 9-10; cf. Ginsberg 2001; Weidenfeld 2006).

actual contribution of learning to the overall development of the EU can be gauged. Thus, looking through the lens of learning theories provides a change of the analytical perspective; it ought not be treated as a mono-causal explanation but rather as a credible contributing factor alongside other (e.g. interests-, values- or events-based) approaches.

Against this backdrop, this study centres on two topics: the learning of a political body like the EU, and the EU Special Representatives (EUSRs) as an expression of European foreign policy. I will briefly introduce the two and their relationship for this work.

The fact that, over the past fifteen years, European foreign policy has witnessed rapid and substantial growth is undisputed. Formerly vested with only a loose body coordinating national foreign policies, the European Union has turned into an international actor involved in the entire spectrum of foreign policy activities: From engaging in diplomatic negotiations with Iran about its nuclear program to conducting military operations in Congo, from gradually stabilizing the European neighbourhood to providing development assistance to more than 160 countries. While there are still many insufficiencies in terms of effectiveness and outcome of its policies (and thus the EU's overall relevance on the global scene), the EU's actual actorness, i.e. its ability to act in international affairs, is hardly questioned, as the many scholarly works that have appeared in recent years show.[4] The EU's newly gained international importance is most visible in the rising number of operations under its European Security and Defence Policy (ESDP), which is an integral part of the Union's Common Foreign and Security Policy (CFSP). From the EU's first ever military operation in Macedonia and its police mission in Bosnia and Herzegovina in early 2003, their number has risen to a total of 20 (ongoing or completed) missions.[5]

A less-known area of activities is the work of the EUSRs. Born from a provision of the 1993 Maastricht Treaty, they nevertheless predate the main CFSP institutions like the High Representative and instruments such as ESDP operations. EUSRs are appointed by the Council of Ministers (or Council, in short) to represent the Union and its foreign policies in certain crisis regions around the world. Their mission is targeted to ensure a coherent EU presence and effective policy implementation. The number of EUSRs has risen from two in 1996 and four in 2001 to eleven at present, extensively covering the major regions of concern of the EU: the Western Balkans, Central Africa and the Middle East, as well as the Caucasus and Central Asia.

---

4   The following monographs and edited books can give an idea of the richness of research in this field: Bretherton/Vogler 1999, 2006; Cameron 1999; Carlsnaes et al. 2004; Carlsnaes/Smith 1994; Elgström/Smith 2006; Ginsberg 2001; Hill/Smith 2000; Hill/Smith 2005; Krahmann 2003; Mahncke et al. 2004; Nuttall 2000; Rhodes 1998; Smith 2002a; Smith 2003; Smith 2004; Tonra/Christiansen 2004; White 2001; Whitman 1998; Zielonka 1998.

5   As of 27 July 2008. For a concise summary of the EU's military, police, and rule of law missions until 2007, see Ginsberg/Smith 2007, 275–280. For an up-to-date overview of ongoing and completed ESDP operations, see: <http://www.consilium.europa.eu/cms3_fo/showPage.asp?id=268&lang=en&mode=g>.

It is not only the EUSRs' institutional age and their geographical scope as well as their focus on security policy and crisis management that make them an exemplary case for the EU's foreign policy. The envoy is one of the oldest instruments of inter-state diplomacy; what is more, being equipped with diplomatic representatives and having them recognized by other entities can be regarded as a sign of statehood, or at least actorness (see section 2.1). An EU Special Representative is, thus, by default not much different from the envoys of states (such as the United States) or international organizations (such as the United Nations); indeed, the EU may plausible have learned from the latter when setting up its own envoys. In addition, EUSRs have—metaphorically as well as practically speaking—become 'a face and a voice' of the European Union (EU Council Secretariat 2005, 1), embodying the Union's fundamental values (see subsection 2.2.3). Still, and surprisingly, hardly any scholarly work on Europe's envoys can be found.[6]

Given that the EU is a foreign policy actor with reasonably young institutions, a practical 'learning by doing' approach can somewhat be expected.[7] This should be particularly true for the EUSRs that emerged early in the lifetime of CFSP but remained on its fringes for a long time. Nevertheless, the 'business' of foreign policy seems too serious to merely try and err. References to learning by politicians could therefore mean only one of two things: Either it is a post-hoc euphemism for weak performance. Or there may be some truth to the word and the EU has learned some serious lessons.

To look at European foreign policy and, more concretely, the EUSRs through the learning lens can be justified on various grounds. First of all, a limited number of scholars corroborate the view of those politicians whether from the national or EU level that refer to the Union's 'lessons' from the Balkans.[8] Some even see the development of the European Union as a whole as "the most obvious supporting example" of the occurrence of international learning (Knopf 2003, 197).[9] Yet, it is one thing to claim that learning has occurred "but quite another to specify when certain actors learn what types of lessons from what events" (Levy 1994, 280). More importantly, while factors such as changes in the international or domestic distribution of power are certainly plausible

---

6   The Chaillot paper "Pioneering foreign policy: the EU Special Representatives" (Grevi 2007) was the first to fill this void. Later, a policy paper investigating the role of EU envoys in the Balkans appeared (Jaanson 2008). Previously, a study on the role of the EUSR for the Middle East Peace Process was published in Germany (Dietl 2005).

7   For a comparison of the difference between everyday and professional use of the word 'learning', cf. Breslauer/Tetlock 1991a, 5-8.

8   "[The] EU clearly has learned from the Balkans case, largely in the form of several institutional changes [...]" (Smith 2004, 196). Though critical on the substantive part of learning, the June 2008 issue of the monthly journal 'Internationale Politik,' (titled 'Balkan Blues: Europe's unlearned lessons') uses the same vocabulary (cf. Internationale Politik 2008).

9   However, Knopf does not analyze the development of the EU using his model of international learning (explained later, see subsection 3.1.2) but merely makes an illustrative example of it. Interestingly, with regard to the EU's Eastern enlargement and its neighbourhood policy as two contexts located between internal and external policies, it is rather academics than policy-makers that speak of a transfer of lessons; for a thorough evaluation, see Kelley 2006.

triggers of development in EU foreign policy, they fail to indicate how the EU reacted and why it did so in the way it did and not in any other way. Reference to these factors therefore remains an indeterminate explanation of institutional change in general and of the development in EU foreign policy in particular (Legro 2007, 11). Learning, in contrast, offers some conceptually fruitful insights by examining the internal processes of how an actor reacts to such outside changes. By looking at how individual cognitive processes shaped by the organizational culture become institutionalized, learning offers a link between individual performance and organizational development. Thus, because it takes into account this 'subcutaneous' level, OL can better explain the way in which an organization reacts than other approaches like path dependence (Pierson 2000) or incrementalism (cf. Hall 1993, 280).

OL's explanatory power has been revealed in management studies and sociology; in contrast, most theoretical approaches to institutional change in the EU do not give credit to the learning approach. Be it with a functionalist (Haas 1958, Schmitter 2004), realist (Hoffmann 2000), intergovernmentalist (Moravcsik 1993), or constructivist (Checkel 2005, Tonra 2001) orientation, many authors disregard the question of how an institution or organization can learn from its environment and, in particular, from its own actions.[10] In contrast, countless volumes have been published in the field of management science on how companies can better adapt to a changing environment and can learn from their own mistakes as well as from their competitors' successes (or vice versa) (Cyert/March 1963; Senge 1990). Similarly, theories of organizational (or institutional) learning have a long history in the fields of sociology (Argyris 1992; Dierkes et al. 2001; March/Olsen 1976), although less with a focus on efficiency but rather with a concern for questions of legitimacy and power (Barnett/Finnemore 1999, 702). The explanatory potential, displayed by these two disciplines, should not remain untapped by political science—if only to tell us whether the European policy-makers' talk of 'learning lessons' is in fact more than just rhetoric: whether actual learning has been taking place at the level of EU institutions.

The obvious neglect of learning as an explanatory factor, let alone as a prescriptive model is in itself puzzling: Given that political scientists hardly investigate the possibility that learning does take place in international institutions, the occurrence of actual organizational learning becomes a least likely case. This would therefore strongly substantiate the claim to take learning into consideration as one explanatory factor. Assuming for a moment that, in the case of the European Union, learning would take place, a second puzzle emerges: Apparently, the EU has always learned the same lesson, i.e. to expand its foreign policy. Could not the war in Bosnia have 'taught' the EU that the North Atlantic Treaty Organization (NATO), of which most EU members were also part, was the more appropriate alliance to deal with such crises? Similarly, could the EU not have 'learned' from Kosovo about the benefits of a particular burden sharing with the United

---

10 Jeffrey Checkel does analyze a process he calls 'social learning' (cf. Checkel 2001). This process, however, has more to do with how individuals adapt within an organization ('socialization') than with what the organization itself can learn via these individuals.

States—here: military operations, there: post-conflict reconstruction—rather than trying to build up its own defence force?[11]

Unfortunately, neither sociology nor management science has so far produced a generally accepted definition of organizational learning.[12] This may be one of the reasons why learning approaches have not found their way into political science in general, or IR or European integration theory in particular.[13] Another may be confusion about terminology, which is not uncommon when talking about a transfer of a theoretical approach from one discipline to another. Sociologists prefer 'organizational learning' as a broader term encompassing all sorts of organizations (including firms, groups etc.). Political scientists, on the other hand, may give preference to the term 'institutional learning.' In their discipline, the 'institution' is the more extensive expression covering all sorts of conventions, organizations, regimes, and networks.[14] In addition, authors seldom give an explanation for their use of either term, organizational or institutional learning.[15] Precisely because this analysis looks at learning in a concrete organization rather than an abstract institution like a regime, a convention, or a network, the term 'organizational learning' is adopted here.

Jargon aside; this work represents a first attempt to fill the theoretical 'learning gap' in political science and IR. The study's epistemological interest (Erkenntnisinteresse) is the basic question whether the EU as an organization did learn, and if so, why, how, and what? From this follow two research questions, one more general and theoretically framed, the other more specific and policy-oriented. First, what are the mechanisms and conditions of organizational learning at the EU level, i.e. the question of why (causal mechanisms) and how (scope conditions) learning takes place? Finding an answer to

---

11   Some authors argue that the military role "remains better performed by other actors in the international arena" (Rhodes 1998, 9); or that increased militarization of CFSP could "hardly have been the right lesson" from the "debacle in Bosnia and Herzegovina and Kosovo" (Rohloff 1999, 42; author's translation).

12   Both Breslauer 1991, 825, LaPalombara 2001b, 557, and Levy 1994, 280-81 regret this fact in a similar way.

13   Cf. Bennett/Howlett 1992, 276. Hardly any standard volume on political science or International Relations, for that matter, treats learning as a distinct field of study, the notable exception being Etheredge's (1981) article "Can Governments Learn?" in Long's 'Handbook of Political Behavior'.

14   See Simmons/Martin 2002, 192-4, Hasenclever/Mayer 2007, 14, and Csigó 2006, 65; cf. the two standard definitions of institutions or regimes in political science: Institutions are "persistent and connected sets of rules (formal and informal) that prescribe behavioral roles, constrain activity, and shape expectations" (Keohane 1989, 3); regimes "can be defined as sets of implicit or explicit principles, norms, rules, and decision-making procedures around which actors' expectations converge in a given area of international relations" (Krasner 1983, 2). Others disagree and claim that the "scholarly literature lacks a widely accepted definition of international institutions" (Duffield 2007, 1).

15   An exception is Haas/Haas 1995, 259: "**Organizational** learning is the process by which the learning becomes ingrained in [International Organizations]. **Institutional** learning is the broader international process by which state entities and other actors learn and assimilate some of these lessons" (emphasis added).

these questions would provide a reason why organizational learning should be considered in the explanation of European foreign policy at all. This also leads to the second, the policy-oriented question: What has the EU learned, from the years of EUSR activity, about the use of this instrument? After all, social science's task is also to think about alternative political solutions (Sandschneider 1996a, 29), i. e. to occupy a middle ground between what is commanded by politics and a theory-only approach that is distant from the political world.

The study therefore has two aims, one academic and the other policy-oriented.

- On the academic side, it aims to contribute to the development of middle-range theories of learning (a theoretical blind spot) by offering an explanatory and evaluative study of the EU Special Representatives (an empirical blind spot).
- On the policy side, it aims to present the EUSRs as an important foreign policy instrument of the EU that is symptomatic of the Union's strategic development.

This study does not offer a single theory of OL or test learning theories in order to prove or disprove them. Instead, by introducing learning theories into the scholarly debate about European foreign policy, it strives to make these theories available for pluralistic, multidisciplinary research. Delineating what exactly the EU has learned in its foreign policy, and how it has achieved this, the study contributes to turning "vague notions such as learning" (Zürn/Checkel 2005, 1048) into a more tangible analytical category. Once established as an analytical category, OL can then properly be taken into account as one factor of change with regard to a certain policy field, and its interaction with other factors—such as power relations, international norms, or domestic groups—can be thoroughly analyzed in a broader theoretical framework.

Because existing approaches do not provide clear-cut hypotheses, the study follows an exploratory (or abductive) research design, combining induction from an historical account of the work of EUSRs (chapter 1) as well as a comparison of the EUSRs with other international envoys (chapter 2) with deduction from the literature on organizational learning (chapter 3). Hence, 'learning' is conceived as a two-phase process of organizational development where organizational learning (phase one, defined for this work as a rewriting of rules as a result of reflection) may be followed by organizational change (phase two). This implies a shift in focus where first the occurrence of OL needs to be analyzed, and then the potential impact of OL on subsequent organizational change is assessed. By doing so, a body of OL occurrences can be established regardless of whether they have led to change, and how eventual change is judged.

This understanding of the learning process as a value-neutral category also differentiates OL from approaches like lesson-drawing (Rose 1991 and 1993) or policy transfer (Dolowitz/Marsh 2000; Stone 2001). Those are concerned with how policies, ideas or institutional arrangements that are thought to be 'successful' can be transferred from one actor or political setting to another (Dolowitz/Marsh 2000, 5). A theoretical approach, however, ought not be guided by normative considerations such as success or failure.

On this basis, the study makes a first attempt by applying an analytical framework of OL to the work of the EU Special Representatives and how it developed between 1996 and 2007. It focuses both on institutional aspects (such as the establishment of EUSRs in the first place and the subsequent expansion and refinement of their structures) and on the policy level (i.e. the EUSRs' operational activity and input into policy-making).

The empirical analysis feeds into the study's aim with regard to the political arena, i.e. to provide valuable insights into the mechanisms of a foreign policy instrument like the EUSRs and to elaborate their importance as a contributing factor to the EU's strategic development. EUSRs, though in existence for more than a decade now, remain an understudied phenomenon—a striking point given their presence in all crisis regions of concern to the EU and their enormous contribution to factual and analytical knowledge about these regions.

The expected results of this exercise of applying theories of organizational learning to the development of European foreign policy are again twofold, relating to its scientific as well as its political significance. A first result should be a contribution to the explanatory strength of organizational learning theories vis-à-vis international institutions. Can OL theories identify learning steps of the EU with regard to the EUSRs, and can these in turn help explain the foreign policy behavior of the EU? The political significance of the project can be seen in its contribution to the ongoing process of developing and refining the strategic actorness of the European Union. By shedding light on a particular player within European foreign policy, it shows whether and how the EU has built up one important CFSP instrument. Moreover, by analyzing processes such as learning, one should arrive at conclusions about the cognitive drivers of the EU's foreign policy extension, i.e. the EU's self-image or its international identity.

Following the theoretical, empirical, and political aims outlined above, I will develop my argument in three steps: In a first part, I will introduce the research subject and develop the analytical framework and model to be employed (theoretical exploration: chapters 1 to 3); part two applies the analytical model to the EUSRs by looking at instances of organizational learning that may be followed by organizational change (empirical analysis: chapters 4 to 6); the third part will summarize the findings (conclusion: chapter 7).

The first chapter presents the research subject by providing a detailed historical account of the development of the EUSRs from 1996 to 2007. So far, no academic work has analyzed their role in the external action of the EU. This 'history of EUSRs' is put into the perspective of the overall development of CFSP, and problematized with a view to organizational learning. The second chapter explains why the EU Special Representatives have been chosen as a case study. It sets out with an analysis of how special envoys operate as diplomatic instruments in different contexts and by different actors. The EUSRs will be compared to the Special Representatives of the Secretary-General of the United Nations (UN) and the Special Envoys of the President of the United States of America (U.S.) with regard to five characteristics: their legal basis, their function, the individuals holding these posts, their institutional relations, and their relevance. Preliminary inferences from this comparison will serve to outline both what differentiates these envoys and which general roles they share. These inferences also serve as an inductive basis for the third chapter, which presents the theoretical framework used, analyzing different approaches from organizational learning theory as well as alternative explanations from IR theory. After this comparative theoretical review follows the elaboration of an analytical framework by looking at the subject, environment, and processes of learning. The chapter finishes with the presentation of the analytical model, its main hypotheses and their operationalization, as well as details on how the study is conducted.

Empirical analysis in the second part begins by establishing a body of organizational learning experiences treating OL as the dependent variable. Chapter 4 will look at instances of learning at the structural and procedural levels, i.e. the invention of the EUSRs and their increase in numbers, their integration into CFSP structures and the establishment of their own structures, and budgetary issues; as well as cooperation and coordination with the Commission and with member states, general mandate provisions, the selection of personnel, and the introduction of lessons-learned seminars. For each instance, the processes of learning are identified ('reflection' and 'rewriting of rules'). Chapter 5 takes a look at instances of learning at the operational and ideational level, i.e. the expansion of EUSR tasks, their basis of operation, coordination of ESDP missions, cooperation with third parties, and double-hatting; as well as the EUSRs' input into policy-making, considerations of the EU's strategic role, the question of path dependence and flexibility, and inference from the work of EUSRs for the future EU foreign service. Again, for each instance, the processes of learning ('reflection' and 'rewriting of rules') are identified in detail. The study then turns to the question whether these learning instances did lead to change. The sixth chapter thus analyzes learning-based organizational change in European foreign policy both at the institutional and the policy level and potential barriers that might inhibit such change. It turns out that more often than not, institutional barriers such as different competencies between the Community and CFSP, or power interests from member states prevent some of the lessons learned from being implemented.

Finally, the third part (chapter 7) provides conclusions and recommendations at the level of both theory and policy-making. Theories of organizational learning represent the lens through which EU foreign policy is examined in this work. What can we see through this lens that other perspectives do not reveal? What do we fail to see? The study finishes with a critical outlook both on the subject and on the theoretical approach and opens up issues for further discussion.

Chapter 1:
Pushing the Frontiers of European Foreign Policy

For more than a decade, the EU Special Representatives have continuously been pushing the boundaries of the EU's foreign policy, exploring, as pioneers, hitherto uncharted territory.[16] Strange enough, this contribution of the EUSRs is not covered in the academic literature. Consequently, I start out this study with an historical account of their work, linking it to different phases of development as well as to changes in the overall setting of European foreign policy.

EUSRs were not only an expression of the extending reach of European foreign policy, but they also foreshadowed some of its very developments. The Maastricht Treaty of 1993 had created a European 'foreign policy' on paper but failed to provide the Union with the instruments to actually pursue strategic aims or intervene in conflicts that threatened the stability of the continent. This became most obvious in the wars following the break-up of Yugoslavia that had left the EU inept to stop the fighting.

The European Union failed in the Balkans on two grounds: a lack of policy and a lack of instruments. The policy divisions between member states that prevented a firm response need not be elaborated here; they have found an eloquent expression elsewhere (see e.g. Ginsberg 2001). Moreover, such policy differences remain to the present day, to which the debates over Iraq in 2003 and, more recently, over the recognition of Kosovo bear witness. But the EU also lacked the institutional mechanisms to interact with international partners and conflicting parties alike, i.e. the means to push through a position (provided it had one).

What is of interest here is the availability to the EU of foreign policy instruments, a quasi-precondition for international actorness that would, in addition, be easier to acquire than policy unanimity. In the Yugoslav conflict, the system of revolving presidencies—the EU's mechanisms for external representation—had soon shown its limitations. Already in 1991, the European Community (EC) had named former British foreign minister, Lord Carrington, to broker a ceasefire for what was then still Yugoslavia (Haine 2004, 38). Later, the Union nominated two successive special envoys, Lord Owen and Carl Bildt, as its representatives at the International Conference on the Former Yugoslavia, with Cyrus Vance and, later, Thorvald Stoltenberg as their UN counterparts (Allen/Smith 1996, 64; Jaanson 2008, 4). The function of these envoys, however, was limited to the representation of the EU in diplomatic negotiations. They could not establish a greater role for the EU, and it was left to the United States to end the war[17] in 1994/95 both through military intervention (by NATO) and coercive negotiations (led by the presidential envoy, Richard Holbrooke). The EU, in contrast, was doubly sidelined: On the one hand, the U.S. took the initiative in what was thought to be the 'hour of Europe,'

---

16   Ajello 2000, 121; cf. the title of Grevi 2007.

17   Cf. the title of Holbrooke 1998.

as the oft-quoted saying attributed to the unfortunate foreign minister of Luxemburg, Jacques Poos, goes. On the other hand, despite being represented at the Dayton negotiation table in a position formally superior to the three member states present (United Kingdom, France, and Germany), it was the latter which helped formulate the Peace Agreement (Schwegmann 2000, 7). It would take nearly a decade before the EU could seriously claim a leading position in the stabilization of Bosnia and Herzegovina, not coincidentally after the High Representative for this country was double-hatted as EU Special Representative.

In a situation where the EU had failed the foreign policy test on its doorstep, EU Special Representatives emerged in the African Great Lakes region and for the Middle East Peace Process, furthering the development of European foreign policy. In the following it will be shown to what extent "the deepening of the institutional foundations of CFSP and the evolution of the instrument of EU Special Representatives carry mutual implications" (Grevi 2007, 29). The 12-year period from 1996 to 2007 is divided into four phases: Invention (1996–99), Formalization (1999–2001), Expansion (2002–05), and Consolidation (2006–07). This underlines how the EU, after periods of nearly unrestrained growth (invention, expansion), has tried to hedge in and institutionalize the EUSRs in order to gain better control over this foreign policy instrument (formalization, consolidation). The latter are also periods with an increased occurrence of organizational learning.

Furthermore, as it appears, the EUSRs have consistently been ahead of the institutional and political developments in European foreign policy: They were dispatched before their function was enshrined in the Treaty; they represented the EU's political approach to a region before there was anything like a common policy; and they became a test case for double-hatting long before the future Foreign Minister will wear his (or her) two hats. It is in this sense that they have been breaking new ground for EU foreign policy.

1.1   The early years: Invention (1996–1999)

For once, it was not the Western Balkans—the "cradle of ESDP" (Grevi 2007, 81)—that effected a catalytic change in European foreign policy, but a place in Africa. For a long time Europe had neglected the worries of this continent, presumably in a mixture of commendable hesitation to intervene due to its colonialist past and sheer lack of ability to face the crises there that in part all have their post-colonial legacy. Nonetheless, the EUSRs as they are known today were invented, as 'EU Special Envoys', to respond to crises on the African continent—both with a view to engage in conflict resolution as such and to increase the EU's profile as an international actor.

1.1.1. The Great Lakes

In the winter of 1995/96, a political and humanitarian crisis befell Rwanda, Eastern Zaire and Burundi. To a certain extent, this was a continued effect of the 1994 genocide in Rwanda and Burundi, yet at the same time the crisis was an expression of the long-standing fragility of the region (Fiedler 2004, 325). During that period, millions of refugees settled in Eastern Zaire; their presence threatened to destabilize the whole 'Great Lakes region.' This name most commonly refers to the region around the Central African lakes Albert, Edward, Kivu, Tanganyika, and Victoria. The region spans the territories of Rwanda, Burundi, and Uganda as well as portions of the territories of the Democratic Republic of Congo (DRC, formerly Zaire) and Tanzania.[18]

Figure 1: Map of the African Great Lakes Region[19]

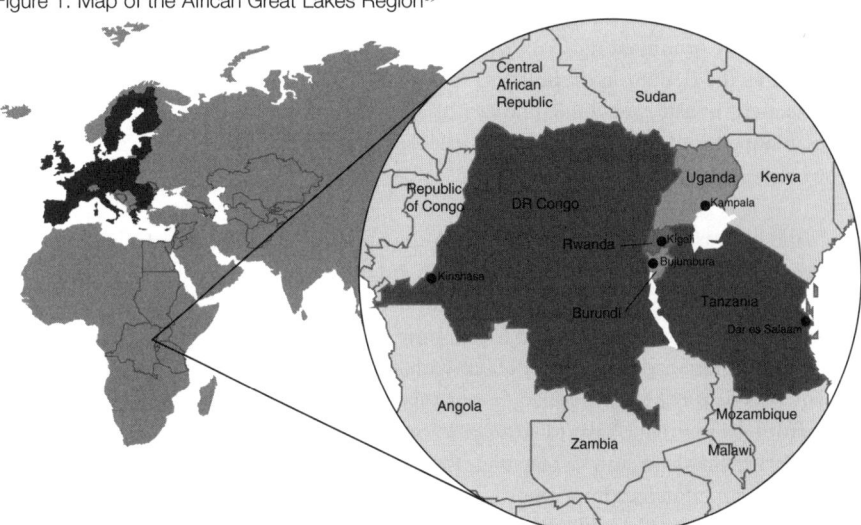

For want of any better policy, the international community tried to alleviate the suffering mainly by providing humanitarian aid. The flow of money into the region reached a rate of one million U.S. dollars a day, more than half of it emanating from the EU (the Community plus member states) (McLoughlin 1998, 1). It was clear, however, that such aid would not provide a solution to the underlying political problems. In this situation, three insights dominated EU discussions aimed at halting the crisis: First, it was acknowledged that the roots of the crisis were not found in just one state but stretched across boundaries; second, the crisis was seen as another periodic upheaval that was part of a long-term predicament plaguing the region; and third, if the EU wanted to have an impact on

18   There is no agreed definition, neither geographically nor politically, of the territory that the Great Lakes region encompasses. Some authors include Congo (Brazzaville) on political grounds (cf. Fiedler 2004, fn3, 317; Moller 2002, 31). Interestingly, the EUSR mandate has never defined the exact area of responsibility.

19   I am very grateful to Simon Burkhardt and Johannes Bister who drew this and the other maps and generously provided me with them.

the situation itself, it needed a political visibility commensurate with its economic commitment (ibid., 2). Such reasoning may have been motivated by more than a utilitarian desire not to waste money. It also followed the logic of a spillover effect from one domain (economic aid) to the other (political influence).[20] While it was clear that, at that time, the EU with its still infant CFSP had little to no influence on the ongoing crisis, the assumption was that any given political presence would be bolstered by the existing economic assistance—and vice versa.

In this situation, the first 'EU Special Envoy' was nominated for the Great Lakes region in March 1996. Following a proposal from the Commissioner for Development, João Pinheiro, the Council passed a joint action on the basis of Article J.8.5 of the new Maastricht Treaty (Treaty on European Union, or TEU). This article provided nothing but a very implicit justification for such an envoy, referring to two duties of the newly established Political Committee (PoCo), namely to monitor the international situation and to contribute to the definition of policies (Art. J.8.5 TEU).[21] Neither the Commission nor the Parliament questioned the legitimacy of this action, and so the former UN Special Representative for Mozambique, Aldo Ajello, became the first EU Special Envoy for the Great Lakes region.[22]

The mandate was simple, broad, and open to initiatives on the part of the envoy. Its objective was to assist the countries of the region in resolving the crisis, complementing rather than competing with existing international initiatives such as those of the United Nations and the Organisation of African Unity (OAU) (Article 1 of the Joint Action). Given the inexperience of member states with such an instrument, the EUSR's working mandate was deliberately left broad, if not vague: to support the ongoing crisis management efforts by international and African actors; to establish and maintain close contacts with all parties involved; and to help with the preparations of a peace conference (Article 2). Article 3 contained an important element stipulating that the envoy "may make recommendations to the Council on measures which the Union might undertake to fulfill its objectives in the region." This phrase captured a potentially proactive role of the EUSRs, providing relevant policy input rather than only reporting to the Council, as the previous sentence of that article suggested.

---

20 For two groundbreaking works on the spillover effect in European integration and its functionalist logic, see Haas 1958; Schmitter 1969: "Spillover refers […] to the process whereby members of an integration scheme […] attempt to resolve their dissatisfaction [with performance in one sector of cooperation] either by resorting to collaboration in another, related sector (expanding the **scope** of mutual commitment) or by intensifying their commitment to the original sector (increasing the **level** of mutual commitment) or both" (Schmitter 1969, 162 [emphasis in original]). For a neofunctionalist explanation of different scopes of integration in the external and internal security policies of the EU, see Börzel 2005.

21 The rationale to establish the position of an envoy based on the monitoring duty of the Political Committee resembles the introduction of UN envoys based on the fact-finding competence of the Secretary-General; cf. subsection 2.1.2.

22 Council Joint Action 96/250/CFSP of 25 March 1996.

The EUSR's main policy function, however, was not contained in the mandate: Because an EU strategy towards the Great Lakes region simply did not exist,[23] the envoy's efforts to narrow the considerable policy differences in EU member states' approaches to this region were to be of great importance. Especially former colonial powers like France, the United Kingdom, and Belgium had particular, oftentimes diverging interests in the region.[24] Initially, the EUSR mandate was limited to eight months (Article 5), though it was to last, through periods of violence and relative stability alike, until the present day. After less than four months, the Council decided to extend the mandate by an additional eight months and to include a review clause.[25] Before the mandate elapsed, the Council extended it for another year, following the demanded review and based on the assumed necessity to keep the envoy active in the region;[26] similar decisions were taken in 1998 and 1999.[27]

Much of the EUSR's work was directed at active conflict resolution, though without being able to pacify the region substantially; at least, it helped the EU gain a place in the international arena. Fighting broke out again in 1998 after Laurent Kabila, with support from Rwanda, Uganda, Angola, Burundi, and Eritrea, had ousted President Mobutu of Zaire in May 1997 and renamed the country as Democratic Republic of Congo. Other neighbouring countries were drawn in,[28] turning the conflict into what commentators dubbed "Africa's first world war."[29] The EUSR intensified his support of international mediation

---

23 Cf. Fiedler 2004, 330; Grevi 2007, 112. A little more than two weeks before Ajello was dispatched, the Commission had issued a Communication to the Council titled "The European Union and the Issue of Conflicts in Africa: Peace-Building, Conflict Prevention and beyond" (European Commission 1996). This document, however, does not amount to a political strategy to deal with the conflicts at stake, let alone a unified position of member states' foreign policies.

24 While Belgium used to be the colonial power in Zaire (now: DR Congo) and Rwanda-Burundi, the neighbouring countries were colonies of the United Kingdom (Uganda and Tanzania in the East) and France (Congo-Brazzaville in the West), respectively. See also Fiedler 2004, 318; Fiedler adds Germany to the list of former colonial powers. While this is of course true, Germany had nonetheless lost its colonies (including today's Burundi, Rwanda and Tanganyika/Tanzania) already during the First World War and this distant past no longer played an appreciable role in German politics in the 1990s. Likewise, Portugal is sometimes mentioned as a former colonial power in Africa (Krause/Schlotter 2007, 353), but it does not have such close ties to the countries of the Great Lakes region.

25 Council Decision 96/441/CFSP of 15 July 1996, Article 1: "The application of Joint Action 96/250/CFSP is hereby extended to 31 July 1997. The Joint Action shall be reviewed six months after the date on which this Decision is adopted." The budget increase made necessary by the mandate extension followed later (Council Decision 96/589/CFSP of 1 October 1996).

26 Council Decision 97/448/CFSP of 16 July 1996.

27 Council Decisions 98/452/CFSP of 13 July 1998 and 1999/423/CFSP of 28 June 1999.

28 "At one level it is a conflict between two regional alliances—a 'Great Lakes' alliance of Rwanda, Uganda, and Burundi, versus one of Angola, Zimbabwe, and Namibia. On another level, it is a violent mixture of national civil wars, including those of Rwanda, Uganda, Burundi, and Angola, all of which are partly fought on Congolese soil" (International Crisis Group 2000, 1).

29 Cf. also Doyle 1998; or the comments of U.S. Secretary of State Madeleine Albright at the UN Security Council, quoted in CNN 2000. Others use the term "Africa's Great War", e.g. Shearer 1999

efforts led by the UN and OAU; however, without succeeding in organizing the regional conference intended to bring the parties at war together (Schmidt 1998, 267; Malu-Malu 1998, A26). At the end, the EU was involved, both politically and economically, yet it was in no better position to stop the fighting than the other international actors, both African and non-African, and their myriad of special envoys (Krause/Schlotter 2007, 362).

1.1.2 The Middle East Peace Process

In the early- and mid-1990s, not only the wars in Central Africa were of major concern to the EU but also the developments in the Middle East. At their meeting in December 1993 just days before the new Treaty on European Union entered into force, the EU heads of state and government defined five areas of priority in which the new CFSP instrument of joint actions should be applied. One of these areas was to accompany "the Middle-East peace process by use of the political, economic and financial means provided by the Union"[30] in support of the 1993 Oslo Peace Accord between Israel and the Palestine Liberation Organization (PLO). This plan was widely greeted with enthusiasm as it presumably opened the way into a new era in this conflict-ridden region. The EU supported the Palestinian democratization process by sending observers to the elections to the Palestinian Council, the first democratic elections in the autonomous territories.[31] However, the assassination of Israeli Prime Minister and Noble Peace Laureate Yitzhak Rabin in November 1995 stymied most people's hopes for peace.

Against this background of rising tensions and growing European involvement, the EU nominated its second Special Envoy in November 1996.[32] Miguel Angel Moratinos, a career diplomat who shortly before had been appointed Spanish ambassador to Israel, became the EU's envoy for the Middle East Peace Process (MEPP). The nomination followed a decision by the European Council a month earlier. The fact that a Spaniard was chosen for this post seems to correspond with the role that Spain, in the early 1990s still a 'new member state', had taken up with regard to the EU's relations with the South: The Madrid conference of 1991 was an important milestone for the Oslo Peace Accord (and for EU involvement in the MEPP), and the EU-Mediterranean Partnership was initiated under the first Spanish Presidency in 1995, with a conference in Barcelona.[33]

---

and Moller 2002, 35.

30 European Council 1993. The other areas were: Promotion of stability and peace in Europe; South Africa; Former Yugoslavia; and Russia. Thus, the African Great Lakes region was not an area of priority for the EU.

31 Council Decision 95/403/CFSP of 25 September 1995.

32 Council Joint Action 96/676/CFSP of 25 November 1996; for a detailed account of the situation surrounding the appointment of the EUSR, see Dietl 2005, 99-111.

33 Cf. Dietl 2005, 104. For an analysis of the interconnectedness of the Barcelona Process and the Middle East Peace Process, cf. Peters 1998. Tom Gross gives a very negative account of Spain's role in the Middle East, accusing it of anti-Zionism (Gross 2001).

Figure 2: Map of the Middle East

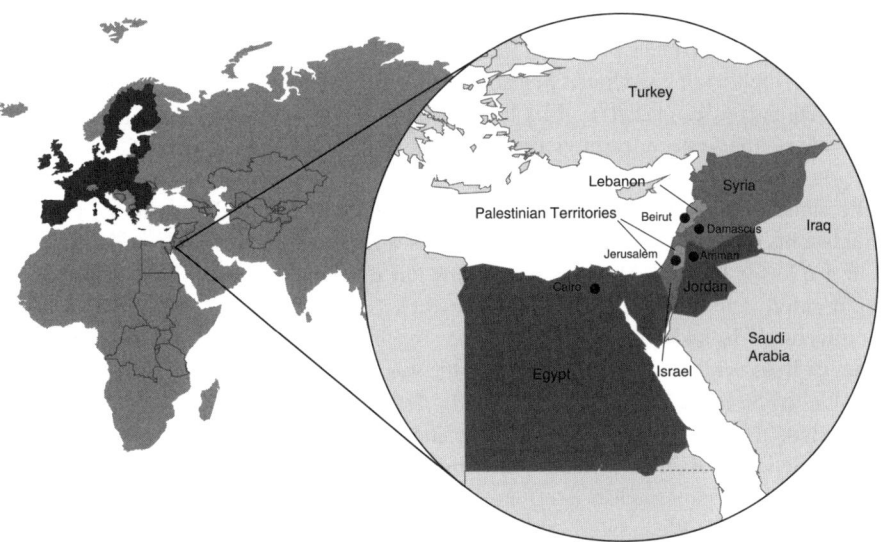

The motivation to appoint a second EUSR was similar to that of the first one: to achieve political representation proportionate to the EU's economic aid.[34] In fact, following the Oslo Accord, the EU had taken on the lion's share of the financial support of the Palestinian Authority (PA).[35] Without this European financial aid, the PA could not have survived for long. To accompany such engagement on the political level was the main task of the EUSR; the EU should not be disregarded again as it was when the United States failed to consult their European partners prior to the Clinton-Arafat summit of October 1996 (Ginsberg 2001, 149). That said, just like in the Great Lakes Region, while it joined the mediation efforts of other actors (such as the United States or the United Nations) the EU could not actually contribute to resolving the crisis.

---

34 The Joint Action itself mentions the EU's "readiness [...] to play an active part in promoting the peace process, commensurate with its interests in the region" (Council Joint Action 96/676/CFSP). Cf. also Soetendorp 2002, 289: "The large financial assistance to the Palestinians in the West Bank and Gaza created pressures for deeper involvement of the EU in the peace process. [...] To add force to their claim for a much larger share in the political leadership of the peace process, the EU member states decided in November 1996 to appoint a Special Envoy, Miguel Moratinos, to the Middle East peace process with a broad mandate." Similarly argue Dietl 2005, 102–3, and Ginsberg 2001, 195. In contrast, Patokallio (Patokallio 2004, 8) argues that the appointment of the Special Envoy was prompted by events on the ground.

35 Between 1993 and 2000, the EU and its member states were the largest donors of financial and technical aid to the Palestinian Authority as well as to the MEPP in general, providing more than 50% of all international assistance (Asseburg 2003b, 175). From the Oslo conference to the end of 2001, the EU alone had committed about one billion Euro in grants and loans, plus an additional 407 million Euro in contributions to UNRWA, the UN relief and works agency for Palestinian refugees, as well as in food aid and other humanitarian assistance. To this sum, one must also add bilateral assistance provided by EU member states (Soetendorp 2002, 288). By 2005, providing a total of around 500 million Euro each year, the EU remained the biggest donor (cf. European Commission 2005 a, 2).

This political ambition notwithstanding, neither Israel nor the United States welcomed greater involvement on the part of the EU (Dannreuther 2002, 9; also Regelsberger 1997, 217). While Israelis perceived Europeans as biased against them and preferred the exclusive support of the United States, the latter did not see a significant actor in the EU (Dietl 2005, 106-7; Tocci 2005, 13-14; cf. Mideast Mirror 1998). Establishing the EU as a credible partner was conceivably the foremost, though not an easy, task of the EUSR.

The initial mandate had a one-year duration and broadly included five different tasks,[36] but like his colleague of the African Great Lakes region, EUSR Moratinos had to carve out a role for himself. Most of his actions did not receive much public attention, as he began to familiarize himself with the main actors of the region, trying to gain their confidence.[37] In addition, the United States too had its envoy, U.S. special coordinator Dennis Ross, who led the negotiations. This was not only due to the greater weight of the United States in general, but also to the fact that Ross was more experienced than Moratinos: He had been in this position since the George H.W. Bush administration. Consequently, Moratinos worked quietly but decisively in the background, for example during the successful mediation efforts that took place early during his mandate, in January 1997, aimed at the withdrawal of Israeli troops from Hebron.[38]

One of the first major achievements of the new Special Envoy was to arrange, together with the Dutch presidency, a meeting of the Israeli Minister of Foreign Affairs Levy with the President of the PA Council Arafat, on the margins of the Euro-Mediterranean Conference in Malta in April 1997 (Regelsberger 1997, 217; Nolan 1997). This took place following a long period of frosty silence, when Israelis and Palestinians refused to speak with each other on an official level. One year later, in April 1998, the European Union and the Palestinian Authority adopted, on Moratinos' initiative, an agreement to

---

36   The main tasks were to establish contacts with the parties and other relevant actors; to offer advice and good offices to the parties; to help implement agreements reached by the parties; to develop and pursue the EU's own initiatives; and to monitor compliance (or non-compliance) of the parties with international norms and their possible actions prejudging a final peace settlement; cf. Council Joint Action 96/676/CFSP of 25 November 1996, Article 2. Following an extension for twelve months in 1997 (Council Decision 97/475/CFSP of 22 July 1997), which left the mandate itself unchanged, the Council modified the mandate in the fall of 1998 in order to include cooperation on security issues with the aim of assisting the Palestinians to meet their commitments on security under the Oslo Accords (Council Decision 98/608/CFSP of 26 October 1998). The mandate now included the task "to develop joint cooperation on security issues within the EU-Palestinian Permanent Security Committee set up on 9 April 1998" (Article 2).

37   Still in the year 2002, a BBC presenter was able to introduce the EU Special Envoy by saying: "You may never have heard of Miguel Moratinos. But he's been the EU's special representative in the region for the past six years;" BBC 2002. Cf. also Dannreuther 2002, 9: "[Moratinos] assumed a deliberately low-level and uncontroversial profile which aimed to build up trust and to project a constructive EU role."

38   Cf. Soetendorp 2002, 290: "Through quiet diplomacy, Moratinos helped the Americans to encourage Yasser Arafat [...] to sign the Hebron Agreement. [...This was] the first time that the EU was actively involved in the US peace diplomacy and was able to demonstrate its value to the peace process." For a newspaper account of the Hebron deal, see Makovsky 1997, 1.

establish an EU-Palestinian Joint Permanent Security Cooperation Committee, including the installation of an EU security advisor with the EUSR's staff.[39] Likewise, in the following year, the envoy promoted the establishment of an EU-Israel Forum (Patokallio 2004, 9).

Another important contribution of EUSR Moratinos concerned the proceedings of the March 1999 Berlin European Council. At that meeting, the heads of state and government advanced a two-state solution to the Middle East conflict, which made the EU the first international actor to promote this proposal (European Council 1999, Part IV). However, at that time, discussions were overshadowed by the North Atlantic Alliance's bombardment of the Federal Republic of Yugoslavia in order to end the crisis in Kosovo.

1.1.3   Former Yugoslavia

The years 1998/99 were dominated by events in the Federal Republic of Yugoslavia, more precisely by the outbreak of violence in the Serbian province of Kosovo. This shifted much of the EU's attention from the 'wider neighbourhood' (Middle East and Africa) to its immediate vicinity. Given the predominance, for Europeans, of the conflict in former Yugoslavia, it does not come as a surprise that successive appointments of EUSRs were made to that region—culminating, by mid-1999, in four special envoys for a region of less than 20 million inhabitants (Allen/Smith 2000, 104).

In June 1998, Felipe González, a former Spanish Prime Minister, became the EU Special Representative for the Federal Republic of Yugoslavia (FRY). His mandate, limited until the end of the year, was to heighten the EU's political profile in the emerging conflict in Kosovo by enhancing the effectiveness of its contribution to conflict resolution.[40] EUSR Gonzalez worked in close cooperation with the President of the Organization for Security and Co-operation in Europe (OSCE), whose personal representative he was, and with U.S. envoy Robert Gelbard (Jaanson 2008, 4).

Mr Gonzalez was soon joined by the Austrian ambassador to Belgrade Wolfgang Petritsch, who was nominated EU Special Representative for Kosovo at the Council meeting in October 1998. The latter nomination took place informally in the Presidency Conclusions rather than by a Joint Action, tasking the serving ambassador of a member state with negotiating on behalf of the Union.[41] This showed the high degree of flexibility that the EU applied to this new instrument. Moreover, it displayed the EU's increased

---

39   Ginsberg 2001, 139. Two generally positive reports on the Special Envoy's work during these years are Pelletreau 1998 and The Economist 1997.

40   Council Joint Action 1998/375/CFSP of 8 June 1998.

41   Cf. Council Conclusions, C/98/322, Luxembourg, 5 October 1998: "The Council has appointed the Austrian Ambassador to Belgrade, Wolfgang Petritsch, as EU Special Envoy to act on the spot for the EU under the direction of the Presidency and in close coordination with the EU Special Representative for the FRY."

willingness to lend a 'voice' and 'face' to the emerging CFSP given the continued crisis in former Yugoslavia (Regelsberger 1999, 248). It took nine months until, at the end of March 1999 and after the NATO air campaign had begun, the Council formalized Mr. Petritsch's nomination by means of a Joint Action, providing him "with the human and logistical resources needed to carry out his functions."[42]

Figure 3: Map of former Yugoslavia

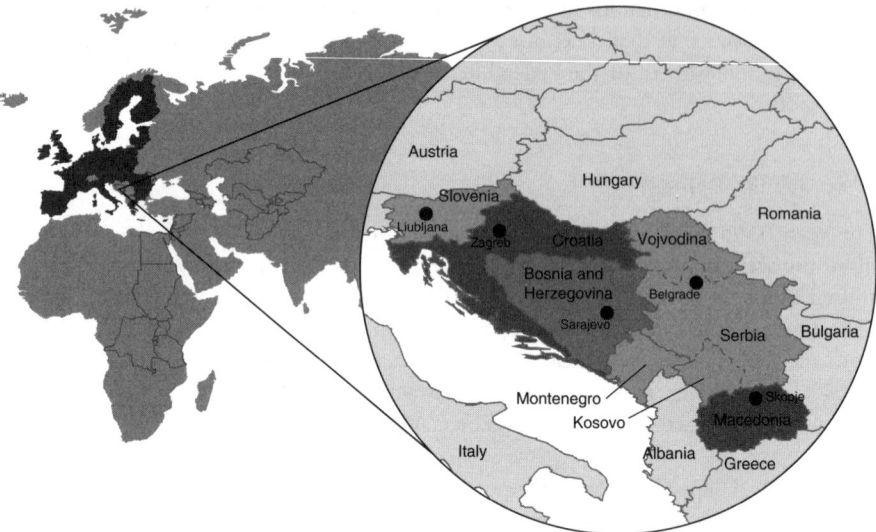

A third Balkan-related Special Representative was the Greek Minister of the Economy and Member of the European Parliament, Panagiotis Roumeliotis. He had already been the Coordinator of the 'Royaumont Process' on stability and good neighbourliness in Southeast Europe before being appointed, in May 1999, as the EU Special Representative for this same process.[43] The Royaumont Process was a by-product of the 1995 Paris peace conference for Bosnia and Herzegovina, representing all the states of ex-Yugoslavia, the neighbouring countries (Albania, Hungary, Bulgaria, Romania, Turkey), the EU member states, Russia and the U.S.[44]

After the end of hostilities in Kosovo in June 1999, the EU appointed an EUSR to act as coordinator of the new-born 'Stability Pact for Southeastern Europe.'[45] This new international framework was the last in a series of trial-and-error policy proposals of

---

42   Council Joint Action 1999/239/CFSP of 30 March 1999.

43   Council Decision 1999/361/CFSP of 31 May 1999.

44   The European Commission and the European Parliament were also associated with the process, as were the OSCE and the Council of Europe; for more information on the Royaumont Process, see Ehrhart/Schnabel 1999.

45   Council Joint Action 1999/523/CFSP of 29 July 1999.

the EU in its efforts to come to terms with the violent break-up of former Yugoslavia (Bendiek 2007, 218; cf. Jaanson 2008, 3). It was worked out hastily, and mainly on European initiative, in the final weeks of the Kosovo war in order to form an international coalition of more than 40 states, organizations, and regional groupings with the aim of supporting regional recovery from the recent set of wars in former Yugoslavia.[46] The Pact's main promise to the countries of the region was that they could conclude Stabilization and Association Agreements (SAA) with the EU that were modelled after the Europe Agreements for Central and Eastern Europe, thus containing the perspective of eventual membership (cf. Allen/Smith 2000, 109). German politician Bodo Hombach became the first figure to preside over this intergovernmental gathering.

The mandate for the Stability Pact envoy was also the first to make deliberate use of another innovative development, that of 'double-hatting.'[47] In a personal union, Bodo Hombach acted both as Special Representative of the EU and Special Coordinator of the Stability Pact. The problems, and benefits, that this arrangement brought with it, spanning the intergovernmental and supranational sphere of the EU, were quite visible from the early days of this arrangement.[48] They were not, at least initially, eased by the new CFSP institutions that were to come.

1.2 Still young: Formalization (1999–2001)

Following the inventory phase, the European envoys entered a period of formalization. Most visibly, they figured as EU Special Representatives in the recently passed Amsterdam Treaty. More importantly, though, their relation to new CFSP institutions like the High Representative and the Political and Security Committee needed to be clarified. Still, two new mandates were added to the list, while those in former Yugoslavia proved to be short-lived. In the end, the combination of formalizing EUSR activities and introducing new CFSP institutions has led to the EU being more visible, and respected, as a mediator in international crises. The next period (cf. section 1.3), coincidentally, showed a continued demand for such crisis management activity.

1.2.1 Treaty changes in Amsterdam and Nice

The Treaty revision of Amsterdam brought significant changes in the area of EU foreign policy, most importantly the creation of the post of a High Representative (HR) for CFSP (double-hatted with that of Secretary-General [SG] of the Council Secretariat).[49]

---

46 For more details see <http://www.stabilitypact.org>; cf. Jaanson 2008, 5–6. The office of the Stability Pact was closed in February 2008 and transformed into the Regional Cooperation Council.

47 In fact, EUSR González had been nominated personal representative of the OCSE Chairman in office prior to his being an EUSR, thus he occupied two functions at once (Jaanson 2008, 4). This, however, was more coincidental than intentionally chosen as a form of double-hatting.

48 Bendiek 2007, 224-5; double-hatting is described in greater detail in sections 5.8 and 6.17.

49 For an overview of how ESDP emerged and how it works today, see Howorth 2005a and Smith

The appointment of Javier Solana as the first SG/HR in October 1999 was preceded by a month-long tug of war about the new person's seniority and political standing (Regelsberger 2000, 238). To support him, a Policy Planning and Early Warning Unit (soon, in parlance, shortened to 'Policy Unit') was created.[50] In addition, the Treaty of Amsterdam, by "explicit confirmation of previous practice" (Council of the European Union 2000, 2), formally gave rise to the EU Special Representatives,[51] as the special envoys were henceforth called.[52]

Only one and a half years later, the Nice Treaty created the Political and Security Committee (PSC, or COPS as the French acronym is preferred in Brussels corridors). This new "linchpin of ESDP" as it was described (Duke 2005, 17) built on the Political Committee stemming from the times of European Political Cooperation and comprising the Political Directors from member states' foreign ministries and a Commission official. The PSC was established, in January 2001, as a body of national officials in ambassadorial rank (plus a Commission representative) permanently located in Brussels.[53] In addition to the function—already fulfilled by PoCo—of monitoring the international political situation and making appropriate policy recommendations, the PSC ambassadors' main new task was to "exercise, under the responsibility of the Council, political control and strategic direction of crisis management operations,"[54] including the EUSRs. Consequently, future extension of the EUSRs' mandates also took account of the new function of the PSC.

The appointment of the High Representative and the creation of the PSC fundamentally changed the structure in which EUSRs operated. The first two of them, for the African Great Lakes and for the Middle East Peace Process, respectively, had been working in relative freedom from precise instructions from—if not to say neglect by some—member

2004, and Missiroli 2004, respectively.

50   Interestingly, no major academic work has to date analyzed the role of the Policy Unit in European foreign policy-making.

51   Already, the nominations for Felipe González and Wolfgang Petritsch made use of the term 'EU Special Representatives.' Yet the Council inconsistently retained the term 'Special Envoy' for extensions of the Great Lakes and Middle East mandate until the end of 2000, when the original Joint Actions from 1996 were repealed.

52   Art. 18 (5) TEU then reads as follows: "The Council may, whenever it deems it necessary, appoint a special representative with a mandate in relation to particular policy issues." Another, though minor novelty from the Treaty of Nice was that, as a derogation from the unanimity principle prevalent in all substantial CFSP matters, the Council shall appoint EUSRs by qualified majority (Art. 23 (2) TEU, third indent). Previously, EUSRs were appointed on the basis of unanimity. For more information on the legal basis of EUSRs, see subsection 2.1.1.

53   For a detailed account of the transformation of PoCo into PSC, see Juncos/Reynolds 2007, 131-135. They find it "worth noting that political directors do continue to meet, often in the sidelines of European Council meetings, and whenever they do so they are, in legal terms, sitting as the PSC" (ibid., 134).

54   Art. 25 (2) TEU. For a list of the committee's tasks and responsibilities, see Duke 2005, 17; for an illustrative study of the working methods and culture in the PSC, see Juncos/Reynolds 2007, 135–144.

states. By 2000, however, they had become a more purposeful instrument of the Union's CFSP: The pioneering phase was over, as Aldo Ajello himself put it (Ajello 2000, 121). Consequently, and in addition to their mere formalization through the Amsterdam Treaty, the Council adopted guidelines on the appointing procedure of and administrative arrangements for the EUSRs (Council of the European Union 2000).[55] They established a clear hierarchy between the High Representative and 'his' Special Representatives, placing the latter under the authority of the former plus giving Solana the right to propose candidates for nomination by the Council (Regelsberger 2001, 249).[56] This was the first major instance of internal guidelines and arrangements that intended to regulate the activity of EUSRs, and, as will be shown later (cf. section 4.3), reflected a high degree of organizational learning.

1.2.2 New mandates: Macedonia, Afghanistan

Unfolding events in the Republic of Macedonia[57] in 2001 demanded that the new EU crisis management institutions be put to a test before being solidly established. Once more it was proven that political crises do not wait for mechanisms to be operational. Following violent attacks by Albanian extremists on Macedonian government institutions, the EU engaged in a shuttle diplomacy hitherto unseen: Series of EU emissaries travelled to Skopje, from EUSR Hombach to External Relations Commissioner Chris Patten to the EU Presidency to High Representative Solana (Reichwein/Schlotter 2007, 261; Schneckener 2001, 92).

The small and young country of Macedonia soon became a testing ground for the new EU foreign policy instruments, including experimenting with different representatives. An SAA, the new bilateral agreement on the road to EU membership, was initialled in April 2001, shortly after the outbreak of the crisis, in order to strengthen the government in power. To uphold its influence, however, the EU held back the SAA's benefits until the government agreed to make concessions to the Albanian side (Piana 2002, 212). To be represented in the crisis mediation efforts, the EU at first nominated, in an ad hoc

---

55   The need for a revision of the rules was already stated in the minutes of the Council meeting that passed Council Joint Action 1999/822/CFSP of 9 December 1999, where it said: "The Council agrees that the Council Joint Actions concerning the EUSR will be updated, as necessary, [...] and aims to complete this revision in the first quarter of 2000;" see Council of the European Union 2000, 2.

56   From 2000 onwards, mandates placed the EUSRs "under the authority of the Presidency, assisted by the Secretary General/High Representative;" cf., for EUSR Moratinos, Council Joint Action 1999/843/CFSP of 17 December 1999; for EUSR Ajello, Council Joint Action 2000/347/CFSP of 22 May 2000, reads similarly. See also Council of the European Union 2000.

57   The country is officially recognized by the EU as "former Yugoslav Republic of Macedonia," or fYROM. In this study, however, either the full constitutional name (Republic of Macedonia) or a shorthand designation (Macedonia) will be used. For an extensive account of how the EU, for four years, unsuccessfully tried to agree on recognition of the country, see Reichwein/Schlotter 2007, 241–252.

arrangement, the British ambassador in Skopje as Solana's representative on the ground.[58] This position was upgraded, in June 2001 and with a view to having a counterpart to the respective U.S. envoy (Jaanson 2008, 7), by the appointment of former French Defence Minister François Léotard as EU Special Representative.[59] His original task was to closely monitor the developments on the ground and to support political dialogue between the parties with the objective of contributing to a settlement (Grevi 2007, 92).

Figure 4: Map of Macedonia

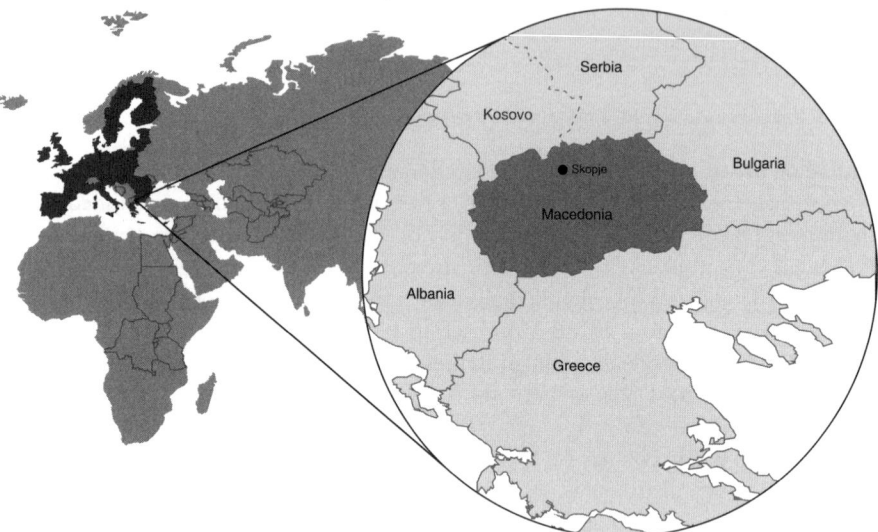

A breakthrough was reached in August 2001 when the Macedonian government and Albanian leaders met in Ohrid for negotiations under American and European supervision. The talks eventually produced a Framework Agreement outlining, among other things, a constitutional reform giving more representation to the Albanian minority. EUSR Léotard was instrumental in this mediation effort, both acting in his own capacity as a respected former politician and in support of High Representative Solana.[60] To implement the disarmament part of the Ohrid Agreement, two consecutive NATO operations were deployed, even though the EUSR had proposed an EU force.[61]

---

58   This was regarded as an important innovation by bringing "in behind the work of the High Representative all of the analytical resources and the broad assessments of the UK [United Kingdom] government" (International Crisis Group 2001, 40).

59   Council Joint Action 2001/492/CFSP of 29 June 2001.

60   Reichwein/Schlotter 2007, 262-5; for a newspaper account of the EUSR's work, see Finn 2001.

61   Operation Essential Harvest was deployed on 27 August 2001, aiming to disarm ethnic Albanians. As a follow-up, operation Amber Fox was dispatched on 23 September 2001, mandated to protect the international monitors in Macedonia; for more information on these NATO operations, see Stefanova 2003; Yesson 2003. The proposal by EUSR Léotard is discussed in Beeston 2001; Castle/ Huggler 2001; and Wood/Norton-Taylor 2001.

Successful mediation did not bring an end to the EUSR's mandate, though—only a change of guard. At the end of October, Alain Le Roy replaced his fellow countryman Léotard. Given their different backgrounds—one a politician and 'trouble-shooter,' the other a career diplomat—this change of personnel reflected the progress made on the way to pacifying the conflicting parties. Le Roy's main task was to supervise the agreement's implementation on behalf of the international community, thereby facilitating further progress towards European integration (through the Stabilization and Association Process, SAP).[62] Today, EU action in Macedonia is often hailed as a successful example of, if not conflict prevention, then at least crisis management, based on the lessons of Bosnia and Kosovo and in close cooperation with the United States and NATO.[63]

Figure 5: Map of Afghanistan

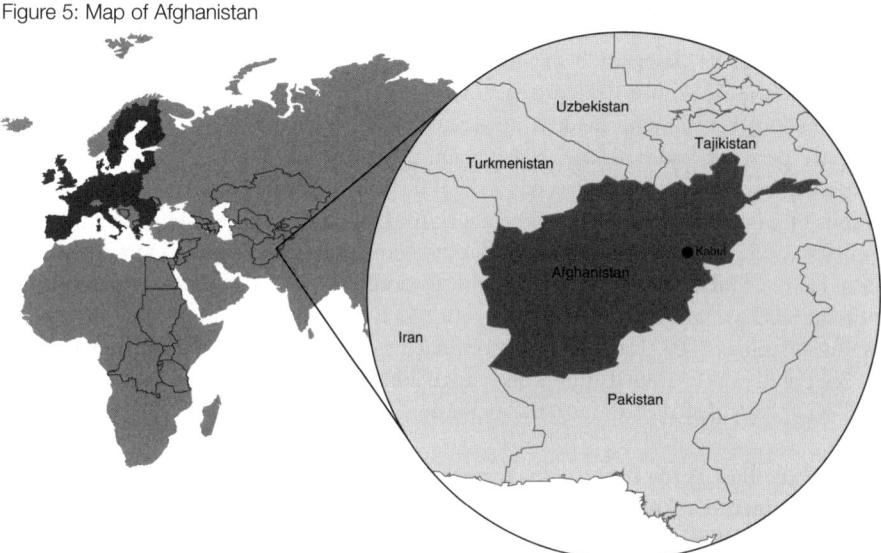

The year 2001, however, will be remembered not so much for the fairly successful crisis management in Macedonia but instead for the terrorist attacks of September 11 and the ensuing war against the Al Qaeda network in Afghanistan. When the international coalition had toppled the Taliban regime, the UN was tasked, at the Petersberg Conference in November 2001, to set up an interim administration (United Nations Assistance Mission in Afghanistan—UNAMA), which the EU aimed to support by means of a Special Representative. At about the same time, the UN Security Council authorised the deployment of an International Security Assistance Force (ISAF), in addition to the separate, U.S.-led operation Enduring Freedom that continued to fight the remaining Taliban and Al Qaeda forces (Klaiber 2007, 8).

---

62 Council Joint Action 2001/760/CFSP of 29 October 2001; Grevi 2007, 93-94.

63 Piana 2002, 212-3 and 216: "NATO and EU collaboration on the matter was remarkably good and close, something that one could not have imagined two years previously" (216).

In December 2001, German diplomat Klaus-Peter Klaiber, a former NATO Assistant Secretary-General, was appointed EUSR for Afghanistan with the task of, inter alia, supporting "the establishment in Afghanistan of a stable and legitimate broad-based multi-ethnic Government agreed upon by the political forces associated with the UN process."[64] Given that the United States was in the lead in all things military, it was of great importance for the EU to be represented adequately among the international organizations involved in the administration and reconstruction of the country (Regelsberger 2002, 233). Its primary means to this end was the EUSR.

1.2.3 Mandates continued, and ceased: Great Lakes, Middle East, former Yugoslavia

Existing mandates demanded a great deal of attention too, with the Great Lakes region, and mainly the DRC, remaining instable. The Lusaka Peace Agreement of 1999 formally brought a ceasefire and a commitment to withdraw all foreign troops (Moller 2002, 35). The EU supported the follow-up to the Lusaka Agreement, which Special Representative Ajello had helped to negotiate, with the establishment of a Joint Military Commission. Yet, fighting between different rebel groups, most of them with foreign support, persisted and both the ceasefire and the troop withdrawal were largely ignored (International Crisis Group 2000, 2; Fiedler 2004, 323). When President Laurent Desiré Kabila of Congo was assassinated in January 2001, his son, Joseph Kabila, took over and embarked on a process of national dialogue, democratization, and economic liberalization. He concluded peace agreements with Rwanda and Uganda as well as the most important rebel groups; in the wake of this effort, a large number of foreign troops left the country (Krause 2003, 166). The EU continued to support this process mainly through its Special Representative (Edmonton Journal 2001, A4), whose mandate was extended[65] and, later, amended according to the institutional changes in Brussels.[66]

The Middle East Peace Process was marred by the outbreak of the so-called second Intifada in September 2000 and the breakdown of the last-ditch effort in Israeli-Palestinian negotiations in Taba in January 2001. In this highly political situation, it was the—natural rather than legal—authority of the High Representative, i. e. Javier Solana's commitment to mediate on behalf of Europe, that strengthened the EU's influence on parties in conflict.[67] Simply having a high-level political 'backup' like Solana (the 'S option') also enhanced the EUSR's standing among the players in the region (Grevi 2007, 43). At the

---

64   Council Joint Action 2001/875/CFSP of 10 December 2001, here: Article 2 a); cf. International Crisis Group 2002, 3.

65   Council Joint Action 2000/347/CFSP of 22 May 2000.

66   Council Joint Action 2000/792/CFSP of 14 December 2000. This mandate was again extended, namely by Council Joint Action 2001/876/CFSP of 10 December 2001.

67   Regelsberger 2001, 247; Dietl 2005, 111; Asseburg 2003b, 184; Ortega 2003, 53. Tellingly, Solana, while frequently travelling to the Middle East, visited the Great Lakes region only in 2003 (Fiedler 2004, 334), thus involuntarily underlining where EU policy priorities lay and, implicitly, weakening the EU's political weight in this particular region.

same time, Solana provided the personal continuity at the Brussels level that Moratinos himself was able to give on the ground.[68]

Indeed, in a change from the previous desire for a visible political role (in addition to its existing economic importance), the EU now used the presence of its Special Representative to demand a more active and responsible role in the conflict resolution efforts. Simultaneously, trust of the EU among regional leaders grew (Dannreuther 2002, 10), although Israel in particular remained wary.[69] At the Taba talks, in the lack of any U.S. presence, the EUSR was the only outside observer and "the resulting Moratinos 'non-paper' became the jointly recognized record" (Nonneman 2003, 39).[70]

The gradual emergence of the Middle East 'Quartet' in 2001 and 2002 gave another boost to the EU's presence in the international arena. The Quartet assembled representatives of the United States, Russia, the United Nations, and the European Union as the main actors mediating the Israeli-Palestinian conflict.[71] While initially regarded as a fig leaf for the U.S. administration's unwillingness to deal with the conflict actively, the Quartet soon began to develop its own positive dynamic and policy proposals (Neugart 2003, 284).

In the Balkans, during this period of formalization, three EUSR mandates were revoked—for the first and so far only time. Mr Petritsch's mandate, limited until 30 September 1999, was in effect repealed already on 22 July 1999, given that the United Nations had begun deploying their mission in Kosovo (UNMIK).[72] Likewise, the Council relinquished Mr. Gonzalez' mandate in October 1999,[73] following the express wish of the EU Special Representative himself and his difficulties in implementing the mandate

---

68 Neugart 2001, 266. The mandate for EUSR continued to be extended; see Council Joint Action 1999/843/CFSP of 17 December 1999 and Council Joint Action 2000/794/CFSP of 14 December 2000. The later extension of December 2000 explicitly tasked the EUSR to "contribute to a better understanding of the EU's role among opinion leaders in the region" (Article 2 (h)).

69 See Asseburg (2003b, 184) who speaks of a "deep mistrust of Israeli policy-makers as well as the Israeli public with regard to European motivations and perceived one-sided pro-Arab stances." Ortega reports on two incidents showing the difficulties between Israel and the EU: "Specifically, at the height of the conflict the Israelis made it quite plain that they were rejecting any EU role, for example when the Israeli Army shelled Arafat's headquarters at the very moment that Special Envoy Miguel Moratinos was holding discussions with him on 6 March 2002, flouting the most sacrosanct rules of diplomacy, and again when Ariel Sharon declined to meet Javier Solana at [sic!] the same period" (Ortega 2003, 56).

70 Moratinos' unofficial account of the Taba talks was published by the Israeli daily Ha'aretz in February 2002 (Moratinos 2002).

71 Dietl 2005, 242. The more formal launch of the Quartet took place in April 2002 in Madrid during the Spanish EU presidency with a meeting of the four principals; until then, only the respective special envoys had met as the Quartet. Cf. also <http://www.un.org/unsco/UNSCO/Quartet.htm>.

72 Council Decision 10363/99 of 22 July 1999.

73 Council Joint Action 1999/665/CFSP of 11 October 1999. The mandate had previously, in January 1999, been extended until 31 January 2000 by Council Decision 1999/75/CFSP. See also Regelsberger 1999, fn 27, 250.

in the face of Yugoslav defiance.[74] The mandate of the Coordinator of the Royaumont Process was revoked one year later in June 2000 when the whole process was integrated into the Stability Pact and its Working Table 1 on democratization and human rights.[75] While the latter two mandates are generally seen as failures, Mr Petritsch's tenure is regarded as successful in that it placed the EU next to actors like the United States and Russia, for example at the Rambouillet conference (Jaanson 2008, 5 and 13).

All other mandates have continuously been extended to the present day. This included, until recently, the mandate for the Special Coordinator for the Stability Pact, although he was no longer called 'Special Representative.' Following a reorientation of the Stability Pact in November 2001, former Austrian Vice Chancellor Erhard Busek took over as EUSR after Bodo Hombach.[76] Busek continued to serve as Special Coordinator and supervision of his work became, gradually and naturally, more of a Commission competence (Bendiek 2007, 215-6).[77] In February 2008, the Regional Cooperation Council replaced the Stability Pact.

1.3 Troubled growth: Expansion (2002–2005)

Just like CFSP and ESDP, the EUSRs experienced a period of expansion (Grevi 2007, 29). Not only were their individual mandates broadened by involving EUSRs in all ESDP missions to come. EUSRs also extended the Union's geographical reach to areas hitherto unconsidered by ESDP. Within some three years, the EU more than doubled the number of its Special Representatives, sending envoys to Bosnia and Herzegovina, the South Caucasus, Central Asia, Sudan, and Moldova, respectively.

1.3.1 New missions, new mandates

The year 2003 began with a blatant exposition of the EU's differences over how to respond to the Iraq crisis, and in particular whether or not to side with the United States over intervention. While the effects of both this internal split and the American-led invasion of Iraq are easier to judge in hindsight, one concrete—and surprisingly positive—outcome of these discussions was the EU Security Strategy. Hammered out by top EU officials in the spring of 2003, and following a public consultation period in the second half of the year, it was finally endorsed by the December 2003 European Council (European Council 2003). For the first time, EU member states agreed on a

---

74 As an example of the Yugoslav refusal to cooperate, suffice to mention that EUSR Gonzalez was not even granted a visa to travel to the country (Jaanson 2008, 4).

75 Council Common Position 2000/387/CFSP of 16 June 2000.

76 Council Joint Action 2001/915/CFSP of 19 December 2001.

77 Thus, while still being in office in his original function as Special Coordinator, the official EUSR web site of the Council lists Erhard Busek as a "former EU Special Representative;" cf. <http://www.consilium.europa.eu/>. Busek ended his activities with the transfer of the Stability Pact into a regional arrangement in June 2008.

joint situation analysis (indeed, their analysis was not so different from the one the U.S. had made earlier[78]), defined the goals they aim to achieve, and designated the necessary steps on that path. More by happenstance than by calculated aspiration, the EU Security Strategy should prove to be the foundation for the expansion to come, a "roadmap for considerable policy developments" (Grevi 2007, 29).

The EU's internal crisis notwithstanding, 2003 also marked the beginning of a number of ESDP operations. At the December 2001 Laeken Council, the EU heads of state and government had declared ESDP mechanisms ready.[79] Later, following intense and difficult negotiations, the EU reached an agreement with the North Atlantic alliance giving the Union access to NATO assets for crisis management (also called 'Berlin plus' agreement; see Gnesotto 2004b, 24).[80] The latter made it possible for the EU to take the lead in missions previously led by NATO, first in Macedonia and later in Bosnia and Herzegovina (cf. Hansen 2006, 42-45).[81] Prior to that the EU had already shown that it could deploy a military mission (Operation Artemis in Congo) even without the support of NATO (Missiroli 2004, 58). Also important, in institutional terms, were the establishment of a European Defence Agency in 2004[82] and a European Security and Defence College in 2005.[83] While the former was designed to improve defense capabilities and armaments cooperation, the latter is a network of national institutions that holds courses on ESDP for civilian and military staff.[84]

The rise in ESDP operations was preceded, however, by the appointment of another EUSR. In anticipation of the deployment of an EU Police Mission to Bosnia and Herzegovina, the existing international representative, guardian of the 1995 Dayton Peace Agreement, was to also be EU Special Representative, thus giving the long-standing reconstruction effort in Bosnia and Herzegovina a distinctive CFSP mark.[85] The Brit Lord Ashdown followed in the footsteps of Carl Bildt, Carlos Westendorp, and (former EUSR for Kosovo) Wolfgang Petritsch to become High Representative of the international community, while at the same time treading a new path for an EUSR: He wore the first 'European-international double-hat' (Bendiek 2007, 225)—an arrangement that his predecessor had proposed (Jaanson 2008, 9) and that aimed to complement the 'hard power' of the international HR with the 'soft power' of the EUSR (Grevi 2007, 82).

---

78   For a comparison of the two security strategies see Berenskoetter 2005.

79   See Annex II to the Presidency Conclusions (European Council 2001).

80   NATO-EU relations were once humorously described as those of two organizations inhabiting the same city but different planets (cf. Hunter 2002, fn3, 73). Others use stronger words, calling them a "frozen conflict" (Hofmann/Reynolds 2007, 1).

81   For a good overview of ESDP's 'first five years', see Gnesotto 2004a.

82   Council Joint Action 2004/551/CFSP of 12 July 2004.

83   Council Joint Action 2005/575/CFSP of 18 July 2005.

84   Hansen 2006, 34. For an overview of the current state of the EU's 'security architecture', see Biscop 2007.

85   Council Joint Action 2002/211/CFSP of 11 March 2002.

Figure 6: Map of Bosnia and Herzegovina

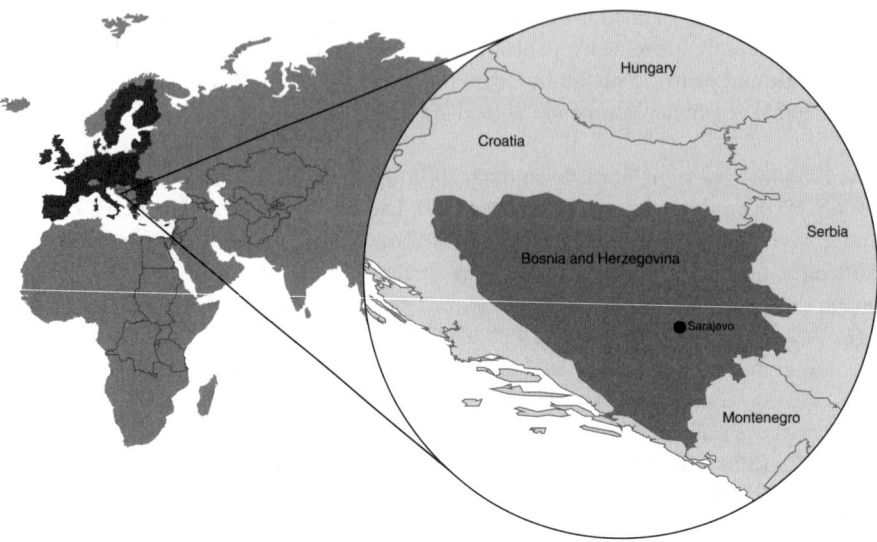

With an enhanced EU presence on the ground, ways had to be found to integrate the EUSR into the existing command structures. Ashdown was therefore included in the chain of command of the soon-to-deploy EU Police Mission (EUPM)[86] and granted authority to give direction to the EUPM Police Commissioner.[87] Indeed, the mission that was to start in January 2003 was one of the reasons why the EUSR was appointed in the first place (and mandates were effectively passed on the same day), based on an "aspiration to take a comprehensive view of the EU engagement in the field of rule of law, across institutional divides" (Grevi 2007, 83). Nearly two years later, Operation Althea was launched, in December 2004, as a successor to NATO's Stabilization Force (SFOR), stationed in Bosnia and Herzegovina since 1996.[88] Consequently, and in addition to the EU Police Mission there, another ESDP operation was active in the area of responsibility of EUSR Ashdown.[89]

Another new EUSR was Heikki Talvitie, a seasoned Finnish diplomat and, of importance with regard to his appointment to the South Caucasus, a former Co-Chairman of the Minsk Conference of the OSCE aiming to resolve the conflict between Azerbaijan and Armenia over Nagorno-Karabakh.[90] While the Union's involvement in the region

---

86   Council Joint Action 2002/210/CFSP of 11 March 2002.

87   Article 2 (3) of Council Joint Action 2002/211/CFSP of 11 March 2002.

88   Council Joint Action 2004/570/CFSP of 12 July 2004; on the same day, the EUSR mandate was extended by Council Joint Action 2004/569/CFSP.

89   Further extensions were passed in 2005 by Council Joint Action 2005/97/CFSP of 2 February 2005; Council Joint Action 2005/583/CFSP of 28 July 2005; and Council Joint Action 2005/825/CFSP of 24 November 2005.

90   Council Joint Action 2003/496/CFSP of 7 July 2003. A first proposal to appoint an EUSR to this

dates back to the early 1990s (Grevi 2007, 55), the appointment of an EUSR, in July 2003, was also a sign of the EU's "willingness to play a more active political role in the South Caucasus."[91]

Figure 7: Map of the South Caucasus

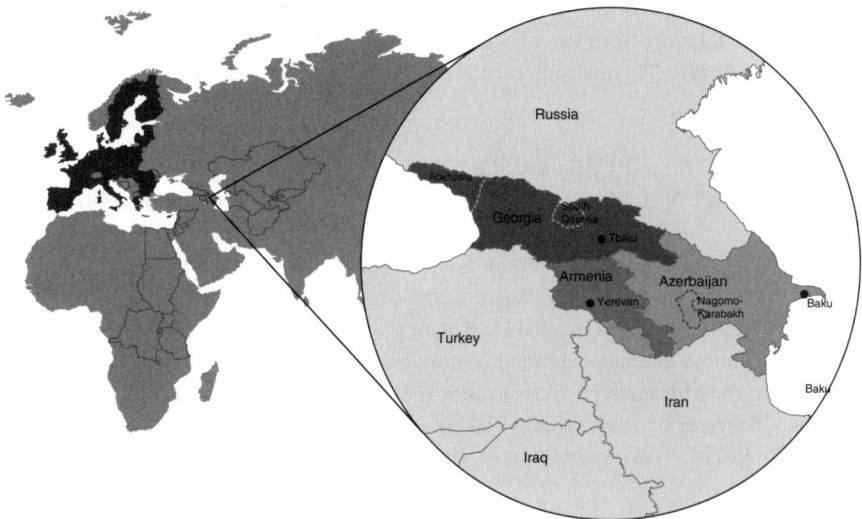

Because the EU did not have an explicit policy towards this region (Coppieters 2003, 159), the Council opted for a more innovative approach when passing the EUSR mandate: Rather than working according to a pre-defined strategy, the EUSR "would play an idea-generating and strategy-formulating role, and his report would be discussed by the Political and Security Committee, after which a more targeted mandate would be adopted" (Lynch 2003, 185-6). The EUSR's regular visits to the region soon "transformed the quality and quantity of the EU's political dialogue" with the South Caucasus (Council of the European Union 2004b, 38). As in the case of the African Great Lakes region, the EUSR was at the same time an expression of a lack of policy, an obligation for the Council to devise one,[92] and a means of helping member states to do so.

EUSR Talvitie started his work just before the sweeping events that unfolded in Georgia in November 2003. The 'Rose Revolution' brought down the government of President Eduard Shevardnadze, and the new President, Mikhail Saakashvili, elected in January 2004, promised a pro-Western policy of democratization and economic liberalization.

---

region was made by the German government in 2001 (Coppieters 2003, 159).

91   Preamble of Council Joint Action 2003/496/CFSP of 7 July 2003. See also Lynch 2003, 172.

92   Cf. Coppieters 2003, 163-4: "In order for the EU voice to carry, Brussels must define new common positions on the region […].The EU Special Representative will thus have to work on different regional levels, which will necessitate a common EU position on delicate geopolitical questions."

The EU supported this course, both by launching its first-ever rule of law mission (EUJUST Themis) in 2004,[93] and by including the country, alongside Armenia and Azerbaijan, in the new European Neighbourhood Policy (ENP).[94] Indeed, this extension of the ENP took place only one year after the policy's creation (then dubbed 'Wider Europe') and the explicit exclusion of the South Caucasian countries from its geographical reach.[95] Following the closure of the OSCE border-monitoring mission in Georgia in the summer of 2005 due to Russian objections, an EUSR support team was created.[96] Its task was to take up, from the OSCE, the responsibility to assess the border situation and, from operation Themis, supervision of the reform of the criminal justice system (Grevi 2007, 57–8).

In 2005, a set of three EUSRs saw the light of day, covering countries and regions as diverse as Central Asia, Moldova, and Sudan. Central Asia, for a long time outside the radar screen of European policy-makers, made it to the headlines in the spring of 2005. In March, President Askar Akayev of Kyrgyzstan had to resign following demonstrations protesting against allegedly rigged elections. Only two months later, in the Uzbek city of Andijan (or Andijon in local language), police cracked down on protesters killing, according to some estimates, several hundreds of people (International Crisis Group 2005b, 1). In the aftermath of these events, the Council appointed the Slovak Ján Kubiš, a former Chairman of the OSCE, as EUSR for Central Asia covering Kazakhstan, Kyrgyzstan, Tajikistan, Turkmenistan and Uzbekistan.[97]

While some argue that the appointment of the EUSR for Central Asia was merely reactive (International Crisis Group 2006a, 18), it appears more convincing that Kubiš was deployed as a strategic means to acquire the overall political strategy that the EU had lacked up to this point to deal with this region.[98] The five Central Asian countries were

93 Council Joint Action 2004/523/CFSP of 28 June 2004. On the same day, the EUSR's mandate—previously extended by Council Joint Action 2003/872/CFSP of 8 December 2003—was amended by Council Joint Action 2004/532/CFSP of 28 June 2004.

94 The European Neighbourhood Policy (ENP) applies to countries that border the EU but do not have a membership perspective, including Ukraine, Moldova, Armenia, Azerbaijan, and Georgia, as well as Israel and the Palestinian Territories, which are also within the area of responsibility of an EUSR. The ENP is a Community policy designed and implemented by the European Commission. For more information, see European Commission 2004a.

95 "Given their location, the Southern Caucasus therefore also fall [sic!] outside the geographical scope of this initiative for the time being" (European Commission 2003, fn2, 4). See also Lynch 2003, 171: "In seven months, the South Caucasus moved from the footnotes to being included in the same breath as the Balkans and the Congo in discussions of ESDP by the High Representative."

96 Council Joint Action 2005/582/CFSP of 28 July 2005. Previously, the mandate had been extended by Council Joint Action 2005/100/CFSP of 2 February 2005 and amended by Council Joint Action 2005/330/CFSP of 26 April 2005.

97 Council Joint Action 2005/588/CFSP of 28 July 2005.

98 Cf. Grevi 2007, 121. The Council, in its annual report, claims that the appointment was "in line with the EU's wish to play a more active political role in Central Asia and in order to ensure coordination and consistency of Union's [sic!] external actions in the region" (Council of the European Union 2006a, 52).

not included in the European Neighbourhood Policy (Matveeva 2006, 87), despite 15 years of bilateral relations, including support through the TACIS (Technical Assistance to the Commonwealth of Independent States) programme and, with some of the countries, the conclusion of Partnership and Cooperation Agreements (PCA).[99]

Figure 8: Map of Central Asia

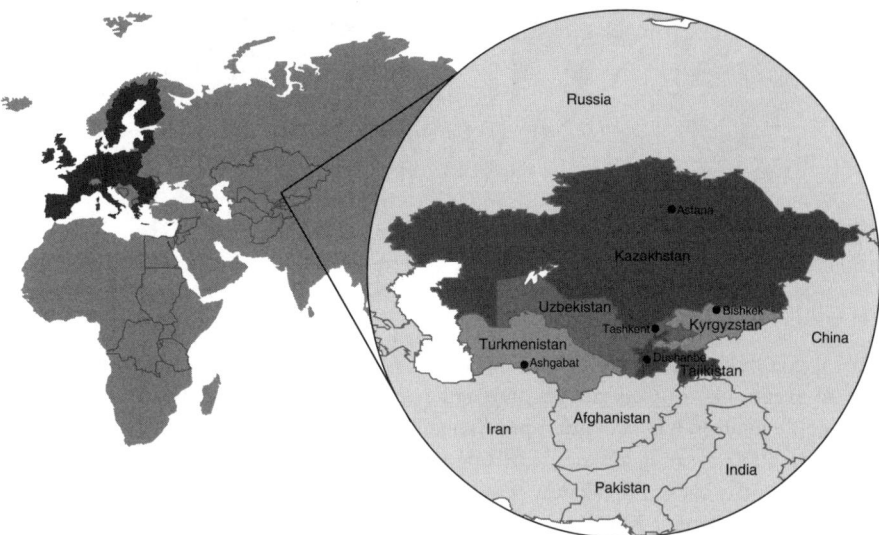

One major reason why the EU did not have any strategy towards the region was an acute lack of information and intelligence. While major players such as Russia, China, and the United States had long taken an interest in this energy-rich corner of the world, half of the EU member states did not and still do not have a single embassy there (Grevi 2007, 122). Even the Commission was represented, until 2007, by a full delegation only in Astana (Kazakhstan), with smaller offices in Kyrgyzstan and Tajikistan.[100] The EUSR was therefore given not only the usual information-gathering role, but his explicit task, being a more "idea-generating and strategy-formulating one" than usual (Matveeva 2006, 93), was to contribute to the formulation of an EU Central Asia strategy.[101]

---

99 PCAs with Kazakhstan, Kyrgyzstan and Uzbekistan entered into force in 1999. PCAs with Tajikistan and Turkmenistan have been signed but are pending ratification due to human rights concerns. EU relations with the latter two countries are based on Trade and Cooperation Agreements, which are not as comprehensive as PCAs, regulating only bilateral trade relations (Matveeva 2006, 85). For an overview of current EU relations with these countries, see the Commission's website: http://ec.europa.eu/external_relations/ceeca/pca/index.htm.

100 As part of the overall effort to increase the EU's presence in the region, the Commission is set to open Commission delegations in all five Central Asian countries; see European Council 2007, 16.

101 Interestingly, both Lynch (2003, 186) and Matveeva (2006, 93) use similar language to describe the role of the EUSR for the South Caucasus and for Central Asia, respectively.

43

Figure 9: Map of Moldova

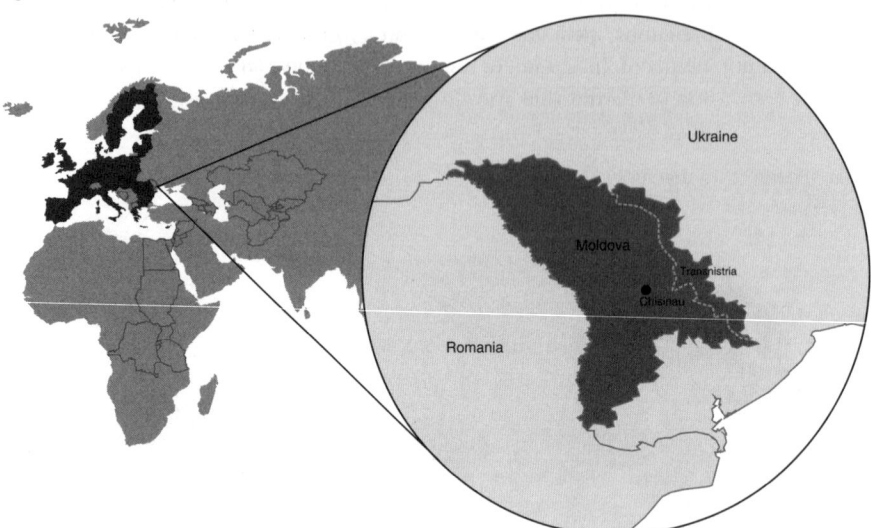

The appointment of an EUSR for Moldova in March 2005[102] was preceded not by critical events like in Central Asia, but rather by positive regional developments. The Orange Revolution had brought a pro-Western government to power in Ukraine in the winter of 2004, creating a window of opportunity to take up the dispute over Transnistria, the Russian-backed breakaway republic on Moldovan soil (Grevi 2007, 65). Shortly thereafter, in February 2005, both Ukraine and Moldova adopted bilateral ENP Action Plans under the EU's neighbourhood policy, thus paving the way for closer cooperation with the Union. In line with the European Security Strategy, appointing an EUSR was seen as a means of intensifying the EU's efforts to contribute to the solution of the Transnistrian conflict (Council of the European Union 2006a, 46).

Consequently, the main task of EUSR Adriaan Jacobovits de Szeged was to "strengthen the EU contribution to the resolution of the Transnistria conflict," while he was also asked to "assist in the further development of the EU's policy towards the Republic of Moldova and the region."[103] Given that Moldova is covered by the ENP under Community competence, the Dutch diplomat had to work closely with his Commission counterparts. Cooperation on the ground was greatly enhanced when the Commission opened its delegation in the Moldovan capital of Chisinau in October 2005, realising a pledge made in the ENP Action Plan. A joint fact-finding mission by the Council Secretariat and the Commission, led by EUSR Jacobovits at the end of 2005, helped pave the way for an EU Border Assistance Mission (EUBAM) to Moldova and Ukraine (Council of the European Union 2006a, 46). The mission's aim was to establish an international customs control on the Transnistrian segment of the Moldovan-Ukrainian state bor-

---

102 Council Joint Action 2005/265/CFSP of 23 March 2005.

103 Article 3 (1), paragraphs a) and d) of Council Joint Action 2005/265/CFSP of 23 March 2005.

der.[104] EUSR Jacobovits was involved in all political negotiations concerning EUBAM, enhancing the portfolio of what an EUSR is tasked to do. And while EUBAM officially is a Community mission financed under the Rapid Reaction Mechanism (RRM), its head is double-hatted as the EUSR's senior political advisor (Grevi 2007, 68-9).

Figure 10: Map of Sudan

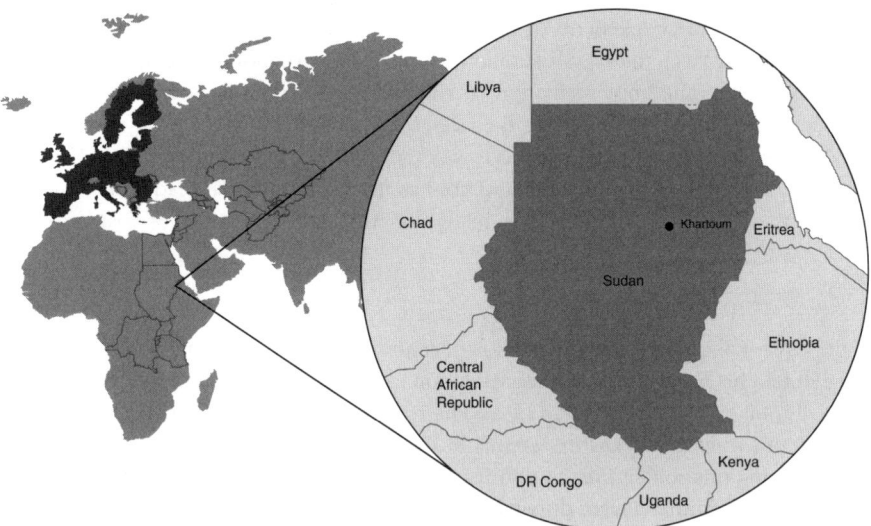

Also in the summer of 2005, nearly ten years after the first EUSR was deployed to the Great Lakes region, another EUSR was sent to Africa. Within the scope of its growing involvement,[105] the EU engaged more intensely in Sudan, both to assist implementation of the peace agreement for the conflict in the South and to assist conflict resolution in the Eastern Sudanese region of Darfur. For the latter, the EU supported the ceasefire commission monitoring the situation in Darfur as well as the African Union Mission in Sudan (AMIS), whose number of military and police continued to rise as hostilities persisted (Faria 2004, 17). In response to a joint AU/EU/UN assessment mission in early 2005, all parties stepped up their engagement: The African Union launched AMIS II with more than 7,000 police and military personnel, and the European Union dispatched

---

104 Cf. European Commission 2005b, establishing the EU Border Assistance Mission, and Council Joint Action 2005/776/CFSP of 7 November 2005, amending the EUSR mandate accordingly.

105 The EU had gradually scaled up its commitment to the neighbouring continent, both in terms of economic cooperation, by the latest (Cotonou Agreement) in a succession of traditional conventions (Yaoundé, Lomé), and with regard to crisis management issues, most notably following the transformation of the OAU into the African Union (AU) in 2002. The latter had sparked increased cooperation in the field of security: In late 2004 the EU adopted an 'Action Plan for ESDP support to Peace and Security in Africa' (Council of the European Union 2004a), followed, in December 2005, by a broader strategy 'EU and Africa: Towards a Strategic Partnership' (Council of the European Union 2005c).

a civilian-military supporting action to this mission.[106] Simultaneously, the latter issued the mandate for another EUSR, the former Finnish parliamentarian and Minister for the Environment, Pekka Haavisto.[107]

Discussions about the EUSR's mandate centred on the question of how robust the civil-military supporting action should be, and whether the EUSR should focus on Sudan only or on the African Union as a whole.[108] Eventually, in both cases the 'lighter' options prevailed, enriched by "elements of novelty and […] experimentation" (Grevi 2007, 103). On the political level, the EUSR should support the international mediation efforts for Darfur as well as the implementation of the peace agreement in Southern Sudan. On the operational level, he was, from the outset, integrated in the chain of command of the AMIS II support mission. For this to work, double-hatting came into play again: The head of the military component also worked as the EUSR's Military Adviser,[109] and the head of the EU Police Team acted as his Police Advisor.[110]

1.3.2 Tenures extended

In the Great Lakes region, EUSR Ajello concentrated his efforts mostly on the DRC, and there shifted his focus from conflict resolution to sustaining a fragile peace and a delicate political transition (Grevi 2007, 112-3). His responsibility increased with the EU's first autonomous military operation Artemis in Eastern Congo, conceived as a three-month long 'bridging mission' in preparation for the launch of a UN operation.[111] 1400 troops under French command were dispatched to protect civilians that had fled the fighting in the area bordering Uganda and Rwanda (cf. Faria 2004, 48). Ajello's task was to provide political support to the mission, which he did not see as an end in itself but rather as "the start of something bigger" in the framework of CFSP (Astill/Norton-Taylor 2003, 13). He was right to the extent that soon two more ESDP operations followed, in 2004 and 2005, respectively, one supporting Congolese police (EUPOL Kinshasa) and another dealing with security sector reform[112] (EUSEC RD Congo).

The three missions marked the second element in the new focus of the EUSR's work, i. e. a shift away from building a policy consensus among member states to "managing the

---

106 Council Joint Action 2005/557/CFSP of 18 July 2005.

107 Council Joint Action 2005/556/CFSP of 18 July 2005.

108 Cf. Grevi 2007, 102-3. In a way, it thus anticipated the nomination of an EUSR for the African Union in December 2007; see section 1.4.

109 PSC Decision Darfur/1/2005 (2005/653/CFSP) of 29 July 2005.

110 PSC Decision Darfur/2/2005 (2005/654/CFSP) of 29 July 2005.

111 For an extensive analysis of operation Artemis in Bunia, the capital of the Ituri province in North-eastern Congo, see Faria 2004, 47-55.

112 EU engagement in security sector reform, or SSR, has developed only quite recently, with the EU Security Strategy of 2003 as the first document to mention SSR missions as part of its institution-building activities (European Council 2003, 12). The mission in Congo was in fact one of the first to test the EU's new approach (cf. Law 2007, 10-11).

growing EU projection in the field" (Grevi 2007, 113). It therefore does not come as a surprise that the Council, during these years, continued to extend the mandate of Ajello. The EUSR, by his extensive experience and the respect he commanded from regional and international actors, had become a most valuable asset for the Europeans.[113]

Developments in the Middle East during this period got off to an unspectacular start but in the end were shaped by two key events: The death of the Palestinian President, Yasser Arafat, in November 2004, and the unilateral withdrawal of Israeli forces from the Gaza strip, in August and September of 2005. In 2002, the Council had decided to give EUSR Moratinos more freedom to present his own policy proposals and amended the EUSR's mandate accordingly,[114] not least bolstering his role as the Union's representative in the Middle East Quartet. This body's most important output of that time, other than continuous multilateral meetings and shuttle diplomacy, had been the agreement on a 'road map,' in October 2002. The document, which on the substantial side envisioned a peaceful two-state solution and, procedurally speaking, reaffirmed U.S. commitment to the MEPP, clearly bore a European stamp (Asseburg 2003a, 23–24; Tocci 2005, 14).

In July 2003, Ambassador Moratinos handed over his position to Marc Otte, a Belgian diplomat who had previously worked as Solana's advisor on defense and security policy.[115] This experience served him well when, in late 2005, the EU deployed its first two ESDP missions in the Middle East requiring him to build a bridge into the security sector: An EU Border Assistance Mission was sent to monitor operations of the Gaza-Egypt border-crossing point at Rafah (EUBAM Rafah), and an EU Co-ordinating Office for Palestinian Police Support (EU COPPS, headquartered in Ramallah) was established to provide support to the Palestinian Civil Police. In both cases, the Head of Mission received guidance from High Representative Solana through EUSR Otte.[116] The fact that, with EUBAM Rafah, Israel had accepted the EU as a partner in the field of security policy was in itself considered a success and a sign of the EU's increased international reputation.[117]

---

113 Council Joint Action 2002/962/CFSP of 10 December 2002; Council Joint Action 2003/447/CFSP of 16 June 2003; Council Joint Action 2003/869/CFSP of 8 December 2003 (taking into account the 2003 Guidelines); Council Joint Action 2004/530/CFSP of 28 June 2004; Council Joint Action 2005/96/CFSP of 2 February 2005 (considering the EUSR's role within EUPOL Kinshasa); and Council Joint Action 2005/586/CFSP of 28 July 2005 (considering the EUSR's role within EUSEC RD Congo).

114 Dietl 2005, 109-110. See Council Joint Action 2002/965/CFSP of 10 December 2002.

115 Council Joint Action 2003/537/CFSP of 21 July 2003.

116 Council Joint Action 2005/796/CFSP of 14 November 2005. Marc Otte's mandate had previously been extended by Council Joint Action 2003/873/CFSP of 8 December 2003; Council Joint Action 2004/534/CFSP of 28 June 2004; Council Joint Action 2005/99/CFSP of 2 February 2005; and Council Joint Action 2005/587/CFSP of 28 July 2005.

117 Neugart 2006, 279; for contemporary accounts of the difficulties that EUSR Otte had to face at the beginning of his term, see Beatty 2003, and Keinon et al. 2003.

In Afghanistan, Spanish UN official Francesc Vendrell succeeded EUSR Klaiber in June 2002,[118] heralding the beginning of increased EU involvement in the reconstruction of the Afghan state. Vendrell had been Personal Representative of the UN Secretary General for Afghanistan and Head of the United Nations Special Mission to Afghanistan (UNSMA), the predecessor of the current UNAMA. Engaging in his intensive travel activities from Kabul rather than from Brussels, EUSR Vendrell was crucial in bringing to the table the EU's contribution to the Afghan state-building process, including the passing of a new constitution and the holding of presidential and parliamentary elections in 2004 (Grevi 2007, 73 and 75)—indeed the first time ever that Afghans selected their head of state by way of competitive elections. The EUSR's mandate has been extended accordingly.[119]

EUSRs also continued to serve in the Balkans, and although Macedonia has seen high turnover, they contributed to the country's gradual stabilization, including through ESDP missions. At the end of October 2002, Alain le Roy handed over to the Belgian Alexis Brouhns.[120] This change of nationality in the person of EUSR also marked the end of a special regime by which, "given the urgency of the situation, and exceptionally," administrative expenditure of the EUSR was covered mainly by France.[121] The financing of an EU foreign policy instrument was brought to the CFSP budget and thus under the control of all member states plus the Commission. EUSR Brouhns served in Skopje for a little more than year, and it was during his turn that ESDP operations Concordia, a military stabilization operation, and its successor Proxima, a police-monitoring mission, were deployed to Macedonia.[122] In both cases, the EUSR acted as the primary interface between the ESDP head of mission and local political authorities, as well as to coordinate the missions with other EU activities on the ground (Grevi 2007, 93).[123] In early 2004, Sören Jessen-Petersen, a former Assistant High Commissioner at the Geneva headquarters of the UN High Commissioner for Refugees (UNHCR), took over.[124] In the summer of the same year, Jessen-Petersen was called to lead the civilian administra-

---

118 Council Joint Action 2002/496/CFSP of 25 June 2002.

119 Council Joint Action 2002/961/CFSP of 10 December 2002; Council Joint Action 2003/448/CFSP of 16 June 2003; Council Joint Action 2003/871/CFSP of 8 December 2003; Council Joint Action 2004/533/CFSP of 28 June 2004; Council Joint Action 2005/95/CFSP of 2 February 2005; and Council Joint Action 2005/585/CFSP of 28 July 2005.

120 Council Joint Action 2002/832/CFSP of 21 October 2002.

121 Article 3 (1) of Council Joint Action 2001/492/CFSP of 29 June 2001.

122 Council Joint Action 2003/92/CFSP of 27 January 2003 (for Concordia) and Council Joint Action 2003/681/CFSP of 29 September 2003 (for Proxima).

123 Council Joint Action 2003/446/CFSP of 16 June 2003 and Council Joint Action 2003/870/CFSP of 8 December 2003. Previously, the mandate was extended by Council Joint Action 2002/963/CFSP of 10 December 2002.

124 Council Joint Action 2004/86/CFSP of 26 January 2004, extended by Council Joint Action 2004/531/CFSP of 28 June 2004.

tion of Kosovo as SRSG. The Swedish diplomat and former ambassador to Yugoslavia and Macedonia Michael Sahlin followed him, serving in this post for over a year.[125]

A major innovation was the appointment in October 2005 of Erwan Fouéré, a Commission official of Irish nationality, as the new EUSR for Macedonia and, simultaneously, Head of the Commission delegation.[126] The two mandates were of course distinct, but intended to be complementary: They both aimed at ensuring a lasting stabilization of the country and supporting the transition from post-conflict reconstruction to pre-EU accession. Nonetheless, following various double-hattings of sorts (e.g. that of Javier Solana as High Representative for CFSP and Secretary-General of the Council Secretariat, or of Paddy Ashdown as EUSR and High Representative of the international community in Bosnia and Herzegovina), this was the first time that such a personal union spanned the first and second pillars of EU policy as they were created under the Maastricht Treaty.[127]

The double-hatting could be regarded as a real-life test case of one of the provisions of the Treaty establishing a new Constitution for Europe (TCE) that was signed two years earlier. The Treaty foresaw the post of an EU Foreign Minister who was also Vice-President of the Commission, thus wearing a similar 'intra-EU' double-hat. This should bring the two main instruments of EU external relations—broadly speaking, diplomacy and aid—closer together (Everts/Keohane 2003, 171). The negative referenda in France and the Netherlands on the Treaty in the spring of 2005 stymied all further discussion on this topic and the TCE never entered into force. The new EUSR in Macedonia, however, put this pillar-spanning arrangement into practice at a different level.

1.4 Establishing themselves: Consolidation and new tasks (2006–2007)

Eventually, it took almost a full decade to consolidate the foreign policy instrument of EUSRs. The Treaty of Amsterdam had brought about the formalization of their existence; yet, as it is often the case with 'constitutional amendments', actual praxis was needed to work out a modus operandi that could not be enshrined in a single legal sentence. Thus, the EUSRs witnessed a period of consolidation—much of it achieved by means of organizational learning—at the same time that CFSP was put on "more solid institutional and policy grounds" (Grevi 2007, 29). That said, new tasks demanded flexible responses, including by improvising on the EU's envoy model.

---

125 Council Joint Action 2004/565/CFSP of 26 July 2004, extended by Council Joint Action 2005/98/CFSP of 2 February 2005 and Council Joint Action 2005/589/CFSP of 28 July 2005.

126 Council Joint Action 2005/724/CFSP of 17 October 2005.

127 The 'first pillar' contains all Community policies as defined by the Treaty establishing a European Community (TEC). Pillars two and three refer to the two new policy areas introduced by the Treaty on European Union (TEU) in Maastricht in 1993, i.e. CFSP and Justice and Home Affairs (JHA), respectively.

1.4.1   Internal consolidation

Efforts to integrate the EUSRs into the structures at the Council Secretariat received a new boost about ten years after the invention of this instrument. A first set of guidelines, concerning the appointing procedure and administrative arrangements (e. g. budget and reporting lines), was passed as early as 2000 (cf. section 1.2 above), considering in particular the role of the new High Representative (Council of the European Union 2000). Moreover, the argument was made, amongst others by the Council Legal Service, that for reasons of political accountability the EUSRs should be placed under a contractual obligation to the Council and their expenditures charged to the Council's administrative budget (ibid., 2-3). This first document was revised in 2003, mainly to return financial accountability to the CFSP budget and, consequently, to the Commission. The objective was to "create a solid basis for funding while allowing optimal flexibility and a high degree of responsiveness to evolving needs on the ground" (Council of the European Union 2003b, 2).

In 2006 and 2007, new guidelines were issued as part of a major internal reorganization effort. They extended the mandate duration to one year, setting reporting duties at regular intervals,[128] while limiting tenure of office to four years and generally strengthening the evaluation process "with a view to assessing the renewal of an EUSR mandate in light of achieved policy objectives" (Council of the European Union 2007c, 1). Besides, the guidelines reinforced the role of EUSRs in promoting political coordination in the field with a view to ensuring a coherent engagement of all EU actors. In addition to these new regulations, they set up a Coordination Unit within the Directorate-General (DG) E of the Council Secretariat and introduced an administrative toolkit as well as a one-week induction course for new EUSRs and their staff (Grevi 2007, 24).

Important as these measures of institutional and procedural consolidation were, they still fell short of the 'support cell,' a joint administrative team designed to help EUSRs strengthen their secretarial and budgetary capacities. It was mentioned in the 2007 Guidelines (Council of the European Union 2007c, 2) but so far has not materialised. Likewise, the envisaged creation of an 'EUSR Management Committee', comprising all relevant services from political desks to the press service to personnel matters has not yet been implemented (Grevi 2007, 36). Instead, EUSRs became lightly integrated into the structures of the Council Secretariat by designating two top officials, the Director of DG E and the Director of the Policy Unit, as senior contact points.

Finally, the creation of a Civilian Planning and Conduct Capability (CPCC) in the course of 2007 removed the EUSRs from the chain of command of ESDP operations. Ever since ESDP was introduced in 1998/99, there was a military bias buffered by a civilian dimension only due to Nordic insistence (Petrov/Dijkstra 2007, 7). The new CPCC was thus conceived as the civilian equivalent of the EU Military Staff (EUMS) and meant to

---

128   The regular cycle now was the following: Beginning of new mandate in March, progress report by the end of June, mandate implementation report by the end of November, and Council decision on Joint Action by the end of January; cf. Council of the European Union 2006c, 9–10.

professionalise civilian crisis management. Prior to this reorganization, it had been the Directorate for Civilian Crisis Management within DG E that worked as an informal operations centre. Now, the new head of CPCC—called the Civilian Operations Commander—would report directly to the High Representative, just like his military counterpart, the Director-General of EUMS (Grevi 2007, 38). It remains to be hoped that, as a consequence of these measures, EUSRs will "be more flexible and, arguably, dispose of more time to fulfill their central political and diplomatic roles of representation, reporting and coordination" (Grevi 2007, 39).

In sum, these innovations have tried to consolidate the political role of EUSRs, either by easing their administrative obligations or by freeing them from operational responsibilities in civilian ESDP missions. Based on these consolidation efforts, all nine EUSRs continued their work during this period, and even a tenth mandate was issued at the end of 2007.

1.4.2   Mandates continued

Before handing over to his successor, EUSR Ajello oversaw another EU mission in the DRC, this time to support the elections there (EUFOR DR Congo).[129] After four successive ESDP missions in the country, it is fair to say that, given the multiplicity of the means employed on the ground, the DRC has become, together with the Western Balkans, "the largest laboratory for EU crisis management" (Grevi 2007, 114; for the Balkans, see Calic 2008, 27). In all this, it was the permanent presence of EUSR Ajello as a coordinating authority which helped politically prepare as well as smoothly run these missions (Grevi 2007, 116; Council of the European Union 2007a, para 290). After nearly eleven full years in office, Aldo Ajello, the first ever and longest-serving EUSR, passed over, in February 2007, to Roeland van de Geer, a Dutch career diplomat with considerable experience in Africa.[130]

In the Middle East, victory of the Hamas party in the Palestinian elections in January 2006 put a freeze on Middle East diplomacy, effectively stopping an until then fairly successful EU policy and the EUSR's work (Tocci 2006, 8). As a reaction, the EU resorted to holding back its support funds for the Palestinian territories.[131] Moreover, the war between Israel and the Lebanese Hezbollah in the summer of 2006 severely tested European diplomacy, eventually leading not to an ESDP mission there but to a UN mission with strong European ingredients (UNIFIL). In this deteriorating situation, EUSR Otte continued to negotiate as a member of the Quartet, as well as to bring about practical

---

129 Council Joint Action 2006/319/CFSP of 27 April 2006.

130 Council Joint Action 2007/112/CFSP of 15 February 2007. Previously, Ajello's mandate had been extended by Council Joint Action 2006/122/CFSP of 20 February 2006.

131 By the time, EU funding had reached around 500 million EUR per year, over half of which provided by the EC budget and the remainder bilaterally by EU member states; cf. European Commission 2005a, 2.

improvements in direct talks with the conflict parties, such as the reopening of the Rafah crossing point in July 2006.[132]

Good news initially came from Sudan, where, in May 2006, a peace agreement was reached for Darfur. EUSR Haavisto had attended the peace talks in neighbouring Abuja, also working closely with the envoys of individual EU member states (Grevi 2007, 105).[133] Likewise, he engaged, also in cooperation with the EUSR for the Great Lakes, in negotiations on dispute settlement at Sudan's Eastern border with Uganda, which led to his taking over a monitoring responsibility there (ibid., 106–7).[134] In April 2007, Pekka Haavisto handed over to Swedish diplomat Torben Brylle.[135]

The Western Balkans, the South Caucasus, and Central Asia showed a steady degree of EU and, thus, EUSR involvement. In Bosnia and Herzegovina, the international mediator and former German politician Christian Schwarz-Schilling succeeded Paddy Ashdown at the beginning of 2006 in the two positions of EUSR and HR.[136] Unlike Ashdown who is said to have neglected his assigned European role in favour of his international hat (Jopp 2006, 236), Schwarz-Schilling had pledged to strengthen the EUSR and even phase out the Office of the High Representative.[137] While effectively doing the former, he did not achieve the latter in a situation where the Bosnian authorities failed to adopt the constitutional amendments deemed necessary by the international community to cede its supervisory function (Grevi 2007, 89). He thus passed over, in June 2007, to Miroslav Lajčák, a Slovak diplomat and former Personal Representative of Solana for the Montenegro referendum.[138]

Phasing out was more successful in Macedonia: There, the police advisory team (EUPAT), successor to operation Proxima, terminated its work in June 2006 and thus concluded five years of ESDP involvement in the country.[139] With the European Council having granted Macedonia candidate status (European Council 2005), EUSR Fouéré started to concentrate on supporting important steps on the way to European integra-

---

132 Cf. Grevi 2007, 138. The EUSR's mandate was extended by Council Joint Action 2006/119/CFSP of 20 February 2006, and Council Joint Action 2007/110/CFSP of 15 February 2007, respectively.

133 The EUSR's mandate was extended by Council Joint Action 2006/468/CFSP of 5 July 2006.

134 This new task was included in the mandate by Council Joint Action 2007/108/CFSP of 15 February 2007, which also extended the EUSR's mandate.

135 Council Joint Action 2007/238/CFSP of 19 April 2007.

136 Council Joint Action 2006/49/CFSP of 30 January 2006.

137 This pledge was also mirrored in a change to the EUSR mandate, as effected by Council Joint Action 2006/523/CFSP of 25 July 2006. Therein, he was tasked to "support planning for a reinforced EUSR office in the context of the closure of the Office of the High Representative (OHR)" (Article 1). EUSR Schwarz-Schilling confirmed this in an opinion article for the International Herald Tribune, cf. Schwarz-Schilling 2006.

138 Council Joint Action 2007/427/CFSP of 18 June 2007. Previously, the mandate had been extended by Council Joint Action 2007/87/CFSP of 7 February 2007.

139 EUPAT was established by Council Joint Action 2005/826/CFSP of 24 November 2005 with a duration of six months.

tion, including reform of the judiciary, and on coordinating the various EU actors on the ground.[140]

Mandates for Moldova and the South Caucasus basically remained the same, as did EUSR involvement in crisis management activities there. EUSR Jacobovits and his successor, the Hungarian former UN official and Assistant UN Secretary General Kálmán Miszei,[141] engaged in difficult negotiations over the conflict in Transnistria (cf. Zerkalo Nedeli 2007). In the South Caucasus, Swedish diplomat Peter Semneby took over from his Finnish colleague Talvitie, in February 2007.[142] Shortly afterwards, the EUSR support team handed over responsibility for criminal justice reform to the Commission, and reconstituted itself as Border Support Team (BST) (Grevi 2007, 58).[143]

During this time, Central Asia witnessed the emergence of a new policy approach of the EU, brought about not least by the EUSR. In May 2007, at the end of and with considerable contribution from the German EU presidency (Grevi 2007, 127), the Council passed an EU Central Asia Strategy (European Council 2007). Its main aim, in addition to making the EU a respected partner of Central Asian countries, was to bring together policy initiatives from member states and the EU level, as well as to strike a balance between a regional approach and assistance to the individual Central Asian countries. EUSR Kubiš and his successor as of October 2006, French diplomat Pierre Morel, had been tasked to prepare a first draft of this document in close consultation with individual member states, the Council Secretariat, and the Commission.[144] After the strategy was passed, the EUSR was assigned a role in monitoring its implementation, in cooperation with the Presidency and the Commission.[145]

For the EUSR in Afghanistan, duties in both international monitoring and ESDP coordination increased. The period started with the London Conference that passed the 'Afghan Compact', which was designed as an overarching policy framework, setting binding targets for both the Afghan government and international actors in fields like security, governance, economic development, and counter-narcotics.[146] To implement this

---

140 Cf. Grevi 2007, 96. The last mandate extensions were made by Council Joint Action 2006/123/ CFSP of 20 February 2006; and Council Joint Action 2007/109/CFSP of 15 February 2007.

141 EUSR Miszei was appointed by Council Joint Action 2007/107/CFSP of 15 February 2007. Previously, Council Joint Action 2006/120/CFSP of 20 February 2006 had extended the mandate.

142 Council Joint Action 2006/121/CFSP of 20 February 2006; a mandate extension was passed by Council Joint Action 2007/111/CFSP of 15 February 2007.

143 At the same time, an agreement was concluded with the Government of Georgia regarding the status of the EUSR and his team; cf. Council Joint Action 2006/366/CFSP of 20 March 2006.

144 EUSR Morel was appointed by Council Joint Action 2006/670/CFSP of 5 October 2006; prior to this, EUSR Kubiš's mandate had been extended by Council Joint Action 2006/118/CFSP of 20 February 2006.

145 Council Joint Action 2007/634/CFSP of 1 October 2007; previously, the mandate had been extended by Council Joint Action 2007/113/CFSP of 15 February 2007.

146 Afghanistan Compact, adopted at 'Building on Success—The London Conference on Afghanistan', London, 31 January and 1 February 2006.

Compact, a Joint Coordination and Monitoring Board (JCMB) was created, on which the EUSR, jointly with the Commission, represents the EU.[147] The work of EUSR Vendrell continued to focus mainly on the rule of law, security sector reform, and human rights. It thus suited this focus well when the EU was asked, in spring 2007, to 'Europeanise' the police mission until then led by Germany. After EUPOL Afghanistan was established,[148] the EUSR was tasked, as in previous cases, to provide the Head of EUPOL with local political guidance[149]—which is expected to give the EUSR more clout vis-à-vis the Afghan authorities (Grevi 2007, 78).

1.4.3 New and different tasks

The last mandate passed in the period under analysis in this study (1996–2007) was preceded by long discussions about the EU's involvement in crisis management in Africa in general, and its relations with the African Union in particular. In the end, the second (intra-EU) double-hatted EUSR was created, acting as both the Special Representative of the Union for and the Head of Delegation of the European Commission to the AU. Such engagement was in line with the EU's commitment to support the AU, last recognized in the EU Africa Strategy of December 2005. The new EUSR was chosen from within the Council Secretariat staff: Koen Vervaeke, of Belgian nationality, had been Head of the Africa task force of the Policy Unit prior to his appointment.[150] His task was to strengthen the EU's influence on the dialogue with the AU on all CFSP/ESDP issues.[151]

While the instrument of EUSRs faced some internal consolidation during this period, it should also be noted that the EU returned to a flexible and inventive use of representatives other than those nominated on the basis of Article 18 (5) TEU. In October 2003, the first of now three Personal Representatives of the Secretary-General/High Representative was appointed. They are members of Solana's cabinet without Council

---

147 Previously, the mandate had been extended by Council Joint Action 2006/124/CFSP of 20 February 2006. A year later, it was extended again by Council Joint Action 2007/106/CFSP of 15 February 2007.

148 Council Joint Action 2007/369/CFSP of 30 May 2007.

149 Council Joint Action 2007/732/CFSP of 13 November 2007.

150 Council Joint Action 2007/805/CFSP of 6 December 2007. A day earlier, the Commission had adopted Koen Vervaeke's appointment as Head of the Commission Delegation to the AU located in Addis Ababa.

151 Another new EUSR mandate was passed in February 2008 for Kosovo, just a fortnight before the declaration of independence of the former Serbian province (Council Joint Action 2008/123/CFSP of 4 February 2008). A planning team had been working since April 2006, proposing both an ESDP mission as a follow-up to the UN administration and the NATO force, and a double-hatted post of EUSR and International Civilian Representative, following the Bosnian rather than the Macedonian model (Council Joint Action 2006/304/CFSP of 10 April 2006). As talks about the province's 'final status' remained inconclusive all through 2007, the province declared itself, in close cooperation with the EU and the United States, independent from Serbia, and invited both the EUSR and an ESDP rule of law mission into the country. For an overview of the transition process towards 'supervised independence,' see International Crisis Group 2008.

approval, covering issues like non-proliferation of weapons of mass destruction (Annalisa Gianella, since 2003), human rights in the area of CFSP (Riina Kionka, since 2007), and parliamentary affairs in the area of CFSP (Michael Matthiesen, since 2007).[152] They mark another dimension of expansion during this period (i. e. that into functional or horizontal issues), but are not studied here.

In addition, two new types of representatives came into being, informally coordinating the EU's policies towards Kosovo and Myanmar, respectively. First, German ambassador to the Court of St. James's in London, Wolfgang Ischinger, was nominated to represent the EU, alongside the United States and Russia (the so-called troika) in the last round of negotiations on the future status of Kosovo in the second half of 2007 (International Crisis Group 2007, 2). While remaining German ambassador in London, and with his expenses covered by Germany, he participated in the troika talks on the EU's behalf. Above all, he reported back to the member states, giving impulses for the negotiation process. Secondly, the crisis in Myanmar in August 2007 prompted the delegation of the Italian Parliamentarian and former Minister of Justice, Piero Fassino, to the region.[153] As a Special Envoy, his task was to support the UN representative there and to coordinate the member states' activities, thus also giving political visibility to the EU.[154] These two appointments not only brought back the initial name, but also the national financing last used in 2001 and 2002 for the French EUSRs to Macedonia.

This increase of ad hoc and non-institutionalized instruments points to a potential future development. In December 2007, EU heads of state and government agreed upon a Reform Treaty, putting a (preliminary) end to years of discussion about institutional reform.[155] One of the new provisions is the creation of a European External Action Service (EEAS), or EU foreign service (although this latter expression is barred from official usage due to sensitivities about national sovereignty in some of the member states). Again, as in the case of the EUSRs, so far there nothing exists but a meagre Treaty reference, explaining that the new 'High Representative for foreign policy' should have a quasi-diplomatic service at his or her disposal.[156]

---

152 From 2005 to 2007, Michael Matthiesen was Personal Representative for Human Rights in the area of CFSP, i. e. Riina Kionka's predecessor. Furthermore, Miroslav Lajčák, today's EUSR for Bosnia and Herzegovina, acted as Solana's Personal Representative for the referendum in Montenegro, with a term lasting from December 2005 to June 2006. For information on the Personal Representatives, see <http://www.consilium.europa.eu/cms3_fo/showPage.asp?id=942&lang=EN&mode=g>.

153 Declaration by Javier Solana, "EU High Representative for the CFSP appoints Piero Fassino as EU Special Envoy for Burma/Myanmar," S315/07, Brussels, 6 November 2007.

154 In addition, between 2001 and 2007, there was a representative of the EU presidency for the International Contact Group on the Mano River Basin. Created under the Swedish presidency, this post was held by Hans Dahlgren, then State Secretary for Foreign Affairs of Sweden, for thirteen consecutive EU Presidencies.

155 Treaty of Lisbon amending the Treaty on European Union and the Treaty establishing the European Community, signed at Lisbon, 13 December 2007, published in the Official Journal of the EU 2007/C 306/01.

156 Under point 30) of the Treaty, a new Article 13a is inserted in the existing TEU, stipulating, inter alia,

Given that the mandates of all representatives taken together not only mirror CFSP priorities but also the central role taken on by the High Representative in defining and implementing these priorities (Regelsberger 2006, 247), the question arises how the EUSRs will be integrated into this broader diplomatic framework. The institutional powers of this new service as well as its (institutional and physical) location will have to be hammered out between the Council, the Commission, and the European Parliament once the Treaty is ratified. Yet the possibility of integrating the existing EU Special Representatives into the EU foreign service shows that there is still a new stage to come in the development of the EUSRs.

The first chapter showed how the EU Special Representatives developed from their invention in 1996 to 2007. This historical account already alluded to some potential learning instances, especially in the formalization (e. g. establishing formal hierarchies with the new CFSP institutions) and consolidation (e. g. passing guidelines on EU coordination in the field, including the ESDP chain of command) phases.

The next chapter of this thesis will begin with a short summary of the EUSRs' basic characteristics, before comparing their work with what other special envoys, i. e. those of the United Nations Secretary-General and the United States President, do. This comparison will lead me to analytical inferences about the work of envoys and their potential function in processes of organizational learning. On this basis, I will illustrate the various roles they can take on and then explain why I chose the EUSRs as the object of this study.

---

that "3. In fulfilling his mandate, the High Representative shall be assisted by a European External Action Service. This service shall work in cooperation with the diplomatic services of the Member States and shall comprise officials from relevant departments of the General Secretariat of the Council and of the Commission as well as staff seconded from national diplomatic services of the Member States." This is the same wording as Article 27 of the TCE.

Chapter 2:
Comparing Special Envoys: Different Models, Similar Roles

The previous chapter showed the historical development of the EU Special Representatives over more than a decade. After being invented as 'substitutes for policy' in 1996 and formalized by the Treaty of Amsterdam, the instrument of EUSRs experienced a significant period of expansion before entering a consolidation phase around the year 2006. The preceding extensive presentation of the research object was intended to familiarize the reader with an instrument of EU foreign policy that has so far remained literally unmentioned by the academic literature; it additionally highlighted some potential instances of learning.

This chapter aims to clarify why the EU Special Representatives have been chosen as an object of study. A comparative overview puts different models of envoys—those of the UN Secretary-General and of the U. S. president—next to each other according to their basic characteristics. From this comparison, I will then draw inferences for their European counterparts, including with regard to their function in learning processes, analyze the various roles special envoys can assume, and justify the selection of the EUSRs as a case for study. This lays the foundations for the theoretical model to be developed in chapter 3.

2.1 Comparing envoys

While in EU foreign policy terms an institutional history of more than a dozen years appears a considerably long time, the history of diplomatic envoys[157] dates back much longer, of course. Thucydides already mentions them in his masterpiece about the Peloponnesian War.[158] They re-appear on the European secular scene with the advent of Medieval and, later, Renaissance diplomacy,[159] a more famous example being Niccolò Machiavelli of Florence.[160] Later, envoys were fully involved in another epoch-making event of the time, the Treaty of Westphalia. Indeed, the diplomats of the modern world

---

157 Unless otherwise designated as an official title (e. g. Special Representative of the Secretary-General), the terms envoy, representative, and agent are used interchangeably in this chapter.

158 Cf. Thucydides 1978, Book 5 Ch. 4: "About the same time Phaeax, son of Erasistratus, set sail with two colleagues as ambassador from Athens to Italy and Sicily." This was an early, though unsuccessful effort in coalition building against Syracuse; see also Madsen/McGregor 1979, 325; Bachteler 1997, 319.

159 For a classical work, see Mattingly 1955: "By 1300, [...] the secular powers of Christendom had already learned all they could from the papacy about the machinery of diplomacy, as about other kinds of governmental machinery" (15). For the influence of papal diplomacy on its worldly counterpart, see Queller 1960.

160 For an analysis of Machiavelli's diplomatic communication as a special envoy to the Papal Court, see Wiethoff 1981.

were first envoys (or messengers) before they became more permanent ambassadors after the 14 th century.[161]

When looking for cases of envoys comparable to the EU Special Representatives, common sense suggests a limitation to the time after World War II where we find two possible predecessors: special representatives of the United Nations, and envoys sent by the United States. The two types make a good case for a comparative inspection because they are different enough in their appearances while sharing some basic characteristics. Moreover, they seem to be located at two ends of a governance spectrum, somewhere on which the EU can be found as well: One is a unitary state with a dominant role in world affairs, the other an international organization with a global membership.[162]

Unfortunately, though, neglect similar to that of the EUSRs seems to have also befallen the representatives of other states and organizations. There is little analysis of the role of these envoys available, other than the autobiographic accounts of some of them.[163] Given the amount of academic inquiry that is devoted to both the foreign policy of the United States and to the politics and policies of the UN system, this is, at the very least, astonishing. These limitations notwithstanding, this section attempts to provide a rough overview of such antecedent cases.

With regard to each set of envoys, observations are made on five different aspects:

– Rationale and legal foundations: What was the original rationale of dispatching an envoy? Which is the present legal basis for their deployment and how rigorously is it applied?
– Function: Which are the formal tasks of the representatives and what is their actual policy contribution?
– People: Who are the individuals on the job, what are their qualifications, and how are they selected?
– Institutional relations: What is the location of the envoys in the overall foreign policy system and who are the closest collaborators?
– Relevance: Have there been periods of changing relevance in the past 60 years and, if so, how could they be explained?

---

161 Mattingly identifies the first resident ambassador in the year 1375 (Mattingly 1937, 427). Following the peace of Westphalia, the accreditation of permanent diplomatic representatives between independent European states became the rule; in fact, "the right to send and receive embassies began to be considered a test of sovereignty" (ibid., 423).

162 For these reasons, I do not compare the EUSRs to envoys either from EU member states or from regional organizations like the OSCE or NATO.

163 To cite only two recent examples, see the reports of Richard Holbrooke, former U.S. envoy to Bosnia and Herzegovina and, most recently, U.S. envoy to Afghanistan and Pakistan (Holbrooke 1998), and Ahmedou Ould-Abdallah, former UN Special Representative for West Africa (Ould-Abdallah 2000). One former UN special representative, Cyrus Vance, also contributed to an academic analysis; cf. Vance/Hamburger 1997.

First, a brief descriptive summary of the basic characteristics of EUSRs is given based on the account of the first chapter so as to make them comparable to the envoys of other international actors, which are presented afterwards and in more detail.

2.1.1 The EU Special Representatives

Rationale and legal foundations

Among the initial reasons, as they have been presented, for sending an EU Special Representative to a given country or region the following are most prominent: To achieve political representation commensurate with existing economic engagement; to gain information about an ongoing conflict; to influence international mediation efforts with respect to a crisis; and to develop a policy towards a given country or region.

The legal basis for sending an EUSR is a Joint Action based on Article 18 (5) TEU: "The Council may, whenever it deems it necessary, appoint a special representative with a mandate in relation to particular policy issues."[164] Joint Actions are one of the primary instruments of the Union's foreign policy, in addition to common strategies or common positions (Article 12 TEU). With these instruments, the Union aims to achieve the objectives it has set for its Common Foreign and Security Policy (Article 11 TEU). EUSRs are an instrument of the Union's CFSP, and reference to these objectives often can be found in their mandates. While EUSRs are appointed by the Council of Ministers, it is the European Commission that legally contracts them as CFSP advisors.

Function and task

EUSRs represent the Union in a given country or region; being a face and a voice of the European Union,[165] they (passively) stand for and (actively) inform others about EU policies. Other than the European Community with its 130 or so delegations to third countries and International Organisations,[166] the EU itself does not have any 'embassies.' The EUSRs thus increase the EU's visibility and profile, especially compared to the rotating Presidency.

The focus of their work is on security policy and crisis management: They offer advice and support to the conflicting parties with the aim of effectively implementing EU policies and terminating the crisis or conflict. To do this, they have a range of—primarily diplomatic—means at their disposal, e.g. proffering good offices, mediation, facilitation, and the like. EUSRs also closely cooperate with third parties, be they states (like Russia or the United States) or International Organisations (like the United Nations, the African

---

164 For a thorough description of the legal and budgetary framework of the EUSRs, see Grevi 2007, 17–28.

165 "EUSRs provide the EU with a visible and practical presence in critical countries and regions. To a considerable degree they are a 'voice' and a 'face' of the EU and its policies on the ground" (EU Council Secretariat 2005, 1).

166 For an overview of 50 years (1954–2004) of external representation of the Community, see European Commission 2004c; for a current overview of where delegations are located, see <http://ec.europa.eu/external_relations/repdel/>.

Union, or the OSCE). More often than not, international crisis management efforts are managed through a 'group of friends', as the informal setting bringing together interested states and organizations are often called.

The EUSRs have important internal roles too. Functionally, the Special Representatives can be considered, in analogy to the anatomical metaphor used previously, the 'eyes and ears' of the EU. They provide information about and analysis of the current situation in their mandate area. Based on their findings, EUSRs can develop policy proposals that they feed into the Brussels policy-making process. Another important role is that of internal coordination, given that the Union, in the realm of foreign policy, has to rely on the consensus of 27 member states and that the Commission does not have the policy-unifying role it has in the first pillar. Therefore, EUSRs strive to coordinate national policies of member states and ESDP operations as well as the activities of the Commission, aiming to achieve the greatest coherence possible (cf. Grevi 2007, 46).

People

Most often national diplomats hold the post of EUSR, or those with a career in international organizations (like Aldo Ajello, Ján Kubiš, and Kálmán Mizsei). Some Special Representatives were active politicians before their term (for example François Léotard, Paddy Ashdown, and Pekka Haavisto), usually bringing a different standing to their mandate. More recently, a number of EU officials, either from the Council or the Commission side, have been chosen as EUSR (like Marc Otte, Erwan Fouéré, and Koen Vervaeke).

Institutional relations

The EUSRs' institutional relations have evolved in parallel to the gradual build-up of CFSP structures themselves.[167] At the beginning, they reported directly to the Council that had nominated them; at the working level, there was a small foreign policy structure in the Secretariat with twelve detached national diplomats, one for every member state. The Amsterdam Treaty codified this small office as the Policy Planning and Early Warning Unit, a more structured body with seconded staff from the member states, the Secretariat, the Commission and the WEU under the guidance of the High Representative.[168] In early 2001, the Political and Security Committee became operational (Missiroli 2004, 63–64). This has resulted in a marginalization of capital-based instances, such as the working groups, where national diplomats appear in Brussels once a month for a meeting and then go back to their ministries (Duke 2005, 29).[169] Instead, PSC ambas-

---

167 For a good overview of how European foreign and security policy was institutionalized, see Smith 2004.

168 Allen/Smith 1998a, 72. From the outset, member states were "divided on the size of the unit, about how closely it should be integrated into the existing Council structures and about how it will relate to the Political Committee. Political directors, based in the national capitals, may feel that the new unit represents yet another move towards the 'Brusselisation' of the CFSP process" (ibid.).

169 While to the detriment of member states' capitals, this 'Brusselisation' nonetheless served as a counterweight to the Commission's efforts to consolidate its hold on external relations (Allen/Smith 1999, 90).

sadors, with their continuous presence in Brussels and daily interaction, actively shape the overall foreign policy system (Juncos/Reynolds 2007, 146).[170] Into this organically grown foreign policy structure the EUSRs, having been created before these new CFSP bodies came into being, had to be fitted in.

Today, the EUSRs' main points of contact are the Political and Security Committee and the High Representative. The PSC provides strategic guidance to the EUSRs (as to every ESDP mission as well) and follows their work with the help of the Policy Unit and the Council Secretariat, while the SG/HR is put in control of the operational direction.[171] EUSRs may, on the recommendation of the PSC or the SG/HR, also report directly to the Council. The actual working level contacts are mostly with the Council Secretariat and the High Representative's Policy Unit. EUSRs report regularly to the Council working groups, thus also reaching the staff in member states' permanent missions and the relevant Commission units.

Figure 11: The EUSRs within the CFSP Structure

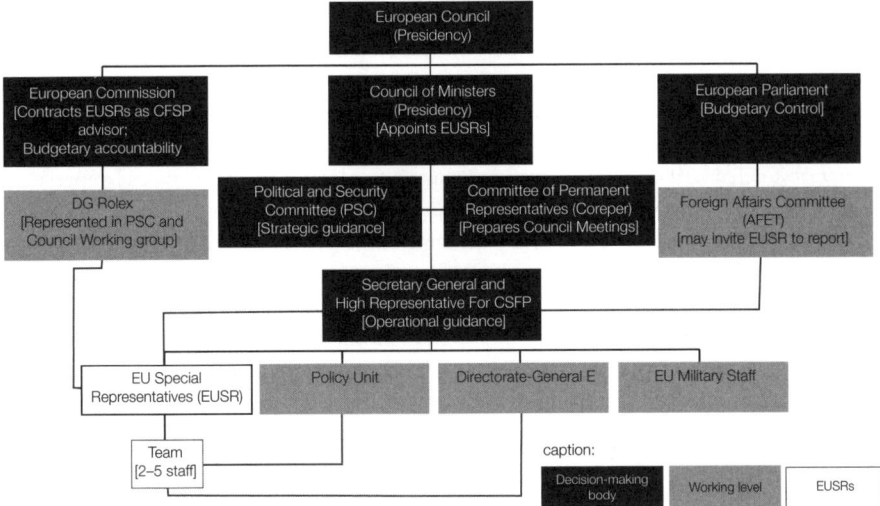

Consequently, the EUSRs are closely linked to all three major players in EU foreign policy—the Council, the Commission, and the member states—in all phases of their work. Their nomination by the Council follows a selection procedure that involves the Council Secretariat, the Policy Unit, and the Presidency on behalf of the member states. Due to

---

170 Not surprisingly, the atmosphere among PSC ambassadors has been compared to socialization among Coreper, establishing a 'we-feeling' and a 'coordination reflex' (cf. Juncos/Reynolds 2007, 142–144; similarly, Duke 2005, 28).

171 These rules have been contained in the guidelines (cf. Council of the European Union 2003b), and they are additionally reproduced in each EUSR mandate.

their status as CFSP Advisors paid from Community funds, they are accountable to the Commission for the budget allocated under the financial statement for their missions.

The preceding graph (p. 61) depicts the location of EUSRs in the CFSP decision-making system.[172]

Relevance

A full, qualitative assessment of the EUSRs' relevance can, of course, be made only at the end of this study, yet some indications on the frequency and magnitude of their use can be given. As outlined in the previous chapter, the number of EUSRs has risen from two in 1996 to eleven in 2008, extensively covering the major regions of concern to the EU: the Balkans, Africa, the Middle East, the Caucasus, and Central Asia. Moreover, their mandates have been considerably extended, now covering the full range of crisis management as well as diplomatic activities. Compared to the early days, their relevance has thus greatly increased.

2.1.2 The UN Special Representatives

As mentioned previously, there is a dearth of academic literature on special envoys, including on the special representatives of the UN Secretary-General. Only a few authors have discussed their role in an analytical fashion. One of the first was Donald J. Puchala in his 1993 contribution to a book about the 'Challenging Role of the UN Secretary-General' (Puchala 1993). His assessment that "the phenomenon of special representation on behalf of the Secretary-General remains an academic mystery [...and that there] is virtually no literature on the subject" remains broadly valid today.[173] Four more works have appeared since, two more academically-oriented, the others more practically-focused: The first is a report by the Carnegie Endowment's Commission to Prevent Deadly Conflict (Vance/Hamburger 1997), the second another contribution to an edited book on the UN Security Council (Peck 2004). Third, the Peace Implementation Network (PIN) issued a report on the management of UN Peace-Building Missions (PIN 1999). Finally, the United Nations published a handbook on peace-keeping operations, in which the first chapter is devoted to the role of the Special Representatives of the Secretary-General (United Nations 2003).[174]

Rationale and legal foundations

The special representatives do not find a single mention in the UN Charter; they have rather developed in the course of the actual practice of, mainly, the Secretary-General and, to a certain extent, of other principal organs such as the Security Council and the

---

172 The graph does not, of course, pretend to fully reflect existing hierarchies within CFSP but aims to simply give an indicative picture of where the EUSRs are located in the EU foreign policy structure.

173 Puchala 1993, 82; cf. Vance/Hamburger 1997, 8; and Fröhlich et al. 2006, 19.

174 Another contribution is a working paper by Manuel Fröhlich (Fröhlich 2006), that has, however, not yet appeared in a journal.

General Assembly. The umbrella term that is used for these envoys is Special Representative of the Secretary-General (SRSG), even though they can take different labels under this heading, like personal representatives, envoys or advisors (Peck 2004, 337–8 [footnote 1]). The denomination by itself, however, does not lend a certain function or responsibility.

The UN Charter provides for different ways of appointing SRSGs, either by the Security Council or the Secretary-General. Typically, the strongest mandate derives from a nomination by the Security Council based on Article 98 of the Charter.[175] In such cases, the Security Council includes the nomination of an SRSG in its mandate for a peacekeeping operation, for the former to run the latter on the ground.[176] Such a representative usually bears the official title of a Special Representative of the Secretary-General.

Lacking the request from a principal organ of the UN, the Secretary-General can all the same appoint his or her personal envoys, implicitly based either on Article 99 or on a combination of Articles 97 and 101 of the UN Charter.[177] In the first case, the Secretary-General uses his right to bring to the attention of the Security Council any situation that, in his opinion, may threaten the maintenance of international peace (Art. 99). In order to fulfill this early-warning function, it is generally understood that the Secretary-General needs to gather information about a crisis, for which he may need to send an envoy on a fact-finding mission.[178] The second case is based on a simple personnel decision of the "chief administrative officer of the Organization" (Art. 97) who is entitled to appoint his staff (Art. 101). The latter may then include personal representatives of the Secretary-General, who are usually designated a topical rather than geographical responsibility. In both cases, however, the legal basis is less clear than with a Council request (Vance/Hamburger 1997, 8–9). Despite the different—and sometimes constructed—legal bases, all three types of SRSGs have become commonplace in the UN's business of diplomacy.[179]

---

175 Art. 98 of the UN Charter (UNCh): "The Secretary-General shall act in that capacity in all meetings of the General Assembly, of the Security Council, of the Economic and Social Council, and of the Trusteeship Council, and shall perform such other functions as are entrusted to him by these organs. The Secretary-General shall make an annual report to the General Assembly on the work of the Organization."

176 In principle, the General Assembly could do the same; however, cases are rare in which it has mandated a peace operation.

177 Art. 97 UNCh: "The Secretariat shall comprise a Secretary-General and such staff as the Organization may require. The Secretary-General shall be appointed by the General Assembly upon the recommendation of the Security Council. He shall be the chief administrative officer of the Organization." Art. 99 UNCh: "The Secretary-General may bring to the attention of the Security Council any matter which in his opinion may threaten the maintenance of international peace and security." Art. 101 UNCh: "1. The staff shall be appointed by the Secretary-General under regulations established by the General Assembly."

178 Similarly, Article 33 of the Charter has been interpreted in a way to allow for the Good Offices of and mediation by either the Secretary-General or his designated representatives; cf. Vance/Hamburger 1997, 9.

179 The resulting three different types of SRSGs were put into three respective "categories" (A, B, and

Function and task

The formal nomination procedure already points to different roles and functions that the SRSGs may have, i.e. either in crisis management, mediation, or information gathering. If tasked by the Security Council, SRSGs will administer a peace operation on behalf of the Secretary-General ("executives in the field"[180]). If it is the Secretary-General appointing the SRSG, the job is either to provide Good Offices to disputing parties ("mediators and conciliators") or to seek information about developments in certain regions ("eyes and ears for the Secretary-General") (cf. Vance/Hamburger 1997, 4).

In addition to these three external roles, SRSGs, they have an internal function as an engine for creating international consensus around policy proposals. In particular with regard to the Security Council, the main UN decision-making organ in the field of international peace and security, special representatives help to shape international consensus and sustain the momentum of conflict resolution (cf. Vance/Hamburger 1997, 4–5). Moreover, they act as focal point for various UN bodies with regard to a specific crisis region or issue (cf. 'institutional relations' below). Another contribution of the SRSGs is on the conceptual level, where they provide, from an informed and impartial perspective, formulas for a potential settlement of the conflict (cf. Puchala 1993, 87–8). Thirdly, as representatives of the international community, they can promote the normative goals enshrined in the United Nations Charter.[181]

It is difficult to determine when particular UN Special Representatives were exceptionally successful in their mission. This is mostly due to the subdued nature of their work.[182] Moreover, it would usually be either the Secretary-General or the United Nations itself that would be credited with eventual success.[183] In general, SRSGs have often been granted "wide latitude" in their actions and the freedom to fill a deliberately vague mandate with their own initiative and creativity (Puchala 1993, 24). Given that each case

---

C) in a report by the then UN Secretary-General, Boutros Boutros-Ghali: "As at 31 July 1996, the number of these officials totalled 32 in the three categories as follows: Category A: Five Under-Secretaries-General and 11 Assistant Secretaries-General; Category B: Eight Under-Secretaries-General, one Assistant Secretary-General and two Directors (D-2); Category C: Four Under-Secretaries-General and one Assistant Secretary-General;" cf. United Nations 1996, 2.

180 This term and the following two terms in brackets are borrowed from Puchala 1993, 84–92. Similarly, the UN in its handbook on peacekeeping operations highlights four broadly different responsibilities of the SRSG: "Facilitator of a political process; Head of UN presence; Head of Mission; and Interim or transitional administrator" (United Nations 2003, 13).

181 Puchala first mentions this point "speculatively," but then cautions: "the normative influence of the [SRSGs] remains ambiguous, and the issue demands further research" (Puchala 1993, 89).

182 "Information about the roles of special representatives and personal envoys is sparse because these missions typically are undertaken without publicity by practitioners of 'quiet diplomacy' who tend not to reveal what they do and how they do it" (Vance/Hamburger 1997, 8).

183 Cf. the Nobel Peace Prize awards to the United Nations (2001), the United Nations Peacekeeping Forces (1988), or to the late UN Secretary-General, Dag Hammarskjöld (1961).

is regarded as being different from previous ones, this approach places a great deal of responsibility on the individual.[184]

People

SRSGs are a long-standing and prominent crowd. Count Folke Bernadotte, mediator of the Secretary-General for Palestine in 1948, and his erstwhile assistant, Ralph Bunche, are considered the first-ever UN envoys.[185] Since then, a number of both high-profile and low-key emissaries have served in this function. The long list of SRSGs includes prominent names such as Olof Palme, former prime minister of Sweden, Martti Ahtisaari, former president of Finland, and Cyrus Vance, former U.S. secretary of state.

Confidence and acceptance are the two basic criteria that have always been paramount for the nomination of an SRSG, in addition to a multitude of desirable qualities. The envoys need to have the full confidence of the Secretary-General, and they must be acceptable to the disputing parties (Puchala 1993, 83). The latter criterion is especially important when the emissary is primarily engaged in mediating a dispute (cf. Vance/ Hamburger 1997, 14). Building on these basic premises, the skills that are demanded from the individual representatives are numerous: They need diplomatic experience as well as familiarity with negotiating techniques, plus a wide-ranging knowledge both of the region in conflict and, if possible, of the procedures of the UN system. Being able to take criticism, even if undeserved given a vague mandate or insufficient means, is certainly an asset—as is "a superabundance of optimism, persistence, and patience" (Peck 2004, 328). To put it briefly, "shrewd political skills" have been a crucial qualification for any envoy of the Secretary-General (Vance/Hamburger 1997, 14).

People with the needed skills can be found inside or outside the UN system. Both backgrounds, of course, have their advantages and limitations. While insiders have in-depth knowledge of the UN machinery and may more easily appear impartial to the conflicting parties, they often are not relieved from their normal duties, i.e. have only limited capacities. Outsiders often bring additional experience, funding, and sometimes backing from certain member states, but may be less apt in pulling the various organizations of the UN family together (cf. Puchala 1993, 82–3).

The selection procedure still is very ad hoc and improvised, though in the end most people selected are united by their multilateral backgrounds. Indeed, "successive Secre-

---

184 "Appointed on an ad hoc basis, in exceptional circumstances, an SRSG's role could be said to be defined by its lack of definition. SRSGs must act with ingenuity and flexibility consistent with a policy framework generally received from the Security Council and often characterized by only a weak consensus concerning the UN's role. In such a context, individuals matter greatly, and the success or failure of UN initiatives can rest on an SRSG's performance" (PIN 1999, 29). Cf. also Puchala 1993, 84.

185 The former was assassinated in action, the latter received the Nobel Peace Prize in 1950 for his (and the late Count's) mediation efforts in Palestine (cf. Puchala 1993, 81; Vance/Hamburger 1997, 8). Thus, the first two UN envoys already covered the entire spectrum of possible consequences of their work.

taries-General have resisted formalizing, institutionalizing, or in any sense routinizing" the procedures of appointing and dispatching a special representative (Puchala 1993, 84). In a system where each Secretary-General had to re-establish his office vis-à-vis the institutionally strong Security Council, it is natural that he maintains this freedom of choice. An overview of those candidates chosen to be an SRSG reveals a certain pattern: They are mainly (former) diplomats or UN civil servants; many of them either worked as SRSGs before or sat on an international commission; and they are predominantly male and on average 63 years old (Fröhlich 2006, 12–13).

Finally, the UN system has reacted to the growing importance of SRSGs by providing training to them, in preparation for a mission as well as following the termination of one. The United Nations Institute for Training and Research (UNITAR) now runs a programme for the briefing and debriefing of Special and Personal Representatives and Envoys of the Secretary-General, including interviews, the distillation of lessons learned, and media like a handbook and a video (Peck 2004, 325). Since 2001, seminars with SRSGs and senior Headquarters and Agency staff have been held on a regular basis to foster the sharing of experiences and networking both among SRSGs and between them and senior staff.[186]

Institutional relations

In institutional terms, the SRSGs are embedded in a web of actors engaged in peacemaking, both in New York and in the field. Their closest relation, understandably, is with the Secretary-General, the full trust of whom they need to carry out their work. There is no hint that this relation might differ according to the three nomination procedures, as those SRSGs who are appointed by a Security Council resolution also primarily work with the Secretary-General.[187] In addition, the SRSG has close links with the Secretariat and its important departments such as for Political Affairs and Peacekeeping Operations.[188]

Still at the New York headquarters, there is the Security Council with its 15 members and their respective permanent missions and, though less involved in the work of the SRSGs, the General Assembly with its various committees. The relation between the Security Council and the SRSGs resembles that of a company's board of directors with its senior staff, one author suggests: While the board may have the power to direct its staff via the executive director (here: the Secretary-General), it would usually refrain from microman-

---

186 Cf. the information provided on UNITAR's website: <http://www.unitar.org/peacemaking/PPD1. htm>. Fröhlich et al. call these seminars "a relatively new way of trying to learn and improve from experience" (Fröhlich et al. 2006, 21).

187 "The SRSG reports to the Secretary-General through the Under-Secretary-General for Peacekeeping Operations" (United Nations 2003, 9).

188 "The SRSG reports to the Under-Secretary-General for Peacekeeping Operations and through him or her keeps the relevant offices at Headquarters fully informed of developments in the field [...]. The Department of Peacekeeping Operations (DPKO) also undertakes or facilitates consultations with other offices and departments at Headquarters level, in particular the Department of Political Affairs (DPA)" (United Nations 2003, 10).

aging the day-to-day work (cf. Peck 2004, 337). The SRSGs themselves seem to cherish the opportunity to report directly to the Council and its powerful members, as UNITAR determined in its interviews with them.[189]

The institutional picture becomes even more complex in the mission area with its myriad of different actors from ambassadors to UN missions, and from relief agencies to the media. First, especially when heading a peacekeeping operation, SRSGs must work closely with those ambassadors whose countries sit on the Security Council. They usually establish regular meetings with a group of relevant national ambassadors to "share information, brainstorm solutions to problems, and engage in joint strategizing," with a view to both engaging member states themselves and harmonizing the recommendations sent back to their capitals.[190] Then, the special representative has different UN organizations and bodies to deal with as well as the conflicting parties, other international bodies, non-governmental organizations, and the media. Add to this the World Bank and other international financial institutions plus the representatives of other international organizations, and the picture of 'the' international community turns rather fuzzy.[191]

Given that the UN side alone usually has various actors in the field, the practice has evolved to make the SRSGs the "principal coordinators of international involvement in complex emergencies" (Vance/Hamburger 1997, 11). He (or she) then has to coordinate bodies like the United Nations Development Programme (UNDP), the United Nations Children's Fund (UNICEF), and the UNHCR. Making it more than just a title on paper, the envoy's real authority comes from the actual coordination effort he or she fulfills.[192]

Relevance

Special Representatives have seen a rise in their numbers and importance since the early 1990s. Before that time, only a few envoys had been sent on behalf of the Secretary-General, mainly on fact-finding missions and to mediate interstate conflicts (cf. Vance/Hamburger 1997, 3). While in 1980 there were only four such representatives, their number had more than doubled by 1996; in 2006, there were no less than 63 exemplars

---

189 "SRSGs were very enthusiastic about appearing in person before the Council. They reported that the opportunity to brief the Council and answer members' questions enabled them to highlight issues of importance and to go into much more depth on key topics. SRSGs and Secretariat staff also noted that oral briefings allow discussions to be more candid and allow issues that cannot be published in a public document to be raised and discussed" (Peck 2004, 332).

190 Peck 2004, 332. Aldo Ajello, when acting as UN special representative, established such a group of ambassadors that he called a "mini-Security Council" (ibid., 333).

191 A UN handbook lists the following "key partners": "Countries contributing personnel; Other Member States; UN agencies, funds and programs; Donors; Regional military or police forces; Regional and sub-regional organizations; Bretton Woods institutions; Inter-governmental organizations; Non-governmental organizations (NGOs); and International media" (United Nations 2003, 11); cf. Vance/Hamburger 1997, 10–11.

192 Cf. also PIN 1999, 25: "Even though an SRSG is nominally the head of all UN operations in the mission area, his or her real authority is limited by the decentralized nature of the UN system where agencies enjoy a considerable degree of independence from the Secretariat. Bringing coherence to the UN presence in the field is a major challenge faced by any SRSG."

of this species.[193] This increased activism has made the Special Representatives "one of the most intriguing and promising aspects of UN diplomacy of the post-Cold War era" (Vance/Hamburger 1997, 2; similarly Peck 2004, 325).

Two different, albeit related, developments are responsible for this increase: The UN's involvement in peacekeeping operations and its activity on global issues. The end of the Cold War has brought the well-known changes to the structure of international conflicts, demanding in response a set of complex, or 'multi-dimensional', peacekeeping operations on the side of the UN;[194] these were usually headed by an SRSG.[195] In addition, the surge of UN involvement in global affairs has brought a flow of topical personal representatives: There are Special Envoys or Advisors on Children in Armed Conflict, for HIV/AIDS in Africa, on the Alliance of Civilizations, and for Tsunami Recovery, to name but a few.[196] They all share the goal "to raise awareness of such major problems, to develop relevant policy, and to work with member states and the UN system to ensure that the problems receive appropriate attention and action" (Peck 2004, 328–9).

Taken together, all UN special representatives are emblematic of the growing importance and the new role that the United Nations play in the post-Cold War world, whether in trying to resolve crises or find solutions to global problems. They may still not appear in the world organization's Charter, but they are an integral part of its efforts to bring peace and stability to the real world.

2.1.3 The U. S. Special Envoys

Different from the United Nations, the United States has a lasting tradition of sending all sorts of foreign policy envoys dating back long before World War II. More than that, the emissary is an "old-fashioned American institution" that came into existence even before the country's independence (Fullilove 2005, 18; cf. Plischke 1986, 112; Waters 1956, 127). That said, the following analysis limits itself to the time after 1945 and to envoys of the U. S. president as head of state. It does not cover other representatives of the broader administration.

Despite this long history of envoys, the literature we find on them is sparse. Two early journal articles from the middle of the century (Waters 1956 and Wriston 1960) are complemented by one book section (Plischke 1986) and two recent contributions to the

---

193 New Zealand 1980, 1996, 2006, 162–4; for similar figures, see Fröhlich et al. 2006, 20.

194 "[A] growing number of UN peacekeeping operations have become multidimensional, composed of a range of components including military, civilian police, political, civil affairs, rule of law, human rights, humanitarian, reconstruction, public information and gender" (United Nations 2003, 1).

195 Cf. United Nations 2003, 2. Prior to 1990, there was only one complex mission: UN mission in the Congo (ONUC) from 1960 to 1964 (cf. Vance/Hamburger 1997, 3). After 1990, more than three dozen such operations took place (cf. United Nations 2003, 4). For an updated list of peacekeeping missions, see <http://www.un.org/Depts/dpko/list/list.pdf>.

196 A list of all current SRSGs can be obtained from <http://www.un.org/News/ossg/srsg/table. htm>.

'Foreign Affairs' journal (Kennan 1997, Fullilove 2005). The latter two already point to an interesting distinction of the U.S. envoys as they delineate them as external to the established American diplomatic service.

Rationale and legal foundations

The legal basis for sending an envoy is rather weak; its actual practice may strictu sensu even be against the letter of the constitution. In Article II, Section 2, the U.S. Constitution asserts the right of the president to appoint, with the consent of the Senate, ambassadors and all other officers of the United States.[197] Despite this clear provision, the president has never requested the approval of the Senate when nominating a personal envoy. Thanks to "congressional acquiescence," this procedure—the only exception to the rule that all ambassadors, ministers, and consuls need Senate approval—is now the established legal practice and therefore deemed constitutional (Plischke 1986, 111).

By appointing his (or her) personal agents, the president thus makes use of one of his prerogatives in foreign policy. He has the freedom to appoint envoys as he sees fit, giving them titles (agent, commissioner, envoy, or representative; usually preceded by the denomination of either "special" or "personal") and tasks according to need. Such practice is possible due to the fact that the president's envoys are not seen as 'government officers' in a legal sense (cf. Plischke 1986, 111; Waters 1956, 127). They are thought to have "an employment, not an office" (Wriston 1960, 221). The president may, of course, send a person who already holds an office, such as the secretary of state or an ambassador-at-large. The latter, however, will have received confirmation from the Senate when nominated in the first place.

Function and task

With such discretion by the head of state, one possible functional distinction is the degree to which the president sees the envoy as an agent of his office, or rather of his person. One group of envoys can be seen as official presidential representatives, while others, embodied with the full trust of the officeholder, "not only in form, but in fact, represent the President personally" (Wriston 1960, 223). The latter group is most important when it comes to emulating the actual relation between heads of state: In this respect, a personal envoy embodies "the significance of individual idiosyncrasies and personal rivalries, of mutual trust or suspicion, among statesmen" (Wriston 1960, 226).[198]

---

197 U.S. Constitution, Article II, Section 2: "[The President] shall have power, by and with the advice and consent of the Senate, to make treaties, provided two thirds of the Senators present concur; and he shall nominate, and by and with the advice and consent of the Senate, shall appoint ambassadors, other public ministers and consuls, judges of the Supreme Court, and all other officers of the United States, whose appointments are not herein otherwise provided for, and which shall be established by law: but the Congress may by law vest the appointment of such inferior officers, as they think proper, in the President alone, in the courts of law, or in the heads of departments." Congress has never vested the appointment of 'inferior officers' in the President; cf. Plischke 1986, 108. Initially, the president even had the freedom to appoint consuls and diplomats; however, over the course of the 19th century, Congress arrogated to itself this right (cf. Waters 1956, 124).

198 This special relationship is made clear in the account of one U.S. envoy, Harry L. Hopkins, as Elmer

To rely on a fully trusted person "is the most important and distinguishing motivation for using the special agent" (Plischke 1986, 114).The broader function of an envoy therefore depends more on what the president thinks he may want to use him or her for than on any legal provision.

Today's practice covers "virtually any type of diplomatic assignment that the president wishes to handle outside of conventional channels: Gather information, conveying presidential views or policy, negotiating, serving as special resident representative, troubleshooting, mediation, attending conferences, and the like" (Plischke 1986, 64; cf. Fullilove 2005, 15; Wriston 1960, 234–7). In addition to these customary diplomatic functions, the president may—in stark contrast to the more issue- or region-based role of EU or UN Special Representatives—send an envoy on a ceremonial mission, e.g. to attend a coronation, royal wedding, or independence celebration. On such occasions, it is usually the first lady, the vice-president or a former president who personally represent the head of state (Plischke 1986, 75–77 and 91).

The president is also free to send more than one envoy to the same region or country in an effort of concerted diplomacy (Wriston 1960, 235). One example of this strategy was the 1966 Vietnam 'peace offensive' of then President Johnson: With this initiative, the president "set in motion a comprehensive process of policy promulgation, public and confidential exchanges, informal and formal meetings, and a flow of special envoys, with the White House captaining the massive diplomatic venture" (Plischke 1986, 88).

Finally, presidential envoys also have an internal function. Despite the foreign policy prerogatives of the president (Primat der Außenpolitik, as Kennan calls it; cf. Kennan 1997, 204), in today's complex web of international affairs, many ministries or government agencies entertain relations abroad. A personal agent might then be used to coordinate and, if possible, harmonize different views and voices from within the U.S. government in order to represent the overall interest of the United States (Plischke 1986, 113).[199]

People

The very first American special envoy was dispatched on a mission before the United States had declared their independence: Benjamin Franklin, "America's first career diplomat," embarked to London as the emissary of Pennsylvania (and later as joint envoy of Pennsylvania, Massachusetts, New Jersey, and Georgia) in 1757 to negotiate with colonial Britain (Plischke 1986, 68). Other early envoys included John Adams and Thomas

---

Plischke chronicles: "Hopkins reported that in one conversation, he told the Soviet leader [Stalin] that his mission was not diplomatic, because his representations were informal, personal, and man-to-man rather than government-to-government. This represents the purest form of personal diplomacy at the summit by means of the special envoy" (Plischke 1986, 101).

199   This point on internal coordination is also made by Wriston, interestingly in a language that resembles talk of the EU's lack of external coherence: "Between 20 and 30 government agencies have people operating abroad. As a practical matter, it is impossible for all of them to work through the Department of State. Yet the United States should speak abroad, if not with one voice, at least with a harmony of voices" (Wriston 1960, 235).

Jefferson, who should later become successive U.S. presidents subsequent to George Washington. After the Second World War, one of the most visible envoys was certainly Henry Kissinger, whose extended missions were not limited to his tenure as secretary of state from 1973 to 1977 (Plischke 1986, 104–08).

Most envoys in recent times were drawn from the group of government officers (Plischke 1986, 66 and 85), even though the president of the United States has the leeway to choose as his envoy whomever he likes. He even has the possibility to appoint close friends or even family members, like the first lady or a brother,[200] as envoys. The closer a person is to the president, the more he or she will be seen as credible surrogates of him, as "almost an alter ego" (Wriston 1960, 223). Yet, due to the sheer number of envoys on which a president relies and who cannot all be from his closest circle, diplomats and other officers make up the majority of the network of representatives.

The list of qualifications that a U.S. envoy should possess is hardly different from that which is expected of other high-ranking emissaries: Personal standing, acceptability to the host government, proven negotiating or mediating skills (including "an aptitude for evoking goodwill"), special preparation for the respective mission, and substantial presidential personal trust (cf. Plischke 1986, 114). However, there seem to be no formal training capacities for them, other than the usual diplomatic training with the State Department. This is an expression of the remarkably low degree of institutionalization of the U.S. envoys.

Institutional relations

Among the institutional relations of a presidential envoy, those with the Department of State and the Senate are of particular importance (in addition to the aforementioned relations with the president and the White House). The State Department is the body that is typically tasked with the execution of foreign policy, for which it entertains the diplomatic service. Still, the United States was very slow in appointing resident envoys, let alone full ambassadors to third countries; thus, the replacement of regular diplomats by special envoys has a long tradition.[201] However understandable this may have been until a full diplomatic service was established in the early 20th century,[202] the use of

---

200 President John F. Kennedy, for example, sent his brother, Robert Kennedy, attorney-general at the time, on a goodwill trip around the world in 1962 (Plischke 1986, 83).

201 "From 1789 to 1800, conventional resident missions were accredited to only five countries [...]. By 1830, after almost half a century, this country was dealing through traditional resident emissaries with merely 15 countries, while diplomatic relations with others continued to be handled by special envoys and commissioners" (Plischke 1986, 70–71). This parallels, two to four centuries later, the aforementioned development of European diplomacy in general. "Presidential envoys were 'special' because the new Republic had no regularized diplomatic relations with many countries. Moreover, for more than a century, ranking U.S. diplomats, designed 'ministers' rather than 'ambassadors,' lacked superior diplomatic stature abroad; the White House sought to offset this by appointing special presidential agents for important missions" (Plischke 1986, 116).

202 Until 1924, two separate services, a diplomatic and a consular one, were in charge of the United States' foreign relations: "The diplomatic service was designed primarily to provide staff support

envoys to bypass conventional diplomats has continued to the present day. Whenever a president felt uncomfortable with his secretary of state or with a particular ambassador, or with the diplomatic service as a whole, he has resorted to his prerogative to appoint personal envoys (Wriston 1960, 224; Plischke 1986, 112).

The increased practice of sending an envoy has thus put a strain on the White House's relations with the State Department. Most regular diplomats resent the presence of a personal representative as it implies that normal personnel are somehow inadequate or incapable.[203] The host authorities, of course, recognize this implied lowered standing of the accredited corps, regarding the presidential personal emissary as the "primary spokesman of the United States" (Plischke 1986, 116; similarly, Fullilove 2005, 16). This is especially problematic because, according to diplomatic customs, the accredited ambassador is the official representative of the head of state (cf. Kennan 1997, 204). Such damage done to professional diplomats is probably the greatest danger of the increased reliance on special envoys. In response, one author observes a conciliatory trend to send ambassadors-at-large (who have Senate approval) rather than ad hoc envoys on special missions (Plischke 1986, 96).

The second institution of great relevance to the special envoys is the legislature, which raises both principled and practical questions. Following the quarrels about whether the president can appoint envoys at his own will or only with the Senate's consent, there was a debate about whether he can appoint a member of the Senate as envoy.[204] One argument against this was founded on principle, i.e. whether this is a violation of the separation of powers. Members of the legislative body should certainly not accept orders from the executive, even if only for a specific mission. This dispute was solved with a modus vivendi built on the fact that envoys were indeed not officers of the government but could act freely within their mandate—and could resign if they saw an infringement upon their independence (Wriston 1960, 229–34).

In addition, there was the practical issue that, because the Senate is the body within the U.S. Congress that must ratify any international agreement, a conflict of interest might occur: What if a senator, as presidential envoy, helps negotiate a treaty, on which he or she must later vote? In the end, because the inclusion of senators in a negotiating team

---

for senior envoys, ambassadors, and ministers charged with the U.S. government's regular communication with its foreign counterparts. [...] Consular officials and their professional staff, far more numerous than the diplomatic one, were stationed in major ports and other commercial centers abroad [...]. Their tasks consisted mainly of providing passport and visa services and protecting the interests of private American citizens living, travelling, or doing business in that region" (Kennan 1997, 199–200).

203 Wriston 1960, 237. Others speak of a "professional prejudice against outsiders" (Fullilove 2005, 16). Plischke argues: "The conclusion has been reached by some, [...] that the very existence of this [special envoy] practice throughout U.S. history evidences the fact that the traditional diplomatic establishment has been inadequate to the challenge of its responsibilities" (Plischke 1986, 116).

204 For two opposing contributions to the original debate, see Flanders 1894 and Thorpe 1894; for a summary of the legal debate, see Plischke 1986, 109–10, and Wriston 1960, 229–34.

might be helpful with regard to the approval of an international treaty by the Senate[205] and with the considerable influence senators had on the U.S. negotiation position, such involvement was esteemed more important than the eventual conflict of interest of that one person.

Relevance

Two trends can be discerned with regard to the varying relevance of special envoys, one general and one specific. The general trend is that their numbers have increased substantially throughout the 20th century, even though there are no exact figures available as no official records about their names and assignments are kept.[206] However, it seems safe to assume that their overall number is in the thousands (cf. Waters 1956, 127; Wriston 1960, 221). The increase is commonly attributed to two factors: First, "the progressively more direct participation of the President in international relations" (Wriston 1960, 226);[207] and, second, the "developments in communications and transport technology and the United States' emergence as a world power" (Fullilove 2005, 14). Naturally, the U.S. role during the Second World War, following a period of isolation after World War I, and in particular after the fall of the Iron Curtain, has brought with it a multiplication of international contacts and, consequently, the extended use of presidential envoys.

The overall increasing trend, however, cannot be regarded in a linear fashion because—and this is the specific trend—subsequent administrations have valued the use of diplomacy differently. As a result, they engaged either more or less in diplomatic activities, be it through regular channels or through special representatives. In this regard, one author remarks a stark difference between the "proliferation of special envoys under President Bill Clinton" and the "little sustained interest in deep diplomatic engagement with the world" displayed by President George W. Bush, at least during his first term (Fullilove 2005, 13).[208] More precisely, the Bush administration, in its effort to downscale the use

---

205 "The failure to name a Senator handicapped the Treaty of Versailles when it was brought up for advice and consent" (Wriston 1960, 230).

206 Cf. Plischke 1986, 79: "Until the election of President Franklin Roosevelt and the world economic and political crises of the 1930s, the appointment of special emissaries remained occasional. However, Roosevelt commissioned [...] a host of [...] personal representatives, setting the pace for a substantial and continuing increase in the use of this diplomatic practice." Later, with regard to the Vietnam war, Plischke recounts: "During the Indochina crisis, [...] Presidents Eisenhower, Kennedy, Johnson, and Nixon [...] employed a corps of special envoys to represent U.S. interest" (ibid., 85). Already in 1960, Wriston stated that: "International conferences have become the most prolific sources of special envoys. The United States now participates in about 350 such meetings each year" (Wriston 1960, 235).

207 It is interesting to note how things have changed in this regard. It was only in 1956 that one could write: "Presidents do not go abroad often or for a protracted period. [...] Presidents, therefore, are not likely to interfere with the status of ambassadors. Secretaries of State are a much more difficult problem. It used to be the rule that they seldom went abroad. [...] Better transportation and communication made such stringent limitations unnecessary. Indeed, a whole series of influences have tended to swing the pendulum to the opposite extreme and make the Secretary of State our most peripatetic government official" (Wriston 1956, 110–11).

208 To be fair, the Clinton administration also received criticism for its heavy use of special agents in

of special agents, reportedly tried to explicitly distance itself from the 'Clinton way' of solving problems by sending an envoy.[209] The Obama administration, in contrast, started with a bold diplomatic offensive, including the dispatching of high-ranking envoys to the Middle East, to Afghanistan and Pakistan, and, most notably, to Iran, thus bringing back a "hallmark of the Clinton years" (The Economist 2009) or indeed, of Franklin D. Roosevelt's times. The normative question here therefore rather refers to the importance an administration places on diplomacy in general than to the specific (American) values that the envoys may or may not embody.

2.2 Roles and role models

There are common patterns as well as discernable differences between the special representatives of the UN Secretary-General and the envoys of the United States president. As they precede the development of CFSP by quite some time, it should be insightful to infer some conclusions from this comparison with regard to the subject matter, the EU Special Representatives. As part of this study's exploratory approach, these preliminary observations each lead to a set of questions, which will serve as inductive input for the next chapter where I will develop the research hypotheses and determine the cases (learning instances) to study.

2.2.1 Analytical inferences from antecedent envoys

Rationale and legal foundation

With regard to the origins of the respective envoys, the fact that the EU Special Representatives were initially appointed without an explicit Treaty reference[210] is in no way singular. The institutions of both UN and U.S. envoys have been formed by persisting political practice rather than by their legal foundation. Indeed, in all three cases the envoys filled a vacuum at the outset: The young U.S. republic did not have permanent ambassadors; the UN Secretary-General was without fact-finding capacities; and the EU did not have any outside representation. What is more, both the UN and the EU used the same justification based on the monitoring duty of the UN Secretary-General and the EU's Political Committee, respectively, to introduce envoys.

---

that it disregards the traditional tracks of diplomacy: "there has recently been a tendency at higher levels in Washington to underrate the importance of the bilateral relationship fostered by the ambassador, as compared to other means of international interaction," e.g. sending a special envoy to multilateral deliberations (Kennan 1997, 207). Kennan criticizes that, while most likely being an expert in his or her field and having the full support of the president, the envoy is oftentimes unaware of the wider, long-term American national interests.

209 This observation is made in reference to the Macedonia crisis of 2001; cf. Kirkconnell 2002, 4 and 12.

210 This is not to imply that there was no legal basis for sending them; they were properly dispatched based on a Joint Action. However, this was an improvisation and the Treaty at that time did not foresee an instrument such as EUSRs.

This leads to questions about the invention of EUSRs: Some seem to believe that an instrumental transfer took place, suggesting a link between the successful model of SRSGs and the dispatching of the first EUSR (Fröhlich 2006, 18–19). What was the reasoning of dispatching the first EUSRs? Did either the UN Special Representatives or the U.S. Special Envoys serve as a model after which the EUSRs were built? To provide a full answer, however, more research is needed.

Due to the legal framework, envoys of the U.S. president and the UN Secretary-General have a more personalized, trust-dependent relationship with their bosses than EUSRs do. The U.S. president has unparalleled freedom in determining both the individual and the job in question— "an almost perfectly free hand in means and methods" (Wriston 1960, 222). As the head of state, he also has ceremonial obligations, which he may choose to delegate to a substitute. The UN Secretary-General, in contrast, is not the supreme body of his organization; especially with regard to the area of international security, he must observe the powers of the Security Council. On global issues, however, he has used his freedom to appoint 'surrogates' on any issue he deems important and cannot attend to exclusively by himself (Puchala 1993, 82). In the European Union it is not a single person (the Secretary-General or the president, respectively), but a 27-member-strong body (the Council) that nominates the envoy. As a consequence, selection of personnel is organized along an institutional procedure involving all major stakeholders. In particular, EUSRs do not formally represent the EU's High Representative for CFSP, Javier Solana, despite the fact that they have been nicknamed 'Solana's deputies'. Thus, the issue of personal trust should be less prevalent for the EU as the envoy is not anyone's alter ego.

The politicized nature of the sending system is greatest in the case of the United States, where a partisan president can dispatch his personal representatives with little care about others' views. He is even free to bypass the State Department—which faces "entrenched political control" at the ministerial level and itself has a weak political constituency anyway (Kennan 1997, 203 and 205)—and its network of accredited ambassadors who are, by default, already his personal representatives. The UN Secretary-General, quite the reverse, ought to be an impartial personality, partisan only to the case of international peace and security. Similarly, political preferences can be expected to be much less relevant with regard to the EUSRs and their institutionalized selection procedure. Rather, it is the usual horse-trading between member states about whose candidate is most suitable for the job that should take place.

From this, interesting questions appear with regard to the CFSP structures and the selection of EUSRs: The formal relation to the Council notwithstanding, what working relationships do EUSRs and their teams entertain both with the Political and Security Committee (as a surrogate of the Council) and with the High Representative himself? Moreover, an analysis might reveal member states' influence on nomination and mandate formulation—marking the 'partisan' dimension in EU affairs.

Function and task

The business of special envoys—diverse as they are in individual cases—is, in principle (and maybe not surprisingly) alike across institutions: They engage in all forms of multilateral diplomacy, usually aimed at diffusing international crises, and they have considerable room for manoeuvre. Differences appear with regard to the duration of an envoy's mandate, its specificity, and its operational quality. Especially in the U.S. case, mandates may be as short as only a few weeks to solve a particular issue ('trouble-shooters'); in such a case, the mandate would be rather precise. The instructions given to EUSRs, in contrast, tend to be broad and long-term so that they can fill them with their own initiative. Likewise, SRSGs have a rather large timeframe and vague instructions, slowly and creatively drilling thick boards, to borrow Max Weber's famous term.

Not surprisingly, this leeway enhances the role of the individual vis-à-vis the institution, which is not without consequences for the learning process (Byman/Pollack 2001, 141; Fröhlich 2006, 17). SRSGs and EUSRs differ insofar that the mandates of the former tend to be more operational with regard to a certain crisis management operation they are in charge of; in that sense, their work is more action-oriented than that of EUSRs.

Both the U.S. president and the UN Secretary-General can engage envoys for anything from secret missions to public diplomacy, something the EU cannot do in a comparable manner. With the discretion to appoint envoys without formal involvement of other institutions, both U.S. and UN envoys can make use of their high profile and try to strengthen public support for a particular policy or mission. Alternatively, secrecy may be used for a fast and frank exchange of views (Fullilove 2005, 16; Wriston 1960, 219). Such secret diplomacy is not available to the EU, at least not in the function of the EUSR. Council decisions must be made public; thus, any new Special Representative and his or her mandate will instantly be known. This does not, of course, prevent an existing EUSR from conducting his or her business in a low-profile or even covert way. In addition, the EU's more complicated bureaucratic processes need not always be disadvantageous when it comes to preparing a mission. One observer criticized the frequent and usually short-term use of envoys by the U.S. president: "Missions are often rushed; envoys can lack specialist knowledge and important contacts; the publicity attending their visits can arouse excessive or premature expectations; personalizing a particular policy sometimes robs it of wide bureaucratic support; and operating through personal agents can demoralize regulars in the diplomatic service."[211] The time that the appointment of an EUSR takes should at least assure a fair amount of preparation of the mission.

Not surprisingly, from these observations flow questions regarding the different tasks of EUSRs: How have they evolved over time? Are some roles more open to influence by the individuals than others, i.e. do they leave room for manoeuvre and encourage

---

211 Fullilove 2005, 16; similarly Kennan 1997, 207–8. Cf. also on the SRSGs: "Each mission is considered sui generis; each is instructed ad hoc, staffed as fully or meagerly as resources allow and executed as ambitiously or cautiously as the Secretary-General thinks appropriate" (Puchala 1993, 84).

learning? How do the EUSRs operate in practice and with whom do they cooperate in the field?

People

In order to fulfill all these demands, envoys need a broad range of skills and experience. Thus, not only the business but also the background of special envoys is fairly similar. Nationality notwithstanding, they are, in principle, drawn from the same pool of highly professional, diplomatically qualified people. This is exemplified by EUSRs like Aldo Ajello and Francesc Vendrell, who had been Special Representatives of the UN Secretary-General prior to their EU post, or the early envoy for Bosnia and Herzegovina, Carl Bildt, who later became first the High Representative of the international community in that country, and then the UN SRSG for Southeastern Europe.[212]

On top of these professional virtues, the people appointed to the post of special envoy usually have the full confidence of the office holder, and they enjoy a good reputation with the conflict or issue in question. Neither U. S. nor UN envoys are appointed based on a formal selection process. While the UN has engaged in training and networking activities for its special representatives, these are lacking on the U. S. side.

These thoughts lead to questions about personality as the basis for personnel selection: What is the role of the personal qualities of an envoy beyond the mere statement that all cases are different? Do officeholders need to be on good terms with their boss and important member states, be acquainted with the procedures of the sending institution, or have thorough expertise of the conflict in question? Or all of the above?

Institutional relations

With regard to institutional relations, it appears that all envoys regularly have to deal with a complex set of independent bodies already on their own side. For the United Nations, these are not only the Security Council and the General Assembly, but also the multitude of operational organizations in the field. In the American system, in addition to the State Department as primary competitor of the special envoys, there is a whole government bureaucracy with different ministries involved in turf battles. These are mirrored by a web of ministerial agencies and delegations abroad that, even for an allegedly unitary actor such as the United States, add to a chorus of different foreign policy voices. The EUSRs are therefore not alone in having to deal with a number of counterparts, both in Brussels and in the field.

The high degree of internal (e. g. inter-ministerial or inter-agency) coordination that rests upon the special representative is, thus, a common feature. As a result, one of the foremost tasks of the envoys is to establish themselves, with the status of the one who

---

212 Likewise, the former U. S. ambassador to the DR Congo, William Lacy Swing, became the UN Secretary-General's Special Representative for that same country in 2003. Moreover, former U. S. Presidents George Bush senior and Bill Clinton today are UN Special Envoys for the South Asia Earthquake and for Tsunami Recovery, respectively.

sent them, as the unifying authority to third parties. Yet this may appear odd because they might actually add to the confusion simply because they are another actor representing the sending institution or state.

An interesting research question stemming from this fact concerns internal coordination, i. e. whether and to what extent envoys have a unifying function in this system: Are they, due to their standing as representatives of a supreme body or person, in a position to coordinate other actors in the field?

Another observation relates to the effect of the co-existence of a professional foreign service and separate special envoys, a situation in which the U. S. is, the UN is not, and the EU wishes soon to be. In the United States today, presidential envoys exist parallel to and even in competition with the Foreign Service. This service already features a host of politically appointed ambassadors at important posts around the world. Some even speculate that the use of envoys at times had a systematic trait, circumventing the Foreign Service.[213] This has created the described demoralizing effect and resulting mistrust of envoys on the part of the diplomatic corps. In contrast, neither the United Nations nor the European Union has its own diplomatic representations, let alone intelligence-gathering capabilities. SRSGs and EUSRs are a means to make up, at least to some extent, for the lack of a similar service in their organizations.[214] For the UN, this is likely to remain the same for the foreseeable future. The EU, however, has begun deliberations about an EU foreign service, or European External Action Service as proposed in the Constitutional Treaty of 2003 and the Reform Treaty of 2007.[215] This would hardly have been conceivable back in 1996 when the first EU envoys received their mandates.

These developments inspire a future-oriented research question for the new EU foreign service: Based on the findings of this study, what are the lessons to be learned from a decade of EUSRs for the EEAS?

The prospect of an EU foreign service raises the question whether this new body should succeed and, thus, replace the existing EUSRs. While this point will be discussed in more detail in the conclusions, one remark is apt already at this stage. Despite the sometimes-tense relation between the U. S. envoys and the diplomatic service, the two fulfill different

---

213 "The more such emissaries are used, and the more they succeed in their missions, the more they will be relied upon. In the past, it is alleged, this sometimes led to the appointing of unsuitable ambassadors with the expectation of recruiting special agents to make up the deficiency, and there is danger that this practice may become commonplace" (Plischke 1986, 115).

214 "Some have suggested that while the ad hoc information-gathering network constituted by the Secretary-General's special representatives posted to trouble spots is helpful, it hardly substitutes for a UN consular system of official intelligence facility" (Puchala 1993, 91). Fullilove sees the U. S. envoys not as substitutes but as complements to the Foreign Service; cf. Fullilove 2005, 17.

215 Both treaties make reference to an EU foreign minister/high representative for foreign policy who is supported by an External Action Service (Art. 27 TCE and Art. 27 of the Lisbon Reform Treaty, respectively). For a first proposal of how such an EU foreign service might work, see Grevi/Cameron 2005.

objectives. Thus, in the same way that a functional U.S. diplomatic service has not made the special envoys superfluous (cf. Plischke 1986, 117; Fullilove 2005, 17), EUSRs need not be abolished once a European External Action Service will be in place.

Relevance

Special Representatives are relevant in a quantitative as well as qualitative sense. As for the former, a clear tendency in international relations to increasingly rely on the use of special representatives is discernable. Both the United Nations and the United States have seen a surge in the numbers of these agents over the years, irrespective of the potential differences between one U.S. administration and the other that was alluded to earlier. Moreover, in both cases, there is one common factor: The rise of multilateralist fora following the end of the Cold War.

The entry on the world stage of the EU Special Representatives and their development in recent years can be seen as part of this multilateral wave. Both the UN and the EU were freed, in a sense, from the limitations imposed by the bloc confrontation. However, while the one had no choice but to engage (the UN was directly tasked with an increasing number of peace operations), the other had the freedom to become more active when and where it thought appropriate (although there was, of course, a certain pressure on the EU to take on responsibility). What one author said of the SRSGs seems to be true for all envoys: that they represent a type of actor that is indispensable for successful diplomacy under today's complex conditions (Fröhlich 2006, 19).

Against this post-Cold War background, a difference in the role of the special envoy becomes clear: The SRSG travels abroad not to bolster the international reputation of the UN but to engage directly in a peace operation. EUSRs, in contrast, have more leeway in defining their role, including how best to enhance the actorness of the EU.

One question would therefore concern the increase of EUSRs: Is this rise driven by internal factors or by external demand? Moreover, what is the weight of prestige-related considerations in dispatching an EUSR compared to those that refer to the crisis in question?

From this aspect of strengthening one's standing flows the qualitative aspect of the envoys' relevance, i.e. their impact on the sending authority. Especially the UN Secretary-General has greatly enhanced his fact-finding capabilities using Special Representatives. What is more, beyond this technical improvement, the use of SRSGs has effectively increased the Secretary-General's "power and autonomy vis-à-vis other UN organs [...thus contributing] to the evolution of the Secretary-General's office as a political-diplomatic agency" (Puchala 1993, 95–6). Likewise, as mentioned before, envoys helped the U.S. president to bypass the State Department and take direct influence on foreign affairs, thereby securing his foreign policy prerogatives (Wriston 1960, 222). While for the United Nations envoys are most useful in sustaining, in the mid- to long-term, an ongoing peace process, for the United States they have also been very useful in high-profile negotiations aimed at achieving an actual peace agreement or other dispute settlements.[216] Thus, in general, special envoys have also had a beneficial effect on the international standing of both the U.S. president and the UN Secretary-General, which would justify their increased use of the former.

A similar benefit might exist for the EU, i.e. that the use of EUSRs, beyond their direct contribution to EU crisis management, might impact on the EU as a foreign policy actor as a whole. The last set of questions thus deals with the EU's strategic role: What has been the influence of EUSRs on the EU as an international actor? Have they contributed to its conflict resolution capabilities; have they enhanced its standing?

2.2.2 Different roles of special envoys

Extending the above made comparison of the function and tasks of the different envoys, a more structurally grounded analysis of the various roles they can assume is attempted here. These roles are not meant to be prescriptive or in any way defining of what an envoy should (or should not) do. They rather serve as a means of dissecting the activity of EUSRs, in order to be able to analyze it through the lens of learning theories.

It has become clear that all envoys fulfilll external as well as internal roles: Despite being deployed on a mission abroad, they also work to the inside of the sending institution. This is the case for envoys of the EU or UN (where they have to lobby member states and to unify them around a common position), as well as of the United States (where they have to deal with different administrative bodies, in particular with the Department of State).

In addition to their internal and external dimensions, the roles of envoys can be structured around their degree of activity. The latter is here portrayed in two forms: presence and actorness. The concept of 'presence' was introduced by Allen and Smith to describe the status of the EC/EU without referring to it being an international actor equal to states or international organizations (Allen/Smith 1990).[217] Presence is more about 'being' than 'acting' (Bretherton/Vogler 1999, 33), whereas the 'being' part can be further divided into factual presence as its most basic form, and informational presence where the presence is used to either gather or distribute information. 'Actorness,' in contrast, builds on concrete 'acting', either individually or intersubjectively.

---

216 Plischke notes that "the primary means by which the United States extricated itself from the Vietnamese quagmire was through the use of presidential personal emissaries—to create viable channels of communication, to negotiate at the [1973] Paris conference table, and to engage in confidential exchanges" (Plischke 1986, 89). Similarly, "the freeing of the U.S. hostages [in Iran in 1981] eventually was achieved indirectly by presidential personal representatives through an intermediary government [of Algeria]" (ibid., 91).

217 With regard to the EU's presence and actorness until the end of the 1990s, scholars concur that it has the former (because it is visible in international fora), but only some elements of the latter (because in some areas it is an international actor, but not in others) (Ginsberg 1999, 432).

Building on these categories of presence and actorness in an internal and external dimension, one can distinguish eight different roles that envoys can fulfill.[218] Internally, presence refers to the fact that by their mere existence, envoys oblige their sending institution to provide political guidance for them, i.e. to agree at least on a minimal policy. In addition, their presence on the ground provides information for policy analysis. Their internal actorness finds an expression in the ability to make policy proposals and to coordinate different agents of the sending institution. Externally, presence implies that the visibility itself of an actor raises expectations of third parties and, thus, can exert influence. This includes the dissemination of information insofar it is not intended to have direct effect.[219] External actorness is expressed both by individual activity and by cooperation with third parties. Here again, presence may also lead to a more operative policy (i.e. actorness) simply because there is someone present in the field to execute it (Regelsberger 1997, 221).

The following matrix summarizes the main functions special envoys have:

Table 1: Eight Different Roles of Special Envoys

	Presence		Actorness	
	Factual presence	Informational presence	Individual Actorness	Intersubjective actorness
Internal – In capitals/headquarters – From and in the field	Obligation	Analysis	Proposals	Coordination
External – Towards conflict parties – Towards third parties	Visibility	Dissemination	Activity	Cooperation

Just a few examples from the historical overview of the previous chapter shall illustrate these different roles with regard to the EU Special Representatives:

– The obligation to devise a policy was felt in the cases of the Great Lakes and the South Caucasus, when the work of the respective EUSRs necessitated common EU positions.
– Political analysis (i.e. information for policy) has been a constant feature of all mandates, from the far-away Great Lakes to small and nearby places like Moldova.

---

218 Grevi (2007, 141–144) distinguishes six roles for the EUSRs: information providers, policy-makers, crisis managers, lynchpins of coordination, networkers, and agents of multilateralism. Despite the fact that these roles are developed less in a systematic but seemingly intuitive way, they resonate well with six of the eight roles described here (i.e. omitting 'obligation' and 'visibility', the two roles stemming from the EUSRs' factual presence). Dietl (2005, 135–39), for one, distinguishes only two roles: bridge-builder between parties, and catalyst of a negotiated solution. However, she limits her focus to conflict management in general and to one region in particular (the Middle East).

219 Cf. Bretherton/Vogler 1999, 5: "Presence does not connote purposive external action, rather it is a consequence of internal policies and processes."

– Delivering policy proposals was an early by-product of this information-gathering activity; it was explicitly mentioned in the mandates of, for example, the EUSR for the South Caucasus or for Central Asia.

– Internal coordination is of major importance in any theatre, given the presence of different actors like Commission delegations, ESDP operations, and member states embassies. It becomes vital in places like Bosnia and Herzegovina and Macedonia, where EU agencies abound on the ground.

– Gaining external visibility was an important element for the EU in the Middle East Peace Process or vis-à-vis the actors already engaged in Central Asia.

– Likewise, the Union used the EUSRs for policy dissemination (or information on policy) in certain places, like in the South Caucasus and, again, within the Middle East Quartet.

– Activity-oriented mandates are needed for different instances of conflict resolution that are part of all mandates in one form or the other, be it in former Yugoslavia or for Sudan.

– Finally, cooperation with international actors is the name of the game especially in post-conflict situations like in Bosnia and Herzegovina, the Great Lakes, or Afghanistan.

Obviously, the lines between these different roles are often blurred, and usually a combination of these roles can be found in mandates. In addition, envoys may assume different roles over time, depending on the stage of the conflict; this will be elaborated in more detail in the empirical part about the EU Special Representatives (cf. in particular sections 5.1 and 6.10). But before, I will justify the selection of the EUSRs as an object of research. Reasons why, in addition, they are a useful case for the study of organizational learning processes will be given at the end of the next chapter.

2.2.3 Case selection: Why study the EUSRs?

The preceding inferences from a comparison of special envoys and their roles provide an answer to the question why I chose to study the EUSRs in the first place. I will briefly summarize this thinking in the following.

First of all, it has become clear that the EU Special Representatives—like their colleagues from the UN and the U.S.—are an understudied phenomenon with an expansive reach. Given the prominence they now have in European foreign policy, this alone would make them a worthwhile object of study. Besides, the Special Representatives cover a broad range of EU foreign policy, with mandates in the EU's major regions of concern: The Western Balkans and Southeastern Europe, Central Africa and the Middle East, as well as the Caucasus and Central Asia. Both the rise in numbers and in geographical scope of the EUSRs led the High Representative for CFSP, Javier Solana, to remark on the occasion of the first joint EUSR seminar:

"You as EUSRs are the visible expression of the EU's growing engagement in some of the world's most troubled countries and regions. The list of where we have EUSRs is, in part, also [a] list of where our foreign and security policy priorities lie." (Solana 2005b, 2).

The following map shows the geographical reach of EUSR mandates in the wider European neighborhood, stretching to Central Asia and Central Africa:

Figure 12: Geographical Reach of EUSR Mandates[220]

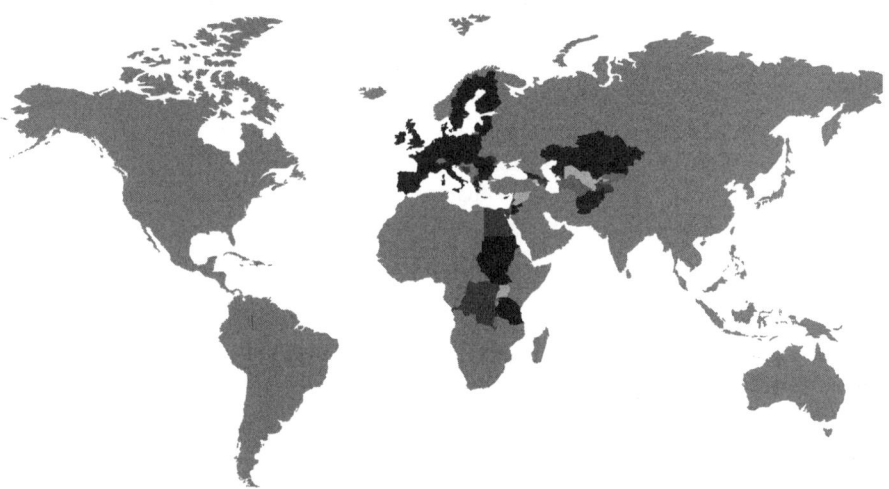

In addition, the EUSRs precede institutions like the High Representative and the PSC by several years; thus, analyzing their origins can give evidence of the founding years of CFSP. Later, EUSRs became closely interwoven with the recent surge in ESDP operations: As it happens, military and/or civilian ESDP operations have been deployed to all the mandate areas of EUSRs except Central Asia. Put the other way around, almost all ESDP operations have taken place within the area of responsibility of an EUSR (the missions in Indonesia, Iraq, and Guinea-Bissau being the exceptions to this rule). The most recent appointment of an EUSR for Kosovo and, at the same time, the deployment of the EU's largest ever ESDP operation to the same region therefore do not appear to be merely coincidental.

Another reason why EUSRs are worth studying is that they may embody fundamental EU values. One author assumed that UN envoys, through their work, could promote the overall goals of the world organization (Puchala 1993, 89). UN Secretary-General Kofi

---

220 Areas covered by an EUSR are colored in different light grey tones, whereas the EU-27 is represented in dark grey. The mandates of the EUSRs for the African Union and for Kosovo, respectively, are not depicted in this map, as they are not part of this study.

Annan called the SRSGs the "personification of the United Nations in the country or region in which [they] serve" (United Nations 2001, 1). Similarly, other authors find that sometimes an envoy can represent the U.S. interests more directly than an ambassador.[221] Transferring this reasoning to the EU not only points to the question of the values and world-views of EUSRs as individuals, making their cognitive maps an object of study (cf. Fröhlich 2006, 20). Such reasoning also leads to the heart of the matter of a foreign policy identity of the European Union.

Finally, the EUSRs are also an interesting subject in institutional terms. This study does not investigate decision-making at the leadership level, but rather bureaucratic processes in a 'thick' institutional environment. The EUSRs and their teams provide a mixture of ambassadorial-level entrepreneurs and administrative officials from the Council and member states with their different socialization backgrounds.[222] At the same time, an analysis of the EUSRs and their immediate counterparts involves a limited number of agents only. This avoids the pyramid (or 'Rashomon') problem of large bureaucracies when top officials do not know the situation on the ground, while lower-ranking employees cannot see the full picture involved in political decisions (George/Bennett 2004, 103).

Selecting the EUSRs as an object of study is therefore the result of a mixed purposeful sampling strategy (Patton 2002, 244). They are a typical case to the extent that they represent the broad spectrum of EU foreign policy, in both geographical and political terms, and embody the EU's fundamental values. In addition, EUSRs can be seen as a politically important case (cf. Van Evera 1997, 83): They work closely with the High Representative and the PSC; they enjoy relative strength vis-à-vis a majority of member states that are not at all or only sporadically represented diplomatically; and with the advent of an EU foreign service, their work has become more important as a model to build upon.

For all these reasons, it seems justified to undertake this first major study of the EU Special Representatives as a case to analyze the EU's organizational learning. How exactly this analysis is conceptualized is the topic of the next chapter.

---

221 Cf. Plischke 1986, 133. One author critical of this view is Kennan 1997, 207–8. His call for the ambassador as main guardian of the national interest appears weak, however, given Kennan's own admittance that "what constitutes the national interest varies with time and circumstance. Essentially, considering the president's preeminence in policy-making, it is what the present occupant of the Oval Office thinks it is and can gain acceptance for among the public and the government establishment" (ibid., 207). This and the fact that a personal envoy is usually closer to the president than a resident ambassador make the envoy a fairly direct expression of the U.S. interest.

222 On socialization processes, see the 2005 special issue of the journal 'International Organisation' (e.g. Checkel 2005), in particular Lewis 2005, who analyzed the work of member states' permanent representatives in the EU's Committee of Permanent Representatives, or Coreper.

Chapter 3:
Theoretical and Methodological Approach

The two previous chapters have shown the complexity of the EU as a foreign policy actor as well as the importance of the EUSRs as an instrument of the EU's external actions. Features of the former worth mentioning are its complex institutional structure, the rise of ESDP in the second pillar, and the development of a distinct approach to foreign policy in general (effective multilateralism) and to crisis management in particular (bringing a broad range of civilian and military means to use). As concerns the EUSRs, one could note their function as an expression of the EU's international actorness, their relative age with respect to CFSP, and their emblematic approach to international mediation. Moreover, they occupy a critical position between certain constitutive actors of the EU (the Council, the Commission, and the member states) well as at the nexus of the EU and its international partners; this renders them, in an organizational sense, internal and external 'boundary spanners.'

It is in this setting that I will devise the theoretical and methodological approach in this chapter. In the following, I will first establish a theoretical framework with a working definition of OL derived at building on the commonalities and differences of existing approaches. Considering alternative explanations of foreign policy change and how learning is conceived in political terms, I will then present my own definition of OL. Based on these deliberations, I will develop the analytical framework and model used for this study. Finally, I will explain the methodology employed and justify the selection of EUSRs as a case study for the empirical analysis in the second part.

3.1 Theoretical framework

"The concept of learning is difficult to define, isolate, measure, and apply empirically," Levy (1994, 280) admits. Others agree that it should not be seen "as a neat linear process with causal antecedents but as a messy, dynamic, interactive process" (Stein 1994, 172–73). What makes engagement in learning theories difficult to start with is that there is no common or in any way prevailing concept in the theory of organizational learning. Instead, a wide range of definitions exist, many emphasizing different aspects of the learning process (see Argyris/Schön 1978, Dierkes et al. 2001, Haas 1991). Worse still, in his overview of the literature, George Huber criticizes that scholars do not even try to build on each other: "The researchers who have studied organizational learning apparently have, to a surprising degree, not used the results from previous research to design or interpret their own research" (Huber 1991, 107).

Due to this lack of a unitary approach that could provide testable hypotheses, an exploratory research design is chosen for this study. It combines induction from the presentation of the EUSRs (chapter 1) and the comparison of special envoys (chapter

2) with deduction from the existing literature on organizational learning as well as from learning methods ('lessons learned' or 'best practices') in the foreign policy arena (chapter 3). This approach, designed to detect the mechanisms of organizational learning in European foreign policy-making, also promotes "the dialogue between theory and data" (Zürn/Checkel 2005, 1046).[223] Heeding Huber's call for more cross-referencing, it also aims to promote the dialogue between researchers by elaborating and building on the commonalities of various existing learning concepts.

3.1.1   A working definition of organizational learning

OL can be defined by referring to its two constitutive elements: Organization and learning. There is little disagreement among the cognoscenti of the matter about the first ('O') part: An organization is a "goal-directed, boundary-maintaining, and socially constructed [system] of human activity" (Aldrich 1999, 2), or in short: a group of people organized for a particular purpose. At this stage, it does not make a difference whether this group acts in the political, economic, or cultural sphere, although this will be of importance later when defining the subject of learning (subsection 3.2.1). Agreement about what constitutes an organization in fact goes so far that most OL works do not even bother to explain, let alone define their understanding of it.

In contrast, descriptions proffered are much more diverse (and disputed) with regard to the second ('L') part. What most definitions have in common is that they see learning

- as a cognitive process in which a group of people reaches,
- a collective understanding about new or newly assessed information,
- which can take place at different levels.

They differ primarily in terms of

- whether they place emphasis on the individual or on the organization as a whole,
- whether they focus on information acquisition or on how knowledge is socially created from such information,
- and whether they see (successful) change as inherent to learning or not.[224]

I will address each of these points consecutively.

Learning can be considered a cognitive process when the environment does not directly influence a person's behavior. Instead, external stimuli are mediated "by images or plans, maps or schemes, or generally spoken, by cognitive structures and processes" within the

---

223   Benner et al. (2007) use a similar approach for their analysis of organizational learning in UN peacekeeping operations, as does Kathrin Böhling in her work on the European Commission: "To cope with the dearth of literature on the European Commission as a product of its organizational dynamics and with the lack of empirical research on organizational learning, an exploratory research strategy is chosen for this study" (Böhling 2007, 19).

224   For an introduction to the related field of system transformation, see Sandschneider 1996b.

individual (Klimecki/Lassleben 1998, 15). Learning is also rational, although limited by the fact that actors do not possess all information necessary or possibly available, and that they are bound by certain norms and values (bounded rationality).[225] While learning is a psychological process at the individual level, it becomes a socio-communicative process at the collective level when information is exchanged between different members of an organization and, thus, shared knowledge is created (cf. below).

The main element of organizational learning consists of the internal processing of external information. This is generally seen to take place in four steps: At first, an organization acquires information from the environment, which it, secondly, distributes internally and, thirdly, interprets with its cognitive structures (or vice versa). Fourthly, the interpreted information is stored in the organizational routines.[226] The processing of information thus takes place at a collective level, i.e. when individual learning experiences become engrained into organizational practices.[227] This adding or altering of information is not a mechanistic process (like changing written rules); instead, it builds on establishing a common understanding (rather in the way unwritten rules emerge and develop). How exactly this is done, will be developed in subsection 3.2.3.

Organizations do not have to rely solely on their own experiences to acquire new information but can learn from others (LaPalombara 2001b, 143), a process that is also called 'vicarious learning' (e.g. Huber 1991, 96; Stern 1997, 70). Such learning might have taken place at the EU with reference to prior experiences of the UN or U.S. envoys. What is more, organizations can even anticipate potential future changes based on present information and try to adapt well ahead of them, without any role models (Malek et al. 2002, 10). In both cases, it is environmental information (about another's experience or about potential future developments) that is interpreted and stored in the organizational routine. Importantly, it is not relevant whether this information is accurate or 'true.'

A differentiation between two levels of learning is generally made, although different authors have labelled them differently.[228] Chris Argyris and Donald A. Schön (1978, 2–3) distinguished between single-loop and double-loop learning, building on Karl Deutsch's

---

225 See Haas 1990, 32, and Smith 2004, 29; for an introduction to the concept of bounded rationality, see Jones 1999 and Simon 1991. The effect of cognitive structures is further elaborated in subsection 3.2.3.

226 Huber 1991, 90; see also subsection 3.2.3 on the processes of learning. Other authors distinguish three steps: "The cognitive process incorporates perception, analysis and choice" (Starbuck/Hedberg 2001, 333).

227 Levy 1994, 287; similar arguments can be found in Levitt/March 1988, 320, Argyris 1992, 8, and Hedberg/Wolff 2001, 537.

228 For an earlier overview of the different labels for "higher-level" and "lower-level learning", as they call it, see Fiol/Lyles 1985, 810; for the elaboration of such concepts, see for example Coopey 1996, Levy 1994, March/Olsen 1976, Miner/Mezias 1996, Nye 1987, Senge 1990, and Weick/Westley 1996. Hedberg is an exception in that he distinguishes three types of learning: adjustment (similar to single-loop), turnover (a middle-type), and turnaround (similar to double-loop) learning (cf. Hedberg 1981, 9–10).

differentiation of simple and complex learning (Deutsch 1966, 92). Simple learning can be characterized as an adaptation within the structure and processes of the present system, i.e. changing the means but not the ends of an organization.[229] Complex learning, in contrast, includes a change of the ends of an organization, i.e. a change of the system rather than merely within it, a process that others call "reframing" (cf. Hedberg/Wolff 2001, 538).

Widespread as it is, the distinction between these two levels does not constitute a fundamental added value to the learning concept. Not only is complex learning thought to be quite rare (Haas 1990, 37).[230] In the case of the EU, it would imply a change of its foreign policy goals and system, e.g. from a multilateral approach to more unilateral policy-making or from applying a comprehensive set of instruments to focusing only on the military.[231] What is more, the question whether a change of organizational routines is simple or complex is of subordinate relevance. Huber, for one, agrees that the distinction is important conceptually but doubts the practical difference between the two learning types (Huber 1991, 93). He is right insofar as, given the lack of empirical evidence of organizational learning and the fact that neither of the two types can be regarded as better than the other per se, finding evidence for either type of learning would in itself be an important first step.

Agreement on these three points does not prevent approaches to differ in three other main aspects. As previously mentioned, organizational learning is a socio-communicative process so the emphasis placed on the role of the individual makes a useful distinction (Friedman 2001, 398). One group of scholars sees 'learning' as an exclusively individual process and its use in the organizational context rather as a metaphor: "All learning takes place inside individual human heads" (Simon 1991, 125). Proponents of this approach contend that organizations learn not by themselves (which would mean to anthropomorphise them) but only through individuals (Levy 1994, 287; cf. Argyris 1992, 8; Hedberg/Wolff 2001, 537). Individual learning alone, however, does not yet guarantee learning at the organizational level (Levy 1994, 311; Nye 1987, 381).[232] Other authors

---

229 Interestingly, the difference between two levels of learning resembles the differentiation by Krasner about change within a regime (change of rules and procedures) and change of a regime (change of principles and norms); cf. Krasner 1983, 3–4.

230 LaPalombara argues that complex learning is even less frequent in public organizations than in the private sector (LaPalombara 2001a, 565). Others are more optimistic, arguing that such learning is at least more probable in organizations than in individuals (Hedberg/Wolff 2001, 546).

231 Not even the inclusion of security policy, a long-time taboo, into the EU's foreign policy by the Maastricht Treaty could even superficially be judged as double-loop learning, because "at a time of major structural change (the end of the Cold War) [...], EU states managed only to rationalize and codify existing EPC procedures, and refused to include more robust, unequivocal provisions concerning defense cooperation, majority voting in the CFSP, Commission responsibilities, and [...] involvement [of the European Court of Justice]" (Smith 2004, 244).

232 It is particularly insufficient to look only at the learning of the leaders, as some early studies of political decision-making did: "No explanation of individual learning, even by a senior leader in a hierarchical system, can explain foreign policy change. Institutional and political processes must intervene to build the political support to transform individual learning into changes in foreign policy

stress that organizational learning is more than the sum of learning by each member of the organization (cf. Fiol/Lyles 1985, 804). They take "organizations as entities which are able to think and act" and, thus, learn by themselves (Malek et al. 2002, 7). Without denying the importance of individual learning, these authors nevertheless stress the importance of communication processes between the individuals of an organization and of the organizational routines that absorb individual learning experiences (Klimecki et al. 1999, 7–8). This is particularly important with regard to personnel turnover, which organizational learning must endure over time (Levitt/March 1988, 321).

Given the common understanding of OL as a collective process, this study builds on individual learning as an important but not as a necessary element: Individuals are critical in setting learning processes in motion (Friedman 2001, 399), but evidence of individual learning is not required to speak of organizational learning. In view of the complexity of the organization under study here, the EU, with different levels of decision-making (national, European) as well as different institutional competencies (pillars), there would be no use in declaring learning at the individual level a conditio sine qua non for organizational learning. On this point, one could also argue with the 'father of European integration,' Jean Monnet, who is often quoted as having said: 'Nothing is possible without men; nothing lasts without institutions'. In the same vein, organizational learning is only possible with individuals but it needs an organization to hold.

The consideration of individual members of an organization leads to a second differentiation of approaches, i.e. whether they focus on informational input to the learning process or on social interaction to create common knowledge. One group of authors stresses the importance of factual information from the organizational environment.[233] Consequently, they give more consideration to the acquisition stage of the information processing activity than, say, to distribution or interpretation. Other approaches place more emphasis on the latter two processes and how knowledge is constructed collectively from ambiguous environmental information. For them, information is not 'raw data' but constructed by human interpretations of social and physical phenomena.[234]

In this work, preference is given, on both theoretical and practical grounds, to the latter approaches that stress the collectively constructed meaning of information. Firstly, for learning to take root, sufficient consensus needs to be built around different interpretations (cf. Malek et al. 2002, 10). Thus, it is more important how information is perceived and treated than what precisely it meant when it was acquired. Secondly, in an organization like the EU, it would not be feasible to trace when exactly a piece of information was received and by whom. Moreover, because the information dealt with here is political-ideological in its content and because the EU itself has undergone profound changes

---

behavior" (Stein 1994, 180).

233 This group is sometimes labelled 'reflectionist' for they see knowledge as reflected from an external, objective reality (Klimecki/Lassleben 1998, 19–20).

234 Haas 1992, 4; consequently, these approaches are also called 'constructionist' (Friedman 2001, 407).

in the period under consideration, it will be much more telling to analyze the way this information is handled and processed within the organization than to trace back the precise information received. What remains essential for learning, though, is a change of organizational routines, i. e. that new information is added and/or old information is altered or discarded on the basis of commonly interpreted information.

Finally, approaches vary substantially in their assessment of change and/or success.[235] For some, behavioral change as a result of learning is needed in order to speak of a complete learning process (Nye 1987, 378). Others go even further and give OL a normative notion by claiming that, for learning to have taken place, processes (or policy) must have been improved "through better knowledge and understanding" (Fiol/Lyles 1985, 803; see also Argyris/Schön 1978, 323; Tetlock 1991, 27–38). With the assumption that learning is a primarily cognitive process, however, this behaviorist position has lost ground. In addition, the inclusion of change or even successful change into the definition of OL would mean to overlook cases where learning (at the cognitive level) takes place but cannot be translated into the desired outcome (i. e. policy change or other). The differentiation of learning and change as distinct is therefore "important for normative or policy purposes as well as for the scientific study of foreign policy" (Levy 1994, 290).[236]

Against this background, and simple though it is, it appears important to note that organizational learning does not necessarily include organizational change. It is critical to separate understanding from doing, and to regard each as a distinct step in organizational development if one wants to examine the impact of new knowledge on behavior (Suhrke 2000, 2). Change does not need instances of organizational learning to precede it; nor do such instances necessarily ensue organizational change. In this work, I will therefore follow Levy's two-stage process in which, first, organizational learning must be detected and, second, this learning may then be translated into organizational change.[237]

In sum, based on the common ground of the different approaches identified above, I regard organizational learning as a cognitive practice of collective information processing leading to a change of organizational routines, i. e. the written and unwritten rules

---

235 For an early consideration of the difficulty of declaring a policy successful or not, cf. Jervis 1976: "This determination [of success or failure] is usually made by applying a simple standard, such as whether the actor was better off at the end of the encounter than it was before. With a successful outcome, relatively little attention is paid to the costs of the policy, the possibility that others might have worked even better, or the possibility that success was largely attributable to luck and that the policy might just as easily have failed" (ibid., 232). Still today, "IOs often lack clearly defined standards for success or failure and have no unambiguous instrument for measurement, which might lead to quick and unequivocal feedback. This usually leaves the organization without any measures for efficiency or effectiveness that go beyond the political judgments of the involved actors" (Breul 2005, 25).

236 For Levy's assessment of 'successful learning' (the "accuracy criterion" as he calls it), see pp. 291–94; Knopf explicitly distances himself from such a value-neutral stance (cf. Knopf 2003, 206).

237 The actual research process, of course, works just as well the other way round: When policy change is detected, this might be traced back to an initial learning process.

that govern how an organization works (phase 1—organizational learning). This learning process has to be analytically separated from eventually ensuing change, i. e. a change of the organization's shape or behavior based on a change of the organizational routines (phase 2—organizational change). To avoid the value-loaded notion of 'learning,' I simply label the two phases together as 'organizational development.'

With this preliminary definition of the two phases of organizational development established from the existing literature, it is worth asking how those who study foreign policy in particular (rather than learning processes in general) perceive learning and change.

3.1.2 Learning and change—alternative explanations

Two broad research fields in political science/IR will be examined in this subsection: First, whether and how researchers conceptualize learning, and second, how they explain change. While the former provides some useful points for the development of an analytical framework that will be summarized at the end, the latter does not give much input to learning in political organizations.

For one, organizational theory and organizational learning "have rarely attracted the attention of political scientists," laments LaPalombara in his contribution to the renowned 'Handbook of Organizational Learning and Knowledge' (LaPalombara 2001b, 8), a publication from the field of sociology as should be noted. Whereas their colleagues from sociology focused on learning rather than on organization, it was only the 'O' part of OL that received interest from political and IR scientists, namely in work on international regimes and, to some extent, on international organizations (IOs).[238] Even there, however, little attention is given to the everyday routines of international bureaucracies, as Barnett and Finnemore realised: "To understand how international organizations work, we found ourselves turning to theories of organization rather than theories of international politics."[239] The 'L' (or learning) part has been disregarded outright by the mainstream of research; even in an International Organization Special Issue covering articles from 1986 to 2000 (Martin/Simmons 2001), the term 'learning' does not appear.

Some noteworthy exceptions exist, though, as a number of authors applied the concept of learning to political science and, more specifically, to foreign policy.[240] However, they

---

238 For two important early contributions, see Keohane 1984 and Krasner 1983.

239 Barnett/Finnemore 2004, viii. See also the telling title ('Political Science and Organization Theory. Parallel Agendas but Mutual Disregard') of Olsen 1998. Levy contends in a hopeful footnote that "[the] literature on learning in foreign policy has been slow to incorporate the insights of organizational theorists, but that is beginning to change" (Levy 1994, 287). Fourteen years on, however, this change is still in its beginning stages.

240 These include, for example, political learning (Heclo 1974), government learning (Etheredge 1981), nuclear learning (Nye 1987), Soviet learning (Stein 1994, Tetlock 1991), learning in international organizations (Haas 1990), epistemic communities (Haas 1992), social learning (Hall 1993, Checkel 2001), lesson drawing (Rose 1993), advocacy coalitions framework (Sabatier/Jenkins-Smith 1993), policy transfer (Dolowitz/Marsh 2000), and international learning (Knopf 2003). Bennett and

focused on their own neologism rather than trying to create a general approach. In his seminal 1994 article 'Learning and foreign policy', Levy summarizes the various approaches to organizational learning so far and critically assesses their usefulness for an analysis of foreign policy (Levy 1994, 280–82). Since then, further attempts have been made some of which, i.e. those most relevant to studying organizational learning in the foreign policy of the European Union, will be examined briefly in the following.

On a theoretical level, Jeffrey Checkel offers argumentative persuasion and social learning as a bridge between the rationalist and the constructivist answer to the compliance puzzle, i.e. the question of why actors comply with institutional norms (2001, 554). His main hypothesis is that learning from convincing arguments is more probable in a novel, unpoliticized environment and when the actors have few prior beliefs.[241] He nonetheless points to the limits posed by domestic politics, in particular the institutional and historical contexts. Similarly, Jeffrey Lewis has done an analysis of the EU's Committee of Permanent Representatives, or Coreper, responsible for preparing upcoming ministerial meetings of the Council (Lewis 2005). His analysis of the socialization mechanisms at work echoes many of Checkel's findings.[242]

On a practical level, Eric Stern looks at learning in crisis situations, hypothesizing that crises may enable learning and change and may help overcome bureaucratic inertia (Stern 1997). He posits that the experience of crises may contribute to cognitive openness and a re-ordering of the political agenda, thus creating political opportunities for reformers (ibid., 76; similarly Brandstrom et al. 2004, 191–2). His focus on crises as a trigger for OL remains unconvincing, though, as he himself warns that crises may as well produce obstacles to learning: In a crisis, individuals may rely on dominant modes of thought and action, or environments may become politicized and thus diminish the potential insight of lessons learned (Stern 1997, 77–79).

While Stern's argument about crises as triggers for learning remains weak, his research on whether vicarious learning, i.e. learning through the observation of others' experiences, can take place, is important (ibid., 70). This is taken up by Jeffrey Knopf in his essay on 'International Learning,' where he introduces the concept of "shared learning" between states and IOs (Knopf 2003, 186). He advocates a normative stance with regard to learning in international relations as a potential prerequisite to reduce the amount of

---

Howlett provide an evaluation of five of these different approaches (i.e. those of Heclo, Etheredge, Hall, Rose, and Sabatier); cf. Bennett/Howlett 1992.

241 Checkel 2001, 562–3. A decade earlier, Tetlock remarked that it is tactical beliefs at the lower level or strategic beliefs at the medium level that may change, while the fundamental beliefs and policy goals at the highest level remain largely constant (Tetlock 1991, 28).

242 For an in-depth analysis of socialization mechanisms also in the PSC, see Juncos/Reynolds 2007. Some authors have criticized the socialization hypotheses, arguing that extensive exposure to the European level does not necessarily lead to supranational role playing (e.g. Beyers 2005). However, this critique does not apply to the EU Special Representatives who, by their standing and identity, are much closer to the Permanent Representatives (i.e. ambassadors) that Lewis analyzes than to the Council officials under study in Beyers' work.

armed conflict in world politics. For such progress to occur, however, learning by just a single entity will often not be sufficient. Therefore, he proposes a model of shared, cross-national learning (ibid., 193).

While some research has been done on learning in domestic or even foreign politics, the field of international organizations has received particularly scant attention. Most prominently, Peter Haas looks at 'epistemic communities', i.e. networks of knowledge-based experts that infuse new information into the policy-making process (Haas 1992). However, not only are epistemic communities a phenomenon of policy fields with a high degree of specialist knowledge (e.g. environmental policy) rather than of the general politico-diplomatic business. What is more, Haas' take on the autonomy of international organizations makes his approach unsuitable here: He views supranational institutions as mere facilitators of learning by national policymakers, e.g. through the provision of new information or influence on their belief systems, and not as actors capable of learning in their own right.[243]

Yet, contrary to Haas' view of IOs as state instruments, these can also be the location where lessons learned are institutionalized through organizational reform and adaptation, most notably in their secretariats. This view assumes a certain, although limited degree of autonomy on the side of the organizations because without it, there would be no (institutional) capacity for learning.[244] Following this approach, some work has been done on the United Nations family of organizations, on the European Union and its institutions, and on international organizations such as Interpol.[245] What is important in all these works, whether they focus on an organization as a whole or on an operational activity such as peacekeeping, is the strong role of the respective secretariat. These bodies "that constitute the bureaucratic real-life existence of intergovernmental and supranational administrations" (Bauer 2007, 14) are the central locus of learning.

Thus, just as their colleagues from organizational sociology, political scientists lack a common understanding, let alone definition, of learning in politics. Again, the reason for this may be that either they consider learning inexistent or that other theories are able to explain whatever learning may take place in international organizations.

I will therefore now examine alternative explanations put forward in political science and IR theory. As explained before, not all change comes from learning; thus, there is naturally a large area of foreign policy change that cannot be explained by OL theories. Yet again, in the area where organizational learning and change overlap, learning theories

---

243 This facilitation effect of IOs is also mentioned in Simmons/Martin 2002, 199.

244 Building on Max Weber's arguments about bureaucracy, Barnett and Finnemore claim that IOs are independent agents rather than mere structures (Barnett/Finnemore 1999, 699; on IO autonomy, see also pp. 704–6); cf. Benner et al. 2007, 16.

245 On peacebuilding operations, see Benner et al. 2007; on humanitarian aid, see Wright 2003; on environmental actors, see Böhling 2002; on the EU, see Checkel 2001, Jachtenfuchs 1996, Lewis 2005, and Böhling 2007; on Interpol, see Barnett/Coleman 2005.

should be better positioned to explain change than other approaches. This is particularly true for the field of International Relations.

Neither of the main IR strands that theorize policy change can provide an explanation for processes taking place within international organizations. Neorealism (Waltz 1979; Grieco 1988; Mearsheimer 1995) explains state behavior only by reference to features of the international system. As Alexander George rightly stresses (1994, 157–8), it was Kenneth Waltz himself who acknowledged that neorealist theory is not a theory of foreign policy (Waltz 1979, 121–122). In particular, due to the limited scope of neorealist theory, it fails "to understand and promote foreign policy 'learning' by states and their leaders" (George 1994, 159). Likewise, liberalism (Moravcsik 1993), while adding a level of analysis by looking at the interests of various dominant groups within states, cannot explain learning processes within the international bureaucracies, because it does not open up the black box of IOs[246] either. This failure of "orthodox theories of international relations" to explain the EU's role in international affairs is not least due to the broad range of instruments and activities of the Union (Ginsberg/Smith 2007, 268).

Given the inability of traditional theories to explain the EU's rise in foreign policy, a distinct strand promoting the analysis of 'European foreign policy' has emerged. This strand unites a plethora of approaches, which themselves draw on a variety of theoretical methods. This makes it difficult to find common ground among the different approaches, which is why, for example, Walter Carlsnaes refuses to provide a general framework of analysis for the study of European foreign policy: "The very notion of multilevel governance with overlapping jurisdictions and partially pooled sovereignty complicates—perhaps even effectively undermines—the feasibility of the comparative analysis of foreign policy as conventionally conceived" (Carlsnaes 2004, 2).

As it appears, 'European foreign policy' approaches do not pay particular attention to the learning of organizations either, let alone propose a model to study its processes. If they do consider learning, it is rather at the broad, rhetorical level, describing both European Political Cooperation (EPC) and CFSP as a "learning process" (Tonra 2001, 14; cf. Smith 2004, 196) or referring to the "lessons of the immediate past (e. g., the Gulf, Bosnia)" (Allen/Smith 1998b, 54; cf. Nuttall 2000, 10). On a more practical level, some see a form of vicarious learning at play when the EU follows NATO (in going 'out-of-area') and the Western European Union (WEU) (by assuming its 'Petersberg tasks') (Bretherton/Vogler 1999, 213).

In sum, neither mainstream explanations of IR nor European foreign policy approaches put forward a comprehensive theory of learning in political institutions. The previously examined articles that explicitly treat learning, at least, provide some useful elements:

---

246 Cf. the programmatic title of Böhling's work on organizational learning in the European Commission ("Opening up the Black Box," Böhling 2007).

- The considerations about environment and beliefs (Checkel, Lewis),
- The role of vicarious learning (Stern, Knopf), and
- The importance of the organization's secretariat (Barnett/Finnemore, Bauer).

I will integrate these aspects into the analytical framework to be developed in the next section (3.2). Before that, I shall briefly perform a 'reality check' by looking at how the concept of learning is used in political practice, which shall help me to come up with my own definition of organizational learning and change at the end of this section.

3.1.3 The real world: Learning in politics

It is unfortunately true that, to the detriment of the discipline itself, contemporary political science and International Relations do not value policy relevance much (Jentleson 2002, 169; cf. George 1994). Good social science, however, should be aware of the options for action at the disposal of decision-makers (Sandschneider 2005, 12). It is therefore apt to try and make the concept of learning to be used here adaptable to the world of politics.

Such adaptation to real-life models is widespread in some disciplines, though not in political science. Indeed, organizational learning in the fields of sociology and business studies in particular may have had an overdose of practical exposure. Putting on the hat of management consultants, sociologists and economists have analyzed the 'learning company' in all its varieties (cf. Senge 1990). Yet, beneficial as such undertakings may be for in-depth research, "few theoretically meaningful studies have been published after consulting interventions" (Berthoin Antal et al. 2001a, 928). Political scientists, in contrast, have steered clear of such consultancy in the first place.

For an adaptation of the learning concept to political reality, the focus is on practical (or even operational) 'lessons learned' exercises, which international actors (states potentially as much as international organizations) undertake in order to be better prepared for similar events in the future.[247] This is much different from both theory-based approaches of 'lesson drawing' and pseudo-scientific reasoning about the 'lessons of the past.' The former refers to the intended transfer of knowledge about policies, ideas or arrangements from one actor to another (Dolowitz/Marsh 2000, 5; cf. Rose 1991 and 1993; Stone 2001). The latter is satisfied with the "usually rather simple, uncomplicated formulations of causal relationships" by way of historical analogies (George 1994, 152; cf. Nye 1987, 379) with the resulting 'lessons' being "superficial, over-generalized, and based on post hoc ergo propter hoc reasoning" (Jervis 1976, 228).

---

247 Put simply, the aim of these exercises is "to draw out lessons from past [...] efforts as a means of helping to plan future ones" (Knight 2001, 36; see also Benner et al. 2007, 24–25). For a reflection on "policy as a learning system" (not without a normative connotation) by a leading politician, see Steinmeier 2006.

A search of the term 'lessons learned' in any library confirms that the examples of such exercises are plentiful: from conferences and seminars being held to evaluate past (often military) operations or practices of development aid (cf. United Nations 2001; Galama/Tongeren 2002; Folke Bernadotte Academy 2003) to the setting up of more permanent boards, such as the Lessons Learned Unit in the Department of Peacekeeping of the United Nations in 1995 (Knight 2001, 36). Some of these undertakings have also found an expression in the more academic literature, such as a review of the 1999 Kosovo intervention (Spillmann/Krause 2000), an evaluation of the ESDP mission in Aceh/Indonesia (Schulze 2007), and an EUSR's account of his stint in Afghanistan (Klaiber 2007).

Yet, a few lessons learned cannot unearth the more long-term processes of learning and change in foreign policy decision-making systems (Eberwein et al. 1998, 274). What Benner et al. have to say about lessons learned in the UN peacebuilding bureaucracy is, unfortunately, true for all areas of politics: "[We] lack any systematic analysis of the gathering and application of lessons learned" (2007, 9). Moreover, as was pointed out in the introduction, talk of 'learning' in the political field does have a drawback: Grandiose lessons-learned exercises are sometimes more of an effort to demonstrate an institution's willingness to learn rather than to actually apply the 'lessons' drawn.[248]

This calculating, potentially one-off approach to learning points to an important element of learning in politics: its symbolic rather than substantive function. Policy-makers may not have an interest in actually 'learning' about how to do things differently (i. e. doing them better, as learning is commonly understood); though, they may feel obliged to demonstrate exactly this ability to improve their actions through evaluation of past performance. Yet, as defined earlier (cf. subsection 3.1.1), organizational learning is a value-neutral, analytical concept and therefore much different from how 'learning' is used in politics. It can encompass tactics such as strategic calculation and role playing (Checkel 2005, 808; cf. Schimmelfennig 2005) as these may result in an altering of organizational routines. At the same time, organizations may learn without their leaders saying or even knowing so, while policymakers' claims to have 'learned a lesson' do not necessarily imply that organizational learning actually took place.

The way forward proposed here is the middle ground between a purely instrumental use of 'learning' that is often found in politics and the lofty definitions from the field of OL that are distant from the world of policy-makers (Jentleson 2002, 181).[249] After all, what sense does it make—especially for a practical concept such as learning—to analyze

---

248 Another such term is 'best practices' and their frequent identification as model cases to follow.

249 For example, one seemingly practically oriented publication concludes to envisage the learning process "as a never-ending self-critical and self-correcting progressive, spiralling process that questions data, seeks to attain insight into or understand the data, makes judgments about factual truth and normative validity of the data, and responds to the consequences of acting on those judgments" (Knight/Masciulli 2001, 242). Desirable as such an ambitious complex process might be, it is utterly unrealistic in politics as it would slow all other activities, ultimately rendering an organization entirely self-referential.

whether or not an organization has learned from its actions, if these findings do not relate to the reality perceived by the officials in that organization?[250] As George proposes in his effort to bridge the gap between the worlds of scholars and practitioners, what is of importance here is how knowledge can be turned into action (1994, 166)—and this is what is at the heart of the analysis of learning processes.

3.1.4 Defining organizational learning and change

In order to achieve this middle ground between theory and practice, I will break down the working definition of OL elaborated earlier (cf. subsection 3.1.1) into its most basic elements and propose a definition that is grounded in theoretical postulates, while at the same time considering the ambiguity of the political process. It should thus be fit to serve the two functions of analysis and prescription alike, i. e. the post-hoc dissection as well as prospective guiding of political action.[251]

I propose the following '4R' definition of organizational learning as the basis of this work:

Definition (phase 1)

Organizational learning is understood as the rewriting of rules as a result of reflection.

What was previously termed 'cognitive practice of collective information processing' is defined in more simple terms as the result of reflection.[252] This echoes the focus on the importance of a collective understanding that is reached with regard to certain incoming information rather than the exact processes of how this information is treated at the individual or organizational level. Furthermore, the 'change of organizational routines' is more plainly named a rewriting of rules. These rules are understood as all formal or informal procedures, frameworks, or codes that guide behavior (Levitt/March 1988, 320). Thus, when a collective process of reflection has taken place in an organization and when this reflection has led to a rewriting (figuratively speaking) of organizational rules, then we shall say that organizational learning has taken place.

---

250   Indeed, as Bruce Jentleson rightly argues, "[there…] is much that academics can contribute to policy. There are adjustments to be made, organizational cultures to adapt to, relationships to be built, and different modes of operating to be learned" (2002, 180).

251   I acknowledge that George warns of a "focus primarily on the **prescriptive** utility of theory for policy-making" and instead calls for a contribution to the diagnosis of a specific situations (1994, 155 [emphasis in original]). However, in this context, prescription does not mean to say what an actor such as the EU will learn from future events, but how it should organize its internal processes if it wishes to enhance its capacity for organizational learning in general. This is not least important with regard to the changing international environment: "[Theory] must often struggle to catch up with changing realities; and in the field of international relations, it generally does better explaining what has happened than in predicting it" (ibid., 156).

252   Again, the word 'reflection' is used here in a value-free, neutral way with no normative mearning implied.

Organizational rules operate at different levels, and I will differentiate four such levels: structures, procedures, operations, and ideas. Authors who look at improvements stemming from learning distinguish between effects at the levels of structure, operation, and strategy (Balthasar/Rieder 2000, 250–251). This trinomial distinction, geared very much toward the evaluation of programmes, is used here as a starting point to define a set of four levels of rules present in a political organization:

–   The structural level relates to the organizational setting and to characteristics such as an organizational memory;
–   The procedural level is about decision-making and consultation procedures;
–   The operational level concerns the organization's actions in the environment; and
–   The ideational level refers to the doctrines and strategies of an organization.

This definition of organizational learning is complemented by a definition of organizational change. It rests on the main elements of the earlier working definition as a "change of the organization's shape or behavior based on a change of the organizational routines" (cf. subsection 3.1.1). A change of the organization's shape is understood to result from a change of rules either at the structural or procedural level; it is termed institutional change. In contrast, a change of the organization's behavior is understood to result from a change of rules either at the operational or ideational level; it is termed policy change. Both forms of change are understood in a value-neutral sense, i.e. do not imply any 'improvement.'

Definition (phase 2)

Organizational change is understood as institutional or policy change following from, though not exclusively caused by, a change of the organizational rules.

Based on these two theoretically deduced and practically oriented definitions, the claim is made that if organizational learning takes place (phase 1), it needs to be taken into account as a contributing factor of the organizational change (phase 2). What may sound profane given how this model was developed does gain great importance when it comes to explaining, for example, the development of the EU's foreign policy. Because if organizational learning were discernable in that process, it would need to be taken into account as another (independent, not just intervening) variable alongside other explanations of organizational development that focus on interests, values, or events. This means to eschew any mono-causal temptations, by being "alert to discovering different causal patterns that led to a similar outcome" rather than trying to find a single causal generalization (George 1994, 170).

Having developed these definitions from a theoretical framework that builds on the commonalities of theoretical approaches as well as inferences from the world of politics, I will now explore the analytical framework of organizational learning. Subsequently, I will elaborate a model of analysis that builds on—and should ultimately support—the above made claim of multi-causality.

3.2 The analytical framework of organizational learning

As explained in the previous section, the notion of (organizational) learning is an understudied, if not neglected concept. In addition, neither organizational theory nor political science offers a ready-to-use framework for the analysis of learning in political organizations but provide for a number of distinguishable elements that I will assemble according to the research question proposed here. In developing the analytical framework of this study, I will thus combine deduction from sociology's OL approaches with inductive insights from the political nature of IOs. In particular, the framework will take into consideration the subject, the environment, and the processes of learning. This framework will form the basis for this study's analytical model, to be worked out in the next section of this chapter.

One preliminary remark with regard to the interdependence of subject and environment is apt at this point. While it is analytically important to define the subject as distinct from its environment, in reality a mutual dependence between the two prevails. It is recognized that organizations need to demarcate themselves from their environment as a constitutive act, thus justifying their existence (Böhling 2007, 21). However, it would be short-sighted to deduce from this that the environment of an organization is "everything outside the organization" (Malek et al. 2002, 6) for the simple reason that organizations are not isolated from their environments: They are open to and even dependent upon the flow of information and resources from outside. Not unlike the way in which socio-logical institutionalists consider structure and agency mutually constitutive (Wendt 1987, 338; cf. Barnett/Finnemore 2004; Bretherton/Vogler 1999, 29), recent approaches to learning see the organization and its environment as equally interdependent (Benner et al. 2007, 19).

This relation of mutual influence of the subject and the environment, in particular where the two come together at the boundaries of an organization, will be considered when developing the analytical framework in the following.

3.2.1 The subject of learning

'Who learns?' is an important question to answer when sketching the analytical framework of organizational learning, especially given the lack of definitional clarity described above. This question goes beyond the point discussed earlier about the role of the individual (cf. subsection 3.1.1), as it is part of the broader question of which 'organization' (or 'organizational unit') is defined as the locus of learning. Furthermore, it heralds the question of where to define the boundaries of an actor vis-à-vis its environment (cf. next subsection).

Organizational learning, in principle, refers to the learning of any organization, i.e. any group of persons organized for a particular purpose. Political scientists would further-more narrow the range to those formal groups of people that pursue a political goal, such as governments, parties, unions, and civil society organizations, for example. Their distinctive feature is that they primarily follow normative considerations and power calculations rather than the rationale of utility and efficiency, as private sector organizations do (LaPalombara 2001a, 557–8 and 562). The level of analysis can then be defined in a more narrow way by looking at a particular component of a certain organization (e.g. one department within a ministry) or more broadly by studying a group of similar organizations (e.g. all political parties in a given country).

With reference to what was condensed earlier from other approaches to learning (cf. subsection 3.1.2), one central organizational unit to look at is the secretariat (Bauer 2007, 14). In this analysis, this refers to the inner decision-making and policy-implementing circle of the second pillar of the EU (CFSP), e.g. the Council Secretariat, the High Representative with his Policy Unit, and the Political and Security Committee.[253]

One important aspect is that every organization spans its boundaries and reaches into the surrounding environment. While it is necessary to clearly define the subject of learning and thus differentiate it from its environment, it is similarly important to look at the organization-environment nexus in order to detect the activities of boundary spanners that trigger learning processes within an organization (Böhling 2007, 24–25). What is more, an organization's boundaries should not be regarded as impenetrable because "increasing the permeability of external boundaries makes organizations more responsive to changing demands and conditions in their environment" (ibid., 24). This notion of 'boundary spanners' has also been identified in new patterns of European diplomatic activity, where national diplomats have turned from old-fashioned 'gate-keepers' to mediators and brokers across organizations (Hocking 2004, 103).[254] It will be of importance when looking at the activities of the EUSRs both within the EU and towards third parties.

In sum, the subject of learning is a group of people organized around a political goal, following primarily normative considerations and power calculations. A central element is the permeability of the subject's (formal) boundaries, e.g. due to the presence of boundary spanners, as their activities can enhance the organization's learning capacity. In this study, the focus is on the inner system of CFSP (level of analysis). The EUSRs and their teams (level of explanation) are understood as boundary spanners in this system.

---

253 The Commission is part of this to the extent that it is "fully associated with CFSP" (Article 18 (4) TEU; the Commission is, for example, part of the Troika and also represented in the PSC; cf. Duke 2006, 6–11). In return, when the Commission is acting under its first pillar competence (Relex), it is regarded as part of the environment.

254 However, Hocking mainly refers to national diplomats acting within the EU milieu; still the concept can be applied to the EU's boundaries with the external world.

3.2.2 The learning environment

In the same way that the environment and the subject are not neatly separable, there is no direct link from the outside to the inside of an organization; external information first must be translated by the structures and staff of the organization. In the words of Hedberg, the environment diffuses to the inside of an organization: "The real world provides the raw material of stimuli to react to, but the only meaningful environment is the one that is born when stimuli are processed through perceptual filters" (Hedberg 1981, 8).

Some authors therefore distinguish an inner environment from an outer environment (cf. Breul 2005, 12; Hedberg 1981, 13–16). The outer environment is the 'real world' as it impacts the organization.[255] The inner environment is constituted by the organizational mechanisms that deal with this impact (Breul 2005, 13–14), i.e. the structures, procedures, and culture that may help or hinder the reception and processing of information from the outer environment into internal knowledge. This also mirrors the cognitivist argument of a mediated impact of external information on the behavior of a person. Such a differentiation has consequences with regard to a semantic imprecision that sometimes occurs when describing the exchange of data between an organization and the environment with the terms 'information' and 'knowledge' interchangeably (e.g. Huber 1991, fn1, 89). Instead, there is an important distinction between the two (Böhling 2007, 33–34): Information constitutes the unprocessed data received from the environment, while knowledge is the product of internal sense-making procedures. Knowledge as the product of information processing can then be stored in the organizational routines.

The construct of an 'environment within' is worth pondering as it helps understand the difference between the object of much of the classical OL literature, the firm, and a political entity like the European Union or an international organization. Of course, the outside world, in principle, is the same to all organizations; yet, the same information can evoke different perceptions on the inside of them (cf. Barnett/Finnemore 1999, 703). For example, if the information emitted by the environment is that the price of oil has reached a new high, then companies will react differently (e.g. by looking for profit margins) than political groups (that should worry about their voters). The "ambiguity, messiness, and continuous struggle and conflict" of the political and governmental environment (LaPalombara 2001a, 562) beg for a differentiation from normal theories of corporate behavior.[256] This is one more reason why, in this study, common OL approaches are adapted to learning in a political institution like the EU.

---

255 To be correct, one should presume that there is not one single outer environment an organization deals and interacts with (the real world), but multiple such environments. Thirty years ago, Argyris and Schön maintained, "Our organizations live in economic, political and technological environments which are predictably unstable" (Argyris/Schön 1978, 9). Since then, the degree of environmental complexity and uncertainty has all but increased.

256 This point is also highlighted by Benner et al. with regard to international organizations: "The literature on organizational learning almost exclusively focuses on business organizations, often relying on quasi-Darwinian market forces as explanatory factors while critically under-emphasizing the political factors in organizational processes. The analogy does not hold; international organizations

The notion of an inner environment also elucidates the role of boundary spanners, in particular in politicized environments that make learning, as was mentioned earlier (cf. subsection 3.1.2), unlikely. Active boundary spanning may help an organization to overcome this handicap: What Jeffrey Checkel said about argumentative persuasion, i.e. that it is more likely in a "novel and uncertain environment [... when a person is] thus cognitively motivated to analyze new information" (2001, 562), is just as true for the analysis of new information as part of organizational learning. Here, boundary spanners such as the EUSRs, as part of the inner environment that receives and processes incoming information, not only frequently travel to the outer environment, but also disseminate information widely inside the organization (e.g. to Council working groups, member states, and Parliament).

Furthermore, the two-tiered approach to the environment is deemed useful methodologically with regard to the learning processes under study, including the capacity to improve one's learning. First, it directs the focus on the processes within an organization (cf. following subsection) rather than on the organization as a whole. Second, it bridges the otherwise strict separation between the organization and its environment not only in nominal, but also in analytical terms. This allows, third, for the observation of learning not only from the outer but also from the inner environment.

Reflection about the inner environment may enable an organization to 'learn how to learn,' a process that is called 'deutero learning.'[257] An organization can process information from either its inner or outer environment. Information from the former may lead to a change of organizational rules regarding the internal structures and procedures, i.e. changing the way that an organization receives information from the outer environment. If this changes the actual learning capacities of the organization, e.g. by enhancing the quality of information analysis, improving the organizational memory, or by developing additional expertise (cf. Levy 1994, 287), then this is called deutero learning.

Finally, the concept of an inner environment points to the importance of the organizational culture as framework for the interpretation of incoming information. Barnett and Finnemore describe organizational culture as "the rules, rituals, and beliefs that are embedded in the organization (and its subunits) [...]. [Organizational culture] provides interpretive frames that individuals use to generate meaning."[258] In connection with the previous point about deutero learning, an organizational culture may be particular conducive to learning, or it may favour certain lessons to learned.

---

rarely operate in a market-like environment where they are likely to go out of business based on the forces of supply and demand." (Benner et al. 2007, 17). For a differentiation between an economic and a sociological approach to the environment of IOs, see Barnett/Finnemore 1999, 703–4.

257 Karl Deutsch employed the term deutero learning long before OL came into fashion (1966, 169); later, Argyris and Schön (1978) took up the concept.

258 Barnett/Finnemore 1999, 719. See also Berthoin Antal et al. 2001b, 879; Barnett/Coleman 2005, 595.

Both the subject of learning and the learning environment are sketched in the following figure. It displays how information can be gathered from the outer (political) as well as inner environment, and that it is processed by the sense-making structures (e.g. organizational culture) of the inner environment. If this reflection changes the organizational rules, phase 1 of OL is completed. Particular types of OL refer to learning from other organizations in the outer environment (vicarious learning) and to learning from the inner environment (deutero learning). Similar, phase 2 is highlighted in that it refers to organizational action either within the subject of learning (institutional change) or towards the outer environment (policy change). The impact of such actions (or outcome) is not assessed here.

Figure 13: The Learning Environment and Subject of Learning

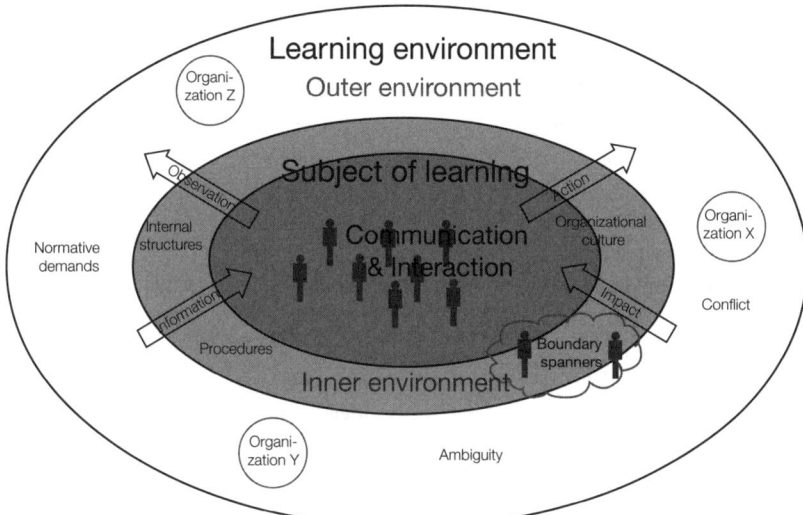

For the purpose of this study of the EUSRs as part of the inner circle of CFSP (subject of learning), the outer environment exists in two different forms: (1) A Brussels environment, comprising the European Commission, the Permanent Representations of member states, the European Parliament, and the delegations of third states and international organizations; and (2) a mission environment, including the respective national and regional authorities, the representations of the member states and of the Commission, other EU bodies such as ESDP missions and the representatives of third countries and international organizations. The mission environment extends to the capitals of both member states and third countries to which EUSRs pay frequent visits.

3.2.3 The processes of learning and change

It was defined earlier (cf. subsection 3.1.4) that organizational learning (phase 1) is the rewriting of rules as a result of reflection. One of the most comprehensive attempts to model this process of reflection and ensuing change of rules is Huber's description of four consecutive stages of OL (Huber 1991). He distinguishes between information acquisition, information distribution, information interpretation, and (storage in) the organizational memory, or rules (ibid., 90).[259] This model's fundamental structure will guide the following deliberations, although it might imply a linear process with one stage building upon the other.[260] In reality, learning is much messier with overlapping processes and feedback loops, producing delays or even interruptions of the process.

Before new knowledge can take hold in the organizational rules, environmental information needs to be acquired, distributed, and interpreted.[261]

–   Information acquisition can be achieved through different means: congenital acquisition (i. e. given from the founding of an organization), experiential acquisition, vicarious acquisition, grafting (or knowledge transfer), or active searching (cf. Huber 1991, 97; Malek et al. 2002, 7).[262] As explained earlier with regard to the complexity of the EU (cf. subsection 3.1.1), this work will not focus on this stage because it will not be traceable when which information was obtained. Instead, the other two stages will be under scrutiny.

–   The distribution and interpretation of new (or newly constructed) information can be impeded by constraints and biases of the individual. A constraint is information absorption capacity: Human beings are "limited-capacity information processors" (Breslauer/Tetlock 1991a, 4); this is accordingly also true for an organization made up of individuals. Biases can include the ideas, socialization, worldview, identity,

---

259 Because he uses the terms 'information' and 'knowledge' interchangeably (cf. above subsection 3.2.2), Huber in fact calls the first stage 'knowledge acquisition': "Knowledge acquisition is the process by which knowledge is obtained. Information distribution is the process by which information from different sources is shared and thereby leads to new information or understanding. Information interpretation is the process by which distributed information is given one or more commonly understood interpretations. Organizational memory is the means by which knowledge is stored for future use" (Huber 1991, 90). Only the latter use of the term 'knowledge' is consistent with the understanding employed in this study, i. e. as cognitively processed information. Huber's fourth construct, organizational memory, is only one aspect of the notion of organizational 'rules' employed here. For a different terminology, cf. Jackson et al. 2005a, 11–14.

260 For an attempt to draw a model where all four stages are interrelated and can happen in any order, see Jackson et al. 2005a, 10. Another critique of Huber is that his underlying conceptualisation of the organization as an information-processing system views information as something objective and transferable. It does not consider the symbolic nature of it, or the way an organization's culture may influence its distribution or interpretation (cf. Böhling 2007, 33); Huber could therefore be called a 'reflectionist' (see footnote 233).

261 For this and the following, see Huber 1991, 90.

262 I refrain from using Huber's terms (congenital learning, experiential learning etc.) here because the use of 'learning' to describe elements in the information acquisition process, which is itself only part of the broader learning process of an organization, is confusing.

or prior beliefs of the individual (Nye 1987, 379). This means that not only the (outer) environment impacts on the cognition of an individual; in addition, the organizational culture constrains or shapes the cognitive maps of an individual (Breslauer/Tetlock 1991a, 11; Hedberg 1981, 6). Consequently, just as different people learn different things from the same situation by applying their individual maps to incoming information (cf. Levy 1994, 283; similarly Levitt/March 1988, 324), groups of people perceive things differently depending on the organizational culture they share.

– Once information has thus been turned into knowledge, in can be stored in the organizational rules to ensure future access. These rules can be decision-making processes, standard operating procedures and manuals, the organizational structure (e.g. organization charts, group structures, and job descriptions), as well as organizational culture and beliefs (Böhling 2002, 10; cf. Jackson et al. 2005a, 14). Only when knowledge (as 'reflected information') becomes engrained into these rules can we speak of learning, because only then is it independent from the individuals that collectively produced it, i.e. available to the organization regardless of personnel turnover (Levitt/March 1988, 328).

What is of primary interest here are the two main filters that impact on the reflection process: The organizational culture that selects and discards information (i.e. the collective bias); and the absorption capacity that limits the amount of information that can be received and stored (i.e. the collective constraint). In particular the strength of culture as an organizational frame of reference (Huber 1991, 93) should not be underestimated, not least because it goes beyond the concept of 'bounded rationality': Indeed, "actors' rationality itself, the very means and ends that they value, are shaped by the organizational culture" (Barnett/Finnemore 1999, 719).

The result of learning is commonly shared knowledge about external events as much as about internal functions, stored in the organizational rules. It is worth noting that the organizational culture as part of these rules can ultimately also be changed through learning. However, this is only conceivable in a very long timeframe because normally it is the culture that influences the learning process in the information distribution and interpretation stage. This harks back to what was said earlier (cf. subsection 3.1.2) about the persistence of fundamental beliefs as opposed to tactical or strategic beliefs that may be influenced by learning (cf. Tetlock 1991, 28; Checkel 2001, 562–3).

It should be stressed again that this first phase of organizational learning is worth studying per se, as neither is learning inherently positive nor is OL-based change necessarily convenient. First, learning itself is value-neutral.[263] The learning process can be completed without afterwards being better able to react to a change in the environment because filters distorted the incoming information (e.g. manipulating it to conform to pre-existing beliefs). In this sense, learning may just as well reinforce beliefs and actually inhibit

---

263 Of course, the 'wrong' organizations can learn too, as two recent studies of organizational learning in terrorist groups by the RAND Corporation suggest (Jackson et al. 2005a; Jackson et al. 2005b).

organizational change.[264] Second, it need not be a 'failure' if change does not follow upon learning. Even if a lesson learned has been judged useful and accurate, applying it straight away may not be good policy: "Policy adjustments may confuse the bureaucracy, erode one's domestic base of support (which, in turn, reduces one's long-term flexibility), antagonize allies, and trigger undesired responses from adversaries" (Tetlock 1991, 38).

Based on the value-neutral results of learning, a separate methodical step analyzes why certain learning instances have not produced organizational change, i. e. it looks at the biases and constraints that act as barriers in phase 2. A learning process may be completed by the change of the rules, but the experiences gathered cannot be put into practice due to domestic, economic, or bureaucratic constraints (Levy 1994, 290). The latter may be based on interest calculations by actors within the organization, or on the actual structures of the organization that may inhibit desired change. I will therefore distinguish two barriers to organizational change: Change resistance on the level of individuals or groups thereof as a bias, and institutional design as a constraint.[265]

With this analytical framework focusing on the subject, environment, and processes of organizational learning, I can now elaborate the model of analysis for this study.

3.3 The analytical model

Derived from the analytical framework of the previous section, I will now develop a research model for the analysis of the work of the EU Special Representatives. First, I will present a model explaining the process of learning, the main object of study. Then, I will elaborate the research variables in response to the research question presented at the beginning. Thirdly, these variables will be operationalized. Finally, the methodology will be explained with regard to the empirical data used for the cases under study, the EU Special Representatives.

3.3.1 Model of explanation

Summing up the insights from the previous section, I arrive at the following two-phase model of organizational development. In phase 1, information is collectively dealt with in a process of reflection, that may lead to a change of the organizational rules. This organizational learning is contingent on two filters: organizational culture and absorp-

---

264 "[…A] great deal of research suggests a strong tendency for people to interpret information in a way that conforms to their prior expectations and world-views" (Levy 1994, 290). This point was highlighted earlier by Jervis in his thorough study of misperceptions in politics: "The process of drawing inferences in light of logic and past experience […] also causes people to fit incoming information into pre-existing beliefs and to perceive what they expect to be there. […] We ignore information that does not fit, twist it so that it confirms, or at least does not contradict, our beliefs and deny its validity" (Jervis 1976, 143).

265 For an early study of how bureaucratic politics and institutional turf battles hinder learning processes, see Allison 1971.

tion capacity. In phase 2, organizational change may follow from learning although two barriers—change resistance as well as institutional design—may limit completion of this process.

The following graphs display this two-phase process, highlighting the main explanatory factors for each phase: Reflection, filters, and rules (phase 1); action, barriers, and change (phase 2). This explanatory model can further be broken down into its constituent variables.

Figure 14: Phase One: Organizational Learning

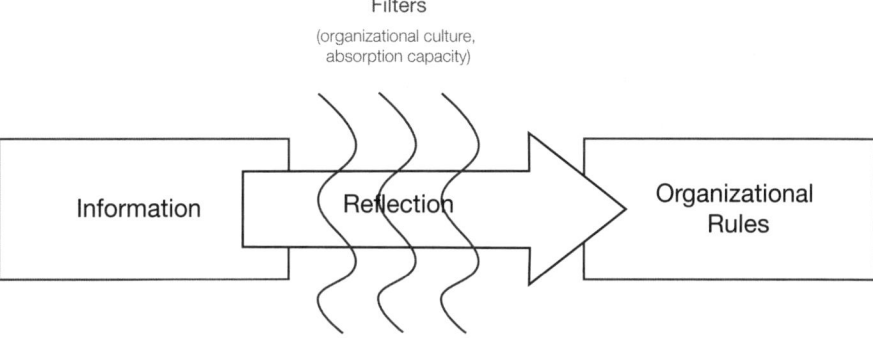

Figure 15: Phase Two: Organizational Change

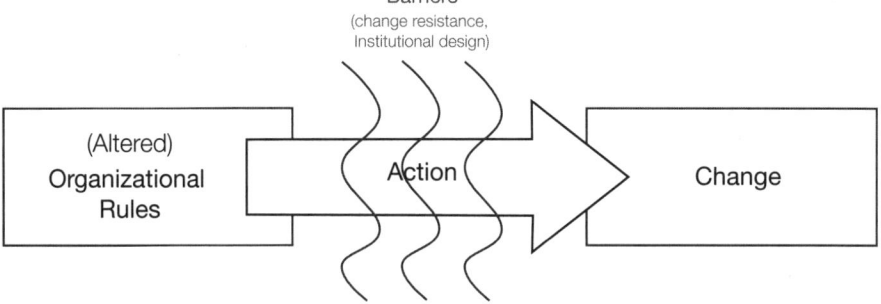

3.3.2 Variables and hypotheses

The detailed model of learning processes presented above provides an answer to the first part of the first research questions presented at the outset of this study, i.e. how learning takes place. The following table mirrors this model by breaking down the theoretical two-phase approach into variables.

Table 2: Variables in the Two-Phase Model of Organizational Development

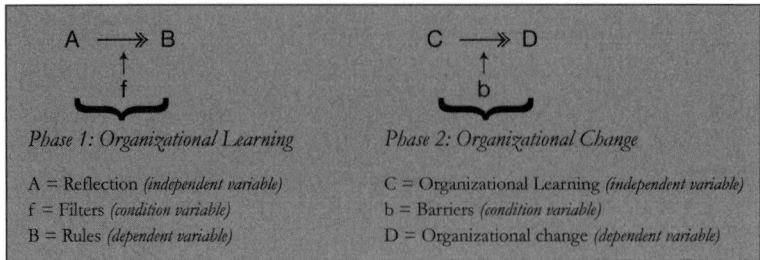

In phase 1, reflection (A), i.e. the collective processing of information from the outer or inner environment, is the independent variable. Filters (f) condition its impact on the rules (B), the dependent variable. When this process is completed, organizational learning is accomplished. The result of phase 1 then becomes the independent variable of phase 2. Organizational learning (C) can produce organizational change (D), although barriers (b), the condition variable, can slow or prevent this result.[266]

This breakdown also displays the causal mechanism at work here:[267] (New or newly assessed) environmental information that is absorbed by the organization is the trigger that sets off the processes of organizational learning (mechanism), as explained above (cf. subsection 3.2.3). This learning mechanism then causes change at the level of the organization (effect). Two things should be noted, however: First, this model corresponds to a mechanism that may be at work; it does not represent a law-like statement such as 'if AB, then CD' (cf. Barnett/Finnemore 2004, 10). Again, this is not about predicting IO behavior, but about explicating past actions and hypothesizing about potential future ones. Second, it does not claim mono-causal validity for OL, but aims to establish learning theories as one explanatory factor of organizational development alongside other, more mainstream explanations.

For phase 1, I will focus on the two elements of reflection and altered organizational rules, whereas for phase 2, I will probe both barriers and change. Enquiring about people's individual cognitive maps or their absorption capacity would exceed the scope of this study. What it can do instead is make inferences from the organizational culture with regard to individual worldviews. Consequently, I will for now simply assume that

---

266 This is not only important to explain the effect of learning on organizational change in this study, but has a broader academic relevance answering the 'so what?' question, as Christoph Knill and Michael Bauer point out with regard to management reforms in IOs: "[We] should not stop at describing and explaining management reforms as the dependent variable. It is rather an important step of further research to take management reforms of international organizations as the independent variable and ask what different particular patterns of reforms make for policy output and policy outcomes. If we know more about these relationships, the discussion of management reforms of international organization [sic!] can be fruitfully linked to questions of policy-making under the conditions of multilevel governance." (Knill/Bauer 2007, 199).

267 For a definition and discussion of different approaches to causal mechanisms, see George/Bennett 2004, 135–149, and Zürn/Checkel 2005, 1048–1056.

filters are at work before later, in chapter 7, taking up this point by approximating the findings with regard to how organizational culture as a bias influences cognitive information processing. With regard to phase 2, in contrast, it is possible to observe the potential barriers that may inhibit change. These two elements, barriers and change, will therefore be under scrutiny for each instance of organizational learning found.

In order to identify the scope conditions under which a particular causal mechanism is set in motion (George/Bennett 2004, 137), I will preliminarily answer the second part of the first research question (i.e. under what circumstances learning takes place) with the following three hypotheses. They are derived from the observations made in chapter 1 about the EUSRs in particular and in chapter 2 about special representatives in general as well as from the theoretical considerations made in this chapter. By tackling the question of how information is acquired, stored in rules and translated into change, the hypotheses also answer the call for more investigation into the properties of the actors, structures, and issues under consideration (cf. Zürn/Checkel 2005, 1055–56).

Each generally formulated hypothesis is explained with regard to its function for the subject of learning, i.e. the inner system of CFSP. Two hypotheses explore the theoretical mechanisms at work in phase 1 (organiziational learning):

Hypothesis 1: Employing a boundary spanner to operate between the organization and the environment raises both the quantity and quality of information and can thus trigger learning in the organization.

❖ In case of the EUSRs, their travelling back and forth between Brussels and the field as well as between capitals of member states and third countries provides the EU with an amount and quality of information hitherto unavailable.

Hypothesis 2: Information provided by a boundary spanner and interpreted internally falls flat if there are no structures in place to retain the newly generated knowledge.

❖ The initial legal limbo of the EUSRs and their only half-hearted inclusion into the Brussels structures weaken the EU's capacity to learn as a foreign policy actor.

The third hypothesis explores the theoretical mechanisms at work in phase 2 (organiziational change):

Hypothesis 3: While the secretariat of an international organization is largely autonomous in its learning, member states and other principal organs will work as barriers when it comes to turning organizational learning into change.

❖ Learning within the Council Secretariat about how to use the EUSRs more effectively will meet resistance from member states if the latter fear that change will tilt the balance in favour of the 'Brussels headquarters.'

The second research question concerns the EU's learning about the EUSRs as a foreign policy instrument. In an initial attempt to answer this question, I arrive at the following two policy hypotheses formulated with direct reference to the subject matter:

Hypothesis 4: While part of a sui generis foreign policy system in the making, EUSRs were developed after the role model of the state (vicarious learning).

Hypothesis 5: Given the EU's claim to learn from its actions and the particular use of EUSRs as boundary spanners, mechanisms should be in place to draw lessons from past activities and to improve the EU's learning capacities (deutero learning).

These hypotheses, both theoretical and policy-oriented, would be easily disproved if the model of organizational learning previously developed were invalid. The null hypothesis for the theoretical hypotheses could be defined as follows: Boundary spanning does not enhance the learning capacity of an actor; established structures to engrain learning are no significant mechanism for organizational learning; and organizational learning, if existent, does not influence organizational change. The policy hypotheses would be falsified if the EU did not also learn from others when developing the EUSRs, or if it had not enhanced its capacities for organizational learning.

3.3.3 Operationalization

In the following, I will operationalize the main elements of the two phases of organizational development (learning and change) under scrutiny here. As mentioned previously, the focus is on cognitively-induced rule adjustment and not on information processing as such (cf. Benner et al. 2007, 61). Moreover, the concept of learning does not contain explicit threshold values, but implies different degrees, as it is procedural by nature rather than quantifiable. The level of analysis is the inner circle of CFSP, i.e. the High Representative with his Policy Unit, the Council Secretariat, and the Political and Security Committee; the level of explanation are the EUSRs and their teams, that act as boundary spanners in this system.

Given the necessity of a manageable operationalization, I will assume that reflection (defined previously as collective cognitive information processing) took place when the information in question was subject of a meeting of officials concerned or was part of a written conversation. This is because there are (at least) two difficulties in gathering empirical evidence for information processing in a political international organization: First, the minutes of meetings are usually not available or cannot be disclosed as 'proof' for who brought forth which idea when and what debate ensued. Consequently, the researcher must rely on the assertions made by his or her interlocutors that a certain item was indeed the subject of a debate, so that he or she can assume its collective cognitive processing. Second, it is unrealistic to ask interviewees to browse their documents to determine when exactly an idea first came about and who exactly proposed it. Again, this work is an academic exercise and not meant to serve as legal evidence.

Organizational rules were introduced earlier as operating at four different levels (structures, procedures, operations, and ideas). They can be further operationalized as follows:

– Structural rules refer to the EU's organizational setup, including the creation of new institutional bodies and their links with existing ones; hierarchies and reporting structures; budgetary allocation; and an organizational memory.
– Procedural rules relate to how different EU bodies cooperate with and consult each other; how decisions about personnel are made; and which evaluation procedures are in place.
– Operational rules apply to how an organization carries out its tasks; how it coordinates in the field; as well as how it cooperates with third parties.
– Ideational rules define the basic strategies and specific policies of an organization and, more fundamentally, its own sense of purpose.

In the second phase, when newly acquired knowledge prompts organizational action, change materializes either at the institutional or at the policy level. Again, such change within an organization does not necessarily equal an effective impact on the ground.

– Institutional change builds on a change of either structural or procedural rules, i. e. what the organization is. It aims to alter the organizational structure in order to use resources more effectively or efficiently. Examples of this include the change of existing or establishing of new decision-making rules (e. g. intra-institutional agreements), budgetary procedures, or evaluation practices (i. e. an internal reorganization of the instrument of the EUSRs).
– A policy change develops from a change of either operational or ideational rules, i. e. what the organization does (or wants to do). It aims to alter the impact of the organization on the outer environment: for example, the mandate of an EUSR is broadened to provide input for strategy development, existing policies (e. g. common positions or strategies) are changed or new ones established, or coordination with member states and the Commission or with third parties is increased.

The barriers that could slow or prevent organizational change can be operationalized according to their formal or informal effect. Formal change resistance would be the opposition, by a member state or an institution of the EU, to putting an established rule into organizational practice. Informally, this could happen by simply blocking or protracting a decision to this effect. Institutional constraints can also be formal (e. g. the pillar structure does not allow for a lesson to be implemented)[268] and informal (by subconsciously making officials think along pillar lines). In the end, change, whether complete or not, eventually translates into new information (via its impact on the environment), thus starting the process anew.

---

268 Ultimately, of course, such constraint could be overcome if the Treaties were changed, which could be said to be a question of mere political will, and the lack of the latter would again be a sign of change resistance.

The two-phase process of learning and change (organizational development) is illustrated in the following simplified model:

Figure 16: The Two-Phase Process of Organizational Learning and Change

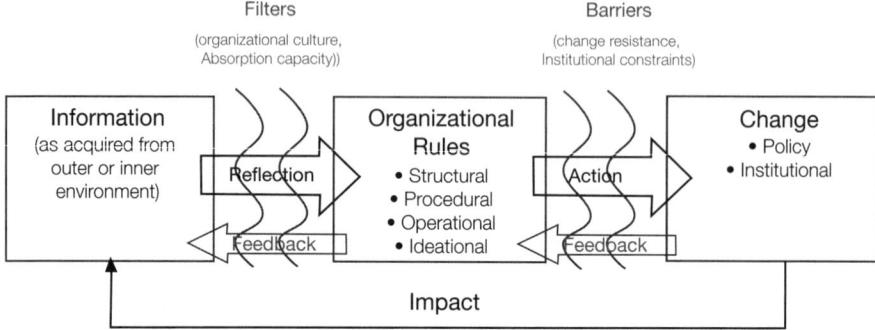

The model does not intend to say that learning occurs in a linear or even circular fashion. To highlight the potential shortcuts or interruptions of the learning process, it therefore includes feedback loops in both the information processing and action stage.

From the previous chapters about the development of EUSRs over time and the comparison with their UN and U.S. counterparts, I can deduce the following eighteen instances that appear to be worth studying as potential examples of organizational learning and change. Each is treated according to the respective level of rules at which changes appear to have been caused:

Table 3: Eighteen Instances of Organizational Learning and Change

Institutional Change	Stuctures	– The invention of EUSRs in 1996; – The increase in their numbers, in particular from 2002 to 2005; – The integration of EUSRs into the evolving CFSP structures; – The parallel establishment of EUSR structures; and – Issues regarding the budget from which EUSRs are paid.
	Procedures	– EUSR cooperation with the Commission and the European Parliament; – Standardisation of general (reporting) provisions of EUSR mandates; – Evolving personnel selection; and – The setting up of 'lessons-learned' seminars in 2005.
Policy Change	Operations	– The EUSRs' tasks; – Their basis of operation; – Political coordination of EU actors in the field; – Changes to the ESDP chain of command; and – External cooperation with partners.
	Ideas	– Policy input provided by the EUSRs; – The calculated use of envoys by the EU; – The issues of double-hatting; and – The EU's strategic role.

For each of the eighteen instances, I will, in part II of this study, first establish how the main variables 'reflection' and 'rewriting of rules' were at play. Then, this body of OL instances will be analyzed with regard to its contribution to organizational change, looking in particular at potential barriers that might slow or prevent such change.

3.3.4 Methodology

The methodology applied is that of process tracing, which has seen a recent revival not least due to Alexander George and Andrew Bennett's highly regarded book on the case study method (2004). Several scholars have noted a relationship between the explanation of causal mechanisms and the method of process tracing (cf. Tansey 2007, 3). The latter is deemed particularly useful when it comes to analyzing how a certain policy decision was generated, in particular when different cases are studied. As George/Bennett themselves succinctly put it in their definition, "[the] process-tracing method attempts to identify the intervening causal process—the causal chain and causal mechanism—between an independent variable (or variables) and the outcome of the dependent variable" (2004, 206).[269] For the present study, this implies an analysis of the processes of learning and change along the variables worked out above.

The role of the EU Special Representatives will be examined over the twelve-year period from 1996 to 2007,[270] seeking empirical data from a combination of qualitative and quantitative sources. A blend of interviews, archival documentation, secondary sources, as well as press releases and media accounts can help reduce methodological biases. Initial research revealed that hardly any documents on EUSR activities are publicly accessible; indeed, most official reports, such as the regular mission reviews, are confidential. However, Council documents such as the Joint Actions stipulating mandate amendments or Guidelines on the EUSRs' work are readily available. With regard to the literature, it was already remarked that the subject matter has to date received very little attention.

Given the scarcity of official reports available to researchers and the dearth of secondary literature on the subject, the study has to mainly rely on interviewing the actors involved in EUSR affairs.[271] Interviews were conducted with nearly all serving Special Representatives plus a number of former EUSRs, and with their staff and the Council

---

269 Critical of the process-tracing approach is one of the leading proponents of the 'socialization school' in international relations, Jeffrey Checkel. He claims that the empirical insight on Europe gained through the method of process tracing is outweighed by a lack of meta-theoretical clarity (Checkel 2006, 8). However, he does not criticize the method as such, but only its underlying positivist and epistemological assumptions.

270 The two recent mandates, for the African Union (of December 2007) and for Kosovo (of February 2008), therefore do not figure in the following empirical part of the study. They have only been considered, for reasons of actuality, in the introductory chapters.

271 Oisín Tansey underscores the usefulness of interviews in such a case: "Other advantages of elite interviews relate to the particular weaknesses of archival documents, as interviews can compensate for both the lack and limitations of documentary evidence" (2007, 767). For a good typology of experts as interviewees and the resulting interview strategies, see Martens/Brüggemann 2006.

Secretariat/Policy Unit staff respectively. In order not to fall into the trap of relying on the opinion of one group of actors only (in this case from the sphere of intergovernmental policy-making), the views from these insiders were balanced by interviews with Commission officials, Members of the European Parliament (MEPs), and experts from think tanks specialized on EU affairs. Moreover, the positions and actions of different member states were taken into account. A list of interviewees is provided in the Annex to this work. Granting officials the freedom to speak, all talks were conducted under conditions of anonymity; thus, I will reference interviews by numbers and not names. Transcripts of the interviews can be made available upon request.

The selection of interviewees followed non-probability criteria, based on a combination of purposive and chain-referral (or snowball) sampling (cf. Tansey 2007). This approach is particularly recommended to examine recent cases, which do not allow the historical methods advocated by George and Bennett, such as archival research, to be employed (ibid., 766). The EUSRs, it appears from the barely available official documentation and secondary literature, are clearly such a case. Finally, with the aim of achieving, in this uncharted and highly political field, as high a degree of objectivity as possible, the views presented in the encounters were again checked against contemporary accounts in the media and other public sources.

All in all, between September 2006 and February 2008, I conducted interviews with 50 different individuals.[272] Starting out from an initially selected set of interviewees, I subsequently relied on a mixture of continuous inquiry as well as informed advice from interlocutors on who else would be well-suited, both by their formal position and by their standing among peers, to provide information on the work of EUSRs. Another reason why this snow-balling method is important in the context of EUSRs is that many officials, both from the EUSR teams and the Council Secretariat, are seconded national diplomats. Thus, when working today in a completely different environment, they are difficult to spot for the researcher, unless former colleagues refer to them.

In line with the demands of the process-tracing method, a semi-structured interview technique was applied. All interviewees responded to queries from a broad set of pre-formulated questions covering three different levels: The EUSRs and their teams; institutional relations within the European Union; and the relationship with both partner countries and international actors, including the role the EU should play in this cooperation. This was done to ensure that interviews remained focused on the theoretical concerns of the research project. At the same time, there was room for both the interviewer and the interviewee to expand, by asking probing follow-on questions or by presenting a hitherto unknown version of events, respectively, so as to allow the researcher to gain a maximum amount of information from the respondent.

---

272 In total, 54 interviews were conducted, as some interlocutors had agreed to be re-interviewed at a later stage. This second interview, however, was not done systematically to review potential developments that had occurred in the meantime but to delve deeper into the research questions than may have been possible at a previous stage.

The data-gathering process thus follows, to the extent that this was possible, the postulates of "empirical triangulation" (cf. Patton 2002, 556), both in terms of sources (broad range of interviewees) and methods (interviews, public documents etc.). Other data collection methods (that of 'participant observation,' for example) were impossible to apply. Regardless of the cost implied by accompanying a handful of EUSRs to trips in their respective countries or regions on three continents, security regulations forbid a researcher to partake in any deliberations at such a high political level.

3.4   Summary of the theoretical approach

This explanation of the methodology concludes part I of this study. In chapter 1, I presented the EU Special Representatives and how they evolved as a foreign policy instrument through four different periods (invention, formalization, expansion, and consolidation), contextualizing this development with the emergence of an overall European foreign policy. Chapter 2 compared the EUSRs with special envoys used by the United Nations and the United States, outlining differences as well as similarities in the different roles they fulfil. This served to explain why the former are a worthy object of study from a policy-oriented point of view. The present chapter then elaborated the theoretical approach taken in this research, highlighting different approaches to organizational learning and presenting a model of analysis for a case study of the EUSRs.

The following part II will present the empirical analysis of the role of EUSRs in European foreign policy. Chapter 4 will establish learning experiences at the structural and procedural level, while chapter 5 will do the same for the operational and ideational level. In chapter 6, I will scrutinize to what extent this body of learning experiences has resulted in organizational change, both at the institutional and policy level.

Chapter 4:
Organizational Learning at the Structural and Procedural Level

The second—empirical—part of this study starts out by collecting occurrences of organizational learning at the structural and procedural level (this chapter) and at the operational and ideational level of EUSR development (chapter 5), before taking all these instances together and analyzing their impact on organizational change (chapter 6).

Looking at the structures and procedures of the EUSRs may not appear to be the most thrilling thing to do, yet it shows the institutional foundation of the instrument and the extent to which it has been progressively consolidated (cf. Grevi 2007, 17). As it appears, the very invention of the EUSRs was already a learning experience, followed by others about their integration into the emerging CFSP structures, about cooperation with the European Commission and Parliament, and about issues such as budgetary accountability and personnel selection.

4.1 Invention of EUSRs

The deployment of the first two EU Special Representatives in 1996 is, of course, the most fundamental change with regard to the research topic. It was preceded by reflections of EU policy-makers about the Union's political visibility both in the conflict of the Great Lakes and the Middle East Peace Process that had led to a change of routines: First as a Joint Action, later in the form of the insertion of a specific article into the Amsterdam Treaty.

4.1.1 Rewriting of rules

The first change of written rules followed the proposal from the Commissioner for Development, João Pinheiro, who had recommended creating a Special Envoy for the Great Lakes region (Interviewee #18). In the second instance, it was a group of EU ambassadors to Israel and Palestine (among them the later EUSR Marc Otte who at that time represented Belgium in Tel Aviv) that made the proposition, aided by the insistence of France and other countries, of sending another European envoy (Interviewee #47; Grevi 2007, 133). Both contributions found their way into the respective Council Joint Actions.[272]

Only a year later, the two posts were formalized in that they were written, under the name of 'Special Representatives,' into the Treaty of Amsterdam amending the Treaty on European Union. Article 18 (5) TEU now reads: "The Council may, whenever it deems it necessary, appoint a special representative with a mandate in relation to particular policy issues."

---

272 Joint Action 96/250/CFSP of 25 March 1996 (Great Lakes) and Joint Action 96/676/CFSP of 25 November 1996 (Middle East Peace Process).

4.1.2 Result of reflection

A variety of reflections preceded the nomination of the first two envoys, some directed at the crisis issue, others more internally motivated. On the internal side, there was an interest of the Union to be represented and to increase its standing in the respective regions (Interviewee #19; Grevi 2007, 133). In the Great Lakes region as well as in the Middle East, the EU was regarded as a mere aid giver, which had led to some frustration on the EU side (Interviewee #47). It therefore aimed at a political role that was commensurate with its economic commitment (Interviewee #18; cf. McLoughlin 1998, 2; Cunningham 1996, 11).[273] In particular in the Middle East, the desire not to play 'second fiddle' after the United States was great (Morrison 1997, A12), although such prominence was consistently denied by Israel (Makovsky 1996, 2; MacAskill 2001, 19).

Lack of international standing was also due to insufficient political representation in the field. Policy-makers on the Council side felt that they could not sufficiently make use, as foreseen by the Maastricht Treaty, of the local Commission delegations (Interviewees #3, 21, and 40).[274] Enhancing the Council's field structures was also a way to increase the amount of firsthand information available to member states, in particular those smaller ones without their own embassies in the region (Interviewee #8). Finally, some people assume that bureaucratic reasons also played a role, i. e. the Council's interest to grow by adding personnel (Interviewee #3).

It is no secret that, initially, EUSRs were deployed as an ersatz for policy (Interviewees #8, 16, and 40; see also Grevi 2007, 41). They were an easy instrument to deploy—a person who can meet the local representatives, but does not commit the Union or the Council (Interviewee #16). At the same time, receiving information from a dispatched envoy turned a substitute for policy into a contribution to a common policy on the EU side, enabling member states to develop a common point of view through a single point of entry (Interviewee #47).

These internal reasons were matched by external pressure from two major crises at which an envoy could be directed. For the Great Lakes, it was the Rwandan refugee crisis in Eastern Zaire (now DRC) that helped bring about the EUSR appointment (Interviewee #18). Foreign aid worth one million U.S. dollars per day was flowing into the refugee camps, yet with no political results (McLoughlin 1998, 1). In the Middle East, the crisis was less acute, but the peace process had taken off without much EU involvement, so the Union wanted to become more effective by providing a single interlocutor for the two parties (Interviewee #47).

---

273 This reasoning was also valid for the later deployment of the EUSR for Afghanistan; cf. Graff 2002, 58.

274 Article J.6 TEU stipulated that "The diplomatic and consular missions of the Member States and the Commission Delegations in third countries and international conferences, and their representations to international organizations, shall co-operate in ensuring that the common positions and common measures adopted by the Council are complied with and implemented."

What is generally valid is that the EUSRs' deployments were based on ad hoc decisions rather than designed after any specific model (Interviewee #44). They were sparked by practical, not philosophical considerations, someone who participated in these discussions claimed: Inventing the EUSRs was not so much a stroke of genius but a question of being more visible (Interviewee #47). It was thought to be natural that, just like there are roving ambassadors in any foreign ministry of member states, a similar instrument should be at the EU's disposal (Interviewees #15, 19, 39, and 44).

Similarly practical considerations also prevailed when the instrument of EUSRs was written into the Treaty in 1997. There had already been discussions about European envoys in the meetings of the so-called Reflection Group preparing the Amsterdam Treaty (cf. Regelsberger 1996, 218). At the time, there were only two envoys, Ajello and Moratinos, whose mandates should receive a more formal backing (Interviewee #15). What is more, in hindsight it appears normal that actual nomination is followed and not preceded by a Treaty reference: The EU has been following a trial-and-error approach by first deploying common instruments like the EUSRs before writing them into the Treaty (Interviewee #47).

4.2 Increased number of EUSRs

Other than the introduction of EUSRs, which was laid down first in a Council Joint Action and later in the Treaty on European Union, the increase in numbers of EU Special Representatives has found no formal expression by way of a doctrine or the like. Nonetheless, the 'unwritten rules' were changed when their abolition was first contemplated but then discarded, as EUSRs generally came to be seen as a useful tool. This reflects different lines of thinking, from the individual change of opinion of Javier Solana to, again, a more institutional reasoning about strengthening the intergovernmental structures within the EU.

4.2.1 Rewriting of rules

After the EUSRs were invented and formalized by the Treaty of Amsterdam, it took quite a while for them to develop their full potential. It seemed expedient to have these few envoys but there was no intention to make this a widely used instrument. Upon taking office, the High Representative gave them good marks, though not much more: In a report to the 1999 European Council written jointly with the European Commission, Solana claimed that "the use of special representatives has allowed sustained [EU] engagement in both the Middle East, Africa and the Western Balkans"—and recommended an evaluation of the use of diplomatic instruments for conflict prevention (including the EUSRs), aiming at a more focused, flexible, and robust diplomatic engagement (High Representative / Secretary General / Commission 1999).

Only gradually did the unwritten rule sink in that EUSRs can be a useful tool for EU foreign policy. Disregarding the short-lived and merely half-successful EUSRs for former Yugoslavia of 1998 and 1999, full five years passed with only two envoys in place, before the next EUSRs were appointed for Macedonia and Afghanistan. After this turning point, the EUSRs were much higher on the agenda, as the 2001 CFSP report of the Council to the EP lists them first among the 'perspectives for future action:' "The Union will continue its efforts to strengthen the CFSP, including by developing and refining the instruments available to it, such as the role of the High Representative and the EU Special Representatives" (Council of the European Union 2002a, 55). By then, policymakers had understood that it is better to use the EUSRs actively rather than to try to abolish them, in particular given the type of crises that the Union is usually faced with, i.e. a multidimensional and protracted conflict (Interviewees #3 and 12). EUSRs were even featured as convenient instruments of crisis management in an early version of the European Security Strategy (Interviewee #6).

4.2.2 Result of reflection

Until he learned about their advantages in actual crisis management, the newly appointed High Representative had no special interest in the EUSRs who predated him (Interviewee #8). Especially the mandate for the Great Lakes was thought to be irrelevant (Interviewee #15). During the 2001 crisis in Macedonia, Javier Solana allowed an EUSR to take his place in the negotiations after an ad hoc arrangement with the UK ambassador was tried first (Interviewee #45). In addition, he lacked an interest in particular world regions: It is fair to say that neither as Foreign Minister of Spain nor as Secretary-General of NATO had Solana developed an interest in the African continent (Interviewee #48). It was not until operation Artemis in Congo that Solana fully learned about the benefits of EUSRs (Interviewees #8, 15, and 48). At that time, he discovered Africa as a testing ground for ESDP, and he understood that, with missions such as Artemis, the EU could actually achieve something (Interviewee #48).

Increasingly, member states also began to see the advantages that EUSRs could offer them. Some of the arguments made most regularly for their great number are the following: They can provide a missing link between member states' heads of mission in the region and the HR/SG in Brussels (Interviewee #12). They can ensure a full-time presence for a given conflict or crisis for which they already have great expertise (Interviewee #12), also opening avenues for additional funding from the Community budget (Grevi 2007, 42). They replace Solana who cannot cover all regions (Interviewees #9, 38, and 48), in particular at the level where important information can be gained from intensively liaising with stakeholders (Interviewee #15). From the point of view of smaller member states, an EUSR is very useful when the cost effectiveness of having an own ambassador is low but the issue at hand is high on the EU's agenda (Interviewee #39). Finally, another added value is continuity because EUSRs are able to build personal relationships, trust, and open communication, which the rotating presidency simply cannot ensure (Interviewees #27, 40, and 44).

These arguments notwithstanding, member states need to be convinced of the advantages of an EUSR in a given situation because the EU option is only one part of their foreign policy calculation. They feel that they can decide whether, on a specific issue, they prefer to pursue the EU track or another track, be it through a different organization or bilaterally (Interviewee #17). This puts pressure on Brussels officials to make the EUSRs an attractive option, an opportunity for action. The availability of a person who can implement a decision or travel to a given region on short notice makes member states more likely to agree on EU action (Interviewee #17).

Institutionally speaking, EUSRs underscore the central crisis management function of the Secretariat. They are regarded as a flexible instrument when an ESDP mission would be too large-scale and politically sensitive to deploy (Interviewee #17). They are therefore the mildest ESDP instrument, securing EU involvement while being fairly easy to direct, with the possibility of following up with a larger mission (Interviewees #12 and 21). In addition, there is again the bureaucratic motive on the part of the Secretariat, which wanted to strengthen its capacities. This became clear in the run-up to the 2005 Sudan mandate, where the ambition to have an EUSR dealing with Sudan and the AU, at Addis, was expressed, to complement the existing Council offices at the UN in Geneva and New York (Interviewee #28).

All this is not to say that EUSRs were not also dispatched around certain external events, such as when the Tulip Revolution in Kyrgyzstan and the Andijan massacre in Uzbekistan served as windows of opportunity for the existing plan of issuing a mandate for Central Asia (Interviewee #1). Another external reason for having an EUSR is the presence, in a given conflict, of special envoys from other actors, such as the United States. This was the case, for example, of the special representatives for Kosovo (1998) and Macedonia (2001) (Council of the European Union 1999; Jaanson 2008, 7).

In sum, following a phase during which the abolition of EUSRs was seriously considered (cf. section 5.7), a number of arguments were made in favour of keeping and even expanding the EUSRs. They have long been considered a 'work in progress', an experiment in itself that is also a precursor to the future diplomatic service (Interviewees #21, 39, and 46).

4.3   Integration into CFSP structures

The integration of EUSRs into CFSP structures must be viewed against the background of a belated setup of these structures, which then had to surpass the existing EUSRs both in terms of institutional strength and hierarchy. Today, the time before 1999 and the appearance of institutions such as the High Representative and the Political and Security Committee resembles the Middle Ages (Interviewee #3) with EUSRs operating in a "relative institutional void" (Grevi 2007, 35). An entire foreign policy machinery had to be built with the Amsterdam Treaty, and the EUSRs needed to be integrated into these structures. Part of this was achieved on the basis of organizational learning: Guidelines were passed and later rewritten, and task forces created. This happened mainly in response to a perceived lack of control over EUSRs, and in order to emulate hierarchical structures that officials knew from their national ministries.

4.3.1 Rewriting of rules

Over the years, four main measures can be detected that were aimed at better integrating the EUSRs into CFSP administrative structures: establishing guidelines, setting up regional task forces, putting Council officials on EUSR teams, and creating high-level contact points within the Secretariat.

The first "Guidelines on appointing procedure and administrative arrangements" of the EUSRs were passed in March 2000 (Council of the European Union 2000); they have been updated three times in 2003, 2006, and 2007, and are being reworked to the present day (Interviewee #16). Back in 2000, the aim was to reinforce political accountability of the EUSRs to the Council and to address the budgetary responsibility for the EUSRs' administrative expenditure. The former meant to clarify reporting lines, including to the newly created High Representative for CFSP (Council of the European Union 2000, 3 [Annex]); the latter implied budgetary changes that will be dealt with in more detail later (see section 4.5). On this basis, the EUSRs' mandates were "brought into a consistent framework providing for operational direction of the High Representative, for a privileged link to the PSC as primary point of contact with the Council, [for] regular reporting and coordination as well as liaison" (Council of the European Union 2003a, 39).

A second measure was the establishment of regional task forces, based on a merger between the Council Secretariat and the Policy Unit (Grevi 2007, 37). These were intended to better control the EUSRs who, without such a connection, would feel too much like self-contained actors (Interviewee #16). A team for Eastern Europe led by the Head of the Policy Unit covers the three EUSRs for Moldova, South Caucasus, and Central Asia, joined by the one for Afghanistan, when appropriate (Interviewee #20). An Africa task force deals with mandates for the Great Lakes and Sudan, as does the Middle East task force with the respective mandate, while for the Balkans, coordination takes place mainly in the field between resident EUSRs (Interviewees #3 and 42).

Moreover, it was established that a Council official works as a political advisor on each EUSR team. These persons are not seconded like national experts but they remain included in the chain of command of the Secretariat, so the person working for an EUSR also covers the same region at the Secretariat or Policy Unit (Interviewees #10 and 44). In this sense, they are also 'spies' watching whether an EUSR follows the political guidance he or she receives (Interviewees #6 and 16). The case of Marc Otte, however, who used to be head of the Middle East task force before being appointed EUSR, is the exception rather than the rule: He is thought to be integrated into the Secretariat due to his previous job and does not have a Council official on his team (Interviewees #6 and 16).

Finally, because EUSRs seemed reluctant to take orders from lower-ranking members of the Secretariat, two senior contact points were established for them. Helga Schmid, the head of the Policy Unit, is thematically responsible for Eastern Europe and Central Asia (Interviewee #3), while her colleague Robert Cooper, Director-General (DG E) within the Secretariat, officially covers the Balkans, the Middle East, and Africa (Interviewees #28 and 39). In addition, operational guidance, which rests with the High Representative, has been officially delegated to Helga Schmid and the Policy Unit (Interviewee #39).

4.3.2 Result of reflection

From the beginning, the ambition of the High Representative and his Policy Unit was to contain the two EUSRs they had inherited from previous times. The latter were seen as acting independently like ministers with a very vague mandate (Interviewees #6 and 41), at times following their own policies like an unguided missile (Interviewees #30 and 44).[275] Javier Solana, in particular, did not appreciate EUSRs pointing to a mandate from the Council in order to underline their independence (Interviewee #39). Instead, he saw himself as a quasi-minister and therefore attempted to incorporate the EUSRs as his deputies or ambassadors, depending on whether they were in Brussels or abroad (Interviewee #3).

The suggestion to have an ambassadorial college of people reporting regularly to decision-making bodies in Brussels (Interviewee #3) reveals that some of the ideas for restructuring were borrowed from the national foreign services. In any bilateral Ministry of Foreign Affairs, a desk officer would give instructions to a high-ranking ambassador in the field. This ministerial normality should also apply to the Policy Unit and the Secretariat, those working there felt (Interviewee #39). Just as there are state secretaries and special ambassadors in national foreign ministries, the EU needs these too, the line of thinking went (Interviewee #48). This feeling was reinforced in contacts with international actors, such as special envoys of the United States who usually have a permanent function in their ministry, e.g. as Assistant Deputy Secretary of State (Interviewee #20). In a context like the Middle East Quartet with envoys from both states and institutions, EU representatives would then look at the U.S. rather than the UN envoy as an example (Interviewee #19). Interestingly, this was not necessarily done to copy the best model available but as an expression of what Secretariat staff members know best (Interviewee #17).

In addition to the Secretariat's desire to control EUSRs better, a streamlining of structures was also meant to enhance the quality of their work (Interviewee #17). It became clear that many of them had been sent on mission not only without a clear mandate, but also with little connection to the CFSP apparatus (Interviewees #40 and 44), other than, for example, Solana's Personal Representatives who are based within the Secretariat (In-

---

275 Indeed, this seems to have been a general feature of the early CFSP day, as the Court of Auditors also criticized the Council's reporting to the Commission as being "irregular, incomplete and unclear" (Court of Auditors 2001, 16).

terviewee #7). However, efforts to control and streamline could run counter to member states' reliance on the EUSRs to be political animals with authority towards the local governments (Interviewee #40). Therefore, a balance had to be struck between controlling the EUSRs' actions at every level and giving them a broad backing so that they could make the EU's voice heard (Interviewee #30). This trade-off between necessary formalization and desirable flexibility is another example of why the whole restructuring process is part of a fluid system still in the making (Interviewee #16).

4.4 Establishing EUSR structures

The enormous attempt to integrate the EUSRs into the CFSP structures at the Council Secretariat stands in stark contrast to the lack of the most basic administrative structures of the EUSRs themselves. While one might say that small teams of about half a dozen people do not need big structures, the relatively high turnover in personnel, the political importance of their task, and the fact that there are nearly a dozen such teams around, comprising some 150 staff in total, would make it opportune to have a better organized working environment. Indeed, not many common rules have been established for those working on the EUSR teams, other than to read past reports from the EU's telex communication network COREU (Correspondance Européenne) and to squeeze one's predecessor in search for information about the job. An organizational memory hardly exists, despite the fact that those involved have reflected on how a common administrative structure for all EUSRs would benefit the work of EUSRs.

4.4.1 Rewriting of rules

In addition to the regulations that come from the Secretariat or the Commission, there are few routines that govern the work of EUSRs, other than to rely on reading COREUs and to speak to one's predecessor. In fact, it is a common complaint that an organizational memory does not exist (Interviewees #16, 34, 36, 39, and 46). Instead, there is only COREU reporting, which can be quite substantial when an EUSR takes over from another person but, in the case of a new mandate, has little direct relevance to the task (Interviewees #26 and 36). Moreover, while the mandate implementation reports can be a good source of information, they provide little evidence of how things really work (Interviewee #42). Especially for Political Advisors (POLADs), therefore, the best bet is to be in good contact with one's predecessor (Interviewee #42), beyond the odd take-over lunch meeting one may have with that person (Interviewee #45).

The idea of establishing a joint administrative team for EUSRs has been discussed and received enough support to figure, as a proposal, in the 2004 Action Plan for Civilian Aspects of ESDP (European Council 2004a) and in the Civilian Headline Goal 2008 (Council of the European Union 2004c), being taken up again in the latest set of guidelines (Council of the European Union 2007c, 2). It has not, however, moved beyond the conceptual stage, in which the Council Secretariat and the Commission are working on the potential modalities of such an administrative support cell. Still today, the EU lacks something as basic as an EUSR handbook (which, by the way, does exist for the United Nations[276]), so seconded diplomats rely on their national networks of former POLADs (Interviewee #33) or on national documentation for information about how to connect with the CFSP machinery (Interviewee #42).

4.4.2 Result of reflection

In general, there has been more reflection on how structures should be improved than developed routines following from this thinking. In different teams, the need for proper documentation was recognized and usually met by hiring an additional assistant (Interviewee #26). Accounting is also underdeveloped in the sense that each team has its own accountant, struggling with Commission oversight of financial reporting (Interviewee #31). One EUSR, upon taking his job, was asked to open a personal bank account for handling his budget (Interviewee #35); others had to commence their work by writing job descriptions for their team members (Grevi 2007, 23).

For these reasons, the idea of an administrative back office has been floated, to deal with the logistical deficits and management shortcomings (Interviewees #31 and 44).[277] Without such structure, people fear that what has been learned individually will inevitably become lost once they leave, and the new staff members will start from scratch (Interviewees #8 and 33). However, such reflection has not been centrally channelled. On the one hand, the political task of an EUSR and his or her team is too important and urgent for them to bother about administrative structures; on the other, teams work in relative separation from each other, and despite their overall number they have not yet joined forces to demand certain changes from the Council Secretariat (Interviewee #29).

4.5 Budgetary issues

A small but significant instance of organizational learning took place with regard to the budget from which the EU Special Representatives are paid. Here, a back-and-forth process could be observed, typical for the trial-and-error period of the early days of EUSR life. Initially, EUSRs were financed from the Community budget, before, in 2000, the Council brought them under its financial control. However, for a combination of legal, financial, and political reasons, it soon had to place them back under Commission authority.

---

276 Although, as one interlocutor suggested, the last thing a newly appointed SRSG would look at is this book (Interviewee #36).

277 The fact that one field-based EUSR did not even have the office facilities in Brussels to receive the author for an interview but had to meet him in a public place, merely illustrates this lack of administrative infrastructure.

4.5.1   Rewriting of rules

Initially, the expenditure of the EUSRs was charged to the general budget of the European Communities under the CFSP heading (B8) that was created in the wake of the Maastricht Treaty on European Union.[278] This practice was confirmed by the Interinstitutional Agreement of May 1999 between the European Parliament, the Council, and the Commission, in which the "Union envoys" were explicitly mentioned as one of the articles in the CFSP budget chapter (B8-013).[279]

In 2000, however, the Council—as part of the broader attempt to establish tighter control over CFSP instruments (cf. section 4.3)—placed the EUSRs under a contractual obligation to the Council as 'Special Advisors.' This contract involved a change in the budgetary responsibility for the financing of EUSR expenditure, which specified that it should be charged to the Council's administrative budget (budget line A-1 1 1 3) from 2001 onwards (Council of the European Union 2000, 3).

Less than two years later, the Council had to give up this arrangement, not least because it was heavily criticized in a 2001 report by the European Court of Auditors on the management of CFSP (Court of Auditors 2001). Therein, it was found that by "defining the costs of EUSR as administrative expenditure the Council has created a situation whereby a legislative body will implement its own political decisions, making a political control difficult" (ibid., 14). Consequently, the auditors recommended reconsidering the classification of EUSR costs as administrative expenditure. Mandate extensions in December 2002 stipulated an in-between solution making the EUSRs "accountable to the High Representative for administrative expenditure and to the Commission for any operational expenditure incurred in respect of activities" while keeping them under a Council contract.[280] In the autumn of 2003, these negotiations were finalized with a view to provide "a solid basis for funding while allowing optimal flexibility and a high degree of responsiveness to evolving needs on the ground" (Council of the European Union 2003b, 2).

From 2003 on, EUSRs were again financed from the CFSP budget and contracted as 'CFSP Special Advisors' of the Commission. This was also in line with the respective Treaty provision stipulating that CFSP operating expenditure should be charged to the budget of the European Communities (Article 28 (3) TEU).[281] This arrangement was fur-

---

278 Cf. the initial mandates for the Great Lakes (Article 4 of Council Joint Action 96/250/CFSP of 25 March 1996) and the Middle East Peace Process (Article 3 of Council Joint Action 96/676/CFSP of 25 November 1996).

279 Interinstitutional Agreement of 6 May 1999 between the European Parliament, the Council and the Commission on budgetary discipline and improvement of the budgetary procedure, Official Journal C 172, 18.6.1999.

280 Cf. Articles 4 and 5 of Council Joint Action (2002/961/CFSP) of 10 December 2002 (Afghanistan), of Council Joint Action (2002/962/CFSP) of 10 December 2002 (Great Lakes Region), of Council Joint Action (2002/963/CFSP) of 10 December 2002 (Macedonia), and of Council Joint Action (2002/965/CFSP) of 10 December 2002 (Middle East Peace Process).

281 Only "such expenditure arising from operations having military or defense implications and cases

ther codified in the Commission's Communication on Special CFSP Advisers, which conceived of the EUSRs as a "category sui generis" (European Commission 2004b, 1) due to "their being entrusted with the implementation of a political mandate" (ibid., 3).[282]

4.5.2   Result of reflection

The initial intention of the Council was a very plain one: to establish full control of the EUSRs, including their financial accountability (Interviewee #8). This also followed from the Council's understanding of how the relevant provisions of the Amsterdam Treaty, which entered into force in 1999, should be put in place: "[In] order to ensure the follow-up of the Treaty provisions at legal/administrative level as well as political accountability between EUSR and the Council, EUSR should be placed under a contractual obligation to the Council" (Council of the European Union 2000, 3). In practice, however, and not least due to an inadequate budget, EUSRs were "often financed in a mixed and improvised way," combining regional programs from the first pillar with an emergency reserve fund and, certainly not least, national contributions (Missiroli 2003, 8).

Both the struggle over control and the unorthodox financing had sparked a legal and political debate. Legally, it was a question of whether the EUSRs were indeed an administrative expenditure (as the Council argued in order to finance them from its budget, claiming that it covered mainly staff salaries and travel expenses) or an operational cost (after all, they were a CFSP instrument and not just additional staff) (Interviewee #9). Not least the Court of Auditors had voiced its misgivings about what it considered an opaque arrangement (Interviewee #41). It criticized the Council for considering the EUSR costs as administrative based on the nature of these costs rather than on the objective of the envoys' activities, because according to Article 14 (1) TEU, any Joint Action addresses specific situations where operational (!) action by the Union is deemed to be required (cf. Court of Auditors 2001, 14).

In the end, it was the politically sensitive question of whether the Council was in fact able to pay for its special representatives that led to considerations of moving the financing of the EUSRs (back) to the Community's CFSP budget (Council of the European Union 2002b, 5). The envoys devoured a considerable budget position of the already slim CFSP budget (Interviewees #38 and 41). Moreover, it is no coincidence that the debate about re-integrating the EUSRs into the Community budget began in parallel to the discussions about the first ESDP operations and their expected cost (Interviewee #38). So it was due to budgetary constraints that the Council eventually let go of the EUSRs' financing (Interviewees #8 and 9; Council of the European Union 2003b, 5).[283]

---

where the Council acting unanimously decides otherwise" should not be paid from the Community budget (Article 28 (3) TEU).

282 In addition, EUSRs were explicitly exempted from the application of the general (i.e. non-CFSP related) Rules for Special Advisers of the Commission.

283 Cf. also International Crisis Group 2005a, 42–43; Bocev 2002.

4.6 Cooperation with the Commission and the Parliament

The way in which EU Special Representatives as a Council institution and instruments of CFSP cooperate with both the European Commission and the European Parliament is naturally a function of the institutional divide that exists under the current Treaty system.[284] In particular the division of labour between the Council and the Commission is often worked out only on a case-by-case basis (Smith 2004, 193). This notwithstanding, some general lessons have been learned from the work of the EUSRs. While little consideration is given to Parliament, it is agreed that EUSRs cannot work effectively without the Commission and its representatives and instruments. Such change of the rules reflects the more politicized role the Commission has acquired over the past decade, the experience of the interdependence of first and second pillar instruments, and the general exigency of coherence.

4.6.1 Rewriting of rules

Gradually, and informally, routines of cooperation between the EUSRs and the Commission have been established, although relations between the Commission and the EUSRs are complex just as the Treaties are complex (Interviewee #40). Today, there is much closer regular cooperation between the two than when EUSRs began their work in the mid-1990s. The main rule is that the two should systematically consult and cooperate with each other, while at the same time respecting (and guarding) different competencies. For liaison in the field, the current set of guidelines stipulates close coordination, including regular briefings and mutual support (Council of the European Union 2007c, 6).

In Brussels, a visible expression of this new cooperation is the system of task forces that has been set up to integrate the EUSRs, the Council Secretariat, and the Commission (Interviewees #16 and 40) in an effort to draw together all sources of specialized knowledge within the central EU institutions (International Crisis Group 2001, 45; cf. Hansen 2006, 41; Grevi 2007 108, 134). In contrast, there is no regular presence of Commission officials in EUSR teams (as it was the case in Ajello's first team), although this is not to be seen as a policy decision (Interviewee #8).

In the case of the EP, it has apparently been engrained into the organizational routines that on CFSP matters Council institutions can largely neglect the assembly, except when it comes to funding matters. Parliament's answer is a continuous critique, taking issue for example with a perceived lack of clear guidelines for creating new EUSR posts (European Parliament 2005, 15), with a "proliferation" of envoys that threatens to weaken the role of Commission delegations (European Parliament 2007, para 61), and with the growing costs of existing missions and offices (Grevi 2007, 21). However, Parliament does not have much of a lever to change things. Only when it threatens to use its bud-

---

284 For a good overview of the Commission's role in European foreign policy, see Duke 2006; for Parliament's (marginal) involvement in CFSP, see Diedrichs 2004.

getary powers will the Council actually budge and compromise, as was the case with the question of regular advance reporting (Grevi 2007, 22; cf. Diedrichs 2004, 33).

4.6.2   Result of reflection

Ever since the introduction of CFSP in 1993, there has been a debate about how to relate the new policy to the long-standing competence of the European Community for external relations.[285] Parallel to the EU's foreign policy arm gradually developing more substance, the Commission has taken on a more and more political role (Interviewee #40). Following the crisis of 1999, sparked by the demise of the Santer College, the Commission began an encompassing reform of its external policies (cf. Nugent/Saurugger 2002). This reform took place at a time when a focus on the civilian aspects of crisis management greatly enhanced the Community's role (European Council 2001). Thus, with the Prodi College the Commission became involved with the EUSRs, while before that time, it had tried to simply ignore them (Interviewee #16).

Today, no comprehensive foreign policy strategy could be developed and no operation should be run without Commission involvement (Interviewees #26 and 40). The Commission believes it has a natural role in conflict prevention and crisis management because fighting poverty eliminates the root causes of conflict, and technical assistance can support reconciliation processes (Interviewee #8). While member states try to protect the 'political' field and relegate the Commission to deal with the developmental and economic aspects of foreign policy, it is clear that the latter's money is always a political factor as well (Interviewee #15).

Therefore, even where it would be possible to distinguish neatly between the Council's political and the Commission's economic role, the Commission's financial aid is instrumental to back up and tangibly support the diplomatic work of the EUSR (Interviewee #39). As a Commission official put it with reference to the direct contacts that EUSR Ján Kubiš had to regional leaders: "He has the access, but we have the instruments to get things done" (International Crisis Group 2006a, 19). Consequently, EUSRs themselves feel they have an interest in cooperating effectively with the Commission in order to use the latter's economic instruments as incentives in their political negotiations (Interviewees #15, 21, 39, and 40). Also, those EUSRs with a background in national diplomacy who might think that the Commission is only there to 'write the cheque' very soon realize that instead, both in terms of resources, information, and contacts, it is an important partner for them (Interviewee #16).

Conversely, the Commission for its part can make use of the 'personified coherence' of EUSRs and their coordinating role (Interviewee #21), as is most visible in the areas under the EU's neighborhood policy. In the South Caucasus in the winter of 2006/07, joint field missions of the EUSR and his team and a number of Commission officials addressed the problem of frozen conflicts, producing a policy paper, together with

---

285 For two early works that discuss this issue, see Jorgensen 1993 and Carlsnaes/Smith 1994.

the Policy Unit, for the PSC (Interviewee #3; Grevi 2007, 59–60). In Moldova, where the EUSR mandate stipulates that he should maintain an overview of all EU activities, notably the relevant aspects of the ENP Action Plan,[286] there is continuous cooperation between the EUSR team and Community actors on border management and other aspects of security sector reform (Interviewees #33 and 37; Grevi 2007, 66).[287] Furthermore, the EUSR can act as a boundary spanner by making the Commission aware of the different policy perceptions in member states and encourage better relations with them (Interviewee #40).

These considerations about necessary cooperation also stem from the working environments both at the headquarters and in the field. In Brussels, foreign policy interaction takes place between the Council and the Commission on a daily basis. The Commission is represented in the Council working groups, the Relex counsellors, and at the meetings of the PSC (Interviewees #21 and 31). This has led both sides to accept the necessity of consultation (Interviewee #28). Moreover, the fact that EUSRs are only half-integrated into the structures of the Secretariat (see section 4.3) leaves them a bit outside of the usual turf war between the Council and the Commission (Interviewee #29).

In the field, the coherent external appearance of the EU is paramount, as there is no point in trying to explain to partners the intricacies of intra-EU competencies (Interviewee #15; cf. Smith 2004, 216). Given that they are not fully on the Council's side, the EUSRs can at times act as an informal mediator between the Council and the Commission in external representation, a role that the Council has tried, but failed, to formally articulate, due to Commission resistance (Interviewee #48). What turns out in practice is a balancing act: As the EUSR cannot give orders to the Commission, what counts in the end is that people find a modus vivendi (Interviewee #31).

The situation is rather different when it comes to relations with the European Parliament. The EP, admittedly, plays only a marginal role in CFSP in general and in the work of the EUSRs in particular (Diedrichs 2004, 33). Usually once, sometimes twice a year, an EUSR appears before the foreign affairs committee (AFET) to report on his work (Interviewee #43), adding up to eleven appearances in 2006 (Council of the European Union 2007d, 6). However, apart from a few exceptions where an EUSR has good relations with Parliament (Interviewee #24), most of them seem to take on the Council perspective that it is very detached from their daily work (Interviewee #28): Their assessments range from little involvement at all due to a lack of information on the EP side (Interviewees #12 and 28) and good discussions but no influence (Interviewee #34) to simply being a nuisance on budgetary matters (Interviewee #28).

---

286 Cf. Article 3 (2) of Council Joint Action 2007/107/CFSP of 15 February 2007.

287 Indeed, ENP is a natural field of cooperation as the mandates of three EUSRs (for Moldova, South Caucasus, and the Middle East Peace Process, respectively) cover seven of the twelve countries with which ENP Action Plans have been adopted (Grevi 2007, 152).

Parliament, in contrast, has only two inroads into the EUSRs' work: Budget negotiations and, stemming from its financial authority, the annual Council reports on CFSP activities. For years now, the EP has criticized the EUSRs in its resolutions on these reports. This was, some allege, in fact more in response to the envoys' institutional location than due to a lack of performance (Interviewee #9). Others stress that Parliament is indeed interested in more forward-looking information about the substance of the mandate (Interviewee #8; cf. Grevi 2007, 22; Diedrichs 2004, 35). Yet, Parliament has no control over CFSP instruments such as the EUSRs other than using its budgetary competence. Even there, the EP cannot block the funding for an individual mandate but only the whole sub-heading on EUSR (Interviewee #9). Still, this is what it did most recently, in order to gain more power for the institutional competition expected after the entry into force of the Lisbon Treaty (Interviewee #28). From this perspective, the EUSRs' work is indeed reflected more as an expression of institutional rivalry than as part of the EU's growing international engagement.

4.7 Standardization of general mandate provisions

In a further effort to streamline the management of EUSRs, the general provisions of their mandates became standardized. These refer to reporting intervals and mandate duration; they could—and should—be the same for every Joint Action, other than the particular references to the region or crisis in question. However, due to the organic growth of EUSR business at the beginning, these provisions were not alike. So, based on some rational thinking as well as the desire to receive more regular reporting, mandates were standardized in 2003, and revised in 2005 and 2007.

4.7.1 Rewriting of rules

In 2003, common guidelines were published that standardized the broader framework of all mandates, most importantly by setting common dates for reporting and mandate renewal. They determined that mandate duration should be "in principle 6 months" and that the EUSR "shall present a comprehensive written report on the implementation of the mandate to the High Representative, Council and Commission two months before the mandate expires" (Council of the European Union 2003b, 5 and 8). These principles, which the PSC and the Council had already agreed in late 2002 (Interviewees # 9 and 10; cf. Council of the European Union 2002b), were then spelled out in a complex evaluation procedure: In mid-May and mid-October, the EUSR has to send his evaluation report to the High Representative, who should pass it to the PSC and to the relevant working group; two to three weeks later, the latter shall make recommendations to the PSC on extending, amending, or terminating existing mandates or on the creation of new mandates, which form the basis of the High Representative's own recommendations that he ought to debate with PSC in early June and early/mid November; finally, in June and December, the Council would take decisions on the respective Joint Actions (Council of the European Union 2003b, 10–11).

To provide a broader focus of the EUSR's mandate, the guidelines also demanded that policy objectives be defined for the given country or region, and that the EUSR's tasks be spelled out in this framework (Council of the European Union 2003b, 5; Grevi 2007, 26). In return, both the reporting of EUSRs and the subsequent evaluation by the working groups were to focus on substantive issues such as policy input and internal EU coordination (Grevi 2007, 25).

In addition, the guidelines introduced "standard wording for EUSR mandates" in contrast to the more ad hoc formulations from the beginning (Council of the European Union 2003b, 3). Now, the 'whereas' plus the 'considering' part of the preamble are distinct for each mandate (containing the political explanation for creating an EUSR) just like, of course, the operational mandate itself (usually given in Articles 2 and 3) (Interviewees #9 and 10). The other parts of the Joint Action are generically drafted (Interviewee #12), built on the standard version that is attached as an annex to the annex [sic!] of the guidelines. This wording was further codified in the 2004 Communication from the Commission on Special CFSP Advisers (European Commission 2004b, 10–11).

Already in 2005, the Political and Security Committee decided that the standard duration of the mandates should be extended to one year, while keeping the necessary flexibility to respond to the specific needs related to a mandate (Council of the European Union 2006c, 1). In light of this, reporting and evaluation intervals were rescheduled, with a progress report now due before the end of June, and a comprehensive mandate implementation report including financial aspects due by mid-November (ibid.). On the basis of these reports, the relevant working groups and the PSC would conduct their evaluation of the mandate, which again would feed into the recommendation from the SG/HR whether the policy objectives contained in the EUSR's mandate have been met and whether the mandate should be extended, amended, or terminated (ibid., 7).

When the guidelines were again revised in 2007, the tenure of office of an EUSR was limited to four years, with the possibility, under "duly justified circumstances, in particular where an EUSR also assumes other functions," of extending this period (Council of the European Union 2007c, 4; cf. Grevi 2007, 26). Moreover, the guidelines introduced additional standard language, going beyond the general regulations on reporting and budgetary responsibility and covering certain horizontal issues such as human rights, gender issues, and children's rights (Interviewee #15; Council of the European Union 2007c, 5). Finally, the established practice of starting a (renewed) mandate on March 1 of each year was confirmed (ibid., 7).

4.7.2 Result of reflection

The emergence of general provisions contained in each EUSR mandate can be considered part of rational process, in which the Secretariat tried to manage the increasing number of mandates (Interviewee #9), which produced an obvious need for regulation (Interviewee #41). At the same time, it was part of an effort to curb the EUSRs by making them report more regularly and introducing a formal mandate review before possible extension (Interviewee #31). However, the initial arrangement of only a six-month duration with various reporting duties at different times became too overwhelming for the Secretariat itself and for the PSC in particular, so the idea was born—in fact during the first lessons-learned seminar in 2005 (see section 4.9)—to renew all mandates at the same time (Interviewees #3 and 31; Grevi 2007, 25).

The fact that, in 2007, tenures were limited to four years had both practical and political reasons. Practically, despite their seemingly never-ending mandates, EUSR are still regarded as a time-bound instrument of crisis management that should not develop into a quasi-permanent institution (Interviewee #12). In addition to this, a sunset clause on the person of an EUSR would make it easier to dismiss an unwanted character without becoming a political issue (Interviewee #12)—as it was the case, for example, when terminating the mandates of Pekka Haavisto or Christian Schwarz-Schilling. Finally, Council staff is very familiar with the system of rotation in the foreign service, which tends to bring certain rejuvenation and a fresh look at things and is believed to prevent people from getting too involved in a matter (Interviewee #12).

4.8   Selection of EUSRs

Two observations can be made with regard to the selection of EUSRs: On the one hand, the selection process has been refined, not least in order to put member states in better control over who should represent CFSP abroad. On the other, rules have emerged about what type of qualities these people should possess. Here, the diplomatic class prevalent in Brussels corridors has greatly influenced the thinking.

4.8.1   Rewriting of rules

Before the 1999 Treaty reform, Special Envoys were nominated directly by the Council, following a Union-wide call for applications and examination of the candidatures by the Political Committee (Interviewee #16; Council of the European Union 2000, 1). Post-Amsterdam, the High Representative began to make proposals for nomination, although this arrangement was more ad hoc and did not receive codification in the 2000 'guidelines on appointing procedure' (Interviewee #6; Grevi 2007, 18). The 2003 guidelines mainly confirmed the existing practice, only replacing the Political Committee by its successor, the PSC, and providing a mechanism to inform member states on the progress in the selection process (Council of the European Union 2003b, 5).

Gradually, from 2004 onwards, the selection process became more complex until, in 2007, a new set of guidelines codified the practice of a multi-stage selection procedure: An initial call for applications by the High Representative is followed by a selection panel composed of representatives of the Presidency, the Policy Unit, and the Secretariat[288]

---

288 The selection body is usually comprised of the Presidency's PSC ambassador, the Director-General E

and a presentation to the High Representative; the panel then makes a recommendation to the PSC, which, if endorsed, should lead to the formal appointment of that person by the Council (Interviewees #10, 16, and 31; cf. Council of the European Union 2007c, 3; Grevi 2007, 18).

On the substantial side, an unwritten rule differentiates between 'diplomats' and 'politicians' as candidates for an EUSR post, giving preference to the former. It is generally assumed that, each mandate being different, personality should be decisive (Interviewee #12). Nonetheless, it seems to have been established that EUSRs should regularly be diplomats, preferably with prior experience not only in the crisis region itself, but also in the Brussels foreign policy machinery (Interviewee #13). Only in exceptional cases should an EUSR be a former politician, e.g. when calling upon a prominent trouble-shooter for high-ranking crisis management. Similarly, while of course a candidate's nationality or sex should not play a role, exceptions were established when it was recognized in 2006 that candidates from the then new member states should be nominated (Interviewees #3, 10, and 12) under the guise of 'equitable regional distribution' rather than proportionality (Interviewee #12). Additionally, with reference to UN Security Council Resolution 1325 on Women, Peace and Security, member states were encouraged to nominate more female candidates (cf. Council of the European Union 2007c, 3).

4.8.2 Result of reflection

Initially, member states were intimately involved in the selection of the first EUSRs, but once Javier Solana had assumed his post as High Representative and started to develop an interest in expanding his reach through the EUSRs (cf. subsection 4.2.2), national capitals became somewhat sidelined. Instead, the Brussels-based PSC gradually became more and more involved in order to control the process (Interviewee #16). However, when member states felt uncomfortable with simply rubber-stamping Solana's personnel proposal in the PSC before passing it to the Council for nomination, they demanded a more transparent process (Interviewee #6), which led to the complex multi-stage selection procedure in place today.

The European Parliament, on a side note, is not involved in the nomination of EUSRs although it would like to be (Interviewee #8). Calls for greater involvement, or at least more information about the selection process—sometimes echoed by the Commission—have so far been countered by the Presidency by referring to the Council's Treaty right (Interviewees #8 and 21; cf. Diedrichs 2004, 37–38).

As regards the professional background of an EUSR, different models have been applied over the years before the 'diplomats preferred' rule was established. Aldo Ajello, for example, was deliberately chosen because he used to be an active politician (a former Italian senator) and because of the merits he had earned as UN mediator in Mozambique (Interviewee #30). Other politicians include former EUSRs for Macedonia, François

---

of the Council Secretariat, and the Head of the Policy Unit (Interviewees #6, 7, and 16).

Léotard, for Sudan, Pekka Haavisto, and for Bosnia and Herzegovina, Paddy Ashdown as well as Christian Schwarz-Schilling. The majority of the remaining EUSRs have come from the diplomatic services of member states.

Those in favour of a more prominent figure argue that an EUSR should be a political animal rather than a fonctionnaire, because their work is extremely political, with hardly any other means at their disposal (Interviewees #16, 43, 46, and 48). In fact, when Léotard was about to leave, there was resistance to having a diplomat succeed him, yet there were no political candidates either (Interviewee #45). France, in turn, did have a candidate, Ambassador Alain Le Roy, and was furthermore willing to provide material support for office structures and security, so this proposal was eventually accepted (cf. subsection 1.3.2).

Others deplore the focus on people from the ministerial level and instead demand from EUSRs real experience on the ground and the willingness to accept working in a team under Solana's guidance rather than on their own (Interviewees #28 and 39; cf. Grevi 2007, 18). While personality can make a difference, it is structures that are ultimately important, they say, and these work better with someone who knows how foreign policy is crafted (Interviewee #28; cf. International Crisis Group 2005a, 44).

As CFSP evolved, former politicians have come to be regarded as too independent-minded, too unwilling to integrate themselves into the hierarchies to be considered for this job (Interviewees #28 and 39). Diplomats, in contrast, are trained to respect hierarchies: For example, different than his predecessor Ajello, EUSR Roeland van de Geer would, from his service in the foreign ministry, know—and accept—that a roving ambassador for the Great Lakes is subordinate to the Africa Director in the Council Secretariat (Interviewees #28, 29, and 30). Moreover, diplomats are of the same breed as the PSC ambassadors and therefore can win their trust more easily (Interviewee #12).

Another consideration that often speaks for diplomats is that EUSRs should be familiar with policy-making at the Brussels headquarters (Interviewees #13 and 46; cf. Jaanson 2008, 11). National politicians typically do not have such experience, thus their propensity to understand the intricacies of intra-EU competition is understandably limited (Interviewee #39), or they may lack the modesty that is advisable when dealing with the Commission (Interviewee #40). EUSR Kubiš had to become acquainted with the 'EU jungle' first (Interviewee #46). His colleague covering Bosnia and Herzegovina, Christian Schwarz-Schilling, felt he had no influence on how his mandate was decided upon, whereas his successor, Miroslav Lajčák, knew the inner EU workings already from his time as Solana's Personal Representative for the Montenegro referendum (Interviewee #32). Another positive and oft-cited example is that of Marc Otte who before becoming EUSR for the Middle East Peace Process worked as head of the Middle East task force in the Policy Unit. As a Belgian diplomat, he also benefits from a culture of cooperation with the Commission. Thus, he is well acquainted with both people and processes in Brussels (Interviewees #13, 16, and 39).

4.9 Lessons-learned seminars

Nine years after the Special Envoys were introduced, a first get-together of all EUSRs with the High Representative took place in Brussels in 2005, in the year when their number rose from six to nine. Inspired by national ambassador conferences, the aim was to exchange experiences and improve cooperation both among EUSRs and between them and their Brussels counterparts in the Secretariat.

4.9.1 Rewriting of rules

The first-ever EUSR meeting, organized in June 2005, followed a general and a particular aim. First and generally, the idea was to take stock of overall EU foreign policy and to discuss what the future priorities should be. Second and specifically, it aimed to reflect on and draw some 'lessons learned' from the EU's experiences with the EUSR instrument (Solana 2005b, 1). This "Seminar with EU Special Representatives," as it was timidly entitled, experienced a follow-up in 2006 (Interviewee #7). From 2007 onwards, 'lessons-learned seminars' as they were then called should be held every six months (Interviewees #16 and 17).

4.9.2 Result of reflection

The idea of having a joint seminar of all EUSRs was inspired by the national ambassadorial conferences that many a Council Secretariat staff knows from their own foreign service (Interviewees #10 and 17). Discussing both political and structural issues in such a setting was regarded as something entirely normal (Interviewee #17). The meeting itself gained prominence once there was a considerable number of EUSRs deployed in the field. By mid-2005, there were nine mandates, even though the EUSRs for Central Asia and Sudan were only nominated after the first seminar took place.

Although the United Nations had started a similar lessons-learned exercise with their SRSGs back in 2001, those familiar with the process stress that it was not a model to follow because of its academic character and limited practical relevance (Interviewee #36). Nonetheless, the EU's motivation to hold such a seminar was similar to the UN's: To promote networking and experience-sharing both among SRSGs and between them and senior staff (cf. subsection 2.1.2 and Fröhlich et al. 2006, 21). For this reason, a report on crisis management recommended a similar exercise to the EU (International Crisis Group 2005a, 38). The latter, however, insists on having had its own idea rather than having heeded someone else's call.

Chapter 5:
Organizational Learning at the
Operational and Ideational Level

The previous chapter explored instances of organizational learning that have altered the structural or procedural routines of the EU. Naturally, most of these were directed at the internal side of EU policy-making. This chapter will now focus on the operational and ideational level, thus bringing in—though not exclusively focusing on—the external dimension of the EUSRs' actions: What they do and where they operate, how they liaise with stakeholders and how they contribute to EU policies, including to the EU's own understanding of its strategic role in world affairs.

5.1 Tasks

Two main routines have emerged with regard to the tasks that an EUSR is asked to complete, i.e. what is written in the operational mandate of a Joint Action. One is to keep this mandate broad and open for a change of events on the ground and to do so deliberately rather than out of strategic weakness; the other is to gradually expand the EUSRs' range of tasks. The reasoning is that a broad mandate that can cover various situations means less work for the supervising authorities, so that only technical changes need to be made when necessary. Moreover, because EUSRs are already active in the field, it is natural to include new tasks if they arise.

5.1.1 Rewriting of rules

The mandates of EUSRs are extensively discussed before an initial Joint Action is issued, deliberately setting a broad framework and covering a vast area of political issues (Interviewees #9 and 31). Within this framework, EUSRs have the possibility to intervene with wide room for manoeuvre and as they see fit (Interviewees #3, 12, 31, and 36). While this was the case already in the early days of Ajello and Moratinos, what has changed is that today, such freedom is granted voluntarily and not out of a certain helplessness, when member states did not know how to deal differently with a conflict other than to send an envoy (cf. subsection 1.2.1).

In fact, the scope of EUSR activities can be anything within an international actor's external relations:

– From classical diplomatic activities, which are sometimes shared with the EU's first pillar, like contributions to the political process of the country or region concerned, extended regional and international cooperation, the supervision of human rights and the rule of law, or programmes under the pre-accession or neighborhood policy heading;

   –   To contributions to conflict prevention and crisis management, including through participation in peace negotiations, supervision of the implementation of international agreements, and the provision of political advice for ESDP missions;

   –   To providing input for EU policy-making, regarding the general strategy as well as new issues such as energy policy.

This broad list of tasks can be fitted into the different—generic—roles of the EUSRs presented at the outset of this study (cf. subsection 2.2.2). Two of them (obligation and visibility) refer to the EUSRs' factual presence, i.e. they are in operation by the envoys' mere existence and prior to whatever task these may be given.[289] The remaining six roles (analysis, proposals, and coordination on the internal side, and dissemination, activity, and cooperation on the external side) can serve as a framework to briefly summarize, in the following table, the broad range of the actual tasks that EUSRs fulfill.[290]

Table 4: Internal and External Roles of EUSRs—Empirical Evidence

Internal Roles	Analysis	General, e.g. through regular reporting	All mandates
		Issue-specific, e.g. rule of law, border control, security issues	Bosnia and Herzegovina, Macedonia, Moldova, South Caucasus, Sudan
	Proposals	General	Central Asia, Great Lakes (2002), Middle East Peace Process, Moldova, South Caucasus
		Issue-specific, e.g. energy, security sector reform, political reform, justice and home affairs	Afghanistan, Bosnia and Herzegovina, Central Asia (2007)
	Coordination	Overall coherence	Afghanistan, Bosnia and Herzegovina (2004), Central Asia, Great Lakes (2007), Macedonia, Moldova, Sudan
		Guidance/local political advice for ESDP and other operations	Afghanistan (2007), Bosnia and Herzegovina, Great Lakes (2005), Macedonia (2005), Middle East Peace Process (2005), South Caucasus (2004), Sudan

---

289 This notwithstanding, to ensure an '(active, effective or continued) EU presence' is at times written into the Joint Action, either as an objective (e.g. for the Great Lakes since 2003, cf. Council Joint Action 2003/869/CFSP of 8 December 2003) or as a task (e.g. for the Middle East Peace Process since 2002, cf. Council Joint Action 2002/965/CFSP of 10 December 2002).

290 The name of a country or region in a given field signifies that the respective task has been part of the EUSR's mandate for this area. A year in brackets indicates the time when this task was added to the mandate in those cases, where this had not been so from the outset.

External Roles	Dissemination	Liaise with all actors	All mandates
		Public diplomacy	Middle East Peace Process (2000), Great Lakes (2002), Bosnia and Herzegovina (2004)
	Activity	Political process, institution-building, elections	Afghanistan, Bosnia and Herzegovina (2004), Macedonia, Middle East Peace Process (2006), Moldova, South Caucasus, Sudan
		Conflict resolution, e.g. peace agreements, mediation	Central Asia, Great Lakes, Macedonia, Middle East Peace Process, Moldova, South Caucasus, Sudan
		Conflict Prevention	Central Asia, Middle East Peace Process, Moldova (2005), South Caucasus
		Security cooperation, rule of law, organized crime	Middle East Peace Process (1998), Macedonia, Bosnia and Herzegovina (2004)
		Community Programmes, e.g. CARDS,* ENP	Bosnia and Herzegovina (2004), Moldova (2006)
		Human rights situation and guidelines	Great Lakes (2004, 2007), Macedonia 2005), Bosnia and Herzegovina (2007), Central Asia (2007), Middle East Peace Process (2007), Moldova (2007), South Caucasus (2007), Sudan
	Cooperation	International collaboration, including multilateral conferences and other fora	Afghanistan, Central Asia, Great Lakes, Macedonia (overall coordination 2002), Middle East Peace Process (Quartet 2002), Moldova, South Caucasus, Sudan
		Regional dimension, neighboring countries	Afghanistan, Central Asia, Great Lakes (2002), Middle East Peace Process (2002), South Caucasus, Sudan

* The Community Assistance for Reconstruction, Development and Stabilization (CARDS) program is the framework for the disbursement of EC financial assistance to the Western Balkans for the period 2000–06 in support of the Stabilization and Association Process launched at the Zagreb summit in 2000. For a brief assessment, see Calic 2003.

Looking at the number of tasks by which the already broad mandates were supplemented in later years, this table confirms the increased involvement of the EUSR in European foreign policy (Grevi 2007, 146). At times, this is merely about changing seemingly insignificant wording, e.g. from 'assisting in' to 'contributing to' conflict management in the South Caucasus, demonstrating a greater interest on the side of the member states (Interviewee #27; European Commission 2006c, 39) or from an 'advisory' to a 'facilitating role' with regard to constitutional reform in Bosnia and Herzegovina (Interviewee #34). At other times, there are more substantial add-ons like the 'energy security and anti-narcotics aspects of the CFSP' that were recently included in the work of the EUSR for Central Asia, together with a broad responsibility for implementing the EU's new regional strategy.[291]

---

291 Council Joint Action 2007/634/CFSP of 1 October 2007.

Even if some issues are not formally included in the mandate, EUSRs have tended to simply incorporate such topics under their existing instructions as they come up (Interviewee #26). This was the case, for example, with water issues and migration in the case of Central Asia (Interviewee #46). Similarly, when the question of regional responsibility arose after the Juba peace talks ending conflict in Uganda, the two EUSRs for the Great Lakes and Sudan pragmatically solved the issue of who should cover the follow-up (Interviewee #31; Grevi 2007, 106).[292]

Looking at which kind of tasks have increased, one finds, besides a growing demand for policy proposals, that the internal coordination role has gained in importance, now often being written explicitly into the mandates (Interviewee #31). After passing the Central Asia strategy, EUSR Pierre Morel was mandated to "promote overall political coordination of the European Union in Central Asia and ensure consistency of the external actions of the European Union in the region."[293] His colleague in Moldova, Kálmán Miszei, has the authority to "maintain an overview of all European Union activities, notably the relevant aspects of the ENP Action Plan."[294] Most prominently, the EUSR for Bosnia and Herzegovina is now tasked "to contribute to reinforcement of internal EU coordination and coherence," inter alia through "chairing a coordination group composed of all EU actors present in the field [...] and through providing them with guidance on relations with the [Bosnian] authorities."[295] Also, the rise of ESDP missions and other operations launched within an EUSR's area of responsibility has increased the EUSR's coordination duties (Interviewees #24 and 39; cf. later section 5.3).

On the external side of EUSR tasks, some mandates have seen additions in terms of public diplomacy, greater involvement in institution-building, or increased focus on the regional dimension. Most significantly, this was the case with the mandates for Bosnia and Herzegovina, the Great Lakes, Moldova, and the Middle East Peace Process. Sometimes, this involves close operational coordination with the Commission. The EU's border mission in Moldova is a Commission-funded activity, not an ESDP operation, and its head of mission serves as political advisor to the EUSR (Interviewee #39). Likewise, responsibilities for the EU mission at the Palestinian-Egyptian border crossing in Rafah are shared between the EUSR and the Commission (Interviewee #12). In Congo, the EUSR has become the EU coordinator for security sector reform, partly because

---

292 Following this informal settlement, it was later written into the mandate of the EUSR for the Great Lakes to closely coordinate with this colleague for Sudan on matters of the Ugandan peace process (Article 3 (f), Council Joint Action 2007/112/CFSP of 15 February 2007).

293 The mandate is, of course, without prejudice to Community competence (Article 3 (1) a of Council Joint Action 2007/634/CFSP of 1 October 2007), a reference that was inserted upon insistence by the Commission, which saw itself sidelined (Rettman 2007).

294 Article 3 (2) of Council Joint Action 2007/107/CFSP of 15 February 2007.

295 Article 3 (e) of Council Joint Action 2007/87/CFSP of 7 February 2007. At the same time, adding substantive issues such as tackling organized crime or supporting the country's constitutional reform proved difficult, due to the delicate political balance between the envoy's powerful international and less elaborate European hat (Interviewee #34). In the end, however, on both issues the EUSR was given a sizeable role.

both the Council and the Commission saw this as part of their competence. In this dispute, the EUSR could provide a neutral territory and act as a buffer between the two institutions (Interviewee #29).[296] However, this role is an unofficial one, because when the EUSR once attempted to make it official, the institutions immediately rejected this (Interviewee #29).

Finally, another remarkable aspect is the addition of horizontal issues such as human rights and the role of women and children in armed conflicts. However, this has less to do with a specific focus on a particular region let alone an increased activity in this regard, but is rather part of an effort to mainstream these topics in all ESDP actions (Interviewee #15; cf. subsection 4.7.1).

5.1.2 Result of reflection

The EUSRs themselves have had a hands-on approach to their work from the beginning: For them, what is written in the mandate has been less important than how they would actually operate (Interviewees #22, 36, 47, and 48). They feel that it is better to have a broad mandate and then do whatever is necessary (Interviewee #39). This is particularly true in comparison to Commission delegations, which may have more competences and resources but are not endued with a flexible foreign policy mandate (Interviewee #32).

Within the Council and the Secretariat, consensus developed that mandates should be uncontroversial and should be kept broad enough so that the EUSR can react swiftly to events on the ground. Changing a mandate is avoided as much as possible, because this is a 'painful' process (Interviewee #39). Especially in a crisis situation, it is not always easy to achieve consensus among 27 member states to pass a new Joint Action (Interviewee #21). Thus, mandates are amended only when clear technical issues so require, such as when the 2005 guidelines introduced new reporting mechanisms (cf. subsection 4.3.1) or when an ESDP mission is placed within an EUSR's regional responsibility (cf. subsection 5.3.1).

In particular the increased inclusion of security-related tasks is, in part, a response to the developing needs on the ground. EU foreign policy is shifting away from a mere CFSP, e.g. a stand-alone ESDP mission, to a more comprehensive method of policy-making in which a variety of means are deployed to a crisis region. This is the case in particular for issues like Security Sector Reform (SSR) and security development that bring different strands of administration together and that nowadays make up the majority of EU activity in areas like the African Great Lakes and the South Caucasus. EUSRs usually are involved as one instrument of the "broad range of civilian and military instruments which are able to support SSR activities" (Council of the European Union 2006b, 3; Interviewee #40).[297]

---

296 The Council's 'Draft Conclusions on a Policy Framework for Security Sector Reform' of 2006 call upon "the Council and the Commission [to] ensure consistency between their activities in accordance with Article 3 of the TEU" (Council of the European Union 2006b, 3).

297 With regard to SSR, the EU relies on two concepts, one each from the Commission (European

5.2   Basis of operations of EUSRs

Contrary to the roving ambassadors from national foreign services to which they are sometimes likened, EU Special Representatives have not always had a clear home base. Different models have been tested over the years: They were based in Brussels, resident in their region, or they operated from their home country. Today, it has become an accepted routine that EUSRs should be located in Brussels and only in exceptional cases reside in their country of responsibility. The exception, however, makes up a third of all cases, i. e. three out of nine EUSRs. The reasons for this gradual establishment of a location rule have to do not only with greater control from the centre, but also with an easier relationship to national ambassadors in the field and a higher standing of the envoy in the eyes of third parties.

5.2.1   Rewriting of rules

The first rule rewritten was that there should be no more 'flying EUSRs', as the early EUSRs for the South Caucasus (Heikki Talvitie) and Moldova (Adriaan Jacobovits) were called (Interviewee #15). This was an established consensus already prior to their departure, and it was confirmed by the 2007 Guidelines: "All EUSRs are either based in the country/region ('field-based EUSR') or in Brussels ('Brussels-based EUSR')" (Council of the European Union 2007c, 6).

The second established practice became the tendency to base EUSRs in Brussels, from where they should travel both to their region and to third countries (Interviewee #9). As a consequence of this, field resources have gradually been increased, in particular for EUSRs that cover a group of countries (Interviewee #27; cf. Grevi 2007, 147).

5.2.2   Result of reflection

The two 'flying EUSRs' should be seen as part of the trial-and-error approach that was prevalent during much of the institutional build-up of EU foreign policy in general and the EUSRs in particular. When Talvitie was appointed EUSR in July 2003, it was initially his home country Finland which covered "exceptionally" the administrative expenditure.[298] However, the arrangement that Talvitie could work from Helsinki was retained even after his expenditure was moved to the Community budget half a year later.[299] Jacobovits, in 2005, chose a similar arrangement, even though his expenses were covered by Community funds from the beginning. By 2006, however, people in the Secretariat felt that EUSRs had little added value if they are headquartered neither in Brussels nor in their respective region (Interviewee #44; cf. International Crisis Group 2006b, 23).

Commission 2006a) and the Council (Council of the European Union 2005b), which together "constitute a policy framework for EU engagement [...], stressing the importance for the EU to take a comprehensive and cross-pillar approach to SSR." (Council of the European Union 2006b, 2).

298   Cf. Article 5 of Council Joint Action 2003/496/CFSP of 7 July 2003.

299   Cf. Article 5 of Council Joint Action 2003/872/CFSP of 8 December 2003.

This, in the end, comes back to the issue of central control from the Secretariat that was elaborated on above (cf. section 4.3).

Arguments that were made with regard to why EUSRs should principally be located in Brussels relate to both an internal and an external dimension. Within the EU, it became clear that non-resident EUSRs pose less conflict in particular with the heads of Commission delegations, as there is less confusion on the side of the host country about who represents the EU (Interviewee #8). This extends to the national ambassadors as well, for whom a resident EUSR would have to be a primus inter pares, something the latter find hard to accept (Interviewee #15). Also from the point of the EUSR him- or herself, there is reason to be closer to the decision-makers. Especially for someone coming from outside of the Brussels machinery, the EU's foreign policy represents a difficult terrain which cannot be understood from abroad (Interviewee #34).

In addition, the Brussels-based EUSR has a higher standing with local authorities: Travelling into and out of a country furthers their work by making them appear as honest brokers (Interviewee #9); their interventions, coming from the perceived higher level of envoy status, gain more political weight (Interviewees #11 and 15; Grevi 2007, 70); and their level is deemed higher than that of the local ambassadors (perhaps with the exception of certain member states), because they represent the whole European Union (Interviewee #17).[300] Conversely, a resident representative should be regarded as the most intrusive version of an EUSR (Interviewee #11).

These principled considerations aside, in each particular case there may be some compelling practical reasons that speak either for or against residency in a given country. A regional EUSR mandate (e.g. for the Great Lakes or the South Caucasus) generally forbids choosing one of the countries concerned for permanent residence (Interviewee #15); EUSRs with such a mandate are therefore usually based in Brussels. At the same time, the double-hat construction makes the EUSR's continued presence in the country necessary. Therefore, the EUSRs for Bosnia and Herzegovina and Macedonia are resident in their respective country.[301] In general, the specific experience from the Balkans underscores the importance of a permanent presence on the ground should the complex EU coordination work well (Grevi 2007, 116).

For all non-resident EUSRs, various field office arrangements have been tried, and usually expanded. Aldo Ajello started out in fact with a resident office in Addis Ababa

---

300 For some, this also speaks against a proliferation of Special Representatives: "If they were to be used so routinely that they were regarded as a substitute EU ambassador, responsible for the entirety of EU contacts with a region or country, potential effectiveness in crisis situations as a sign of EU priority and sense of urgency could be lost" (International Crisis Group 2005a, 43).

301 This rule is confirmed by the new EUSR for Kosovo who is double-hatted with the post of International Civilian Representative. It is, however, contradicted by the EUSR for Afghanistan who is the only resident EUSR without a double-hat. The new EUSR for the African Union, who is resident in Ethiopia, is a hybrid in this sense, because he both double-hatted and covers an entire region. No rule should therefore be seen as too binding.

before moving to Brussels after three months (Interviewee #15); later, the idea of an EUSR location in Kinshasa came up (Interviewee #29). In Central Asia, there is a resident political advisor in Almaty, collocated at the premises of the Commission. Although the main Commission delegation was moved to Astana, the new capital, like all the other embassies, the POLAD kept his base in the former capital Almaty, as it better allows him to pursue his regional mandate (Interviewee #26). The EUSR for the South Caucasus, in contrast, has one POLAD in each of the three capitals in the region (Interviewee #27), while the EUSR for Sudan also enjoys office support in Khartoum, Addis Ababa, and, most recently, in Juba in Southern Sudan (Interviewee #35; cf. Grevi 2007, 108).

5.3 EU political coordination

Over the years, EUSRs have learned to fill the intergovernmental coordination role bestowed upon them. This includes the habit of regularly meeting national ambassadors in the field, liaising with the heads of ESDP missions and paying frequent visits to member state capitals in order to discuss policy. This is based in part on an effective need to coordinate and prepare political decisions as well as on drawing on the UN model.

5.3.1 Rewriting of rules

Even in its external dimension, a great deal of the envoys' work is directed towards internal affairs, for example when the EUSRs have been established as the focal point of EU coordination in the field (Interviewee #44). This derived partly from the experiences made in the Balkans, where in Bosnia and Herzegovina and Macedonia a whole range of EU actors was working on the ground, often with little coordination. In Bosnia and Herzegovina, for example, the EU undertook a case study of EUSR-ESDP cooperation (Council of the European Union 2007a, para 41). As Grevi wrote in his stock-taking of EUSR activity: "The serious problems encountered in promoting coordination between different EU actors in [Bosnia and Herzegovina] triggered a useful, albeit late, lessons learned process [...] a noteworthy example of institutional learning" (Grevi 2007, 88).

The EUSR's coordinating function was codified in the 2007 guidelines that stipulated: "The EUSR will promote overall EU political coordination. He/she will help ensure that all EU instruments in the field are engaged coherently to attain the political objectives set out by the Council" (Council of the European Union 2007c, 6). This is most explicit in the case of Bosnia and Herzegovina, where coordination has become the "defining feature" of the EUSR's mandate, spelling out in detail how he should establish a "'centre of gravity' coordinating EU action" (Grevi 2007, 84).

Similarly, cooperation with national ambassadors had first emerged as an unwritten rule before being incorporated in the same set of guidelines. Non-resident EUSRs hold at least one meeting with national ambassadors (often including the Commission head of delegation) when they embark on a trip to the region (Interviewees #8, 15, 20, and 46).

Such an exchange of opinion could also possibly take place twice per trip: to receive local information prior to meeting the national authorities, and to brief ambassadors pursuant to these talks (Interviewees #15 and 19). The 2007 guidelines specified that the EUSR should provide regular briefings to member states' missions in the field, which in turn should make best efforts to assist the EUSR in the implementation of their mandate (Council of the European Union 2007c, 6). In a regional setting like Central Asia, this was spelled out in an innovative regional conference of EU heads of missions, organized by the EUSR in Astana in autumn 2006 and now held as an annual event (Grevi 2007, 125–6). In addition, many official meetings are attended in the troika format, bringing together the EUSR, the head of Commission delegation, and the Presidency ambassador (Interviewees #27 and 30).

Another instrument is that of establishing a 'core group' of member states with a particular interest in the country or region of concern, which can meet either in the field or in capitals. Aldo Ajello established such an informal group among the national ambassadors in the Great Lakes region (Interviewee #48). In Afghanistan, a country already crowded by the international presence, particular efforts were made to foster EU internal coordination on the ground (Grevi 2007, 73). The latter was complemented by a capital-based group, created by Francesc Vendrell, that meets once every three to four months (Interviewee #36).

Indeed, to travel to the capitals of interested member states in order to explain and discuss the European approach to their mandate area has become a regular activity of EUSRs. Enhancing such inclusiveness towards member states is by no means restricted to the 'usual suspects,' i.e. the big ones, but includes all those with a stake in the respective region (Interviewee #20).

5.3.2 Result of reflection

The 'consultation reflex' has evolved from a necessity in the beginning to an instrument of sound policy as much as politeness. When no common policy existed, EUSRs like Aldo Ajello had to construct an EU position from the bilateral talks they had both in Brussels and in the field (Interviewee #15). Today, there may be a common policy, but consultation with member states is still of prime importance. This not only extends to the larger ones that are usually involved but also to those that have a particular relation with the region, e.g. the Baltic states for Eastern Europe and the Caucasus, or the Nordic countries due to their large shares in development aid (Interviewee #19). It is even more imperative to informally tie ambassadors into the EUSR's activities for atmospheric reasons: As the envoy is, at the least, a primus inter pares, it becomes less interesting for national authorities to talk to bilateral ambassadors (Interviewees #29 and 45); involving them is thus also a sign of recognition. Such coordination is again in the interest of the EUSRs, because they need the ambassadors on board if they want their issues to make it through the Council (Interviewee #20).

Limiting the number of member states involved by forming a 'core group' was based on practical considerations as well as existing examples. Primarily, it followed naturally from the awareness that a meaningful policy discussion is not possible with 27 people around the table (Interviewee #36). In particular, it is important to integrate the more active member states in order to avoid sending conflicting messages (Interviewee #15). Moreover, there was the example of the UN: Already as SRSG for Mozambique, Aldo Ajello had established what he called a 'mini Security Council' of relevant UN member states whose representatives he met with and briefed regularly (Interviewee #48; cf. Peck 2004, 333). Similarly, Francesc Vendrell built on his previous experience as SRSG when modelling his core group after its UN equivalent called the 'group of friends of the Secretary-General' (Interviewee #36).

Finally, demand for coordination among EU actors as well as among member states grew with the number of ESDP operations (Interviewees #12 and 15; cf. next section). In the case of Bosnia and Herzegovina, for example, EU actors abound: The Presidency, the Commission head of delegation, the commanders of EUPM and EUFOR, plus the head of the European Agency for Reconstruction. In such a case, an EUSR with a strong backing from Solana and the PSC is needed for internal coordination (Interviewee #31). Also within an ESDP mission, the EUSR needs to coordinate personnel-contributing member states that want to have a say in the political dimension of the conflict. This was the case for security sector reform in Congo, where the EUSR first had to follow up on the material implementation of a political decision (Interviewee #15) and then, once national contributions were there and the mission operative, provide a certain presence for bilateral ambassadors to showcase their involvement (Interviewee #29).

5.4   ESDP chain of command

The increase of ESDP missions in the regions of responsibility of an EUSR gradually led to an inclusion of the Special Representatives into the chain of command, where they should provide political guidance to heads of mission and ensure overall coordination. However, this rule was fundamentally changed in 2007 when the EU established the Civilian Planning and Conduct Capability (CPCC) at the Council Secretariat in Brussels. This new body took over control of civilian ESDP and placed the EUSRs back outside of the chain of command. The rationale for inserting the EUSRs into the chain in the first place has much to do with striving for coherence, while the most recent decision is based on considerations of the EUSRs' lack of appropriate police or military expertise and the need to reduce the complexity of their mandates.

5.4.1   Rewriting of rules

As for how rules have changed gradually over the years towards an inclusion of EUSRs into the chain of command, the case of Bosnia and Herzegovina is instructive. Not only was the EU Police Mission there the EU's first-ever civilian crisis management operation under ESDP, but it was also conceived jointly with a new EUSR mandate (cf. subsection 1.3.1). The respective mandates of March 2002 stipulated that the Special Representative's position in the unified chain of command is to deliver reports from the police commissioner to the SG/HR and to pass on the latter's guidance to the police commissioner,[302] granting the EUSR "authority to give direction, as necessary, to the Head of Mission/Police Commissioner" of EUPM.[303] Thus, within the overall EU co-ordination with which the EUSR was entrusted, a special emphasis was put on providing a link to ESDP instruments on the ground (Grevi 2007, 83).

This model of providing political guidance to heads of mission was largely followed in later cases of ESDP operations, such as the Police Mission in Macedonia (EUPOL Proxima);[304] the EU police and security sector reform missions in the DRC (EUPOL Kinshasa and EUSEC RD Congo);[305] the EU Coordinating Office for Palestinian Police Support (EUPOL COPPS);[306] the rule of law mission EUJUST Themis in Georgia;[307] and the EU's civilian-military supporting action to the African Union mission in the Darfur region of Sudan (AMIS).[308] It furthermore became enshrined in the Council's "EU Concept for ESDP support to Security Sector Reform" of 2005, which stipulated that "[when] an ESDP action in support of SSR occurs in an area where an EUSR is in place, the EUSR should ensure the overall political co-ordination of EU's actions on the ground" (Council of the European Union 2005b, 18). By 2006, it was therefore fair to say that a pattern had emerged in EU civilian crisis management where the Head of Mission reports to the HR/SG through the EUSR with political guidance flowing in the opposite direction, from the PSC through the EUSR to the Head of Mission (Hansen 2006, 36).

For military operations the language was different, although the task was similar. Most importantly, the military chain of command is separate, with political control and strategic direction exercised by the PSC on behalf of the Council, and military direction provided by the EU Military Committee. This is the case, for example, of EUFOR in Bosnia and Herzegovina,[309] which even has its own legal basis deriving from Annex 1a of the Dayton Agreement (Interviewee #32). Still, the EUSR retains his task to ensure overall EU political coordination in Bosnia and Herzegovina by chairing a coordination group composed of all EU actors present in the field, including the EU Force Commander. The latter "shall, without prejudice to the chain of command, take EUSR local political advice into account, especially with regard to matters for which the EUSR has

---

302   Articles 6 and 7 of Council Joint Action 2002/210/CFSP of 11 March 2002.

303   Article 2 (3) of Council Joint Action 2002/211/CFSP of 11 March 2002.

304   Cf. Council Joint Action 2003/870/CFSP of 8 December 2003.

305   Cf. Council Joint Action 2005/586/CFSP of 28 July 2005.

306   Cf. Council Joint Action 2005/796/CFSP of 14 November 2005.

307   Cf. Council Joint Action 2004/532/CFSP of 28 June 2004.

308   Cf. Council Joint Action 2005/556/CFSP of 18 July 2005.

309   Cf. Articles 6 and 8 of the mandate for EUFOR in Bosnia and Herzegovina, Council Joint Action 2004/570/CFSP of 12 July 2004.

a particular or stated role, and shall, within his/her mandate, endeavour to take into account any request from the EUSR."[310]

With the creation of the CPCC in the second half of 2007, a new civilian command structure was established in Brussels (cf. subsection 1.4.1) and EUSRs have formally been removed from the chain of command. Now, both the Civilian Operations Commander as head of the CPCC—a function previously exercised by the head of DG IX within the Council Secretariat (Interviewee #31)—and the Military Operations Commander, the Director-General of the EU Military Staff, will report directly to the High Representative (Grevi 2007, 38). The EUSR is left with providing "local" (rather than general) political guidance to the head of mission or force commander (Council of the European Union 2007c, 7); he is no longer in the line of reporting, and operational command rests with the CPCC (Interviewee #8). The new rules notwithstanding, any head of mission is well advised to cooperate closely with the EUSR in the field, who remains responsible for the basic political approach to a country or region (Interviewee #31). In Afghanistan, for example, the EUSR not only gives local political guidance, but he and the Brussels-based Civilian Operation Commander "shall consult each other as required."[311]

5.4.2 Result of reflection

Reflection that prompted the gradual inclusion of EUSRs into the chain of command is in line with the demand for external coherence, in particular within the second pillar. EUSRs provide a layer of political coverage that is "closer to local dynamics" (Grevi 2007, 37). Again, the Bosnian case is emblematic, because it shows the strong link between an EUSR and an ESDP mission right from their conception (Interviewee #38). This double-hat was created, because, functionally speaking, the High Representative as an international official could not be in the EU chain of command (Interviewee #44). Moreover, there was the example of the UN, where a peacekeeping mission is placed under the civilian SRSG. This model, however, has never been fully taken up at the EU due to reservations of some member states' military leaders to put their commander under local civilian control (Interviewees #8 and 40). Still, from an institutional point of view, it did make sense to establish a proper relation between two field entities that receive guidance from the PSC and the High Representative.

With the increase of ESDP missions and the additional tasks conferred upon EUSRs,[312] exercising control over these operations soon became overwhelming, especially because EUSRs were not specialists in either security or police affairs (Interviewee #29). More-

---

310 Article 7 of Council Joint Action 2004/570/CFSP of 12 July 2004.

311 Article 1 of Council Joint Action 2007/732/CFSP of 13 November 2007; see also Council Joint Action 2007/733/CFSP of 13 November 2007 for the respective changes to the mandate of EUPOL Afghanistan.

312 Usually, mandate amendments take the form of adding to the list of tasks the EUSR should fulfil; cf. section 5.1.

over, the specific delineation of tasks of the different layers in the command structure proved controversial (Grevi 2007, 38). This at times provoked personality clashes as it did in Afghanistan between the EUSR and the Head of EUPM (Dempsey 2007). In an effort to reduce complexity, it was therefore agreed to remove the EUSRs from the chain of command (Interviewee #8), and, after some fierce fighting, to add a phrase on 'providing local political advice' into their mandates (Interviewee #31).

5.5 External cooperation

Even though most instances of organizational learning reported on so far focused on the improvement of internal processes, such internal streamlining and coordination should also be seen as a precondition for successful collaboration with external actors. In addition to that, learning took place directly in the field of external cooperation. The main rule that has been established here is that EUSRs should participate in international fora for conflict resolution. This is based on the EU's multilateral understanding as much as on its motivation to enhance its international actorness.

5.5.1 Rewriting of rules

From the first mandates in 1996 to the present day, and reconfirmed by general guidelines, EUSRs have systematically engaged with international partners. It was Ajello's first and foremost task to "to support the efforts of the UN and the OAU,"[313] just as his colleague Moratinos should "establish and maintain close contact with all the parties to the peace process, other countries of the region, the United States and other interested countries, as well as relevant international organizations, in order to work with them in strengthening the peace process."[314] This principle was additionally recorded by the 2003 set of guidelines, which—in a very general way, admittedly—stipulated that EUSRs should "liaise with other international and regional actors in the field" (Council of the European Union 2003b, 7).

Today, many EUSRs work through, and sometimes even in explicit support of, international organizations as well as informal fora, as increased reference to international coordination in the different mandates demonstrates:

–   The EUSR for Afghanistan shall "support the pivotal role played by the UN, notably the Special Representative of the Secretary-General" and, jointly with the Commission, "actively participate in the Joint Coordination and Monitoring Board," the body uniting 21 countries and institutions that supervise implementation of the Afghanistan Compact;[315]

---

313 Council Joint Action 96/250/CFSP of 25 March 1996.

314 Council Joint Action 96/676/CFSP of 25 November 1996.

315 Council Joint Action 2007/106/CFSP of 15 February 2007.

- In Moldova, the EUSR is asked to work "in close coordination with the OSCE, representing the European Union through appropriate channels and in agreed fora and by developing and maintaining close contacts with all relevant actors;"[316]
- The EUSR for Central Asia, a region with a high degree of international involvement as of recent, shall "develop appropriate contacts and cooperation with the main interested actors in the region, and all relevant regional and international organizations, including the Shanghai Cooperation Organisation (SCO), the Eurasian Economic Community (EURASEC), the Conference on Interaction and Confidence-Building Measures in Asia (CICA), the Collective Security Treaty Organisation (CSTO), the Central Asia Regional Economic Cooperation Program (CAREC) and the Central Asian Regional Information and Coordination Centre (CARICC);"[317]
- The mandate for the Middle East Peace Process asks the EUSR to "facilitate and maintain close contact with all the parties to the Middle East peace process, other countries of the region, members of the Middle East Quartet and other relevant countries, as well as the UN and other relevant international organizations."[318] Indeed, at the envoy level of the Quartet, EUSR Moratinos is the only EU voice at the table, whereas at the principals' level, both the High Representative for CFSP and the Commissioner for External Relations meet with the Foreign Ministers of Russia and the United States and with the UN Secretary-General.

Multilateral coordination is even more institutionalized in countries that are partly regulated, or at least heavily influenced by, an internationally negotiated peace agreement, such as Bosnia and Herzegovina, Macedonia, and Sudan.[319] Just to give one example, in Macedonia, where early on the United States had left the lead to the Europeans (Interviewee #45) the resident EUSR is responsible for coordinating the efforts of the international community at large.[320] Hence, he holds weekly meetings with the 'security principals' (i.e. the heads of international actors active in the field of security, e.g. the U.S., NATO, and OSCE) and fortnightly meetings with the heads of all international organizations in the country (Interviewee #24; Grevi 2007, 93–94).

5.5.2 Result of reflection

Acting as the face and voice of the Union in international crisis management efforts has been a constant feature of EUSR work, and one of the prime motivations to dispatch them in the first place (cf. sections 1.2 and 4.1). Being represented as an international player alongside other established actors serves the Union's motivational interest. The EU uses international fora to inform about its—common (if there is one)—policy as

---

316 Council Joint Action 2007/107/CFSP of 15 February 2007.

317 Council Joint Action 2007/634/CFSP of 1 October 2007.

318 Council Joint Action 2007/110/CFSP of 15 February 2007.

319 The respective agreements are the Dayton Agreement for Bosnia and Herzegovina, the Ohrid Agreement for Macedonia, and the Comprehensive Peace Agreement for Southern Sudan as well as the Darfur Peace Agreement for Sudan's Western province.

320 See Art. 3 (c) of Council Joint Action 2002/963/CFSP of 10 December 2002.

well as to influence ongoing deliberations (Interviewee #3). By closely coordinating with or even working through such gatherings, it can project its interest less openly (Interviewee #27). Therefore, part of the increased international intertwining is a result of this motivation.

In addition, such international cooperation suits the EU's multilateral longing. In most cases, the EU arrived at the table when the conflict had been going on for a while, so that international organizations (in addition to some individual countries) were already in the lead. This was the case initially in the Great Lakes, which already by 1996 felt a sort of 'envoy fatigue' (Lautze et al. 1998, 88–89), and the Middle East, but also in the South Caucasus, where the OSCE has been an important player dealing with the conflict in South Ossetia (Interviewee #27). It was thus consequential for the EU to support the ongoing multilateral activities and liaise with actors in the field rather than try to push through its own approach.

5.6 Policy input

The tasks of EUSRs have been considerably broadened not only in general terms, as the previous sections have shown, but also in a particular area most relevant for the EU's actions on the international scene: policy formulation. While it is generally acknowledged that some EUSRs were initially deployed because the EU did not have a policy in place for a given country or region, this ideational routine has now changed to actively demand policy input from them. The latter can come in direct form as explicit recommendations, or it may be transmitted more indirectly through continuous reporting and analysis from the field. Reflections about the need to improve the amount and quality of information available as well as to harmonize policy analysis led to this change of routines.

5.6.1 Rewriting of rules

Today's routines stipulate that an EUSR should be sent to a crisis region as an expression of an existing or as an active contribution to a future policy, rather than as a substitute for one (Interviewees #10, 16, and 31). If a policy is not yet in place, the EUSR should first co-develop the EU's approach and then help to implement it (Interviewee #31). This policy-input function of the EUSRs was made explicit in the 2001 annual CFSP report of the Council to the EP (Council of the European Union 2002a, 37). It is also formulated explicitly in some of the mandates:

- From its inception, the mandate for Central Asia tasked the EUSR to "assist the Council in further developing a comprehensive policy towards Central Asia;"[321]
- In the South Caucasus, the EUSR shall "assist the Council in further developing a comprehensive policy towards the [region];"[322]

---

321 Council Joint Action 2005/588/CFSP of 28 July 2005.

322 Council Joint Action 2007/111/CFSP of 15 February 2007; this formulation has been retained in

- The EUSR for the Middle East Peace Process shall "report on the possibilities for European Union intervention in the peace process and on the best way of pursuing European Union initiatives and ongoing Middle East peace process-related European Union efforts;"[323]
- Likewise, the EUSR for Moldova is mandated to "assist in the further development of the EU's policy towards the Republic of Moldova and the region, in particular regarding conflict prevention and conflict resolution;"[324]
- In 2002, the Council added to the list of tasks of the EUSR for the Great Lakes that he should "report on the possibilities for European Union intervention in the peace process and on the best way of pursuing European Union initiatives."[325]

What has thus emerged is that EUSRs, in particular through their regular reporting, are now accepted as focal points for producing policy proposals with relevance to their mandate areas (Interviewee #17). Their accounts, both in written form via COREU and orally to the PSC and the Council working groups, are an important factor in fine-tuning policy (Interviewee #10). Some EUSR teams, with their knowledge of what a desk officer in a foreign ministry needs, have taken to writing short input briefs more regularly, e.g. once a month. They have seen that in this way, they can push topics onto the agenda (Interviewee #33). In particular the EUSRs' biannual implementation reports contain concrete policy proposals, sometimes pre-planned with certain member states so that these can refer to the report at the PSC (Interviewees #12 and 20). Finally, in order to provide input at the highest level as well, EUSR should be systematically involved in both visits abroad and meetings in Brussels that the High Representative or the Presidency hold (Grevi 2007, 43).

5.6.2 Result of reflection

In the EUSRs' early days, devising a common EU position for either the Great Lakes or the Middle East Peace Process was more puzzle work than policy formulation. Ajello identified the policies of key member states, trying to bridge the gap by looking for the nuances between national positions, and to come up with a proposal that was acceptable to all (Interviewees #40 and 48; Ajello 2000, 118). Given the often-diametric positions of former colonial powers like France, Belgium, and the UK (Interviewee #48; cf. section 1.1.1), this clearly was not an easy task. Yet Ajello succeeded, and for the first time member states received a regular stream of political analysis from an EU source in the field (Grevi 2007, 113).

The regular flow of information from the field, tailored to the particularities of intergovernmental decision-making, has thus been a valuable contribution to policy formulation. EUSRs occupy themselves full-time with a particular dossier and often provide a

---

all following mandates. Cf. also Grevi 2007, 57.

323 Council Joint Action 2002/965/CFSP of 10 December 2002.

324 Council Joint Action 2005/265/CFSP of 23 March 2005.

325 Council Joint Action 2002/962/CFSP of 10 December 2002.

regional perspective, different from the national ambassadors (Interviewee #17). Their input also helps to bring all member states to the level of information that the Commission has from the reporting provided by its own delegations (Interviewee #33). This is an important factor when, in Brussels, the Commission and Council working groups or the PSC sit together in the various regional task forces and develop a common policy (Interviewee #16). In Moldova and the South Caucasus, for example, there was no EU policy in place, but the Commission was already fairly engaged. In such cases, the EUSRs make significant contributions to policy development at the EU level (Interviewees #17 and 44).

An additional motivation behind this change of routines was to harmonize political analysis throughout the second pillar, in Brussels as much as in national capitals. EUSRs usually have better access to and therefore more privileged information from local authorities, which they share with the heads of member state missions so that the reporting from national ambassadors reflects this knowledge (cf. subsection 5.3.2). Then, input continues to circulate from the PSC, where ambassadors are "quite appreciative" of such contributions to their debates (Grevi 2007, 45), to member state capitals (ibid, 46). In the end, this renders policy-making easier in Brussels, because it helps to unify the views of the member states (Interviewee #17). Once an actual policy is in place, this in return is an asset to the EUSR himself, as it bolsters his standing vis-à-vis his local counterparts (Interviewee #27).

5.7 Deliberate use of envoys

Over the years, the EU has learned how and when to use envoys in a deliberate, calculated way as time-bound crisis management tools. Officials stress that it should be within the flexibility of member states represented in the Council to either dispatch new EUSRs or retract old ones. An actual phasing out of the mandate was seriously considered in the case of the Great Lakes, before the EU reengaged there with operation Artemis, and in Macedonia, where the double-hat was invented instead. An additional motivation for the 'flexibility rule' was the fact that member states have become wary of the institutional power accumulated by the regular adding of new and continuous prolonging of existing EUSR mandates.

5.7.1 Rewriting of rules

The considerable increase in the numbers of EUSRs due to the EU's learning about their usefulness (cf. section 4.2) was accompanied—or even balanced—by the emergence of an unwritten rule: EUSRs are but a tool that can be employed and suspended according to need. As instruments of crisis management, EUSRs should have time-bound mandates and should not become an institution in its own right (Interviewee #16). The question of whether or not to send an EUSR should be a case-by-case decision (Interviewee #12), and there should be no self-perpetuating mandates (Interviewee #15).

By sending new 'envoys' that are neither labelled nor appointed as EUSRs, the Council has confirmed its flexibility to respond differently to different crises (Interviewee #12). Because sending an EUSR in practice does imply a mid- to long-term commitment, the Council opted for the more suitable impromptu deployment of envoys in the cases of Kosovo and Myanmar in 2007 (cf. subsection 1.4.3). While somewhat new to the EU, this recent tendency to resort to flexible ad hoc arrangements of representatives is nothing new for people who are acquainted with the normal operations of any ministry of foreign affairs (Interviewees #12 and 19).

5.7.2 Result of reflection

After the first EUSRs had been around for a number of years, member states began wondering about the lever they had when they wanted to end a mandate (Interviewee #31). This was, as it happened, a political question, because from a practical or even legal standpoint, they had the power to cease any mandate simply by not extending it any longer. For example, in the first years of this decade, there was serious discussion in the Secretariat about terminating the mandate of the EUSR for the Great Lakes region. However, after Mobutu was thrown out of power and following the first ESDP mission in Congo, decision-makers in Brussels from Solana on downwards learned to revalue this tool (Interviewee #31; cf. subsection 4.2.2). Today, the EU is engaged in a much more intensive way, which also implies that it could not simply withdraw its envoy without major upheavals (Interviewee #31).

The discussion about mandate termination as such underlined once more that EUSRs should only be kept as long as there is a need on the ground, even though they are not dispatched as a short-term intervention in the first place. In the case of the Great Lakes, for example, it is has been repeatedly made clear that the mandate should be limited to the duration of the UN mission there as a reliable indication of how long EU involvement is needed (Interviewee #15). Furthermore, these considerations were also an element of the motivation to introduce evaluation measures in 2003 (cf. subsection 4.7.1). Yet, while it is recognized that Special Representatives should have special functions and that their job should be over at some point (Interviewees #40 and 43), it has also become clear that implementation of an EUSR mandate needs time and flexibility (Interviewees #3 and 31).

Today, officials insist that the Brussels agenda is determined by the member states, taking into account the events on the ground, and not by the EUSRs themselves (Interviewee #31). This also includes flexibility in scaling down the mandate, or merging it with other instruments, as needed (Interviewee #15). This was the case in Macedonia, where after initially debating the closure of the EUSR office, it was instead merged with the EC head of delegation and the double-hat was created (see next section). As a consequence, it can be said that the EUSRs today are used in a rather conscious way (Interviewee #8).

5.8   Double-hatting

Today, it is an accepted ideational routine that double-hatting can be beneficial for a coherent political impact, though it is not regarded as a 'one-size-fits-all' model. The most prominent case of double-hatting is the intra-EU model where an EUSR combines, in his or her personal capacity, both the responsibility of head of Commission delegation and of a CFSP-related mandate with regard to a certain country or region. In 2005, the mandate for the EUSR in Macedonia was amended so as to accommodate for the inclusion of such a personal union. This model was confirmed by reports from the European Commission and Parliament. It reflected the desire for more pillar-spanning coherence in general, and the awareness of hitherto poor EU coordination in Macedonia as well as the aim to scale down EUSR involvement in particular. In addition, there are instances of international double-hatting, i. e. when the second responsibility is one of international supervision, and intra-CFSP double-hatting, for example when the head of an ESDP component is also an advisor to the EUSR.

The learning associated with the development of intra-EU double-hatting spans all forms of organizational routines: It is structural, because it creates, if only quantitatively small, a body that works across the pillar divide; it is procedural in the sense that reporting lines and coordination mechanisms are entirely new; it is operational in the way 'Mr. Europe' acts towards partners; and it affects ideational routines by symbolizing a policy shift from conflict prevention and crisis management to integration and eventual EU membership of the country. In sum, it also symbolizes the EU's wish to appear as a unitary actor and speak with one voice; for this reason, it is considered under the 'ideational' heading here.

5.8.1   Rewriting of rules

While for a long time it was inconceivable to unite first and second pillar competencies in one post, the parallel nomination of Erwan Fouéré as head of Commission delegation and EUSR proved the opposite. This was a "pilot-innovation" (Grevi 2007, 48) that had in fact been recommended by Fouérés predecessor, EUSR Michael Sahlin (House of Lords 2006, 20). At the heart of the matter, there is a personal union, i. e. one person fulfilling two different tasks, or wearing two different hats (Interviewee #24). The amalgamation therefore does not go much beyond the personal level with separate competencies remaining in the CFSP and in the Community field, respectively (Grevi 2007, 48)—a point that will be of importance later.

Although the model character of the new arrangement for other posts was questioned, not least by the Council, the idea was soon taken up in a number of reports and evaluations. The European Parliament particularly welcomed the arrangement, because it brought the EUSR function more closely under Community—and therefore also parliamentary—control. The report by the EP's external relations committee (AFET) on CFSP developments in 2005 consequently calls for an automatic attribution of the functions of all existing country-specific EUSRs to the respective Head of the EU Delegation in that country (European Parliament 2007, para. 8, indent i). This would make the Macedonian case a model for at least all non-regional mandates.

The Commission is less vocal than Parliament in pushing for more double-hatting (Interviewee #16), although the Macedonian model was also featured sympathetically in its communication 'Europe in the World' of 2006 (European Commission 2006b). This report looked—from the Commission's perspective—at practical improvements in strategic planning and cooperation at EU headquarters and in the field, notably within the scope of the existing Treaties. It was timely published at the end of the post-referenda reflection phase and as a follow-up to the October 2005 Hampton Court Summit, which had tasked both the High Representative and the President of the Commission to enhance cooperation on external relations (Grevi 2007, 36). The report asked Council and Commission to propose double-hatting where appropriate, and called upon the two, explicitly drawing on the "positive experience of double-hatting in Skopje," "to unite the EU's presence as far as possible in Sarajevo and Pristina" (European Commission 2006b, 9).

The House of Lords in London prominently considered the Commission's proposals, including by looking at the practice of double-hatting. The Lords heard evidence inter alia from Ambassador Cutileiro from the Commission, one of the main authors of the 2006 Communication, Director-General Robert Cooper from the Council Secretariat, and double-hatted EUSR Erwan Fouéré (House of Lords 2006). They recommended active consideration of "extending this model on a case-by-case basis and adapting it to other situations where a Commission delegation and EUSR are on the ground in the same city, country or region" (ibid, 23).

Most recently, the principle of personal union was confirmed by the call for applications for the (double-hatted) Head of the EU [sic!] Delegation to the African Union, a post combining the functions of Head of Delegation of the EC to the AU, appointed by the Commission, and EUSR to the AU, appointed by the Council. It explicitly spells out that the "individual concerned will work under the authority and operational direction of the Secretary-General/High Representative for the CFSP [...] as far as his/her tasks as EUSR are concerned, and under the authority and operational direction of the European Commission as far as his/her tasks of Head of the EC Delegation are concerned" (Council of the European Union/European Commission 2007, 1).

As these examples show, a consensus rule has now been established that the experience of double-hatting has been rather positive (cf. Grevi 2007, 97), a judgement that is not limited to the intra-EU model but extends to other arrangements too. 'Intra-CFSP' double-hatting exists in the case of the EU border mission in Moldova and the EU support mission to AMIS in Sudan. In addition, the so-called 'international double-hat' from Bosnia and Herzegovina was most recently extended to the mandate for Kosovo. The method of double-hatting has thus become engrained in the EU's organizational routines.

5.8.2 Result of reflection

In Macedonia, two related developments brought about the thinking of a double-hat: The great number of European institutions present on the ground and the increased difficulty in distinguishing between the EUSR's crisis management mandate and the Commission's work under the SAP. The presence of the entire EU bureaucracy in the wake of the 2001 crisis, including programmes run by the European Agency for Reconstruction and under the CARDS programme, resulted in poor coordination of EU policies in the field (Interviewees #8, 10, 16, and 43). While some such tensions could be expected due to the novelty of ESDP missions, "intra-EU turf wars in FYROM, and back at Headquarters in Brussels, proved particularly serious" (Grevi 2007, 94). The overload of EU institutions created not only confusion on the part of the local interlocutors, but also an opportunity for the latter to play one EU actor against the other (Interviewees #10, 16, and 24; cf. House of Lords 2006, 20). In addition, there was confusion about which institution was doing what. At the beginning, the EUSR assisted in political processes and the implementation of the Ohrid agreement. However, after the country had actually made some progress, by 2005 the membership perspective became the centre of attention also for the EUSR, and the lines between him and the Commission blurred (Interviewee #11).

In this situation of an excess of EU institutions and lack of clarity about their different tasks, it was conceivable, and debated, to phase out the EUSR in order to reduce complexity on the ground. The Council, at least initially, indeed wanted to terminate the mandate of then-EUSR Sahlin (Interviewee #25). This was mirrored in the mandate review of May 2004, in which the Western Balkans working party of the Council Secretariat reported that "if positive developments in the country continued, there could be room for a discussion about a possible exit strategy at the next evaluation of the EUSR's mandate" (Council of the European Union 2004d, 2). Phase-out would also coincide with the view of many in the European Parliament who did not and still do not see the need for an EUSR in an SAP-participating country but consider his presence as rather worn out (Interviewees #16 and 43).[326] The Macedonian authorities, in contrast, asked for him to stay so that they could use his presence to exert pressure in internal negotiations about political reform (Interviewee #25).

Double-hatting then appeared as quite an attractive option that would allow the Union to scale down high-level involvement without phasing out the Council's presence in total (Interviewees #11 and 17). As a response to the practical problem of reducing the number of interlocutors, it furthermore helped to convey a single policy line (Interviewee #16; House of Lords 2006, 20). Conveniently, in autumn 2005, tenure of the Commission Head of Delegation was about to finish, and EUSR Michael Sahlin had asked for his mandate to end. This made it possible to bring in an entirely new person,

---

326 This question is considered differently by different actors, according to their political interests: Others regard having a CSFP instrument like an EUSR in a candidate country not as a legal contradiction but merely a philosophical one—and therefore have less difficulties with such an arrangement (Interviewee #11).

avoiding any political signal by having either of the two taking over the job of the other (Interviewee #25).

Beyond the borders of Macedonia, the pillar-spanning double-hat was also of importance for the debate about a potential EU foreign minister. Discussions about the change of mandate for the EUSR ran parallel to the European Convention and the subsequent unsuccessful ratification process. By combining the political authority of the EUSR for Macedonia with the economic assistance programmes of the Commission for that country (Interviewee #17; cf. section 4.3), this new arrangement on the ground was a means to further develop the double-hatting concept for the future foreign minister (Interviewees #17, 19, and 45; cf. Smyth 2005).[327]

The Bosnian double-hat, in contrast, was based on reflections about intra-CFSP coordination as well as international cooperation. As mentioned previously (cf. subsections 1.3.2 and 5.3.1), the EUSR mandate was explicitly designed to establish a unified EU chain of command from EUPM to Javier Solana by way of the international High Representative (cf. Grevi 2007, 83). Initially, some member states were sceptical about strengthening the already considerable powers of the international community's Office of the High Representative (OHR) with an additional EU mandate (Jaanson 2008, 9). Yet those who favoured close coordination, including with Commissions activities, prevailed with the idea "to provide maximum coordination between the peace process and the EU police mission, as well as the EU's overall Stabilization and Association Process in Bosnia" (International Crisis Group 2002, 9). In addition, the arrangement was thought to underline the European dimension of the international reconstruction effort in the country.

5.9 The EU's strategic role

The European Union aims to play a strategic role at the global level. It has done so ever since the Nine Foreign Ministers solemnly affirmed, in 1973, a 'European Identity in Relation to the World' (European Community 1973).[328] Even so, it formally acquired the instruments necessary for such a role only with the launch of CFSP twenty years later. To achieve a truly political (as opposed to merely economic) role in the international arena can therefore be regarded as a principal rule in EU foreign policy. This rule has been confirmed, including by the work of the EUSRs. It is reflected by considerations

---

327 With the renewed impetus from the passing of the Lisbon Treaty in 2007, the same can be said of the double-hat for the AU, even though no one would say so in public (Interviewee #12); for more on the EUSRs' model function for the EEAS, see subsection 7.3.2 in the conclusion.

328 In this Declaration on European Identity, the Nine stated: "European unification is not [...] inspired by a desire for power. [...] The Nine intend to play an active role in world affairs and thus to contribute, in accordance with the purposes and principles of the United Nations Charter, to ensuring that international relations have a more just basis; that the independence and equality of States are better preserved; that prosperity is more equitably shared; and that the security of each country is more effectively guaranteed" (European Community 1973, part II no. 9).

of the particular instruments EU crisis management disposes of, and the function of the EU as a model for reconciliation.

5.9.1 Rewriting of rules

The EUSRs' work has not quite revised but rather reconfirmed the rules of European strategic involvement in global affairs, so in this particular case the definition of learning as a 'rewriting of rules' might not be taken too literally.[329] The EU likes to portray itself as a 'different' power, while the latter is usually qualified as soft, normative, or civilian[330]—as illustrated by recent remarks of the EU Commissioner for External Relations, Benita Ferrero-Waldner, who said: "The EU will become an ever more powerful force for the good in tackling the world's trouble spots. [...The] sort of power we aspire to [is] neither exclusively soft, nor hard, but rather—smart power" (Ferrero-Waldner 2007).

At the broadest level, this ambitious understanding of the EU's global influence is symbolized by the European Security Strategy of 2003, which stipulates: "The European Union is inevitably a global player [...]. Europe should be ready to share in the responsibility for global security and in building a better world. [...] An active and capable European Union would make an impact on a global scale. In doing so, it would contribute to an effective multilateral system leading to a fairer, safer and more united world" (European Council 2003, 1 and 14). This universal approach is translated into regional strategies like the ones for Africa or Central Asia (Council of the European Union 2005c and European Council 2007), and even into country-specific ones like for Bosnia and Herzegovina (European Council 2004b).

More specifically then, the mandates of the EUSRs list the EU's policy objectives with regard to the country or region where they are dispatched, and to whose fulfillment their work should contribute. These objectives centre on the following aspects: The peaceful settlement of conflicts with the help of multilateral institutions; the establishment of stable, peaceful, and pluralistic societies through political reforms (rule of law, democratisation, human rights, and good governance) and economic development; regional cooperation and good neighborly relations; as well as enhancing the European Union's effectiveness and visibility.[331] While the latter objective may be regarded as clearly self-serving—and, on a side note, telling with regard to the motivation behind much of the

---

329 The definition could just as well be understood very literally in the sense that the rules were re-written, i.e. written again. Either way, the altering of the rules in response to reflection signifies that learning did take place.

330 For this terminology, see the discussion of the 'EU's international identity' in the concluding chapter of this work (subsection 7.2.3).

331 Cf. Council Joint Action 2007/87/CFSP of 7 February 2007; Council Joint Action 2007/106/CFSP of 15 February 2007; Council Joint Action 2007/107/CFSP of 15 February 2007; Council Joint Action 2007/108/CFSP of 15 February 2007; Council Joint Action 2007/109/CFSP of 15 February 2007; Council Joint Action 2007/110/CFSP of 15 February 2007; Council Joint Action 2007/111/CFSP of 15 February 2007; Council Joint Action 2007/112/CFSP of 15 February 2007; Council Joint Action 2007/113/CFSP of 15 February 2007.

EU's engagement—the others are the kind of motives that an enlightened actor would have knowing that helping your neighbor ultimately betters your own situation. The Security Strategy put such reasoning in its title ('A secure Europe in a better world'), and this understanding is reconfirmed by the work of the EU Special Representatives.

5.9.2 Result of reflection

The EU's global hallmark is the wide set of instruments that it can employ: from military and civilian crisis management to political strategies such as the neighborhood policy and the Central Asia strategy to specific integration policies like the Stabilization and Association Process for the Western Balkans and the Barcelona Process for the Southern Mediterranean (cf. Grevi 2007, 149). It can choose from a huge toolbox, containing political dialogue, economic cooperation, development assistance, institution-building, establishment of the rule of law, reconstruction work, and both civilian and military ESDP missions (Interviewee #31). The quality and quantity of EU engagement is unparalleled, staffs believe (Interviewee #8).

Moreover, the EU follows a different—some might claim disinterested—approach to international politics. It is described as a partner without selfish interests that rather invests in stability, democracy, and economic prosperity of other countries (Interviewee #46). The European focus on governance and human rights is thought of as the Union's added value (Interviewee #28). Even in the case of energy resources, where the EU has a genuine interest for example in Central Asia, it does not pursue these unilaterally by entering a 'new great game' (Interviewee #46).[332] On the contrary: in what it calls a transparent and non-confrontational approach, the EU has been trying to explain to partner countries like Russia that it does not perceive politics as a zero-sum game (Interviewees #1, 27, 36, and 46). Thus, the EU focuses on the potential for regional cooperation, be it in fighting terrorism and drug trafficking, or promoting education and economic development, e.g. by offering a partnership for investment into high technology (Interviewee #46). In this respect, the question of competition with the United States falls into the larger picture of how the two see the general world order: While the EU favours multilateralism and a regional approach (e.g. to water management in Central Asia), the U.S. relies fully on bilateral relations (Interviewee #1).

European officials claim that the Union has a broad long-term approach based on partnership that is culturally better attuned to local problems (Interviewees #36 and 46). This includes a penchant for institution-building and the support of pluralistic movements, favoring processes not persons, institutions not individuals (Interviewee #36). It does not pursue short-term interests of the monetary or military-strategic kind (Interviewee #46); instead, a 'politique des petits pas' is hailed as what should bring the EU forward (Interviewee # 28). Nevertheless, the deployment of harder ESDP measures is possible

---

332 It was Rudyard Kipling who coined the phrase "the great game" for the 19th-century rivalry between tsarist Russia and imperial Britain for rule over Asia. For the term of the new great game, see for example the programmatic titles of Kleveman 2003 and Rashid 1997.

to support the EU's goals, though these means are not to be used in a hostile environment but only when all partners see such EU involvement as desirable (Interviewee #27). This makes the EU a trusted partner, more so than Russia and the United States (Interviewee #46). The latter—like most other nation states, including many member states—follow a realpolitik approach, looking for resources and riches. The EU as a whole is the only big player that does not do that (Interviewee # 28).

In the eyes of many staffs, this makes the EU a unique civilian or soft power (Interviewees #8 and 27)—if only by the scope of relations it offers to these countries (Interviewee #27)—that is indeed capable of learning. Moreover, it is assumed that the EU serves as a model for other regions in the world, both in terms of its internal developments and its external behavior. The African Union, for example, is said to look to the EU as a role model in crisis management and reconciliation when developing its own peacekeeping capabilities and political mediation processes (Interviewee #35). Finally, when reflecting on the way the EU has developed, some freely resort to describing ESDP as a learning process (Interviewee #8). In particular, reference is made to the Balkans where the EU failed at first, but from this failure it did learn and presumably prevented a civil war in Macedonia (Interviewee #31).

Chapter 6:
Institutional and Policy Change based on Organizational Learning

The two previous chapters scrutinized what was called 'phase one' of the learning-based change model of organizational development introduced in this study. Together, they present eighteen instances of organizational learning in the realm of the EU Special Representatives, i. e. where collective reflection led to an altering of organizational routines. The latter could be of a structural, procedural, operational, or ideational nature.

In this chapter, I will now analyze the second phase of this model, i. e. whether and to what extent these learning instances contributed to organizational change. Additional regard will be given to the barriers that actually did, or potentially could prevent, such change.

6.1 Invention of EUSRs

The very fundamental learning about inventing the EUSRs (cf. section 4.1) has led to the continuous presence of these envoys, adding an important element to the EU's toolbox. Barriers such as diverging policy interests among member states have only slowed, not prevented this process, which also laid the groundwork for the increase of EUSR mandates over the past decade (cf. next section).

6.1.1 Ensuing change

The most visible change from this organizational learning is, evidently, the continued and increased presence of EU Special Representatives in all crisis regions of European concern. The EU's initial and ad hoc learning has equipped the Union with an instrument that now "[provides] a valuable contribution to foreign policy making and crisis management at the European level" (Grevi 2007, 41). EUSRs are quite an institutionalized tool (Interviewee #8), with Aldo Ajello having been the longest serving EUSR before quitting the job in February 2007 after eleven full years in office.

Deployment of the first two envoys added an instrument to the EU's foreign policy toolbox at a time when the latter was still quite empty, sporting mostly toothless declarations and a small number of sanctions. The EUSRs assured the EU's visibility and active presence in two major crisis regions hitherto only poorly considered by the EU, so they have put the EU and its political actors on the map (Interviewees #40 and 48). This contribution is best summarized by one official: "The EUSRs filled an existing need for Europe in a particular crisis. They were the right incarnation, turning a handicap into a virtue. This can be seen most clearly in Africa, where we have come from 'no EU' when the war in the Great Lakes broke out to the EU being a central player ten years later" (Interviewee #40).

Moreover, from being somewhat of a fig leaf in the beginning, both envoys gradually—through their analysis and by identifying political issues—became 'our man abroad' also from an internal perspective (Interviewee #40). Their reporting has come to be the most valuable source of political information for smaller member states lacking an embassy in the respective region and fearing that they might be excluded from EU decision-making (Interviewee #30). Thus, EUSRs have driven CFSP forward (Interviewee #2)—a judgment that will be further justified by the points to follow.

6.1.2 Potential barriers

While some barriers did exist, these did not impede but only slowed change, so that learning can be regarded as successfully followed up on. First of all, there was the evident lack of a common policy. Sending an EUSR without policy guidance can quickly turn into a failure, either because the person cannot do anything or because what he does on his own will not be appreciated by all member states. This leads directly to a second barrier, which is the policy differences between member states that existed not least along the lines of former colonial ties with countries in the Great Lakes region (see also subsection 1.1.1). France in particular was in the beginning very reluctant to intervene there; the government did not want to have a joint European action on the agenda. So the Quai d'Orsay came to be called 'Kigali sur Seine' due to its ties with the Rwandan leadership (Interviewee #18). Lastly, funding could also turn out to impede the development of the EUSRs, a point that will reappear at a later stage (cf. section 6.5). Taken together, however, the EU's organizational learning could still be turned into change.

6.2 Increased number of EUSRs

The EU's learning about the usefulness of EUSRs (cf. section 4.2) has led to a greater visibility of the EU in 24 countries[333] and a strengthened political presence there. In particular, the combination of deploying an EUSR and simultaneously developing a policy has been used. Expanded influence of the Commission, which has general misgivings about this increase, has not prevented such change.

6.2.1 Ensuing change

The main political change resulting from this learning about the use of EUSRs is an increase of the EU's visibility in and access to the various crisis regions (Interviewees #20 and 22). EUSRs compensate not only for the lack of member states' embassies in the regions concerned, but also for the weaknesses of the rotating presidency—which can be compounded by a lack of competence, because member states do not always send their

---

333 24 is the number of countries that are covered by the eleven EUSR mandates that existed on 1 March 2008 if one does not count, for reasons of proportion, all countries of the African Union but only Ethiopia, where the EUSR is based in the capital Addis Ababa. Moreover, Kosovo is regarded as a country too.

best and brightest ambassadors to sub-Saharan Africa (Interviewee #30). Also, partner countries perceive the EU as a more serious foreign policy player, not least because an EUSR stands for decision-making on the Council (i. e. member state) side rather than by the Commission (Interviewee #38).

In particular, the EU continued to use EUSRs as a means to link an existing economic presence to a commensurate level of political visibility, which could already be witnessed in the early days of EU activities in the African Great Lakes. In the South Caucasus, for example, the EU refused to withdraw or diminish its involvement despite disappointing results after spending one billion Euros in the region between 1991 and 2000 (Coppieters 2003, 159). On the contrary, it took to stepping up its political profile, including by sending a Special Representative.

The interplay between appointing an EUSR and following up with another policy instrument could be observed in various cases in which 'pioneering EUSRs' made up for the little guidance and funding they had with teamwork and an active field presence. In Moldova and the South Caucasus, for example, EU missions were created only after the EUSR was present, thus as part of a long-term engagement and not in response to an immediate threat (Interviewee #27). Moreover, the EUSR for Central Asia was sent as a means of strategic involvement (Interviewees #7 and 31); later, his presence helped to sell the Central Asia Strategy to member states, because there was already someone who could be charged with implementing its various measures (Interviewee #20).

6.2.2 Potential barriers

The European Commission has come to be not a real barrier but a factual brake to an increase in EUSR deployment by holding up individual cases for a certain time. With every new EUSR proposed, the Commission fears an overlap of competencies unless the mandate is squarely within the political-security realm or when it has a regional as opposed to a country-specific dimension (Interviewee #8). While the Treaty grants the right to send an EUSR to the Council alone, in practice the Commission has certain influence over whether an envoy will be dispatched or not. It can put conditions on a mandate before giving its informal assent, such as that the EUSR for Sudan would have to work on the Commission delegation premises in Khartoum and that the delegation building should be renovated with funds from the EUSR's budget (Interviewee #28). Until this agreement was made, the Commission had always refused to allow a Council presence in Sudan. So even if member states were in agreement about sending another envoy, they would have to get around the—institutionally or politically motivated—reservations that the Commission may make.

Occasionally, it is the member states themselves that are in the way of appointing another EUSR. Depending on the region concerned, some member states may not have an interest in a coherent EU policy, because they have their own interests there. This was the case, initially, of the EUSR for the South Caucasus (Interviewee #44).

Both barriers, however, the Commission and individual member states, have not ultimately obstructed the overall expansion of this instrument based on an appreciation of its usefulness.

6.3 Integration into CFSP structures

To integrate the EUSRs into the emerging CFSP structures has been a long process—and it is still ongoing. The learning that has come about (cf. section 4.3) has resulted in an increased acceptance of the High Representative's authority among EUSRs, enhanced also by the forced leave of some of their colleagues. However, the machinery works far from perfect, and barriers remain with regard to the physical integration of EUSR offices into the Secretariat and to the varying degree of interest of—and therefore control by—Solana and the PSC towards EUSRs in certain regions.

6.3.1 Ensuing change

A major result of the organizational learning described above is that today the authority of the High Representative, and with him that of the Council Secretariat and Policy Unit, is no longer questioned. If EUSRs were at first an add-on to the system, like extraterrestrial beings, they are now much more integrated (Interviewee #18). Their work is controlled by the Policy Unit and, ultimately, by the authority of the High Representative. PSC strategic guidance, in contrast, is to be understood in the sense of a more hands-off type of supervision: PSC ambassadors follow the EUSRs' work based on regular written reporting, but they are not involved in daily decision-making (Interviewee #3).

In 2006 and 2007 in particular, EUSRs felt their leashes tighten once more (Interviewee #32). In a formal letter, Director-General Robert Cooper called to order EUSR Schwarz-Schilling after the latter had spoken to Members of the European Parliament about policy areas that were not covered by his EU mandate (Interviewees #32, 34, and 43).[334] In February 2007 he was replaced, as were his colleagues for Sudan and Moldova who too had fallen in disgrace with the High Representative: One had failed to respect the limitations of his mandate, the other lobbied against clear-cut policies of some member states (Interviewees #20, 29, and 28; cf. Traynor 2007). As a result, their successors still feel a whiff of suspicion from member states when they present policy proposals (Interviewee #37).

At the working level, the integration of seconded political advisors (the 'spies') produced the desired results. These POLADs see their function as an early-warning system, helping the EUSR to navigate Brussels by pointing not only to what is politically desirable but also to that which is politically feasible (Interviewee #39). Bureaucratically not part

---

334 The issue in question was the importance of education in a war-torn country. In his capacity as High Representative of the international community, education reform was one of Schwarz-Schillings major portfolios; however, not so under his EUSR hat.

of the EUSR team, they ultimately can say 'no' when necessary (Interviewee #1). In addition, by being involved in a "constant path of interaction" with the EU foreign policy machinery (Grevi 2007, 34), these POLADs provide an essential link for EUSRs into CFSP structures.

6.3.2 Potential barriers

Despite all good intentions and year-long efforts to integrate the EUSRs into the Brussels foreign policy system, numerous barriers have impeded learning-based change from being fully implemented. These have to do with personal and institutional limitations of the High Representative, the Secretariat, and the PSC as well as with certain resistance on the part of the EUSRs themselves. Still, while the list of barriers is considerably long, integration has, on balance, been fairly successful. And with the EU External Action Service just around the corner there are even more adjustments to come (cf. subsection 7.3.2).

First of all, the High Representative has limited capacities, which he usually directs at the crisis regions in which he is personally interested. Solana has a lot more to do than to take care of his EUSRs. Apart from the now annual meetings as part of the lessons-learned process (cf. section 4.9), he has little contact with them and has delegated supervision to the Policy Unit (Interviewee #6). Solana's own interests centre mainly around the Balkans and the Middle East (Interviewees #36 and 44), to the extent that other EUSRs are neglected (Interviewee #37). Ironically, competition also takes place among those that can be sure of the High Representative's interest. A sort of institutional rivalry for closeness to Solana emerged between the Secretariat's Middle East task force and the respective EUSR team (Interviewee #42). The head of the task force, Christian Jouret, used to be a member of the EUSR's team, which makes competition an institutional fault line and not a personal issue (Interviewee #42).

Moreover, personal closeness to Solana means less structural control. The team of EUSR Marc Otte for example is presently exempt from the rule that one political advisor should be seconded by the Secretariat. Whether this is because Otte is a former member of the Policy Unit or because he enjoys "one of the closest working relationships with the SG/HR" (Grevi 2007, 134) (with whom he shares a common history at NATO) is irrelevant in this context. His predecessor Moratinos, a compatriot of Solana, was already a close collaborator due to the High Representative's interest in the region (Interviewee #44). The team apparently feels that it does not need an official from the Secretariat to 'spy' on them.

Secondly, the merger between the Secretariat's DG E and the Policy Unit is not complete (Interviewees #3 and 16; Grevi 2007, 32) and structural control over the EUSRs is not fully established. Helga Schmid for the Policy Unit and Robert Cooper for DG E are both heads of structures that remain distinct. Each serves as senior contact point for a group of EUSRs,, because a farther-reaching proposal to create an EUSR management committee did not materialize (Grevi 2007, 36). Also below this level, it is not always clear to outsiders, including staff from the Commission and Parliament, who is responsible for a certain dossier. The administrative level remains particularly opaque to those who come from outside the system, as many EUSRs still do (cf. section 4.8). Thus, to a country-based EUSR, it may appear to be a malfunction of the bureaucracy that sets priorities at its own will when, at the same time, his staff are absorbed by the Council structures rather than concerned with the necessities of the country in question (Interviewee #34).

The imperfect condition of the CFSP system makes the Brussels structures themselves still very individual-based and therefore vulnerable (Interviewee #16). Personality is enormously important when the weak organization of the Council Secretariat—which resembles a design by Trotsky, whereas the Commission has more of a Stalinist structure, as someone ironically suggested (Interviewee #28)—allows everyone to try to enlarge their room for manoeuvre. In the end, because the EUSRs as an institution have developed together with the EU system as a whole, the Council is not equipped to control them fully (Interviewee #16).

This may lead to the impression on the receiving (EUSR) end that, despite official guidance from the HR/SG and from the PSC, there are hardly any requirements on how to integrate their work into the CFSP institutions (Interviewee #29). Even people from within the Secretariat perceive the EUSRs as an institution sui generis that has nothing to do with their structure: While politically tied to the SG / HR, they presumed that the relation did not go beyond in-kind contributions such as providing them office space (Interviewee #41). EUSR teams still appear like 'satellites to the secretarial mother ship' (Interviewee #42). This extended to the fact that when Solana was to visit a region, some EUSRs had the feeling of working in isolation rather than being included by the Secretariat into the preparations of the trip (Interviewee #35).

Interestingly, the question of the physical location of the EUSRs' offices symbolizes as much as perpetuates this incomplete integration into CFSP structures. EUSRs who have their headquarters in Brussels (i. e. who are not resident in the country of their mandate) still have not been integrated into the Council Secretariat's building. Instead, their offices are concentrated in two different locations, one just opposite the main 'Justus Lipsius' Council building, the other a few blocks away on the premises of the Belgian Military School (cf. Graff 2002, 58). Especially with the many trips EUSRs take, it is possible for a Secretariat official not to see his EUSR for months (Interviewee #28). It therefore appears ironic, as one interlocutor remarked, that despite trying to formally integrate the EUSRs into CFSP structures, the former are still physically located well outside of the latter (Interviewee #39). In sum, this "scattering of EUSRs and of their advisors across different offices and different buildings did not help smooth communications between their teams as well as between EUSRs' staff and the various interlocutors in the Council Secretariat" (Grevi 2007, 23-24).

Other observers felt a clear disproportion between the presence of the Brussels bureaucratic apparatus and the lack of political guidance (Interviewee #32). Particularly for staff working in the field, it appeared that Brussels would provide only bureaucratic processes and red lines but no political impulses (Interviewee #32). A similar complaint was made with regard to the PSC, where discussions were not always instructive, failing to provide the strategic guidance necessary (Interviewee #31). Some even felt that discussions in bodies like the PSC were useless, because decisions were pre-programmed by the working level, thus questioning PSC's actual control over its administration (Interviewee #34).

Yet, there are also structural limits to the way member states can take influence. Any operation, even an EUSR, needs to have a single focal point and cannot be run by committee, as the military saying goes (Interviewee #17). Only at certain times did member states clearly keep control over the process, for example in the timing of the departure of three EUSRs in February 2007: Solana had to wait until the end of the Finnish Presidency (which wanted to keep EUSR Haavisto) and the beginning of the German Presidency (who felt that in this position, they could not protect EUSR Schwarz-Schilling so as not to appear to be pursuing national goals) before he could dismiss them (Interviewees #28 and 34).

Finally, the EUSRs themselves also had their share in avoiding full implementation of the integration efforts. Ajello was indeed quite an independent EUSR who did not perceive himself as part of Solana's team, and vice versa (Interviewee #44). Others saw it as their task to tell the PSC what strategic guidance they should give them rather than the other way round (Interviewee #36). Also, a few did not display much willingness to adjust to the complex institutional environment they were propelled into from their national political or diplomatic careers (cf. Grevi 2007, 35).

6.4   Establishing EUSR structures

The huge gap between learning about the integration of EUSRs into CFSP structures and learning about the establishment of their own structures (cf. section 4.4) is reproduced when it comes to subsequent change. The only visible adjustment is that a single coordination post was created within the Secretariat. One major barrier to more change—based on the little learning that exists—is the unwillingness of member states to establish a parallel structure. The frequent rotation of political advisors who are usually seconded by member states can also be seen as an impediment.

6.4.1   Ensuing change

As a consequence of the lack of established rules described earlier (cf. subsection 4.4.1), there has not been much learning-based change (or any other type of change, for that matter). It was only in 2007 that, within the Coordination Unit of DG E in the Council Secretariat, a person was tasked with providing information for and support to the EUSRs (Interviewees #16 and 41). Before, an 'administrative toolkit' had been prepared to provide information on how to start up an EUSR office, giving guidance on issues from personnel recruitment to classified communication and media relations (Grevi 2007, 24).

At the working level, a lack of institutional structures has led to a particular reliance of political advisors on each other. This created a fascinating experience of European collaboration, both among EU states and within the team (Interviewee #45), where staff experienced fairly successful EU coordination rather than rivalry (Interviewee #46). EUSRs too have noted the benefits of working with seconded diplomats from member states. They constitute a multinational team working for a common project, regardless of national policies. This makes them more efficient than national teams, especially because member states appear willing to send good people, when they regard the staffing of the EUSR teams as an investment in personnel (Interviewee #47).

6.4.2 Potential barriers

There are various reasons why it has been difficult—or impossible—to implement a more unified EUSR structure, which is clearly needed. In face of the failure to fully integrate the EUSRs and their teams into the Secretariat, it appears that they should be kept as a separate structure without becoming too powerful themselves. For example, EUSRs cannot dispose of their budget and hire staff at their own will, but instead must compromise with member states on the personnel that the latter choose to second (Interviewees #34 and 36). Indeed, sometimes team members are not even paid out of the EUSR's general budget, e.g. military and police staff who are paid directly by member states or the Commission. In these cases, the EUSR does not even have control over his own team, because his staff members ultimately take instructions from the place their money comes from (Interviewee #35). In addition, regardless of the regional situation (political stability, number of EUSR offices), an unwritten rule exists, supported by both the Commission and the Council Secretariat, that specifies that the budget of one EUSR should not be bigger than those of the others (Interviewees #8 and 35). Here, bureaucratic thinking rules over the political necessities on the ground.

The reliance on detached national experts for staffing EUSR teams, which has the above-mentioned positive characteristics, also makes the establishment of an organizational memory difficult (Interviewee #16). When these people leave, they usually take their knowledge with them (Interviewee #33). Moreover, POLADs in the field often do not have any Brussels experience (Interviewee #39). In this case, if someone is on secondment from the Council Secretariat, that person is automatically thought to ensure a certain level of reliability (Interviewee #45). This situation could be alleviated if there were something like a preparatory seminar for all EUSRs or their POLADs, something simple that, again, every Foreign Ministry offers its diplomats (Interviewee #33).

As for the proposed general administration team at the Secretariat, different provisos from both the Commission and the Council side hold back the formation of such a unit (Interviewee #8). Given that it has not been created so far, and that discussion about an EU foreign service is to restart soon, the idea would probably be taken up in this context rather than be established up front (Interviewee #44). For now, it holds true that, if EUSRs are successful, it is 'malgré la structure,' as one interlocutor put it (Interviewee #22).

6.5 Budgetary issues

The back-and-forth experimenting with budgetary responsibility (cf. section 4.5), where EUSR financing initially came from the Community budget, then from the Council, and from 2003 onwards again from the Commission, has had two consequences. It first led to a change in the status of CFSP advisors, and it eventually granted the Commission a say in the fundamental questions of EUSR business. The main limitation in both instances has come from the constraints of the CFSP budget.

6.5.1 Ensuing change

The first learning instance, the appropriation of the EUSR budget by the Council, had led to a diminished role of the Commission in this field (Interviewee #9). This point was supported by the auditors' report, which found that this arrangement weakened the Commission's role in the implementation of CFSP action (Court of Auditors 2001, 14). Interestingly, however, the Commission itself did not feel so sidelined, because, in its reply to the report, it expressed its general satisfaction with the financing from the Council's administrative budget, only asking for a clarification of the distinction between 'administrative' and 'operating' expenditures (ibid., 37).

The lasting change that flowed from the post-2003 arrangement under which EUSRs are paid from the general CFSP funds, however, is a new division of labour between the main institutions—and one more favorable to the Commission. EUSRs receive political direction from the Council (via the PSC), whereas they are accountable for their budget to the Commission. This has given the latter considerable influence over EUSR affairs, a point that will be elaborated further in the next section.

6.5.2 Potential barriers

A major restraint for both instances was and has remained, banal as it sounds, money. The initial arrangement was barred from taking hold by the budgetary constraints that the Council experienced then. These were only aggravated by its operational difficulties in managing an increasing number of EUSRs at the same time as launching the first ESDP missions (Interviewees #8 and 41). In the second instance, however, change was complete: The Council Secretariat re-learned about how best to arrange the financing of its Special Representatives. Yet even now, limitations come from the still fairly narrow CFSP budget of the Communities: With a growing overall number of EUSRs, an increase in their field presence, plus heightened security requirements, final expenditures have in recent years regularly exceeded the initial commitments made (cf. Grevi 2007, 20-21). Budgetary issues will therefore remain a stumbling stone for EUSRs, practically as well as in their relations with the Commission and Parliament.

6.6 Cooperation with the Commission and the Parliament

Learning about how to cooperate with the Commission (rather than with Parliament—cf. section 4.6) has led to various common activities in and joint reporting from the field, also displaying a different degree of learning between the headquarters and abroad. All this, however, can easily be impeded by persisting institutional differences and a lack of understanding of the organizational procedures of either party.

6.6.1 Ensuing change

Change resulting from the cooperation doctrine with the Commission is most visible in third countries where cooperation between EUSRs and Heads of Delegation has greatly improved (Interviewee #21).[335] EUSRs usually receive logistical support such as office space on delegation premises for their political advisors in the field (Interviewees #28, 33, 38, and 46) or informational support with regard to country-specific contacts (Interviewee #15). At best, this extends to a 'welcoming into the European family' by the Commission staff already present, adding a social aspect to cooperation (Interviewee #33). In return, the EUSR typically includes the Commission Head of Delegation in his activities (Interviewees #15, 36, 38, and 45), thus demonstrating vis-à-vis third parties that the EU is a single entity (Interviewee #27). The two field structures also often coordinate their respective reports to Brussels in order to avoid conflicting messages, while at the same time maintaining their different foci—project work here, political relevance there (Interviewee #38). More specifically, EUSRs now help implement Commission policies such as the Partnership and Cooperation Agreements in Central Asia (Interviewees #1 and 26).

While much of this cooperation takes place at an informal level, other instances are more formal. Early on, the EUSR for the Middle East Peace Process, for example, produced a 'vision paper' as a longer-term strategy for the region together with the Commission (George 2000). Similarly, his colleague for the South Caucasus wrote a joint strategy for Georgia with his Commission counterparts (Interviewee #21). The two also cooperate closely through the Border Support Team (for which they share responsibility) and on issues concerning the Neighbourhood Policy (Grevi 2007, 58). Again, in Africa, the disbursement of the 'African Peace Facility' requires cooperation between the Commission and the PSC, thus building a bridge between the two pillars (ibid., 101). The

---

335 Ironically, in the field sometimes the EUSR and the Head of Delegation get along well, as for example in Afghanistan, but the staff of the two are lacking contacts or familiarity (Grevi 2007, 75).

availability of these Community funds has strengthened the position of the EUSR for Sudan (ibid., 107).

Such cooperation notwithstanding, the relation is not free from competition, although such rivalry between the Commission and the Council about being the number one European representative is much more cultivated in Brussels than in the field (Interviewees #33, 44, 45, and 46). At headquarters, EUSRs are told upon their arrival to keep the Commission out of their area of competence rather than to respect its own (Interviewee #39)—just like a Head of Delegation is instructed by Commission officials to be assertive towards the EUSR (Interviewee #36). Similarly, a new EUSR may be advised not to bother consulting the Commission when trying to devise a strategy (Interviewee #26). Nonetheless, the setting up of joint task forces (cf. section 4.6) has helped to improve coordination in Brussels as well (Grevi 2007, 138). Still, the building of bridges through coordination and cooperation, important as they are, cannot be a "substitute for genuine cross-pillar joint strategizing, joint planning, joint implementation and joint evaluation" (Sherriff 2007, 91), in particular in areas with overlapping competencies such as security sector reform.

To avoid competition, in some cases mandates have been painstakingly formulated. In the case of Central Asia, for example, explicit reference was made to the "energy security aspects of the CFSP" of the envisaged Central Asia strategy—and not just energy policy in general.[336] The mandate for the South Caucasus, in contrast, arguably includes individual first pillar competences, which caused difficulties with the Commission (Interviewee #8). This overlap, nonetheless, has led to the inclusion of the respective EUSR in the three regional ENP action plans[337] as a partner in the implementation of the reforms in the rule-of-law sector (Interviewee #27). This provision was praised for opening new perspectives for closer inter-pillar cooperation in the region, following "the rather constructive experience of coordination between the Commission, the Presidencies and the EUSR in the course of the negotiation of the three plans" (Grevi 2007, 59).

EUSRs have also helped to improve institutional interactions between the Commission and member states. Positively acting as boundary spanners, they have brought the different desks together (Interviewees #21, 40, and 44). As a result, an EUSR "is currently the most streamlined way in which the Commission and member states can coordinate through a single contact point in a complex crisis that threatens to become a conflict" (International Crisis Group 2005a, 43).

Relations with Parliament have also seen some improvements, though not as many as MEPs would like. However, this is not the fault of EUSRs alone but part of the institutional division upheld by the pillar structure. At the broader level of CFSP, the

---

336 Cf. Council Joint Action 2007/113/CFSP of 15 February 2007.

337 ENP Action Plans are negotiated with the country in question and represent important instruments for implementing this Community policy; see also the respective ENP Action Plans for Armenia, Azerbaijan, and Georgia.

introduction of a Personal Representative of SG / HR Solana for Parliamentary Affairs in January 2007 addressed this issue.[338] With the latest set of guidelines, the Council heeded calls by MEPs for more stringent criteria for appointing EUSRs and evaluating their work (Council of the European Union 2007c, 4 and 7; Grevi 2007, 22). Moreover, EUSRs have—encouraged by the High Representative "to update the European Parliament on a regular basis on their objectives and activities"—increased their appearances at parliamentary committees (Council of the European Union 2007a, 36).

Thus, and despite the overall still negative tone of relations with Parliament, Elmar Brok, an MEP and, at that time, the powerful head of the EP's external relations committee, presented a positive portrayal of recent cooperation. In a contribution to a volume analyzing the first five years of ESDP, he declared, together with his co-author, the deputy head of the AFET secretariat, that officials responsible for ESDP operations, including special representatives, are increasingly at the disposal of their committee (Brok/Gresch 2004, 187). Although this does not give Parliamentarians much of a say over how the EU's foreign policy is conducted, it is at least an improvement over the benign neglect the EP had experienced in the early years.

6.6.2 Potential barriers

The main barrier to implementing further change is the persisting Treaty structure that distinguishes between first- and second-pillar competencies. This barrier will remain until a double-hatted superior is created, either at the level of the EUSR (see section 6.17) or at the level of the High Representative for CFSP / Vice-President of the Commission. Before then, there is no way that an EUSR can give instructions to the Commission—nor that the Commission's wish to be rid of the EUSRs (Interviewee #40) will turn into reality.

From this legal division follows a widespread mutual lack of understanding mainly in Brussels. In this milieu, it may already be regarded as a sign of cooperation not to work against the Commission (Interviewee #30), and often an offhand attitude towards Parliament prevails (Interviewee #36). Others may believe they could command the technical assistance they need for conflict resolution from the Commission or think it wise to pull rank (Interviewee #39) instead of heeding the advice from local Commission staff (Interviewee #28). Likewise, the Commission may prefer not to use EUSR reporting for its Country Strategy Papers (Interviewee #2)[339] or loathe accepting the EUSR's coordinating role on the ground (Interviewee #8). Of course, the case pending at the European Court of Justice to decide on competence in the field of security sector reform and small arms certainly does not improve the atmosphere (Interviewee #21).

338 See Press Statement S028/07 by Javier Solana, Brussels, 29 January 2007.

339 The flow of information is similarly disregarded in the opposite direction: "In the past there have been proposals to make use of the Commission's insight into crisis areas or unstable regions by using the Commission's Country Strategy Papers (CSP) more systematically in the planning of ESDP operations. [...] In practice, however, Council staff admit to never having seen a country strategy paper" (Hansen 2006, 41).

The distance, both physical and mental, that is present in Brussels exacerbates this institutional division. The illustrious 'two sides of Rue de la Loi' on which the Commission and the Council are located make it so that, as an institutional reflex, each side will start working on its own proposal before coming together and sharing information (Interviewee #19). Mentally, cross-pillar cooperation demands that super-political diplomats and super-technical bureaucrats overcome their differences (Interviewee #39). The effect of the combined physical and mental distance has been accurately summed up in the famous aphorism that 'where you stand depends on where you sit'[340]—and it holds true for the EU no less.

In the field, both sides often feel unwillingly caught in a process that is dictated by the Treaty and may be contrary to the actual aims on the ground. When the political line is the same for the two sides but institutional infighting is about responsibilities in implementation, operational questions become hostage of institutional arrangements and a good part of an outward-oriented project is directed towards overcoming Treaty barriers (Interviewee #15). For example, the training of the Congolese police ended in permanent makeshift, because it had to be devised in parallel projects due to overlapping competences (Interviewee #48). In this sense, staff members themselves look forward to a Treaty revision that should bring clarity to the division of the different competences, and many regard increased cooperation with the Commission as a step towards the prospective EU external action service (Interviewees #15, 35, and 38; cf. subsection 7.3.2).

Moreover, the willingness to cooperate can be hampered by a lack of Commission delegations in the respective region. This is the case in Central Asia, where at the outset of the EUSR's mandate, the Commission was only represented in Almaty, Kazakhstan (Interviewee #26). Similarly, there used to be only one Commission delegation in the South Caucasus, in Tbilisi, Georgia (Interviewee #26). Conversely, if the EUSR appears to lack political clout, Commission staff might turn to international organizations such as the OSCE or the UN for help rather than to their EU colleague, which happened in the South Caucasus (cf. International Crisis Group 2006b, 23).

Another barrier is inherent in the Commission's responsibility for the distribution of funds, both internally (i.e. to the EUSRs) and externally (to projects and partners). Internally, the Commission may use this power to refuse EUSR reassignment if political priorities change (Interviewee #33).[341] Externally (in the Balkans, for example), there is a clear difference between the Commission's focus on association and enlargement and the still necessary post-conflict institution-building that an EUSR may advocate (Interviewee #34). In addition, financial assistance from the Commission may have a schedule that is different from the policy line dictated by current events (Interviewee

---

340 I am quoting Graham T. Allison on this who, however, gives credit to Don K. Price (Allison 1971, 176).

341 Cf. also Hansen 2006: "[Budgetary responsibility] buys the Commission influence over the strategic political approach and the implementation of ESDP operations" (31) and "the Commission at times uses its control of the budget to position itself or to gain access to leadership positions in the field" (40).

#35). Because payments have been agreed years beforehand, even the head of delegation does not have the freedom to stop transfers at his will (Interviewee #36).[342] For these reasons, opportunities for clashes over funding abound.

The aforementioned differences extend to the European Parliament, only that the barrier here is also a politico-institutional one: Because it has no real power, Parliament can pass long resolutions with little practical content and usually without prior consultation with the EUSR concerned (Interviewee #36).

A general question, however, is whether this division between the political and the economic is something specific to the EU or whether this is not valid for all governments and international organizations. UNDP, for example, would not find fault with a political decision of the UN either but give money regardless, just as the General Assembly may pass ineffective resolutions (Interviewee #36). Likewise, intra-institutional conflicts can be found in any member state's government—for example, between the foreign affairs ministry and the development ministry (Interviewees #33 and 36).

Given this (natural) institutional competition, much therefore depends on the willingness of the EUSRs to overcome this rivalry. Some may concentrate their work on the CFSP components and leave the Commission alone, while others may understand their mandate in a broad sense and thus cooperate closely with the Commission. Yet, despite these barriers, the overall relations of EUSRs with the Commission (and to some extent with the EP as well) have changed for the better, and much of this was based on previous instances of organizational learning.

6.7   Standardization of general mandate provisions

Standardizing EUSR mandates, in particular with regard to lines and intervals of reporting (cf. section 4.7), has led to a less burdensome involvement of the PSC, including fewer debates about new mandates, and generally contributed to the establishment of better EUSR structures (cf. sections 6.3 and 6.4). The new administrative requirements, however, have at times also put a strain on the EUSRs' work, diverting their attention from the political tasks they were given.

6.7.1   Ensuing change

The streamlined reporting has led to regular though less laborious involvement of the PSC, and the review process introduced has helped to better adjust the mandates to the needs on the ground (Interviewee #31). Creating a set of standard language has produced substantial benefits not only by triggering fewer debates in the political bodies

---

342   Cf. also Hansen 2006, 30: "In the past, external activity by the Commission has typically been more long-term and tender processes emphasise thoroughness and accountability. This differs fundamentally from the needs of crisis management."

about working relations, but also by making translation easier for the language services (Interviewee #9).

As for the last adjustment limiting tenure, it is naturally not yet possible to detect any changes, in particular because it is apparently directed more at newly mandated than at long-standing EUSRs: Ajello quit his job after 11 years in office at his own request; likewise, Vendrell, after serving for more than six years, has asked to be replaced by the summer of 2008; and Marc Otte, operating since 2003, is too close to Solana to be thrown out (cf. subsection 6.3.2).

6.7.2 Potential barriers

While change has generally been forthcoming, the overall amount of administrative requirements imposed on the EUSRs may create a severe burden for the latter, thus potentially obstructing future developments. EUSRs become frustrated particularly when they feel that they are driven not by the issue at stake but by a bureaucracy producing many obligations (Interviewee #3). This also harks back to the point made earlier (cf. subsection 6.3.2) that a disproportionate presence of administrative demands compared to political guidance hinders implementation of proposed structural changes (Interviewee #32).

6.8 Selection of EUSRs

The rules described above about how to select an EUSR (cf. section 4.8) have led to greater openness of the process. This produced competition for the available posts, and, indirectly through the personnel selected, brought greater acceptance of the hierarchical structures that the Secretariat wanted to establish (cf. section 6.3). While the formally established system produces good results, some barriers remain in the informal role that either member states or the Commission may play in the process, as well as in the limited number of potential candidates, including female ones, to draw from.

6.8.1 Ensuing change

The introduction of a multi-stage selection procedure involving both Council Secretariat and Presidency has led to a more open process and ultimately, by increasing competition and introducing interviews, also helped to raise the quality of personnel selection (Interviewees #3, 16, 20, and 31). So far, there has not been a shortage of excellent applicants (Interviewees #16 and 31).[343] The post of EUSR is a lucrative, prestigious job that should not be regarded as a sinecure for retired national politicians, even if the new system cannot prevent discarded national politicians from being presented as candidates

---

343 Indeed, in order to attract "highly qualified and experienced candidates" that have "political access at the necessary level," the EUSRs' pay was also raised and standardized equivalent to that of a director-general in the Commission (Council of the European Union 2003b, 3).

(Interviewee #31). A great deal of emphasis is put on the personality of the representative, including his standing in the region to which he will be dispatched (Interviewees #2, 12, 16, 31, and 38). This is particularly important, because the EUSR system is still very person-based (Interviewee #16): "[Success] depends considerably on the personality and political weight of the individual and his ability to gain the respect of diplomatic peers and the parties in the crisis area" (International Crisis Group 2005a, 43).

Another consequence of the EU's learning about how to select its special representatives is that, today, none of the EUSRs is a former politician. Nearly all of them are national diplomats, with the remainder hailing from a career in international organizations. By selecting diplomats with a political instinct rather than mere fonctionnaires, the EUSRs are still one degree fancier than national ambassadors in the field (Interviewee #12). At the same time, their background from national administrations eases the workings of the newly established hierarchies (Interviewee #2).

The fact that most EUSRs are national diplomats may highlight the importance of the internal dimension of their work. Yet many of them also have experience in multilateral diplomacy, thus making them act as boundary spanners to third countries and multilateral organizations. Aldo Ajello as a former SRSG was able to build upon his relations to the UN and the African Union (Interviewee #48). Likewise, Francesc Vendrell, thanks to his previous UN engagement, was well positioned to establish good relations with countries like Russia, India, Iran, and China—states that are not the EU's most natural partners but of great importance to a country like Afghanistan (Interviewee #36). In addition, Ján Kubiš, being the former Secretary-General of the OSCE, had an entrée at a high level with very good personal contacts, including statesmen like the 'sun god' Nazarbayev of Kazakhstan (Interviewee #46; cf. International Crisis Group 2006a, 19).[344] Therefore, their often times multilateral background helps EUSRs to more easily build bridges to third countries and international organizations (Interviewees #2 and 12).

6.8.2 Potential barriers

One main barrier derives from the fact that, although the selection process ought to be transparent and open, member states and even the Commission play a larger informal role than is actually foreseen. While it is natural for member states to lobby for their own candidate (Interviewees #10 and 15), and consequential that those member states with historical ties to a certain region may produce a greater number of qualified candidates (Interviewee #12), powerful member states may still overturn the verdict of the selection panel for political reasons. This was allegedly the case when Pierre Morel was nominated EUSR for Central Asia (Interviewee #37). Likewise, the Commission, though not formally involved in the nomination process, does have influence over the selection by

---

344 Yet, his multilateral experience of trying to forge a consensus of 56 OSCE member states made EUSR Kubiš too cautious in his approach in the eyes of some (Interviewee #1), displaying a "tendency to favour engagement at all costs and stability in relations over innovation and constructive criticism" (International Crisis Group 2006a, 18).

threatening to ultimately block a candidate that it considers unsuitable, e. g. with regard to his views on Community competences (Interviewees #8 and 21).

Another barrier is the limited number of people who usually apply for an EUSR post. While the UN Secretary-General commands a pool of around 100 SRSG candidates, selection for EUSRs is more limited. In the end, about half a dozen people will file an application (Interviewee #10). Some believe that, if the EU could only attract the right characters, it would also have more influence (Interviewee #39). Moreover, just as the whole business of CFSP is male-dominated—with the exception of two Personal Representatives, Solana's entire cabinet is made up of men (Interviewee #20)[345]—there has so far not been a 'Ms Europe,' despite UN Security Council resolution 1325 calling for a greater participation of women in peace operations (Interviewee #21).

6.9   Lessons-learned seminars

Holding joint EUSR seminars to distill some lessons learned can be seen as an effort of veritable 'deutero learning'; the balance of this exercise, however, is mixed at best. What the EU learned about these seminars (cf. section 4.9) has enhanced intra-EUSR coordination in some aspects. However, it has not succeeded in bringing the EUSRs together politically or administratively, due to their heterogeneous mandates as well as a lack of real interest on the part of the High Representative.

6.9.1   Ensuing change

Measured against the claim of the first seminar to "maximize the potential of the EUSRs to contribute to the coherence and effectiveness of the EU's foreign policies" (Solana 2005b, 1), its achievements are not great. An idea to increase administrative support through 'office establishment teams' was floated and regular simultaneous reporting proposed (Grevi 2007, 24 and 26). The latter was put into practice by the guidelines (cf. section 6.7), while the former remains an unfulfilled wish. Moreover, in the wake of the 2005 meeting, regional coordination was enhanced (e. g. between the 'Eastern European' EUSRs) as part of a systematic attempt to bring expertise together (Interviewees #4 and 36), yet this cannot be attributed to the seminar alone.

What could have been the beginning of a major internal evaluation and networking exercise turned into more of an informative event both for EUSRs and for the interested audience in member states.[346] One tangible outcome of the 2005 seminar was a fact

---

345   See also the Council's 'phonebook' (Council of the European Union 2007b, 80).

346   Grevi is less critical in his assessment, saying that the seminars have "proven a useful opportunity to address common problems, enhance synergies and raise awareness of respective challenges" (Grevi 2007, 148). Even if this was the case, it would not necessarily constitute real deutero learning, i. e. organizational learning on how to improve an organization's learning procedures.

sheet on the EUSRs[347] produced by the Council Secretariat for the subsequent press briefing. Also, information provided on the Council's web pages was updated to include the EUSRs (Interviewee #9). However, no lasting change was brought about with regard to the learning character of this effort.

6.9.2 Potential barriers

Most people involved in the lessons-learned seminars are now rather critical of them, albeit occasionally for different reasons. The meetings have been used less to actually share experiences and draw common lessons and more to make EUSRs aware of newly established procedures (such as security regulations) or of the expected consequences of the new Treaty (Interviewees #12, 15, and 37). While some EUSRs would prefer to discuss overarching political questions, others find that their jobs are too heterogeneous to allow for a meaningful discussion (Interviewees #36 and 44).

Time constraints are another key barrier, from Javier Solana's own schedule to the one of every EUSR. Solana himself usually gives only a short introductory presentation, staying for an ensuing lunch but without much of an intake of information from the EUSRs (Interviewee #37). Then, staff members from the Policy Unit or the Secretariat take over, but the whole meeting does not last longer than three hours (Interviewees #36 and 37). On the other hand, even if they wished for more regular—or longer—meetings, it would be difficult for the EUSRs, with all their various trips, to meet more often (Interviewees #15 and 36).

Despite good intentions and the potentially right setting, the EU has therefore failed to establish a mechanism that would enhance its own capacities for organizational learning. A potentially extremely valuable source of information for improvements both at the political and practical level, the lessons-learned seminars have instead become a perfunctory exercise (Interviewee #36), or, put more drastically, a useless sequence of talks that lead to nothing (Interviewee #44).

6.10 Tasks

As a consequence of the EU's learning about expanding the EUSRs' mandates (cf. section 5.1), new issues have steadily been added to the task list, also enlarging the room for manoeuvre that an EUSR has. This, however, has at times made EUSRs too proactive, producing the feeling of a loss of control on the side of the Council Secretariat and member states, which the latter tried to counter by fostering supervision mechanisms (cf. section 4.3).

---

347 The title of the fact sheet is "EU Special Representatives. A voice and face of the EU in crucial areas" (EU Council Secretariat 2005).

6.10.1 Ensuing change

Two broad changes flow from the learning about the tasks of EUSRs, one giving the envoys freedom to fulfill their duties and the other enhancing the overall number and scope of the latter. First, EUSRs enjoy considerable room for manoeuvre in their operations, especially when there is no firm, overarching European policy as in the Western Balkans (Interviewee #16). Member states appreciate EUSRs actively filling the existing niches (like the EUSR for Afghanistan did when he firmly interpreted his mandate with a regional dimension) as long as they do not run counter to established interests (Interviewee #36; Ajello 2000, 119). While EUSRs must obtain backing from member states in regular intervals by seeking PSC directives, it is the standing they gain from providing initiative in areas where most member states lack a political concept that helps them to make their case with the relevant authority (Interviewee #19).

Second, this general freedom to work within the mandate has been extended over time to other policy areas, as the Council saw it fit to task the EUSRs with additional duties. In the case of Central Asia, new issues like water management and energy were added to the EU's strategy upon insistence of the EUSR (who is tasked to monitor implementation of the strategy) and against the will of the Commission, which felt this was within its competence (Interviewee #46). In Macedonia, the EUSR's engagement was initially about ending conflict and negotiating an agreement; despite the fact that the Ohrid agreement could be largely regarded as implemented, the EUSR has continuously been given new tasks to fulfill (Interviewee #17). However, the EUSR's profile has been toned down by the double-hat he wears as Head of the Commission Delegation (cf. section 6.17).

The broadening of mandates has therefore led to a more comprehensive involvement of EUSRs in nearly all aspects of EU foreign policy. Today, they no longer do only political talks and leave all hands-on work to the Commission, but rather they also engage, in what remains very much a case-by-case approach, in concrete projects and operations (Interviewee #22).

6.10.2 Potential barriers

The main barrier to giving the EUSRs even more freedom in their actions is the natural interest of the Council to exercise control over them, a barrier which in itself has been strengthened by various learning experiences (cf. section 4.3). Given the lack of hierarchies with which the system has developed, some EUSRs have become too proactive from the point of view of the Brussels headquarters (Interviewee #16). This, however, has been less the case in places like the Western Balkans, where the EU policy system is thick and the EUSR is part of a massive bureaucratic machinery that can contain eventual incidents (Interviewee #16). In Bosnia and Herzegovina, for example, the EUSR has a specific catalogue of tasks and thus a more restricted mandate with closer connection to Brussels, whereas the international High Representative has a political mandate and more room for manoeuvre (Interviewee #32; cf. Jaanson 2008, 12).[348]

Another barrier is at the technical level of member states' contributions, which may not be as forthcoming as the situation demands or as the mandate stipulates. Crisis management operations rely on experts and equipment typically provided by member states. Consequently, beyond their personal involvement, EUSRs need support from member states in terms of manpower and material when an ESDP operation is deemed necessary (Interviewee #19). This means a great deal of door-to-door canvassing in member state capitals (Interviewee #37)—still, they may end up with insufficient contributions despite sufficient pledges (as was the case with EUPOL in Afghanistan; cf. Dempsey 2007, 3). Thus, mandates can easily grow too large if member states do not at the same time provide the resources necessary for proper implementation (Grevi 2007, 146).

6.11 Basis of operations of EUSRs

The EU's learning about placing the EUSRs, as a rule, in Brussels (cf. section 5.2) has led, together with a gradual expansion of field offices, to increased efficiency at headquarters and an enhanced presence on the ground. The only drawback—short of trying to be everywhere at the same time—is that EUSRs do not have an official deputy.

6.11.1 Ensuing change

The general rule of having EUSRs based in Brussels but with a strong structure in the field has had two positive effects: Their relative integration into the CFSP structures, despite persisting difficulties (see section 6.3), was enhanced by them being Brussels-based rather than 'flying' or field-based (Interviewee #16). In addition, a permanent presence in the respective countries and regions has been created, which receives a regular 'upgrade' when the EUSR flies in (Interviewee #15).

The exceptions to this rule have had their specific justifications and do not diminish the value of having most EUSRs in Brussels. It proved helpful to send a resident EUSR in the direct aftermath of the conflict in Macedonia, for example, where the EUSR was already resident before double-hatting was introduced. There, the EUSR's presence was critical in uniting the conflicting parties and enforcing changes, as the local counterparts registered only a few days of absence (Interviewee #45). To have an established rule should therefore not prevent the EU from responding in a flexible way when circumstances so demand (cf. section 6.16).

---

348 This has also implications for how the double-hatted mandate is fulfilled (cf. section 6.17).

6.11.2 Potential barriers

One barrier to a more efficient division of labour between Brussels and the field is the fact that an EUSR has no official deputy. In this case, it may cause some irritation, for other EU representatives and for third parties alike, if an EUSR cannot, for example, be present in his region due to other obligations (Interviewee #29). This point has become more relevant with double-hatting, where a deputy does exist, but only under one (i.e. the Commission) hat (cf. section 6.17).

6.12 EU political coordination

The EU has learned to use EUSRs for intergovernmental coordination of its various actors, in particular of member states both in the field and in capitals but also of ESDP operations (cf. section 5.3); they have thus become "hubs for coordination" (Grevi 2007, 46). Change resulting from this is seen in a steady flow of information to national foreign ministries, leading ultimately to a convergence of views that paves the way for common and coherent external action. Coordination can, of course, be obstructed by national ambassadors who may lack an understanding of how the EU works or who may follow differing policy priorities.

6.12.1 Ensuing change

The enhanced coordination role of the EUSR has had both internal and external effects, i.e. pulling member states together and presenting a common policy line to the outside. Internally, coordination was sometimes limited to merely stating the existing differences and fabricating a position from them (Interviewee #48). In the end, however, such co-ordination has not only helped to keep member states 'on board,' but more importantly to streamline information flowing from the field into national capitals as well as that of the EU. An explanation by Aldo Ajello, made in a different context and confirmed by respondents (Interviewee #19), may illustrate this effect: "When I briefed [national ambassadors] each week, I was basically dictating the reports they would write to their capitals—which had two good results. First, I knew they were sending the right information. Second, I knew they were all sending the same information at the same time. So, all the capitals were reacting in the same way" (Peck 2004, 333).

Such internal harmonization of positions is important, because EUSRs, in dealing with crises, usually work through international coordination formats where more and more often the EU is present in a way in which the member states are not (Interviewee #17; cf. section 6.14). In these cases, EU core groups headed by the EUSR become the main policy-discussing bodies, helping to develop a unified policy by bringing together the different positions from member states (Interviewees #15 and 36). Operationally as well, EUSRs have played a "catalytic role," for example in the setup of EUFOR in Bosnia and Herzegovina as well as in drawing operational lessons learned from this mission (Grevi 2007, 87–88).

The internal coordination of member states and EU actors is therefore also a function of the EU's external activities. Besides the rotating presidency that normally represents the Union vis-à-vis a host government, EUSRs have the capability, thanks to the continuity of their mandate, to build a trustful and personal relationship with the authorities (Interviewee #15). In the Great Lakes, it was only after the EU had reached internal consensus about its policies, greatly advanced by the EUSR, that it could become active externally, with the EUSR now managing the EU's field projection (Grevi 2007, 113). In addition, they can take a position in the middle ground above perceived national interest: This was particularly significant in the case of Macedonia, where national ambassadors, being based in Skopje and with the government as their main interlocutor, tended to be pro-Macedonian. While they had little understanding for the Albanian revolt in 2001, the EUSR and his team were newcomers with a more balanced view, who could talk to both the Macedonian government and to the Albanian leaders (Interviewee #45).

6.12.2 Potential barriers

EUSRs are meant to bring member states together but they are also submitted to institutional restraints (Interviewee #31), with some being principled (e. g. a lack of understanding) and others being very practical ones (e. g. a lack of embassies). A principled barrier is first and foremost a potential lack of understanding among national diplomats of how the EU works and, consequently, of why the EUSR should be entrusted with EU coordination on the ground (Grevi 2007, 47). The mindset of many a national ambassador who has never worked in Brussels is geared towards bilateral relations, disregarding the fact that his country has already agreed to an EU policy that the EUSR is tasked to implement. Here, it does not suffice to grant a coordinating role on paper, but the latter must be put into practice (Interviewee #15). If conflicts occur, they must be solved in a communication triangle between that ambassador, the respective national capital, and Brussels, which is a clear weakness (Interviewee #15).

An EUSR trying to mediate national positions may thus experience that the PSC ambassador in Brussels and his compatriot ambassador in a third country live in two worlds with regard to the same conflict issue (Interviewee #19). This is partly understandable due to a different policy focus: Bilateral ambassadors pay much more attention to local conditions, to which they are accustomed, and less to the EU's overall appearance (Interviewee #19). In the case of Darfur, for example, national ambassadors in Khartoum were much more interested in the internal developments of the Sudanese government than in actual crisis management, which was more in the focus of ambassadors in Addis Ababa where the AU is based (Interviewee #28). Moreover, national ambassadors receive orders from their ministry to uphold and represent national policies, whereas those working on the EU side are trained to look for consensus (Interviewee #19), an asset in a system where individual wishes are rarely taken into account (Interviewee #12).

The main practical barrier to intensive EU coordination is a lack of representation by member states on the ground (similar to the weak presence of the Commission in some regions, cf. subsection 6.6.2). When the EUSR for Central Asia held the first of what are now regular ambassadorial meetings in Astana in October 2006, many ambassadors flew in from Moscow or from Ankara, providing a measure for how poorly member states are represented in the region (Interviewee #26). With the number of embassies ranging from one in Kyrgyzstan to a little more than a dozen in Kazakhstan,[349] the meeting of all resident national ambassadors can be a small gathering (Interviewee #46). The situation is similar in the Great Lakes region[350] and, to a lesser extent and improving, in the South Caucasus.[351] In principle, however, this is not going to change very soon as member states' resources are limited and, as an ironic effect, they now receive political information through the EUSR himself.

In addition, those member states that are already represented by an ambassador frequently send their own special envoys to a crisis region. Interestingly, the appointment of an EUSR does not lead to fewer activities by certain member states, as one might imagine. In fact, the opposite may happen: Member states dispatch their own emissaries simply to have a national counterpart present who can pursue a more national position (Interviewees #28 and 35).[352] In Sudan, for example, representatives of the UK, Germany, France, and the Nordic countries were active in addition to the EUSR (Interviewee #35; cf. Grevi 2007, 104). As a result, when there are strong national interests present, the EUSR is caught between two stools (Interviewee #28) and EU coordination becomes difficult again—as was the case in the early days.

6.13 ESDP chain of command

With regard to the inclusion of EUSRs into the chain of command of ESDP operations, another back-and-forth learning process took place (cf. section 5.4). While the first step did further a dominant role of the EUSR in the field, the latest decision has at least for-

---

349 The exact figures for 2006 are: 14 EU embassies (of Bulgaria, Czech Republic, France, Germany, Greece, Hungary, Italy, Lithuania, the Netherlands, Poland, Romania, Slovakia, Spain, and the United Kingdom) in Kazakhstan; one (Germany) in Kyrgyzstan; four (France, Germany, Sweden, and the United Kingdom) in Tajikistan; four (France, Germany, Romania, and the United Kingdom) in Turkmenistan; and nine (Bulgaria, Czech Republic, France, Germany, Italy, Latvia, Poland, Slovakia, and the United Kingdom) in Uzbekistan (The Europa World Year Book 2006).

350 Only three member states (Belgium, France, and Germany) have a diplomatic representation in Burundi; nine (Belgium, France, Germany, Greece, the Netherlands, Portugal, Spain, Sweden, and the United Kingdom) have one in the DRC; four are represented in Rwanda (Belgium, France, Germany, and the United Kingdom); and nine (Belgium, Denmark, France, Germany, Ireland, Italy, the Netherlands, Sweden, and the United Kingdom) have an embassy in Uganda (The Europa World Year Book 2006).

351 Eight member states (Bulgaria, France, Germany, Greece, Italy, Poland, Romania, and the United Kingdom) have diplomatic representations in both Armenia and Azerbaijan; and ten (Czech Republic, France, Germany, Greece, Italy, Lithuania, the Netherlands, Poland, Romania, and the United Kingdom) have one in Georgia (The Europa World Year Book 2006).

352 This, by the way, appears to be a regular feature of EU institutional development, where centralized coordination does not make national posts superfluous.

mally strengthened central control by the Secretariat. What could plausibly be expected as a barrier to full implementation of the latter is the fact that EUSRs have gained political weight in their own right, so that force commanders in the field need to consult them anyway, whether this is formally written into the mandate or not.

6.13.1 Ensuing change

The initial learning instance strengthened the role of EUSRs mainly in the field but, circuitously, also in Brussels. Their weight was increased each time a crisis management operation came up by including them in the chain of command (Interviewee #9). This is summed up in a study of the EU's crisis management activities: "The EUSR has gone from being a purely political figure and representative of the HR/SG to taking on a more operational role, where the EUSR is tied into the achievement of an ESDP mission's goals" (Hansen 2006, 36). Conversely, an ESDP mission on the ground can today be seen as a guarantee that the respective EUSR's mandate will be extended (Interviewee #12).

With the new CPCC structures established only shortly before the end of the period under analysis here, it is too early to point to specific changes flowing from the creation of a solid civilian chain of command parallel to the military one (Grevi 2007, 38). What has already become clear is that by taking the EUSRs out of the chain of command, the Secretariat achieved an institutional strengthening of its position vis-à-vis the EUSRs. This corresponds to the efforts of establishing tighter control over them in the first place (cf. section 6.3). Whether the EUSRs' less operational role in civilian ESDP missions also gives them "more time to fulfill their central political and diplomatic roles of representation, reporting and coordination" (Grevi 2007, 39) is less certain. So far, cooperation between the EUSRs and the acting CPCC director, despite being clear on paper, has developed in a grey zone and, in some cases, only following a substantial fight about the lines of reporting (Interviewee #42).

6.13.2 Potential barriers

One main barrier to producing real change is the interdependence of EUSR and ESDP commanders in the field when it comes to the political environment of a mission. For cooperation in the field, interlocutors generally do not expect much to change, simply because work on the ground continues to be based on good relations between the EUSR and the ESDP head of operations (Interviewee #29). A strong, long-standing EUSR would therefore simply assume to be kept, if not in the chain of command, then at least in the flow of information, as he cannot tell partners that he is 'not competent' on a CFSP issue (Interviewee #42). At the opposite end, mission heads may approach the EUSR directly, regardless of the chain of command, because the latter has more leverage on certain issues (ibid.).

Additionally, the new arrangement may not substantially reduce the workload of an EUSR. Given the latter's political coordination function, efforts at including ESDP operation commanders—particularly if the EUSR is seen as being somewhat higher up but not placed above them in the chain of command (Interviewee #32)—may need to be enhanced as well. Numerous meetings, joint press statements, and security assessments will have to be made regardless of the EUSR's position in the ESDP chain of command (Interviewee #32).

6.14 External cooperation

Turning to how the EU deals with partners, the Union's process of learning about external cooperation (cf. section 5.5) has resulted in various EUSRs representing the Union in different 'groups of friends.' The most prominent of these fora that precook multilateral decisions is the Middle East Quartet. Ultimately, this has increased the EU's international standing. What can impede a unified EU representation is mainly the desire of member states to pursue their own policies, at times aided by third countries that may wish to see the EU split on a certain issue.

6.14.1 Ensuing change

The established practice of international coordination brought about increased participation of the EU in international fora, namely the diverse 'groups of friends.' These informal groups of countries and organizations—formed on an ad hoc basis and gradually accepted by the non-represented—have become fairly institutionalized over time. Such groups exist for the Transnistrian conflict in Moldova (the '5+2 negotiations'), for Afghanistan (the Joint Coordination and Monitoring Board), for the South Caucasus (the 'Group of Friends of the UN Secretary-General for Georgia' and the OSCE 'Minsk group'), for the Great Lakes (the 'Friends of the Great Lakes'), for Sudan (the 'Abuja Process' for the South plus the 'Joint Commission' for Darfur), and most prominently for the Middle East Peace Process (the 'Middle East Quartet'). In addition, plenty of lower level technical groupings exist that channel international activity, for example in Afghanistan with its plethora of formal and informal coordination groups, be it on counter-narcotics, joint security analysis, disarming illegal groups, police coordination, or NATO's Provincial Reconstruction Teams (cf. Grevi 2007, 76–77).

These mechanisms of international cooperation are a dynamic environment, with a power of influence rather than a power of decision (Interviewees #27 and 47). If such a group manages to instigate a peace process (as was the case in the Lusaka process in the Great Lakes and the Abuja process for Sudan), the EUSR can be instrumental in keeping close contacts with both the UN and AU, in order to deliver the EU's contribution (Interviewees #15 and 28).[353] This was also attempted when the EUSR joined the

---

353 On the facilitating role of the Group of Friends, including the EUSR, in the Great Lakes, see African Times 2004, 3.

'5+2' talks for the Transnistrian conflict, thus called after the Union and the United States entered the existing negotiation format involving Moldova, Transnistria, Russia, Ukraine, and the OSCE (Council of the European Union 2006a, 46).

Usually, some individual member states are also part of these crisis contact groups. The EUSR as the overarching European authority can then become the policy driver by bringing partners, including first and foremost EU member states (cf. section 6.12), together (Interviewee #40). Moreover, if formal negotiations are gridlocked, an EUSR can use his direct contacts for discreet initiatives aimed at overcoming the stalemate. A member state can also support the envoy in his coordination function, as Spain did when it hosted an international 'brainstorming session' called for by EUSR Vendrell on how partners should engage in the rebuilding of Afghanistan (Harrison 2002, 6).

In addition to these international groups, all EUSRs have established direct relations with partners like the United States and Russia (important for all conflict zones) as well as with regionally significant countries such as Iran, India, China, and South Africa (Interviewees #36 and 44).

As a consequence of these efforts, the international standing of the EU has grown—if self-perception by different EU actors can be an indicator. They find that, thanks to the EUSRs, the EU is perceived as a serious player (Interviewees #30 and 31), and that it has moved from the margins to centre stage in international politics (Interviewee #40). Most partners are thought to appreciate the more active role of the EU, not least in places like Central Asia, where the EU is perceived as the favorite partner—preferred over Russia or the United States (Interviewee #46). Even the latter seem to acknowledge the new strategic role given to the EU by the EUSRs, when, for example, the U.S. Undersecretary of State actively engages his EUSR counterpart in American policy towards a particular region (Interviewee #39).

6.14.2 Potential barriers

The main barriers to this positive international involvement of the EU are the sometimes overly egoistic policies of member states. The EUSR may aim to increase the cohesion of the EU's external representation, but this is regularly undermined by bilateral talks between member states (Interviewee #3). In settings like the 'groups of friends', they act formally in their national capacities and can, without venturing to diverge from EU policies, create room for interpretation of what exactly those policies mean (Interviewee #27). In addition, their tendency to consult their non-represented EU partners ahead of the meetings of the circle of friends is quite limited (Interviewee #27).

These persisting differences are sometimes played on and thus exacerbated by other international actors, mainly Russia and the United States. They may not actively try to disunite the EU, yet the (by no means unusual) occurrence of EU dissent feeds into their prejudices and works to their advantage (Interviewee #36). At other times, it is the various European organizations themselves, such as the EU, NATO, and OSCE, that impede international cooperation with an egoism of their own. Then, as in the case of negotiations over Nagorno-Karabakh in the South Caucasus, the "plethora of European initiatives" can be "confusing and often disheartening, as the missions are uncoordinated and lacking in concrete proposals" (Shaffer 2003, 8).

6.15 Policy input

One of the strengths—and indeed one of the original justifications—of the EUSRs has been their ability to provide firsthand information and analysis from faraway places of which, paraphrasing Chamberlain's dictum, many EU member states know nothing (cf. section 5.6). Smaller member states that normally lack an extensive web of missions abroad have become more involved in EU policy-making due to the information provided by the EUSRs. That is why, today, they "play a significant role in fuelling policy initiatives at the EU level" (Grevi 2007, 33), thus improving the EU's foreign policy at large. EUSR input has been visible in the formulation and implementation of broad strategies as well as in proposals for more operational engagement.

The barriers to putting this learning about the EUSRs' policy input into practice are found in the Brussels headquarters and with member states. Both of these normally see policy formulation as their prerogative and duty, and therefore do not allow others to make their mark. This was even more pronounced when an EUSR was deployed more as a fig leaf than as an instrument of action. In such cases, member states did not want to become active in a situation beyond sending an EUSR, and they would therefore be unwilling to follow the latter's potentially obliging political advice.

6.15.1 Ensuing change

As a general consequence of the EU's learning about an enhanced role of EUSRs in policy-making, the quality of the EU's foreign policy has been improved, observers note (Interviewee #12). This can be shown with the following examples, looking at the EUSR contributions to EU strategies and policies (such as for Central Asia, Africa, and the European neighbourhood) as well as at cases where the EU initiated operational activities based on the proposal of an EUSR.

The EUSR was the main conceiver and feeder of the EU's new Central Asia strategy that was passed in June 2007 (European Council 2007), though leaving the driver's seat to the respective Presidency (Interviewees #1, 4, and 12). He "played an entrepreneurial role" in drafting the paper (Grevi 2007, 126), the idea for which already existed when EUSR Kubiš embarked on his first mandate as it was thought of as a conceptual basis for the new post (Interviewee #46). In 2006, the Finnish Presidency began the process knowing that Germany, the country to take over the Presidency from them and the only member state with a diplomatic presence in all Central Asian countries, wanted to make the region one of the priorities of their presidency (Interviewees #1 and 26). Despite being initially reluctant toward the idea of a strategy fearing it would make him less independent in his work, EUSR Kubiš prepared a first draft (Interviewee #1). Meanwhile, the Commission had finalized its Central Asia Regional Strategy Paper for the period from 2007 to 2013 (European Community 2006). This internal document highlights the democratic, economic, and social issues faced both by the region as a whole and by each country individually and maps out the assistance that the Community will provide.

Because it was never formally decided who should draft the strategy, the EUSR eventually found himself in this position. Pierre Morel, in office since October 2006, took the initiative when it was clear that Germany would push the topic during its term, but would not do so openly as long as the Finns were at the helm (Interviewee #38). With the Commission proposal as a basis, he presented a carefully worded discussion paper on elements for a strategy in late 2006 (cf. Council of the European Union 2006a, 158). He knew he was acting in an institutional vacuum; no one had asked for—let alone endorsed—his initiative, and cooperation with the Commission was not always smooth (Interviewee #1; Grevi 2007, 127). Still, Morel's draft was taken up in Berlin, and the strategy was finalized under the German presidency, meeting the target date of the June 2007 European Council (Interviewee #26).

Cooperation worked extremely well in this case, also because there was no beauty contest between concepts (Interviewee #46). Germany had signalled early on its willingness to pass the strategy under its Presidency, and had also supported the nomination of Morel as the successor to Kubiš, who became an ally in the formulation of the strategy (Interviewee #7). Moreover, France, a strong regional player with embassies in all Central Asian countries except Kyrgyzstan, lent support to 'its EUSR' (Interviewee #38).

Today, the strategy is part of the comprehensive character of the EU's broader approach to the region (Grevi 2007, 121) and the EUSR is tasked to monitor its implementation. This way, he is active in putting into practice some of the proposals he made himself, which had been integrated into the strategy as follow-up measures (Interviewee #46). This gives the post of EUSR a new dimension by structuring the mission and by providing clear terms of reference and a comprehensive roadmap for the EUSR's actions (Interviewee #26; Grevi 2007, 128).

As for the EU's Africa strategy, which was passed in December 2005 (Council of the European Union 2005c), EUSR Ajello contributed to the drafting process as far as the Great Lakes region was concerned (Interviewees #8 and 15). Previously, he had contributed to the 1998 Common Position "concerning human rights, democratic principles, the rule of law and good governance in Africa" (see Fiedler 2004, 328). In general, observers say that the EU never decided to act against Ajello's express wish: When he advised not to follow a certain route, the EU would not do so (Interviewee #30).

In the South Caucasus, the EUSR was instrumental in bringing the whole region under the overarching policy framework of the European Neighbourhood Policy. The latter was also a way of departing from the more defensive approach based on what the EU Security Strategy said about dealing with frozen conflicts (Interviewee #31). When the ENP was first passed in 2003, Armenia, Azerbaijan, and Georgia were explicitly excluded from the new policy.[354] The EUSR at the time, Heikki Talvitie, sensed a strong desire among the countries concerned for closer, more structured relations with the EU. That is why he lobbied strongly, and successfully, together with some Eastern European member states and the European Parliament, for their inclusion in the revised policy proposal made in 2004 (Interviewees #3 and 27; cf. European Commission 2004a, 10). After only one year, the Commission retracted from its earlier 'footnote policy' and advocated the inclusion of these countries in the ENP, citing the Union's "strong interest in the stability and development of the Southern Caucasus" (European Commission 2004a, 10).

From policy input, the EUSR then shifted to actively making operational proposals for how to deal with this volatile region. Inter alia, he proposed the EU's first rule of law Mission in the context of ESDP, EUJUST Themis in Georgia, which was launched in July 2004. Through Themis, senior EU experts supported, mentored, and advised the Georgian authorities on urgent challenges in the criminal justice system (Interviewee #6).[355] When this mission was terminated, the EUSR and his reinforced team took over the monitoring of the implementation of agreed reforms, thus giving "the EUSR position a more operational flavour" (Hansen 2006, 37). EUSR Talvitie contributed, together with the Commission, to formulating a strategy for Georgia (cf. section 6.6), even though, according to the Council Secretariat, "the Commission Action Plan on Georgia only took ESDP concerns into account where they coincided with the Commission view" (Hansen 2006, 41). Moreover, Peter Semneby, Talvitie's successor, helped deescalate the Georgian-Russian conflict in 2006, thanks to his good contacts to Moscow (Interviewee #12; Grevi 2007, 59).

In this sense, political input proved crucial for operational tasks such as crisis management. EUSR Ajello was critical (in particular with his acute knowledge and assessment of the political situation in Congo) in the internal debates over the deployment of the Artemis mission in 2004. He succeeded in making it clear to member states that, without a mission, the EU would risk a breakdown of all structures created since 1997 (Interviewee #15). Equally, his role was crucial in the EU's reaction to the Congo crisis of 2006, when Ajello prepared and accompanied the European electoral mission on the ground, thus taking care of the political dimension of crisis management (Interviewees #12 and 29). As a result of his concise and detailed reporting, a great number of smaller

---

354 Cf. subsection 1.3.1; see also European Commission 2003, 4 (fn2); Coppieters 2003, 168; and Lynch 2003, 171.

355 The mission's mandate is formulated in Council Joint Action 2004/523/CFSP of 28 June 2004. The operation was terminated on 14 July 2005, having "succeeded in at least setting in motion an ambitious plan of reform of Georgia's criminal justice system" (Grevi 2007, 57).

member states was willing to send staff officers to the mission's Potsdam headquarters (Interviewee #30).

Other examples of an active contribution of the EUSRs to operational activities of the Union include the setting up of a border mission for Transnistria and the EU missions in the Middle East. It was EUSR Jacobovits who first proposed the Transnistrian border mission (Interviewee #6). His successor, Kálmán Miszei, succeeded in making visa facilitation part of the Commission negotiations with Moldova, based on the rationale that this would increase the country's attractiveness vis-à-vis the Transnistrian breakaway republic (Interviewee #20). Likewise, EUSR Otte successfully lobbied for more EU engagement in the Middle East, namely through the two ESDP missions there, EUBAM Rafah and EUPOL COPPS (Interviewee #6).[356] Despite all persisting difficulties, both operations have brought about a qualitative leap not only of contacts between Israelis and Palestinians, e.g. by establishing a liaison office for regular communication at the technical level, but also of the EU's presence on the ground (Interviewee #19). It is on such measures that the EU can now build when it promotes its principles of a comprehensive settlement and multilateralism within the Quartet. The international Annapolis conference of November 2007 can thus be seen as a success of European ideas, in that European proposals exert influence through their acceptance by larger groups (Interviewee #47).

In general, the EUSRs have raised the qualitative level of policy deliberations in Brussels by providing EU-made information, thus making decision-making bodies less dependent on information graciously given by larger member states (Interviewees #21, 35, and 36; Grevi 2007, 46). The EUSRs' policy input has had a great impact on those member states that have either no embassy or one with only a skeleton staff in the respective region. These member states have become more active through the EUSRs' COREU and PSC reports, also engaging other EU institutions such as the Commission in policy talks (Interviewees #21, 35, and 36). This does not imply that the EUSRs have become the main source of political thinking in the EU, especially because their exact influence is hard to identify given that it cannot be regarded in isolation from processes in the PSC or the Secretariat.

On the whole, while they are still instruments rather than makers of policy (Interviewees #13, 16, and 30), the EUSRs are helpful in providing a level playing field for all, thus bringing the Union's comprehensive approach to crisis management to fruition (Interviewee #21). They analyze the situation on the ground, identify policy strands in the member states, and propose acceptable policies on the basis of their information (Interviewee #40; Grevi 2007, 142). Similar to what the Policy Unit achieved at the general political level, the EUSRs have thus helped to start a European doctrine, with respect to their regional responsibility, overcoming formerly juxtaposed national positions (Interviewee #47; Grevi 2007, 47).

---

356 For the contributions of EUSR Moratinos to formulating an EU policy, see Dietl 2005.

6.15.2 Potential barriers

The main barriers to change based on the learning about the EUSRs' policy input lie in the sensitivities of member states, and in whether these actually want the EUSRs to deliver meaningful policy. For member states, making policy proposals is very much the prerogative of their national foreign services (Interviewee #12). EUSRs must therefore be careful not to be seen as too proactive, which would offend some member states. A case in point is the current EUSR for Moldova who draws huge skepticism for all of his proposals due to the fact that his predecessor embarked on a collision course with member states over the question of peacekeeping in Transnistria (Interviewees #20 and 33). In practice, however, there are many areas with little EU (or, for that matter, national) policy present, so member states are grateful for the support from EUSRs (Interviewee #44). Ajello, for example, was enough of a politician to know how to prepare a proposal with member states, and how far he could go in such proposals (Interviewee #30).

Beyond national sensitivities, both the EUSR and whatever EU 'policy' is in place may just be a 'fig leaf', or a substitute for real action. Even when policy development is part of the EUSR's mandate, an effective contribution may not actually be expected (Interviewees #8 and 39). All the same, an overarching policy framework such as the EU strategy for Central Asia may not amount to much more than textual coherence while policy differences—and therefore joint inaction—persist (Interviewee #1). Therefore, despite all good intentions of and well-meaning input from the EUSR, the practical terms of EU engagement are a matter for member states—or the Commission, as far as it is within its competence—to decide on (Interviewee #16). These limitations notwithstanding, the input provided by EUSRs has strengthened the EU's foreign policy, in particular in the politico-diplomatic realm.

6.16 Deliberate use of envoys

The 'flexibility rule' that was carved out as an outcome of organizational learning (cf. section 5.7) has been implemented mainly with respect to its first postulate, i.e. to add new EUSRs in a manner allowing for future adjustments. This has increased the EU's freedom in responding to various crisis demands. In contrast, the rule's second stipulation that mandates should not be perpetuated has so far had little impact, because only a few mandates were terminated once and for all. This is due to a combination of institutional interests and external expectations that develop once an EUSR is in place, and which are hard to overcome.

6.16.1 Ensuing change

In following the flexibility rule, the EU has gained leeway in deploying the instrument of an envoy as a targeted response to a crisis and not just in a pre-formed manner. Such flexible use of instruments can be seen in the recent increase of non-Treaty-based Council representatives, i.e. envoys who are not appointed based on Article 18

(5) TEU but instead by simple administrative decisions. This is a regular habit for other institutions to appoint their representatives, such as the three Personal Representatives of Solana who cover topical issues such as human rights, relations with Parliament, and weapons of mass destruction. In addition, the Presidency can appoint representatives, such as the Swede Hans Dahlgren who served as an envoy to the Mano River Basin from 2001 to 2007.

Most recently, in the cases of Kosovo and Myanmar, the Council also reverted to a variable use of the envoy instrument, even though it could have enacted it on the basis of the Treaty. In the summer of 2007, the Council nominated German diplomat Wolfgang Ischinger as the EU's representative in the Kosovo troika talks. The reasoning was to stay flexible, both in terms of budget (Germany covered all costs incurred) and with respect to the limited time frame of the Kosovo negotiations (Interviewee #31). Likewise, the Italian politician Piero Fassino was dispatched, only a few weeks later, as the new Special Envoy (sic!—bringing back the original title) to Myanmar in order to support the UN representative Ibrahim Gambari and to coordinate member states activities. These two nominations together have additionally unravelled existing categories, establishing a new, more flexible level of representatives (Interviewee #12).

Other instances underscore that the EUSRs are not dispatched in a knee-jerk reaction to any given crisis. When Somalia was in unrest in early 2007, sending an EUSR was an option discussed but discarded; instead, the Deputy Director of the Africa Unit at the Council Secretariat, Jean-Christophe Belliard, was internally assigned to be the focal point for events there (Interviewee #12). Similarly, sending an EUSR to Zimbabwe was a topic of discussion among member states. In the end, member states decided against this instrument. The reasoning was that, generally speaking, part of the added value of an EUSR should be access to the government. However, Zimbabwe's current regime was considered the wrong body to turn to; thus, sending an EUSR there would thwart the EU's political efforts (Interviewee #30). Moreover, the European Parliament, despite its general aversion to the instrument, for years had called for an EUSR for Tibet (European Parliament 2003). This request remained unanswered by the Council, despite the fact that the EP even made appropriations for such a post in the 2006 CFSP budget.

Finally, the fact that individual EUSR mandates were indeed terminated at the end of the 1990s (cf. section 1.2.3) underlines their time-bound nature. In the cases of the EUSRs for the Royaumont Process and for Yugoslavia, it was mainly a lack of success—and not the completion of tasks—that led to rather short-lived mandates. The mandate for Kosovo was no longer upheld once the UN embarked to administer the province and the EU had taken over responsibility for the economic pillar of UNMIK. As for the EUSR for the Stability Pact for Southeastern Europe, the initial rationale was to tie the Pact to the Council via the EUSR (Interviewee #44). After a contractual relation between the EU and the Stability Pact had been established, the Council did not hesitate to phase out the mandate. So while some may see the law of institutions at work that makes it increasingly difficult to dismantle an institution once it is created (Interviewee #40), these examples demonstrate that path dependence alone cannot explain this pattern.[357]

6.16.2 Potential barriers

Because member states have learned to appreciate the usefulness of the EUSRs, particularly smaller states that rely on the reporting of the latter (cf. sections 4.2 and 5.6), terminating an individual mandate has become less common. Instead, it is more likely for them to be changed or refocused, as was the case in Macedonia (double-hat) or in the Great Lakes (from a regional crisis focus to one on institution-building in the DRC) (Interviewee #15). In the end, this may result in the extension of mandates beyond a point of clear added value, especially when the political price of termination is considered too high. Such cost may arise from internal factors, such as interested member states, or from outside expectations. Once an EUSR is deployed, third parties come to count on EU involvement in certain crises, so that the retreat of an envoy would send the wrong signal to international partners (Interviewee #31).[358]

In addition, the prospect of the European External Action Service guards against too much flexibility. On the one hand, it makes it improbable that the EUSRs and other envoys would be done away with entirely without any replacement in the form of the EEAS (Interviewee #40). On the other, those member states that fear the gradual building up of a quasi-foreign ministry, for example through the Personal Representatives, may wish to diminish the flexibility of Brussels institutions like the High Representative or the Council Secretariat (Interviewee #12).

6.17 Double-hatting

Most significantly, double-hatting as the combination of the post of EUSR with that of Head of Commission Delegation (cf. section 5.8) has advanced cooperation between

---

357 The following thought experiment should illustrate that there is not even anything like 'instrumental dependence' of the EU on its Special Representatives. The saying 'If you have a hammer, everything starts to look like a nail' can be translated into institutional policies, meaning that once an organization has a useful instrument at its disposal, it will see lots of opportunities to employ it—whether adequate or not. With the EUSRs, things are slightly different: In a world that is full of potential 'nails', the EU with its focus on multidimensional crises is actually searching for 'real' nails to deploy the EUSRs rather than seeing 'nails' where there are none. At the same time, the EUSRs can be used not only in complex crises but in other circumstances too, like promoting the Central Asia strategy among member states. This 'hammer' is therefore at least multifunctional, if it is a 'hammer' at all.

358 Ultimately, the EU is not a state in which a newly elected leader can change the whole foreign policy orientation, including the instrumental toolkit. This is what happened on the U.S. side after George W. Bush was elected president in 2000. In order to distinguish itself from the internationally active policies of the Clinton years, the Bush administration amongst other measures drastically cut the number of Special Presidential Envoys (Kirkconnell 2002, 4). This course was changed when President Barack Obama took office in January 2009 and soon reinstated envoys to the most relevant crisis regions (cf. The Economist 2009).

the Commission and the Council side and brought clarity about who is 'Mr Europe' in a third country. The additional impact that this arrangement has had fuelled the debate not only about the proliferation of the Macedonian model but also about what benefits it could bring at the level of the High Representative / Vice-President of the Commission proposed by the Lisbon Reform Treaty. Barriers to this, however, still exist at the institutional level (the question of personnel statutes) as well as at the political level (when an EUSR would become too powerful due to such an arrangement).

6.17.1 Ensuing change

What the EU learned about combining two posts from different pillars into one personal union, tentatively tried in the case of its presence in Macedonia, produced positive change: "Double-hatting [...] favoured a sea-change in the troubled relationship between CFSP/ESDP and Community instruments and actors, and fostered much closer coordination" (Grevi 2007, 95). The UK's Lordships confirm this view by concluding that "the double-hatting arrangement has been a success in Macedonia, has led to greater visibility for the EU presence, greater impact and coherence [... The] EU now speaks with one voice in Macedonia" (House of Lords 2006, 22).

Indeed, the Macedonian double-hat works well despite initial hesitation about a 'personal union' of two different mandates that have remained separate (Interviewees #8 and 24). In practical terms, the two existing offices were merged to one 'EU mission' but with two budgets, two different staffs, and two lines of command and reporting. In the politico-diplomatic field, advisors are contracted under the EUSR's budget; all others are delegation (i.e. Commission) staff (Interviewee #24). The majority of tasks relate to the accession process rather than to the EUSR's mandate (Interviewee #8). Ironically, even the EUSR's mandate in its standard language about coordination (Article 9) calls for cooperation with the Commission delegation—as if the same person were not heading this delegation.[359] Yet, despite this institutional separation of staff, the exchange of information and overall cooperation has gone rather well (Grevi 2007, 97).

The positive effects double-hatting has had on the ground have brought about closer consultation between relevant officials at headquarters' level in Brussels, who now regard themselves as married to each other (Interviewee #11). Frequent interaction is as much a prerequisite for as it is a result of the double-hatting, "fuelling a common approach across inter-institutional divides" (Grevi 2007, 97; cf. House of Lords 2006, 22). Where there are issues of overlapping competence—and, naturally, there are many in a candidate country—the EUSR/Head of Delegation usually receives joint instructions from both the Council and the Commission (Interviewee #11; House of Lords 2006, 22). The double-hatting has therefore enabled the EUSR to solve—both upstream in Brussels

---

359 For example, the EUSR is asked, as is any of his non-double-hatted colleagues, to "provide Member States' missions and Commission delegations with regular briefings"; cf. Council Joint Action 2007/109/CFSP of 15 February 2007.

and downstream in Macedonia—the serious coordination problems affecting the EU's performance between 2003 and 2005 (Grevi 2007, 96).

Moreover, the combination of posts has increased the EU's visibility and standing vis-à-vis third parties as well as its actual impact. EUSR Fouéré is now commonly referred to as 'Mr Europe', which gives him a more prominent profile locally but also eases coordination with delegations of member states (Interviewee #24; Grevi 2007, 96). This has also made the impact of the EU message, now carried by only one voice, much stronger. Finally, it allows the EU to use community instruments for political purposes, thus reaping a maximum benefit with its interventions (Interviewee #24).

The model has received considerable attention with regard to Bosnia and Herzegovina and the discussions about a transition of authority from the OHR to local authorities (Interviewee #8). In a joint policy paper, Commissioner Rehn and High Representative Solana implicitly included the possibility of double-hatting by stating that such an arrangement could rationalize structures and unify the EU's efforts in the context of closing the OHR (Solana/Rehn 2006, 2). As a first step, the paper explored the co-location of the EUSR offices and the EC Delegation in Sarajevo; a new building is now under construction and, pending the closure of OHR, at least the Commission delegation will move in once the building is ready (Interviewee #32).

However, the 'intra-EU' as opposed to the existing 'international' double-hat model of Bosnia and Herzegovina would only come once the 'Bonn powers' will be phased out, as Commission thinking in particular forbids the EC Head of Delegation to exercise them. The same person should not demand reforms on behalf of the Commission and, at the same time, order the government to implement them under his EUSR-cum-OHR-powers function, as the argument goes (Interviewees #8, 34, and 32; cf. Solana/Rehn 2006). It is also for these reasons that the new Kosovo EUSR follows the Bosnian rather than the Macedonian model—due to the political powers he yields (Interviewee #8).[360]

For the African Union, a process of reflection had been going on for quite some time until an 'integrated double-hatting' was realized in December 2007 (Interviewee #15; cf. House of Lords 2006, 23). While it was inspired not least by the Macedonian model, this second arrangement attempted to go beyond mere copying. Much more than establishing only a personal union at the top, the AU double-hat, with the EU foreign service looming on the horizon, should function as an integrated delegation (Interviewees #31 and 41).

Indeed, considerations of an EU presence at the seat of the AU hark back to when the first mandate of the EUSR for Sudan was issued (cf. subsection 1.3.1), signifying a fairly long learning process. Two alternative models had been discussed prior to deciding in

---

360 Cf. also Jaanson 2008, 12; Grevi 2007, 89-90. For how international administrative structures in Bosnia and Herzegovina served as a blueprint for the setup of UNMIK in Kosovo in 1999, see Graff et al. 1999, 20.

favour of the double-hat: to add an ESDP mission, both civilian and military, to the Commission Delegation at the AU that was planned anyway; or to open a third Council office in addition to the ones in Geneva and New York. The former was not chosen, because it was difficult to combine the Head of Delegation post on the Commission side with the Head of Mission post on the ESDP side. The latter solution would have been too complicated and too expensive, as it would have had to be paid out of the Council's administrative budget (Interviewee #41). Seven years prior, the Council was happy to declare the EUSRs' activities as administrative in order to pay for (and control) them directly (cf. section 4.7); today it is glad to gain an additional presence financed by the Community budget.

Its singular character notwithstanding, the Macedonian model could be regarded as trendsetting in that is has initiated a process of gradually developing its application to other cases (Interviewee #16). Double-hatting is now the rule at operational levels, such as in Moldova, where the head of EUBAM is also senior advisor to the EUSR;[361] in Bosnia and Herzegovina, where the heads of important departments within the OHR also serve the EUSR (Grevi 2007, 84); in Sudan, where the EUSR's police and military advisors are heads of the respective support element to AMIS II;[362] and in the Middle East, where an EUSR advisor is double-hatted as the head of EUPOL COPPS.[363]

6.17.2 Potential barriers

Various technical, legal, and political barriers have prevented the Macedonian case from serving as a model for a greater number of EUSRs. Technically, there are hurdles such as the budgetary responsibility for shared facilities, plus the tricky legal question of how to overcome the obligation of all Commission staff (including the Head of Delegation) not to take orders from any other EU institution or member state, including the PSC (Interviewees #10 and 17). For some time, the argument was also made that a double-hatted EUSR would need to be a Commission official in the first place (Interviewee #31), a condition that Erwan Fouéré fulfilled but which was no longer applied to Koen Vervaeke upon his taking up the AU post. As the Commission was eager to introduce another double-hatting arrangement, the Council had made it a precondition for approval to nominate a person of its choice (Interviewee #31).

While technical questions are time-consuming but eventually manageable, double-hatting of the Macedonian type is also extremely sensitive in political terms due to its potentially precedent-setting character (Interviewee #11). Indeed, member states, in a protocol declaration to the Council meeting that passed the initial Joint Action, explicitly declared Erwan Fouéré's appointment as an "exceptional measure" that should not be "regarded as setting a precedent for the appointment of future EU Special Representatives" (Council of the European Union 2005a, 3). Even though this declaration has been formally

---

361 Council Joint Action 2007/107/CFSP of 15 February 2007.

362 Council Joint Action 2007/108/CFSP of 15 February 2007.

363 Council Joint Action 2005/797/CFSP 14 November 2005.

upheld, member states have by now quietly come to accept the model character of this arrangement (Interviewee #17). However, in order to avoid as much as possible any obliging effect, the precedent was qualified in two ways: Generally, further application of this double-hat model would have to be decided on a case-by-case basis (Interviewees #15 and 31; cf. House of Lords 2006, 23, and Grevi 2007, 97). Regionally, it should for now remain limited to the Enlargement process, i. e. it is only conceivable for the Western Balkans (Interviewee #16; cf. Grevi 2007, 97). In Moldova, for example, double-hatting was considered but not put into practice: While it could have eased tensions with the Commission about the ENP Action Plans (cf. section 5.1), the EUSR there is not a resident envoy and the Commission's role is not as strong as it is in the Balkans (Interviewee #39). Thus, although many see that it works well in the specific circumstances on the ground, this model has not yet been adapted as a best practice that should guide future mandates or gradually transform existing ones.

Political sensitivities are not confined to the CFSP area but also spread to institutional questions such as the Treaty reform proposing the double-hatted foreign minister. Some of the member states were particularly wary at the time of the first mandate to convey to their parliament or public that double-hatting could be seen as an anticipation of this Treaty formula (Interviewee #16). With regard to the new EU foreign service, the Commission had for a long time rejected a Council presence in Addis Ababa that would flow from a double-hatted EUSR (Interviewee #28). When this post was finally created at the end of 2007, the planned integrated substructure underneath the EUSR/Head of Delegation could not be achieved (Interviewee #16).

As mentioned before, there are more obvious practical—i. e. less politically constructed—difficulties as well. Being an EUSR (or a Head of Delegation, for that matter) is already a full-time post, so some simply see a work overload in combining these two posts into one (Interviewee #9). Furthermore, in contrast to the Head of Delegation, an EUSR does not have a deputy at his side. As the double-hat is only a personal union and not a merger of offices, the Deputy Head of Delegation cannot take over duties under the CFSP mandate when the EUSR is not present (Interviewee #24). Then, there might also be EUSRs who would dislike wearing a Commission hat given that it involves lengthy bureaucratic processes rather than discreet political dialogue (Grevi 2007, 48).

Some of the seemingly practical questions can easily be given a political touch, for example in the case of a regional mandate. There, the EU would have to choose a delegation in one particular country to merge with the EUSR mandate; preferring one partner country over the others by establishing the EUSR's residence there would be politically quite sensitive (Interviewee #16; Grevi 2007, 49). In regions such as Central Asia or the Great Lakes, where member state presence is feeble, a double-hat arrangement would also give the respective EUSR too much importance (Interviewee #16).[364] In the

---

364 The fact that now there is a double-hatted office in Addis Ababa does not disprove this point, because a) there is a clear location for where to base the EUSR (i. e. at the seat of the AU) and this location is different from the EC delegation to Ethiopia, and b) relations with the AU are under

end, these barriers have so far been strong enough to prevent all non-regional EUSR mandates from being double-hatted as the EP has demanded (European Parliament 2007, para 8 (i)). Nonetheless, double-hatting has been established as a model for future operational as well as institutional models.

6.18 The EU's strategic role

As explained previously (cf. section 5.9), the strategic role of the EU has a long history. What could be detected in its relation to the EUSRs was not so much a rewriting but a reconfirmation of the rules. Still, no immediate change should be expected from such organizational learning; instead, a long-term effect is rather more likely. What this effect could be will figure more prominently in the conclusions (see subsection 7.2.3). Yet there are some barriers such as a lack of unified policies or of boldness in decision-making that are visible already today.

6.18.1 Ensuing change

Learning about the EU's strategic role will not have an immediate but rather only a long-term effect. Many of the EU's activities in the area of rehabilitation and confidence-building measures will take years to be effective (Interviewee #27). Yet, by working on the internal rather than on the external side of affairs, the EUSRs have actually raised the EU's international profile (Interviewee #40).

Important partner countries have expressed their appreciation of the EU's role. Reportedly, even in a highly security-related area such as the Middle East, the United States has come to accept the EU's soft power, both in development cooperation on the ground and as a partner to forge consensus within the international community (Interviewee #19). Russia too has become more open-minded toward and appreciative of EU engagement through the EUSRs, such as when foreign minister Sergey Lavrov and President Vladimir Putin commended, at a Troika meeting, the EUSR's role in general and his cooperative efforts towards Russia in particular (Interviewee #46).

6.18.2 Potential barriers

The main barrier to the implementation of what has been learned about the EU's strategic role is the oft-cited lack of a unified policy. While there are member states that support the course of making the EU a global 'civilian' power—in Africa for example, these are usually the Scandinavian countries and the Netherlands—other members prefer to point to the 'realities on the ground' and pursue realpolitik (Interviewee #28). This has consequences for the administrative level, which is often not sufficiently equipped to reach the political objectives the EU has set itself, just because member states do not

---

much tighter control from the Council than, say, with the handful of countries located in the Great Lakes region (Interviewee #16).

want the centre—with its penchant for well-meaning policies—to be too strong (Interviewee #34).

Furthermore, a specific political culture seems to have been bred in Brussels: The EU is a cautious and conservative organization that lacks boldness in decision-making, a fact that is aggravated by the need for agreement between 27 member states (Interviewee #39). After all, the Council Secretariat is still a secretariat and not geared towards diplomacy: The rules are made for a technical organization, not for a political one (Interviewee #39). Only in a few cases, like in Moldova and the Balkans (i.e on European territory), does the EU find itself in a leading role, with EUSRs formally involved in the political processes. Already in the South Caucasus, the impact of the EU is very limited (Interviewee #3). This shows that the EU is still far from putting into practice what it has learned and what it claims its global role to be.

Chapter 7:
Learning and Change in EU Foreign Policy—
An Assessment

The only thing we learn from history is that people learn nothing from history.
Georg Wilhelm Hegel, 1830

"The idea is like a pair of glasses on our nose through which we see whatever we look at. It never occurs to us to take them off," is what the philosopher Ludwig Wittgenstein once pointedly remarked (Wittgenstein 1958, no. 103). It is downright impossible for us humans to actually take these glasses off; yet it appears feasible (metaphorically speaking) to change them. This is what I have tried to do by looking at the developments in European foreign policy through the lens of organizational learning theories, examining such an emblematic case as the EU Special Representatives. Thus, I do not claim to present a 'new truth' but rather wish to add to academic discourse by presenting a different perspective. What the latter can contribute is part of this conclusion.

This study set out to introduce organizational learning, a theoretical blind spot, as a contribution to theory development. As a case, the EU Special Representatives, an even more pronounced empirical blind spot, were chosen to provide an alternative history of the development of European foreign policy over more than a decade, highlighting the invention (1996–99) and subsequent formalization (1999–2001) of EUSRs, as well as a period of expansion (2002–05) that was followed by a consolidation phase (2006–07). Comparing the EUSRs—along a set of internal and external roles—with special envoys of both the United States and the United Nations brought preliminary insights into their working procedures. Based on these insights (induction) as well as on a theoretical OL framework (deduction), I then developed the analytical model of this study.

Having analyzed the work of nine EUSRs over a period of twelve years by means of a model of organizational development in the preceding part (chapters 4 to 6), in concluding the research I will now proceed backwards, i. e. from the explanatory character of the model to the broader theoretical implications of OL to the relevance of the EUSRs as an instrument for European foreign policy:

– The first look is at the model of organizational development—elaborated at the end of chapter 3 and highlighting the causal mechanisms of learning—that was used for the empirical analysis of the EUSRs' work: I will summarize the learning experiences that have become engrained in the EU's organizational rules and the organizational change they resulted in. In addition, I will draw inferences on the scope conditions of organizational learning in the EU context (7.1).
– Then, I will turn to the theoretical implications of my research for OL, International Relations, and explanations of European foreign policy (7.2). I will scrutinize the findings that looking through the 'OL glasses' suggests for OL and IR theory, and

assess the explanatory power of OL with regard to other approaches when it comes to explaining European foreign policy. In particular, I will highlight two aspects of how learning impacts on the latter: the centrality of a European (foreign policy) identity as well as the importance of the EU's internal dimension.

–   Finally, returning to the policy considerations from the beginning of this work, I will put forth recommendations on what the EU ought to learn from a foreign policy instrument called EUSR. These recommendations mainly refer to the flexibility of deploying envoys as boundary spanners and, prospectively, to how the planned European External Action Service could make use of Special Representatives (7.3).

7.1   Filling a research gap: An analytical model of Organizational Learning

In the following, I will briefly summarize the instances of organizational learning and ensuing change that had been deduced earlier on (cf. subsection 3.3.3) and were then scrutinized in the empirical chapters of this work (part II). First, organizational learning is treated as the dependent variable, bringing together a collection of learning experiences that have become part of the collective memory of the EU, or of its unwritten *acquis organisationel* (7.1.1).[365] As a next step, instances of subsequent change (i. e. where organizational learning is the independent variable) are reviewed (7.1.2). Both steps then serve to determine the scope conditions of organizational learning in the EU context, i. e. the effects of filters such as organizational culture and absorption capacity, and barriers such as change resistance and institutional design (7.1.3). On this basis, I can evaluate the analytical models' theoretical significance in section 7.2.

7.1.1   Summary of instances of organizational learning (phase 1)

All in all, eighteen instances of organizational learning could be traced with regard to the EU Special Representatives. The summary of these instances follows the previously developed set of structural, procedural, operational, and ideational levels. In addition, I will point out two cases where the EU has broadly failed to learn.

At the **structural level,** the most important instances of the EU's organizational learning in the context of the EUSRs took place at the very beginning: Based on reflections on the EU's standing in the respective regions, on its political weight (or rather lack thereof), and on how to make a contribution to the resolution of two long-standing conflicts (in the Great Lakes region and the Middle East), the Union dispatched its first ever 'special envoys.' Since then, the number of EUSRs has increased, again for a combination

---

365   The French word of the *acquis* (accomplishment) is used here with reference to its meaning in EU jargon: The *acquis communautaire* refers to the sum of Community laws, whereas the *acquis politique* denotes the body of established policies and practices in the field of CFSP (Ginsberg 1999, 436; Mayer 2004, 65). With particular regard to EU foreign policy, Grevi refers to the "*acquis* of institutional practice and experience" that has emerged in CFSP/ESDP policymaking (Grevi 2007, 31 [emphasis in original]).

of both internal (institutional strengthening) and external reasons (usefulness in crisis regions).

A (continuing) major learning process is related to the integration of EUSRs into the developing CFSP structures, trying to fence in these hitherto fairly independent actors. By their mere presence, EUSRs create the need to incorporate them into the Brussels foreign policy machinery. When passing guidelines, establishing task forces, or changing the budgetary location of the EUSRs, more often than not the structures of national foreign ministries provided the model to learn from. At the same time, little has been learned with regard to the EUSRs' own institutional structures, apart from the need to create a central administrative support unit.

In terms of **procedures,** it has emerged as a clear lesson that close cooperation with the Commission is essential for the work of EUSRs—a point that has been driven home to Brussels not least by the envoys in the field. Similarly, how to coordinate the various political EU activities, i.e. of member states as well as ESDP operations in a given country, has become engrained in the EU's organizational memory. Other learning instances relate to how mandates are drafted and to the selection of EUSR personnel (both in terms of transparency of process and of the officeholder's desired qualities). With regard to how the EU should make better use of the experiences made by the different EUSRs ('lessons learned'), there is only little learning to report on.

Concerning **operational rules,** learning is most obvious in the wide range of tasks that current EUSRs are asked to fulfill. In practice, mandates deliberately left broad provide room for manoeuvre for the envoys, not least in order to react to events on the ground. Here, it becomes clear that Brussels institutions have been able to learn two contradictory things at different levels: On the operational level, they want to give EUSRs a fairly free hand; but on the structural level, they try to better control them. Striking the balance between the two then is key, and yet it has not always been easy.

A difficult balance has also been present in the learning processes with regard to the location from which EUSRs should operate (mostly Brussels, it is now thought) and whether they should be included in the chain of command of ESDP operations (they used to be, but no longer are). When it comes to external cooperation, the EU has learned about the usefulness of having EUSRs as representatives in the plethora of international fora that try to organize international assistance for a given crisis region.

The most political of learning instances took place at the **ideational level,** where the EU has learned to employ the EUSRs for veritable input into policy rather than deploying them for want of one. In particular, it has learned to draw on them in a calculated and flexible way, including by using the so-called double-hatted function when necessary, instead of reacting to a perceived demand in an automatic fashion. Last but certainly not least, it is through the EUSRs that the EU has confirmed previous aspirations about its global strategic role, a point that will be taken up again later (cf. subsection 7.2.3).

This long list of learning instances can be contrasted with two observations about short-comings of the EU's learning, i.e. cases where it has failed to learn or has not learned well enough. First, much of the EU's learning appears to be directed towards internal affairs and seems less outward-oriented or policy-relevant than one might have expected (or hoped for). Second, the EUSRs have been an important factor for the EU's learning, but failed to learn themselves due to a lack of organizational capacities. I will address these points in the following.

Different factors may account for the **dominance of internally focused learning,** one being research design and data availability. As most of the policy-relevant material is classified, in this attempt to explain the working of a particular foreign policy instrument I had to focus on the less sensitive and therefore more easily available organizational information. This 'access factor' would make it similarly—or even more—difficult to study in detail the EU's process of learning about world events such as the 9/11 terrorist attacks or external developments such as the Iraq crisis of 2003. Not only would the analysis of information processing and potential learning in these cases be a study of its own, but also would the limited accessibility of empirical material put a huge strain on any research-er's efforts to investigate the EU's internal proceedings in reaction to these events.

Another factor derives from the analytical framework developed earlier with its differ-entiation between an outer and inner environment and in particular the importance of the inner environment's sense-making structures (cf. subsection 3.2.2). There, I alluded to the fact that an organization can learn by processing information from its inner environment. This is what happened in the case of the EU: Its learning about structural and procedural issues such as the invention of EUSRs and their integration into CFSP structures, or internal cooperation with the Commission and personnel selection, is dominant not because the EU is an inward-oriented institution but because it is an organization that needs—like any organization—these sense-making structures of the inner environment.

What is more, learning about the inner environment contributes to the external dimen-sion too. While the EU may not have learned how to solve a particular conflict—which, empirically speaking, is hard to do anyway, and no single international actor can claim to have found such a formula—it has learned how to best receive information about a conflict, feed this into policy-making processes, and at the same time be represented on the ground as well as in international fora. In Alexander George's terminology (George 1994), the EU's learning has produced knowledge with regard to the 'generic theory' of how to use an instrument of conflict management. This generic theory itself needs to be embedded in an 'abstract theory' of International Relations (here: the EU's understand-ing of multilateralism; cf. subsection 7.2.3).[366]

---

366 According to George, both generic theory and abstract theory would need to be additionally com-plemented by 'actor-specific knowledge' about the case in question (George 1994, 161).

Finally, and in addition to these explanations for the predominance of the internal dimension, one should bear in mind that the level of structures and procedures is not necessarily less important as such—witness the Commission's role in EFP, which compensates for its political weakness with its institutional power. Especially a multi-layered institution like the EU will always have to invest more in its internal procedures than do more unitary actors like states (cf. subsection 7.2.3 on the internal dimension). The level of operations and ideas is therefore but one part of where organizational learning can take place.

The other shortcoming—that **EUSRs have contributed to the organizational learning of the EU, but much less learning took place at their own level**—is mostly due to the fact that there is no organizational memory for the Special Representatives. In particular the lack of persistent institutional structures prevents knowledge from becoming rooted in organizational rules. All new EUSRs, not only the first two, had to start their work from scratch. They operate in a broadly permissive—if not neglectful environment—often lacking strategic guidance from member states.

Ironically, whereas the EUSRs are meant to provide continuity to third parties, people at their team level come and go and there are no institutional structures to retain individual learning experiences. Thus, learning may work at the individual level of EUSRs and this contributes to the EU's organizational learning; collectively, however, i. e. at their own (sub-)organizational level, learning is particularly difficult for the EUSRs.

The evidence of a number of instances of learning confirms the actual occurrence of organizational learning. This finding is not derogated by existing shortcomings, i. e. that learning was incomplete in two instances.

7.1.2 Summary of instances of organizational change (phase 2)

Now it is possible to assess the influence that these eighteen instances of organizational learning have had on learning-based change, i. e. on how the EU makes use of the foreign policy instrument of the Special Representatives. In view of the relatively weak position of the EUSRs as outsiders to the system commanding only a small team with little infrastructure plus given the strong role of member states in CFSP, one might not expect a large impact of EUSR-induced learning on policy or institutional change. The analysis effectuated in this work, however, paints a different picture.

It is fair to say that much of what the EU has learned through the EUSRs has led to considerable change, both at the institutional and policy level.

With regard to the **institutional level of structures and procedures,** learning about the usefulness of commanding an instrument such as the Special Representatives has turned them from a fig leaf covering a lack of policy into a flexibly used tool to respond to different and changing crises. The presence of the envoys—and indeed their increasing number—have contributed to the establishment of CFSP structures that render the

EU more operational as an actor, and the streamlining of the mandating process has reduced the workload for the PSC. Interestingly, however, the EU did not establish similarly strong structures at the EUSR level for fear of strengthening their independence vis-à-vis the Brussels institutions.

Cooperation with the Commission has improved a great deal, including on budgetary issues, with differences discernible between the headquarters (where competition is still high due to the persisting pillar structure) and the field (where all parties generally try to be as constructive as possible). The picture is also mixed with regard to personnel selection, where a more open process has increased competition for the EUSR posts, but the basis for selection still remains somewhat small. Likewise, lessons-learned seminars were put in place in response to learning, though they have not yet produced much further change.

Concerning the **policy level of operations and ideas,** one can witness a gradual expansion of the EUSRs tasks. Once they were deployed, they were continuously assigned new duties over the years, sometimes at their express wish and sometimes because the Council thought it wise to use them for additional assignments. EUSRs also enhance the coherence of EU instruments in the field, providing a bridge not only to ESDP operations, but also to other policy areas such as Enlargement policy, the European Neighbourhood Policy, development policy, and, as of recent, energy policy. This has considerably enhanced the EUSRs' position within the CFSP structures, so that for reasons of both pragmatism and power-calculation they were in the end relieved from their function within the chain of command of ESDP operations. Learning about the EUSRs' basis of operation has eventually strengthened their position in Brussels, while allowing them to keep an extended presence in the field, very often with different regional offices. Furthermore, the EU's presence in international fora was given a boost by the EUSRs' function of cooperating closely with external partners in more or less prominent 'groups of friends' settings that predetermine multilateral policies.

Change has also been considerable at the level of how EU policies are made. This primarily concerns the extensive reporting that EUSRs provide on a regular basis, channelling proper EU information into the policy deliberation process, as well as their specific contributions made to the EU's Neighbourhood Policy or its Central Asia Strategy. This change can also be witnessed in operational arrangements such as the coordination of the EU's political activities in a given region. Such close liaisons, in particular with member states foreign missions, have led to more streamlined information being passed on to national capitals.

Finally, what the EU learned about using envoys in a calculated way, including by double-hatting them if opportune, has led to two important changes. Internally, it has set a working example (though formally contested in its precedent-setting character) of how the EU's foreign policy could be arranged across pillars in the future under the personal union of the next High Representative of the Union for Foreign Affairs and Security

Policy and Vice-President of the Commission for External Relations. Externally, it has enhanced the EU's actorness by equipping it with a full-fledged foreign policy instrument that other actors, both international organizations and nation states, dispose of too.

This list of changes stemming from learning instances of EUSR work highlights the importance of taking into account organizational learning as an independent explanatory factor.

On the whole, these changes—together with what the EU has learned about its role in the world but which can only in the long run be translated into change—have enhanced the Union's strategic actorness in international affairs.

Before looking at the theoretical (7.2.3) and practical consequences (7.3) these findings have for European foreign policy, I will first determine the general scope conditions of learning and change.

7.1.3 Scope conditions, or: When and how learning and change occur

It is now time to return to the study's epistemological interest and the research questions formulated at the outset. Based on the instances of organizational learning and change collected in part II (chapters 4 to 6) and summarized above, I can confirm the original assumption and assert that the EU as an organization did indeed learn.

Answering also the more elaborate question of when and how learning and subsequent change occur, I will now identify the relevant scope conditions. The model introduced in chapter 3 highlighted biases and constraints, respectively, for both phases: Organizational culture (bias) and absorption capacity (constraint) are **filters** that impact on information processing leading to **organizational learning (phase 1);** change resistance (bias) and institutional design (constraint) can act as barriers to transforming learning into **organizational change (phase 2).** The question here is whether and how the filters and barriers have conditioned processes of learning and change in European foreign policy?

As for the filters, **organizational culture** is key here for two reasons. On the one hand, from the outset this study did not venture to analyze the individuals' capacity for information absorption that was introduced as additional cognitive filter (cf. subsection 3.3.2). On the other hand, it turns out that, because they face much more information than they are able to process, organizations select the stimuli to which they respond (Hedberg 1981, 8). This implies that an organization does not receive all (necessary or important) information about an event in or a change of the environment. While it may be the case that an organization endures technical difficulties to receive relevant information due to its weak absorption capacity, this tends to be overridden by the fact that the organization is biased to select the information it wants to process with whatever capacities it has available. It is thus appropriate to focus on organizational culture in this assessment of the scope conditions of learning.

Providing the link between the individual and the collective level, organizational culture allows for deductions from one level to the other. Individuals can shape the organizational culture as much as they will adapt to it. Analyzing the organizational culture therefore permits a researcher to draw conclusions about how the (majority of) individuals within an organization think of and perceive broader concepts—which ultimately influences how they learn.

By looking at the factors that shaped the reflection phase of the learning instances reported on in this study, some **characteristics of the organizational culture in the European foreign policy realm** can be discerned.

– One is the recurring desire to achieve greater coherence and to speak with one voice, be it in the coordination of member states in the field (vertical coherence) or in pillar-spanning efforts of cooperation between the EUSRs and the Commission (horizontal coherence). This is in line with the aspiration for greater international standing and for trying to match the EU's economic weight with new political weight, exemplified in the double-hatting of EUSRs.
– Another characteristic is the orientation toward national foreign services and the attempt to build state-like structures that allow for efficiency and control. This is visible in the various guidelines passed as well as in the way EUSRs have been used for the provision of information and analysis that feed into the policy-making process. The interesting element here is that the organizational culture wants to be at the same time different from and similar to member states: It aims to differ in the strategic direction, pursuing a less interest-oriented and more values-based policy, while trying to emulate them in the organizational setup, copying structures from national foreign ministries.
– Moreover, the EU is conscious of the broad spectrum of instruments that it commands (albeit through different pillars). It aims to use them as part of a comprehensive approach to crisis management, in particular in the way ESDP missions (both military and civilian) are intertwined with diplomatic (i. e. CFSP) measures and Community policies, such as security sector reform, border control, or economic support.

In addition to these three practical aspects of organizational culture (external coherence, orientation toward state structures, and a comprehensive set of instruments), a **substantive element of the organizational culture concerning the EU's international role** can also be discerned.

– All respondents referred to the image of the EU being a different type of power in world affairs—and they saw their work as a contribution to achieving this position. The bottom line of the EU's organizational culture is that the EU has a role to play in international affairs, that this role should be different from what states (including member states) or international organizations do, and that in the past, for a variety of reasons that need not be analyzed here, it has failed to take on this role (cf. in particular section 5.9).

From these findings, I can deduce that individual filters of EU officials have the following characteristics:

–   They value external coherence;
–   They look at national models for institutional inspiration;
–   They appreciate the EU's comprehensive set of instruments; and
–   They are aware of the EU's global ambition.

Based on the findings of this study, I can also refine the hypotheses presented in chapter 3.

It is true that the EUSRs as **boundary spanners,** shuttling between the subject of learning and its environment, have both increased the amount of information available to the EU (quantity) and analyzed and bundled the same according to need (quality); **they thus triggered learning** (hypothesis 1). This goes back to the differentiation between an internal and external environment, whereas the former is located within the subject of learning. Boundary spanners as an organizational sub-unit straddle the learning subject's defining boundaries into the external environment (cf. subsection 3.2.2). What is more, not just by their actions but even by their mere presence do they produce reflection on the part of the EU. In other words: The simple fact of having (to use) an envoy, whether or not he or she delivers information, already triggers learning. This also has practical consequences, which I will highlight later (cf. subsection 7.3.1).

The question of maintaining a balance between granting the freedom to collect information and providing the **necessary structures to process and, ultimately, store such information** (hypothesis 2) is also pertinent, although answered to the EUSRs' disadvantage: While Brussels institutions are happy to receive wide-ranging information through the Special Representatives, they have consistently refused to build up stronger structures for them. The continuous lack of such structures has only marginally weakened the EU itself in its capacity to learn as a foreign policy actor, e.g. when specific knowledge gets lost within the EUSR teams due to personnel turnover. In return, it keeps the EUSRs from developing a rival centre of gravity.

In addition to these filters, **barriers** to translating learning into change exist, and they also relate to the question of the EU's international competencies in that they usually curtail the more ambitious lessons learned.

Change resistance, for example, can be found in the unwillingness of member states to grant the EU (i.e. the EUSRs as one of its instruments) freedom to make decisions on foreign policy matters, or at a more practical level in the resistance of national ambassadors to being coordinated by an EUSR. Another example is found at the policy level, when member states cannot agree on a common and coherent policy with regard to a given issue. Such resistance certainly is not only with the member states but also with Brussels institutions when they refuse to exploit the leeway they have, for example by foregoing closer cooperation between the Council and the European Parliament. Furthermore, the strengthening of EUSR structures, if only by a small administrative unit, has met internal resistance from these institutions.

This notwithstanding, when EU institutions are a barrier to change it is usually due to **institutional design**—something that member states as the masters of the Treaties could overcome, if only they wanted to. Pending this, Commission and Council fiercely guard the existing legal-institutional divides, thus preventing lessons that promote cross-pillar cooperation from being put in place.

Ultimately, institutional design as a barrier can thus be subsumed under change resistance of member states, just like (with regard to the filters in phase 1) organizational culture overrides the individual's absorption capacity. These findings largely confirm the third hypothesis: Member states will resist changes that appear to be in favor of the 'Brussels headquarters.' Their power to do so is, however, limited as they cannot directly influence social processes in the organization and therefore have little sway over how staff views develop, including those of national officials. Still, by providing an authorizing environment, they remain an "outer structural constraint" (Woods 2006, 4). Thus, one can say that while IO secretariats are to a large extent autonomous in their learning, member states become dominant as soon as it comes to translating learning experiences into change.

In sum, the research gap of organizational learning has been somewhat narrowed:

Learning does take place in organizations, e.g. in the European Union's foreign policy. It is usefully conceptualized as a two-phase process of organizational development where learning and subsequent change are treated separately. Moreover, organizational culture appears to be the main filter in the first phase (organizational learning), whereas the influence of member states takes prominence in the second phase (organizational change).

These findings have important implications for OL theory (7.2.1), IR theory, and theoretical approaches to European foreign policy (7.2.3). In addition, now that I have established what the EU learned about the EUSRs, I can infer some practical propositions for EU foreign policy-making in general (7.3).

7.2   Theoretical implications from learning through the EUSRs

The *acquis organisationel* of learning and change, presented in the previous section, is by itself no small feat. Confirming both the merits (yes, learning does take place in organizations) and limitations (no, it is not a sufficient explanation for change) of learning, it will now serve to assess the study's overall theoretical contribution to the development of OL as a middle-range theory, to IR theory, as well as to approaches that theorize European foreign policy.

7.2.1 Organizational Learning as a middle-range theory

This study used an exploratory approach due to the lack of a consistent framework for the analysis of the organizational learning of political institutions (cf. section 3.1). Furthermore, given that mainstream approaches in International Relations in general and European foreign policy theory in particular could not explain the processes of learning, a distinct model of organizational development (learning and change) was created. The task now is to conclude this exploratory research and tie this study's results into the broader approach to organizational learning.

Most importantly, the analytical model developed in chapter 3 with its distinction between learning and change has proven to be useful. To begin with, such differentiation appears crucial because, as Levy advances (1994, 290), one would miss important cases studying only learning that produced change (here, for example, one would omit cases such as the EU's learning about stronger EUSR structures or about the model character of the Macedonian double-hat). Moreover, the two phases display different characteristics that, in turn, have important theoretical implications, which I will explain in the following.

With regard to **phase 1,** consideration of the **influence of filters such as the organizational culture is a characteristic element.** The effects of such cognitive filters on what kind of information an organization receives and, consequently, which lessons it learns therefrom, cannot be overestimated. Earlier research on political psychology and organizational behavior showed that a perceptional filter (or worldview, or in Hegel's terms: *Weltanschauung*) "interprets stimuli in a way that is meaningful to an observer. [...] A Weltanschauung [...] influences what problems are perceived, how these problems are interpreted, and what learning ultimately results" (Hedberg 1981, 8). At their utmost, strong worldviews influence human perception to disregard unfavorable lessons (Jervis 1976, 143; Haas 1992, 28).[367]

Put simply, the **EU—just as any other organization—only learns what it wants to learn.** The effect of these perceptional filters is such that only those lessons become engrained into organizational rules that fit its pre-conceived image of a coherent, state-like actor with a broad set of instrument playing an important international role. Information is selected, and acquired information is screened for those elements that

---

367 The same argument could be made for an early—and decisive—experience of European weakness: In 1956, France and the United Kingdom learned different lessons from the Suez crisis in which they were jointly involved. The UK 'learned' to never again not be on the American side; France 'learned' to not always rely on the United States (cf. Smith 2004a, 34). Based on the findings of this work, it is likely that these 'lessons' did not accidentally coincide with, but instead were greatly influenced by the prevailing foreign policy identity of each country.

could prove helpful on its way to becoming a respected actor at the global level, while dissenting voices are discarded.

This focus on the cognitive function of learning renders OL theories more potent than, for example, adaptation approaches that are based on stimulus-response models (cf. Hedberg 1981, 3; Malek et al. 2002, 8). The analysis has demonstrated that it is not just any external stimulus (like the crisis in Somalia in 2007) that triggers the deployment of an EUSR, but that stimuli are mediated by the EU's cognitive structures—and that, based on a previous occurrence of learning, the EU may decide against responding to the stimulus in an automatic way.

What is remarkable about this filtering of unwanted lessons is that the selection process already takes place in the learning phase and at a collective level. Information that appears unfavorable for the EU's global activity—for example that it could be better to uphold the pillar division than to try and overcome it with joint task forces and double-hatting, or to postpone engagement until the EU has developed a policy rather than appoint an envoy to help it develop one[368]—does not even enter the organizational memory. As a consequence, there is no need for a top-down intervention by pro-European politicians or top officials to eliminate negative lessons.

This leads to considerations of the theoretical implications of **phase 2.** The influence of member states over the occurrence of change (as opposed to the autonomy of the central structure—often the Secretariat—with regard to learning) **gives credit to rationalist approaches that perceive the relation between member states and IOs as one between principals and agents.**[369] While in the first phase of organizational learning, ideas of the EU's global role are dominant, the interests of institutional players mark the second phase of putting such learning into practice. However, the influence of states is not as strong as these approaches suggest, stipulating that the agent acts on behalf of the principal due to a grant of authority that is revocable at any time (Howkins et al. 2006, 7). The scope of action of states as principals is limited, as they cannot influence the important cognitive and social processes that form and help maintain an organizational culture.

Still, this understanding of phase two helps to respond to an important normative concern that Michael Zürn and Jeffrey Checkel raised based on their findings of how socialization processes can change the allegiances of national officials. They wonder whether—given these fairly autonomous (socialization or learning) processes—there is still democratic control of and legitimacy in the EU's political affairs (Zürn/Checkel 2005, 1072–74). Without going into the debate about the extent of the EU's 'democratic

---

368 The latter, for example, was the case in the early days when the UK expressed reservations about having a more comprehensive policy on the Middle East before appointing an EUSR; cf. Cunningham 1996, 11.

369 For an introduction to principal-agent theory with regard to international organizations, see Howkins et al. 2006; in the same volume, one article focuses on delegation in the European Union (Pollack 2006).

deficit,'[370] suffice here to say that learning processes do not diminish the democratic credentials of EU policy-making. While OL takes place rather autonomously in the Secretariat and, as a process, is indeed not democratically controlled, **the implementation of learning experiences into change is very much subject to the will of the principals, such as representatives of the democratically elected governments in member states.**[371]

This study highlights the different dynamics of learning and change: The first phase (organizational learning) is conditioned by organizational culture, i. e. the norms, values, and practices that emerge over time from the collective action of the individuals within an organization; the second phase (organizational change) is influenced by change resistance and institutional design, i. e. the different interests of various stakeholders (e. g. member states and primary institutions).

From this follows that, to study the first phase, reflexive theories that involve rationalist elements are more suitable, e. g. constructivist and sociological approaches that include notions of role-playing and persuasion. The second phase, in turn, could be better explained by rationalist theories that take into account the role of ideas.

The EUSRs have thus proven to be a good testing ground for learning theories, making it possible to assert their usefulness (because learning occurs and it does generate change) without advancing claims of superiority. As one author observed, "Learning is generally very rare in any organization. In the case of multilateral organizations, it seems that learning occurs at their initial moment or at crucial junctures throughout their development." (Knight 2001, 33). The opposite was shown in this study: that learning takes place on a regular basis and not just at junctures. This is in itself a valuable contribution to the debate about OL. To what extent these findings also contribute to theories of International Relations as well as to the explanation of European foreign policy, is part of the following two subsections.

7.2.2 Implications for International Relations theory

This two-phase model building on cognitive factors in phase 1 and actor interests in phase 2 underlines that **learning is an interdisciplinary approach** that "cuts across virtually all of the major theoretical and meta-theoretical cleavages in social science" (Stern 1997, 69). After neorealism with its interest-based explanation had gained dominance in IR theory, ideas and identity were relegated to near non-importance as mere rationalizations of underlying interests with no influence of their own (Jachtenfuchs

---

370 For two contrasting views on the presumed dangers of the EU's 'democratic deficit,' see Schmitter 2000 and Moravcsik 2002.

371 With regard to the democratic accountability of what EUSRs do, Grevi notes that "the larger the role of EUSRs, and the more salient the political issues that they address, the more accountable they will be expected to be to the EP" (Grevi 2007, 23).

1999, 67).[372] Now we have come to see a "revival of idea-based attempts to analyze foreign policy dynamics" (Vennesson 2007, 3; cf. Yee 1996, 69).[373] Learning theories can offer a bridge between the call for greater attention to ideas and the focus on institutional development. They provide one means to look into the 'causal nexus' between cognitive beliefs and decision-making behavior (cf. George 1979).

Looking at the dominant meta-theoretical discussion of explanations from either the rationalist or constructivist field, this study lends support to those researchers who wish to overcome "the current gladiatorial posturing typical of the rationalist–constructivist debate" (Barnett/Coleman 2005, 615).[374] Promoting a synthesis of approaches is not done out of a wish for academic harmony though, but because of the shortcomings of each approach and because I do not regard these two approaches as mutually exclusive. Checkel in particular (cf. Checkel 2001; Zürn/Checkel 2005) claims that rationalists, because they stick to a strong form of methodological individualism, cannot grasp the interaction context during which agent interests may change. At the same time, constructivist models focus mainly on elements of cognitive psychology. Thus, neither approach, Checkel deplores, can sufficiently investigate the complex interaction of social learning that shapes the interests and identities of an agent (cf. Checkel 2001, 560–61). In this situation, the concept of learning "constitutes a possible conceptual bridge between scholars in the neo-positivist tradition who privilege structures and those in the constructivist tradition who privilege ideas" (Lebow 2005, 94).[375]

Another important theoretical aspect is **to see the learning result as the independent variable of change and not merely as an intervening variable** as other approaches would have it. The latter see ideas merely as 'switchmen' (in Max Weber's terminology) that can direct the dynamics created by other forces (cf. Goldstein/Keohane 1993). Claiming explanatory power for learning as an independent variable is not to deny that learning works in response to information about external events and that the latter are therefore an important condition of change as well (see Parsons 2002, 49). Yet, if all incoming information is interpreted in a certain (pre-determined) direction, it may in

---

372 The neorealist position is well formulated by Stephen Krasner: "[Ideas] legitimated political practices that were already facts on the ground. [They] have been one among several instruments that actors have invoked to promote their own, usually mundane, interests" (Krasner 1993, 238).

373 One example for the rise of ideas-based explanations in European integration studies is Craig Parsons work on 'The Origins of the European Union' (Parsons 2002).

374 Another proponent of this conciliatory approach is Checkel, who sees himself as part of "an emergent trend, where there is a move away from an 'either/or,' 'gladiator' style of analysis (either rational choice or constructivism) to a 'both/and' perspective" (Checkel 2001, 581).

375 Authors who regard learning in a normative fashion, i.e. as an improvement or progress, would limit the proposed combination of approaches to the level of methodology. Concerning the basic assumptions rationalism (or realism) and constructivism (or idealism) make, they see insurmountable differences: "While realists doubt the possibility of progress, idealists and their more cautious liberal successors seek to identify processes or institutions that could bring about a more peaceful or equitable existence. [...] This suggests that the possibility of learning is integral to the liberal and idealist projects" and not to rationalist or realist approaches (Knopf 2003, 192).

the end be the filter that is more powerful than the triggering event. This reading also confirms earlier research on organizational learning and conflict, where the authors conclude with regard to three conceptual frames of conflict, i. e. resources, interests, and identities, that the identity frame may be much more relevant to OL than the resource or interest frames (Rothman/Friedman 2001, 582).

The possibility that actor learning may generate systemic change has important implications for the study of international relations as it suggests that "structural change may be the product, not the cause, of behavior" (Lebow 2005, 112). With regard to the debate about 'Soviet learning' and the end of the Cold War (Breslauer/Tetlock 1991 and Nye 1987 and Stein 1994), the question is whether Soviet leaders merely learned to adapt to changing material circumstances (as realism holds, granting no causal effect to learning); or whether their learning was genuine and based in part on autonomous ideas, thus not fully endogenous to structural change (as constructivists would argue). In the end, it is reasonable to argue that both, structural change and causal learning, were a necessary condition for the end of the Cold War (Goertz/Levy 2007, 21).

Methodological richness is certainly one of the strengths of OL theories. Better than other approaches, be they classical IR theories like neorealism or liberal intergovernmentalism or from the newly established camp of European foreign policy theories, they can explain the development of the EU as an international actor. Most theories focus on what is considered the second phase in this study. In contrast OL not only offers a different independent variable (instances of organizational learning), but it also provides a model of how to endogenously explain this variable in the first place rather than taking it as an exogenous given. In the words of Ben Tonra, concepts such as learning that are able to explain change in belief systems "can offer a dynamic model of foreign policy and foreign policy change within the EU far richer than that available through strictly rational accounts" (Tonra 2003, 736).

However, one caveat is apt: The organizational learning approach does not constitute a grand theory and can only **contribute to a plurality of explanations,** i. e. in combination with other theories such as institutionalism or intergovernmentalism. As others have proposed with regard to management reforms in international organizations, the idea should be to "combine tools, theories and explanations from the various related sub-disciplines (public administration, international relations, organization theory, political science)" (Knill/Bauer 2007, 199). In this context, organizational learning deserves to be treated as an independent variable (next to others) and need not be relegated to being an intervening variable only marginally influencing other, more powerful factors at play.

In this vein, this study contends that OL theories are particularly apt for bridge-building between IR strands as well as across disciplines. They offer a variety of analytic perspectives by combining constructivist elements (e. g. the cognitive and socially-interactive process of learning) and rationalist postulates (like goal-oriented and strategic behavior of both organizations and individuals) and, of course, elements of organizational theory and political psychology.

7.2.3   Implications for explanations of European foreign policy

This study has shown that organizational learning does take place within the EU and that it produces organizational change; consequently, it needs to be factored in into theoretical explanations of the development of European foreign policy. In the following, I will outline what precisely the EU's learning through the EUSRs contributed to this development. This will also provide an answer to the second, policy-oriented research question of what the EU has learned about how and when to make use of its Special Representatives in particular and about its foreign policy development in general.

It is often said that European foreign policy is a system in the making, developing in a *sui generis* way; as if to confirm this notion, the EU did not emulate any existing set of envoys when introducing the EUSRs. What could be seen is a process of trial-and-error experimentation. **The EU is 'learning by doing' in a very practical sense,**[376] trying and testing concepts before formally writing them into the Treaties or its rules of procedures. Nonetheless, looking through the learning lens reveals two different blueprints that have guided the EU's institutional development in this realm. One is the very ideal image of what kind of an actor in international relations the EU aims to be; I will come back to this in the next subsection when looking at the EU's identity. The other is the real world, where the EU does not find any comparator and therefore picks and chooses from existing models to develop specific instruments that fit its particular situation—it engages in **vicarious learning.**

The prototype for this learning by doing approach is taken **from (member) states rather than from international organizations** (hypothesis 4): When reflecting about how best to mould its special representatives, the EU favored selective copying from national services. The first Special Representative, Aldo Ajello, had held the same position for the United Nations before. Despite this fact, the EU did not look at the Special Representatives of the UN Secretary-General, which could have served as an example of how another international body (whose policy-making similarly depends on the intergovernmental cooperation of its member states) deals with the questions of information gathering and external representation.

The EU's incremental learning from states is surprisingly normal, one could say: It is surprising because member states commonly oppose any move that furthers the EU's statelike qualities; it is however also normal because most often it is national diplomats who prepare decisions at the working level and who look to their own national foreign services for inspiration for how to improve mechanisms and procedures within CFSP. These dif-

---

376   The phrase is used here rather in the sense of Janice Gross Stein characterizing Gorbachev's personal development (Stein 1994) than it its more metaphorical meaning (see Wallace 2005, 439; or the title of Jaanson 2008).

ferent impetuses are bound to cause friction when it comes to translating learning experiences into organizational change (as the debate about 'barriers' has shown above).

Paradoxically, applying learning theories to the EU's development reveals that the latter's claim to learn from its own actions (as typified by the talk of the 'Balkan lessons') is rather baseless; instead, the advancement of the EU continues to proceed by trial-and-error. When it comes to the **EU's competence for deutero learning, or 'learning to learn'** (hypothesis 5), this study finds that the EU has not actively enhanced its learning capacities, neither in the case of the EUSRs nor in the wider realm of the Brussels foreign policy complex. Especially the deliberately set up lessons-learned seminars, held once a year together with the High Representative, have proven to be a futile exercise. While it was—rightfully—thought by some individuals that such meetings could be useful to both the EUSRs and the Brussels headquarters, the way they have been held so far—limited to half a day with an opening speech by Javier Solana followed by briefings about current events or technical issues—have failed to produce any meaningful learning instances. In this regard, the EU probably again rather resembles the states as political actors for which the urgent issues of the day dominate the thinking, and evaluations of what was done yesterday and how it was done are seen as too academic to seriously consider. Therefore, the second policy hypothesis has failed the test: There are still no clear-cut mechanisms in place that could produce meaningful lessons from past activities that would in turn be considered by policy-makers.

The fact that the EU has developed in an incremental, evolutionary fashion points to a general feature of how change has come about: It corroborates the view of those who claim that **external events or critical junctures,** which are often considered as triggers of transformation, **in fact only enable change but do not produce it.** They offer a window of opportunity to bring internal ideas and small-scale changes, like learning experiences accumulated overtime both in Brussels and among national officials, to the foreground. In his thorough overview of the 'institutionalization of cooperation' in EFP, Michael Smith recognizes learning by doing as one of the endogenous factors that are the "ultimate source" of institutional change in the EPC/CFSP system itself; in contrast, major internal or external events like crises or intergovernmental conferences can only "help explain the eventual codification of institutional reforms by EU governments" (Smith 2004a, 242). It is therefore not so much from crises that the EU learns,[377] or that the grand bargains struck at the EU's Intergovernmental Conferences (IGC) actually determine the "institutional trajectory of European integration" (Koenig-Archibugi 2004a, 139). **Both merely help the EU to translate previously acquired learning experiences into change,** thus strengthening the "evolutionary nature" of the EU's foreign policy (Grevi 2007, 34).[378] In contrast to top-down concepts that see EU foreign

---

377 This is what some authors claim, in particular for United Nations peacekeeping missions (Breul 2005; Brandstrom et al. 2004; Stern 1997; Suhrke 2000).

378 The influence of learning is recognized by a special issue of the 'Journal of European Public Policy' dedicated to EU treaty reform: "[Dynamics] such as learning, socialization, and the incremental institutionalization of policy paradigms at the EU level [...] can (re)shape preferences before and sometimes even during IGC negotiations" (Falkner 2002, 2; cf. Christiansen et al. 2002).

policy-making organized in an intergovernmental fashion with member states in the driving seat, it is bottom-up developments that incrementally but ultimately change the way of real-life politics.

In this attention to gradual change and to trial-and-error methods also lies the major advantage of OL theories compared to the theory of Historical Institutionalism (Pierson 2004; Thelen 1999). By focusing on organizations and on how they develop over time, Historical Institutionalism and theories of organizational learning have some common traits; not least, case studies and the method of process tracing appeal to both of them (George/Bennett 2004, 9). However, the two main tenets of Historical Institutionalism, path dependence and critical junctures, do not chime well with the institutional flexibility—and autonomy—assumed by learning theories.

Path dependence suggests that institutions continue to evolve along a trajectory determined by their foundation, with the initial dynamics reproducing themselves through positive feedback (Pierson 2004, 11). The critical junctures argument postulates that it is only possible to depart from such past trajectories at significant moments in an institution's lifetime (Thelen 1999, 387). However, not only has the literature on critical junctures been weak "in specifying the mechanisms that translate critical junctures into lasting political legacies" (ibid., 388). What is more, path dependence cannot account either for those instances in which abolishing individual EUSRs was pondered or for the increase in flexibility witnessed most recently (cf. section 5.7). Learning theories, in contrast, can explain this by referring to how the EU has tested different working models for the EUSRs, even considering the fundamental option of ending the instrument altogether.

Instead of path dependence, other mechanisms are at play here, namely how the idea of Europe taking on its role as a global actor has shaped the EU's organizational culture and with it the various learning instances described in this work. It is therefore appropriate to look at whether and how researchers define the EU's international identity.

7.2.3.1 A 'distinct power,' or: The centrality of the EU's international identity

The development of post-war Europe makes for a fascinating case of identity construction. To the extent that the EU is very often equated with 'all things European' (cf. Risse 2004, 254–55), fifty years of integration have had an undeniable impact on the continent. To answer the main question of how national and European identities can go together (if the latter is not to substitute the former, which does not at all appear to be likely), the image of a "marble cake" (Risse 2005, 296) of intermingling identities was introduced.[379]

---

379 In fact, the 'marble cake' metaphor was already used previously by March and Olsen in an attempt to portray the structure of the EU as "the most highly institutionalized international organization in history" (March/Olsen 1998, 967). Originally, Ira Sharkansky described the relations between the U.S. federal government and those of the 50 States as a 'marble cake' rather than a 'layer cake' (Sharkansky 1981). This is interesting not only for the apparent parallel to the United States, but also because the book in which Sharkansky's article appeared is Paul Nystrom and William Starbuck's 'Handbook of Organizational Design', an early work of organizational theory that also featured Bo Hedberg's article on 'How organizations learn and unlearn' (Hedberg 1981). Belatedly, if probably

National identities are not replaced by an emerging European identity, but the two co-exist. As a result, some authors see the appearance of a European demos, though cautioning that "it is simply too early to talk of an independent, robust, superordinate, and strong European social/collective identity" (Zürn/Checkel 2005, 1067).[380] Thus, when referring to a 'European identity,' it is difficult to avoid one of the two standard reflexes: Either the hastiness of denouncing such identity, or the hyperbole of praising whatever 'we-ness' is evinced. I shall nonetheless attempt to outline some conclusions from this research relating to the EU's emerging international identity, limiting the deliberations on identity in two ways: First to its foreign policy part, and second to the elite group of EU officials. For both, there is some research to draw on.

As for the EU's foreign policy identity, ever since François Duchêne declared the European Community a "civilian power" (Duchêne 1972, 1973) and was later rebuked by Hedley Bull who argued that this was a contradiction in terms and instead pleaded for "a military power Europe" (Bull 1982), a debate about what kind of international power Europe should be has been taking place.[381] While these two treatises were rather normative in nature, more recent contributions have tried to analyze the actual foreign policy behavior—or 'active identity' (Manners/Whitman 1998, 238)—of the EU.[382] They have come up with EU-specific elaborations of Joseph Nye's 'soft power' concept (Nye 1990), proposing for example a civilian superpower (Whitman 1998), a normative power (Manners 2002), a smart power (Ferrero-Waldner 2007),[383] a gentle power (Lucarelli 2006), and, most recently, an ethical power Europe (Aggestam 2008).[384]

Neither taking sides in this debate nor seeking to propose its own 'power wording', this study holds that the concept of a distinctive international identity of the EU does indeed exist,[385] and that this concept of a 'distinct power' has an influence on the EU's own development, for example via the impact of the organizational culture on learning and subsequent change.[386] The EUSRs in particular embody the EU's identity as an

---

unknowingly, European integration theories thus do apply organizational concepts.

380 For a good multidisciplinary contribution to European identity formation, see Herrmann et al. 2004.

381 For an overview of the 'original and current debates' about Civilian Power Europe, see Orbie 2006.

382 The current state of affairs on the question 'what kind of power' Europe is (that it is a power seems to be no longer in doubt) is presented in a special issue of the Journal of European Public Policy (Sjursen 2006).

383 The concept of 'smart power' was also developed by Joseph Nye; see Nye 2006. For Benita Ferrero-Waldner, EU Commissioner for External Relations and Neighbourhood Policy, who took up the underlying idea in the referenced speech, the 'soft power' is a central tenet (Portela 2007, 9–10).

384 An entire issue of the journal International Affairs is dedicated to the question of 'Ethical power Europe,' a concept that encompasses "both civilian and military power, as well as social and material power" (Aggestam 2008, 2).

385 A good analysis of the values, images, and principles (or "VIPs") that the EU's identity consists of, can be found in a recent edited book (Lucarelli/Manners 2006b).

386 For how values, images, and principles influence EU integration in a 'self-learning process', see

international actor: Solana himself, in a speech in 2005, called them (together with his topically-oriented personal representatives) emblematic of what EU foreign policy is all about: conflict resolution, crisis management, tackling the new security threats, standing up for the EU's values and interests, and seeking comprehensive solutions to complex and multi-dimensional problems (Solana 2005, 2). It is in this sense—i.e. in what they do, how they do it, and what they learn from it—that they are a powerful expression of European identity.

The EU's foreign policy identity is influential also because it is not as precarious as other identities related to internal politics. European principles such as continuous integration and good governance face problems when translated into policies due to weaknesses on three accounts: definitional clarity, structural backing, and/or public support (Metcalfe 2005, 25–26). The EU's international identity, in contrast is neither ill-defined nor internally contested but rather finds constant replication in documents ranging from the Declaration of European Identity in 1973 (European Community 1973) to the EU Security Strategy of 2003 (European Council 2003). The institutional structure of CFSP to which this identity is bound may not be as strong and established as, for example, the Commission structure (a fact that accounts for some of the weaknesses of putting the identity into practice); yet it has evolved in a sufficiently robust way to maintain a guiding function for day-to-day politics. Finally, other than some internal market policies, the EU's international identity commands broad social acceptance in the European public as not only the regular Eurobarometer polls show.[387]

For these reasons, it is safe to assume that the EU's international identity serves as a framework for learning as well as that it is continuously reinforced by changes that build on this learning. This may also help to explain one point raised at the beginning of this study, i.e. the EU's adherence to its global ambition in the face of failure. Because investigating the internal processes of learning within an organization can be a means of better understanding why the EU has stayed on this path.

With regard to how the EU elite has developed its own identity, analyzes have shown that socialization processes are at work as concerns national officials active in EU policy-making.[388] The latter have come to not only work at but also to identify with both locations, the member states capital and the Brussels environment, operating "constantly in a demimonde between the national and the EU" (Laffan 2004, 76). Consequently, the permanent representatives of member states as the most characteristic example of these officials describe themselves as "having dual personalities, performing multiple roles,

---

Lucarelli/Manners 2006a, 205–7.

387 For a most recent poll, see European Commission 2007, 28; for an analysis of the experiential base of public support for CFSP, see Schoen 2008. A majority positive view for a common European foreign and defense policy also exists in the United Kingdom; see House of Lords 2008, 21.

388 In addition to some of the contributions to the 'International Organization' special issue on 'Socialisation in Europe' (cf. Checkel 2005), there is an earlier article examining the 'identity and role perceptions of national officials in EU decision-making' (Egeberg 1999).

wearing different hats, even having a 'Janus face'" (Lewis 2005, 939). In a way similar to the EUSRs, officials from member states "act as 'boundary managers' between the national and the European" (Laffan 2004, 92).

Important as these contributions to the debate about the influence of identities are, they do not tell us what the European identity of national officials actually consists of. To know more about the substance of the latter, one would have to go back to the presumed EU identity evolving around the different 'power' concepts described above.

Further research would also be needed with regard to the worldviews of EU officials at large, despite two meaningful contributions to explore this field. A team of researchers at the European University Institute in Florence analyzed the worldview of a handful of top EU officials, including the High Representative for CFSP, Javier Solana, and External Relations Commissioner, Benita Ferrero-Waldner.[389] The studies of these high-ranking individuals prove very insightful and confirm, building on Alexander George's 'operational code' approach (George 1969), a worldview that centers on a greater EU role in the international arena (see e.g. Barros-Garica 2007, 12). Yet, they focus only on the level of EU leaders and not on the broad level of (still fairly high-ranking) EU civil servants in the Council Secretariat and in DG Relex of the European Commission, which are instrumental in processes of organizational learning. As a second contribution, the previously mentioned 'International Organization' special issue on 'International Institutions and Socialization in Europe' (e.g. Zürn/Checkel 2005) features an article analyzing the worldviews of Commission officials (Hooghe 2005). However, the Commission's strong role as the promoter of a collective European interest, as enshrined in the Treaty, is at least weakened if not disputed in the foreign policy realm. Altogether, these individual contributions, while focusing on European views in general and not those regarding its international identity in particular, do not add up to a systematic analysis of how EU officials think about European foreign policy.[390]

If such an all-encompassing study of the identity of EU officials were made, it would be equally interesting to mirror its results with those of an analysis of third-party perceptions of the EU's foreign policy in general and of EUSR activity in particular. In an exercise that followed from the public consultation process of the European Security Strategy, non-European authors from Africa, Latin America, Asia, and Oceania were asked about their impression of the EU's new role in international affairs (Ortega

---

389 Following an introductory paper (Vennesson 2007), contributions analyze the worldviews of Javier Solana (Barros-Garica 2007), Director-General Robert Cooper (Foley 2007), Benita Ferrero-Waldner (Portela 2007), former Commissioner for External Trade Peter Mandelson (Triscritti 2007), and Commissioner for Fisheries and Maritime Affairs Joseph Borg (Coutto 2007).

390 Interestingly, there is a case of an 'EU identity' decreed from above: The mandate for the EUSR in Bosnia and Herzegovina demands that an "EU dedicated staff projecting an EU identity shall be assigned to assist the EUSR to implement his mandate" (Art. 7 ['Constitution of the team'] of Council Joint Action 2007/87/CFSP of 7 February 2007). It is presumably mentioned there because the EUSR, under his other hat of High Representative, has a majority international (i.e. non-EU) staff.

2004b).[391] The conclusions are affirmative: "[No] state or international actor perceives the European Union as a strategic threat, because it represents a new approach to global politics. That approach implies renouncement of military competition, which is replaced by competition in the economic and commercial fields, as well as dialogue and partnership in the political arena. Furthermore, the new approach understands international relations to be a multilateral process in which diplomatic negotiation, the resolution of disputes and respect for international law and institutions are paramount" (Ortega 2004a, 119).

For the moment, these are only individual opinions but they could provide a starting point for a more comprehensive, focused analysis to determine whether the EU's new global role really is welcome among the political elites (or even the publics) of third countries.

Given such research into the nature and strength of the EU's international identity, it would also be possible to estimate how the EU would behave in international affairs: If this identity were a strong enough cognitive filter to deflect unwanted feedback, the EU could be expected to always interpret incoming information in a way that it feels encouraged to become more active.

A final observation is that, interestingly, while the interests of member states may inhibit further integration of European foreign policy, their identities are less in the way of constructing an EU foreign policy identity, be it called soft, smart, civilian or normative power. More and more, the EU has overcome the 'bold talk and little action' stage and instead tries to walk its talk. It actively promotes its holistic approach to international affairs, summarized in the term 'effective multilateralism' of the EU Security Strategy (European Council 2003), as a proactive contribution to global governance (Ortega 2007). Surely, this consensus is far from being part of the *acquis communautaire,* instead constituting only a somewhat weaker *acquis politique* (Ginsberg 1999, 436; Mayer 2004, 65). Still, there is broad agreement among member states of what the European Union ought to do, even if it is not always capable of doing it (more often than not due to a lack of political will on the side of member states).

In sum, the EU's internal identity centers on the notion of being a distinct non-traditional global power; it influences the Union's learning by way of its organizational culture. While the substance of this identity is vaguely determined with reference to a benevolent (e.g. soft, civilian, normative, gentle, ethical, or smart) power, more research is needed to determine the individual worldviews of EU officials. Nonetheless, it appears that the image of the EU's global role commands broad support, including from member states and many third countries.

---

391 Bretherton and Vogler's earlier study also takes into account the views of third country representatives (Bretherton/Vogler 1999).

Built on this common ground, some see a deepening of CFSP as the "logical extension of the origins of the European project" (Solana 2008, 2), as the next big integration project after the creation of the Internal Market, the introduction of the Euro, and Eastern Enlargement. This understanding highlights the important internal dimension of the EU's external policies, which I will briefly analyze in the following.

7.2.3.2   Active abroad for peace at home: the importance of the internal dimension

From the time when Putnam conceptualized what he called 'two-level games' (Putnam 1988), the domestic relevance of foreign policy has been widely recognized. In the context of European integration, however, the importance of these two levels is a different one: Whereas in the world of states (at least in a neorealist reading) the **international** level is about survival, for the European Union survival of the integration project will be determined at the **internal** level. To what extent a growing number of member states ('widening') can continue to integrate their policies ('deepening') will be decisive. Pressure from the international level—for example the weakened weight of member states due to globalization and the rise of new powers such as India and China or the demand for European action in what is perceived as a multipolar world (Solana 2008, 2)—serves as a welcome line of reasoning rather than an existential threat.

It is therefore reasonable to view the EU's growing global engagement not only as a response to external crises, but also as a means to rally member states around a common cause.[392] As early as in the European Single Act of 1986, EU heads of state and government publicly stated the expectation "that closer co-operation on questions of European security would contribute in an essential way to the development of a European identity in external policy matters."[393] Hindsight confirms this ambition to create an identity through common action. From its creation, "the CFSP regime is explicitly linked to the creation of a collective European identity" (Tonra 2001, 15).[394]

The efforts to devise common policies as well as joint operations have, among other things, increased confidence-building among EU member states and helped create common viewpoints within a multilateral frame of reference (Ginsberg/Smith 2007, 269). One of the first to recognize this trend was Ernst Haas, who found that interaction between EU and national officials would lead them to develop common values and

---

392 A different argument highlights intergovernmental cooperation, of nation states in general as well as within the European Union, "as a new *raison d'état*, as a device designed to loosen the constraints imposed on governments in the domestic arena" (Koenig-Archibugi 2004b, 148 [italics in original]). This appears to be an interesting idea that cannot be dismissed out of hand. However, it is not congruent with the basic principles of European integration and thus is not treated further at this point.

393 Single European Act (1986), Title III, Art. 30, N° 6(a).

394 Similarly, Karen Smith stresses the idealist reasons behind the continual CFSP reform efforts, which reflect the EU's "desire not only to improve [its] problem-solving capacity, but also to strengthen collective identification and consequent action" (Smith 2003, 9). Enlargement, too, as part of the EU's external relations and by protecting and promoting human rights and fundamental freedoms, has increased the salience of a particular aspect of EU identity in European foreign policy (Sedelmeier 2003, 6).

cognitive systems and, thus, common interests: "This entire process takes place on the basis of organizational learning. [...] The answer to maximizing the learning process lies in extending the range of participation in practical problem-solving" (Haas 1968, 13). Building on such a *communauté de vue* (de Schoutheete de Tervarent 1980, 49), the permanent interaction in Brussels over time should create a sense of belonging to a common endeavor and to shared ownership of foreign policy initiatives (Grevi 2007, 33).

In addition, by providing a focal point for a given crisis or region and by thus creating the need to give common instructions to them, the EUSRs advance a 'habit of coordination.' This was first noticed with regard to the closed circles of foreign ministers and their political directors in the early days of EPC (de Schoutheete de Tervarent 1980; Nuttall 1992). Later, it was detected in the group of ambassadors assembling as the Coreper in Brussels (Checkel 2005 and Lewis 2003). Most recently, researchers have also applied this 'socialization concept' to the PSC itself (Juncos/Reynolds 2007). Similar socialization processes might be seen in the fact that EUSRs distribute factual information both via national ambassadors in the field and PSC ambassadors in Brussels. These aspects point to further interesting cross-references of organizational learning to the more mainstream fields of European foreign policy analysis.

It is the "fragmented nature of agency at the European level" (Tonra 2001, 39) that justifies the focus of the EUSRs' efforts on the internal side. A malevolent observer might still resort to lamenting that this merely shows the fig leaf character of the EU's foreign policies, that the EU does not have the power for real conflict-solving, or that it is ultimately satisfied with navel-gazing. However, more powerful international actors have not been able to solve some long-standing conflicts either. In addition, the EUSRs have to 'work on' member states and the Commission in order to secure consent for their proactive external engagement.

The instrument of EU Special Representatives therefore confirms the importance of the internal function of foreign policy.[395] Even though the EUSRs' many internal tasks are not always explicitly spelled out in the mandate (cf. section 5.1), it could be shown that in practice these are at least as important as the external tasks:

- Coordinating member states policies as well as ESDP operations on the ground;
- Encouraging the development of common policies by providing information and analysis; and
- Acting as 'boundary spanners' and bridge-builders across institutional and political divides.

The importance of the internal dimension complements the identity driver in explaining the EU's persistent (and puzzling) pursuit of cooperation in foreign and security policy despite its—sometimes evident, at other times alleged—failures in some cases (cf. Smith

---

395 This is, contrary to some estimates (Grevi 2007, 41), what distinguishes EUSRs from national diplomats.

2004b, 4). This leads me to some concrete policy recommendations that could be taken from this research.

7.3 EUSRs and EU foreign policy: Some recommendations

The preceding theoretical conclusions can be complemented by a few considerations of potential policy implications. Much more than a mere case to demonstrate the theoretical mechanisms and practical usefulness of organizational learning, the EUSRs are an instrument of a real-life international actor that aims to devise common policies, to mediate conflicts and solve crises, and to influence political processes.

For the EU, the Special Representatives have become an all-round instrument that it can flexibly deploy anywhere within its political reach (which is, admittedly, still limited to its broader vicinity) and that enhances the synergy between the instruments and resources at its disposal. In terms of crisis management, there is hardly anything EUSRs do not do. In addition, they have provided the Union with effective representation in 24 countries located in regions most relevant to EU security. The continuity of their presence and the visibility of their engagement have raised the Union's political profile in these regions (which is not to say that there is not more to be done). Finally, they build bridges within the CFSP pillar, to member states, and to the Commission, thus furthering the EU's foreign policy effectiveness.

How could this instrument be further improved?[396] Two recommendations stand out, one principled about enhancing the EUSRs' boundary spanning, and the other specifically about the advent of an EU foreign service. The two have in common that they build on the EUSRs' most valuable contributions to the development of EU foreign policy, i. e. their bridge-building function between EU institutions, policies, and partners.

7.3.1 Envoys as boundary spanners

The notion of 'boundary spanners,' introduced as an analytical category to understand how information can be acquired for learning processes (cf. subsection 3.2.1), is now used to describe the political activity of the EUSRs. The latter span boundaries in all senses: The EU's internal and external boundaries as well as the political boundaries of conflict management understood in a narrow sense.

EUSRs have provided bridges within CFSP (e. g. by coordinating member states as well as ESDP operations on the ground), across pillars (e. g. through close consultation with the Commission with the aim of combining the EU's political and economic instruments), and to the EU's international partners (e. g. by liaising with third countries and

---

396 For hands-on, practical proposals of 'Enhancing the performance of the EU Special Representatives,' see Grevi 2007, 145–154. The intention here is to neither repeat nor outdo but simply to conceptually supplement the recommendations made there.

international organizations present in a given crisis region). They have thus contributed to coherence at both the institutional and the policy level (cf. Grevi 2007, 46).

In addition, they have stretched their activities far beyond what troubleshooters and conflict managers conventionally do, embodying in themselves the EU's comprehensive approach to crisis management. In Bosnia and Herzegovina, they—for better or for worse—have authority to safeguard the country's constitutional order, while in Macedonia they supervise the country's transformation into a future EU member state; in both Sudan and the African Great Lakes region, they are deeply involved in operational issues of security sector reform, plus they coordinate overall crisis management cooperation with the African Union as a whole; in Moldova and the South Caucasus, they engage in confidence-building measures, whereas in Central Asia they help devise a whole new policy framework of inter-regional cooperation.

In essence, the EUSRs provide, not least through their boundary spanning function, a valuable contribution to the EU's holistic approach to crisis management. To strengthen the latter, four things need to be done:

(1) Increase the numbers of boundary spanners;
(2) Strengthen the institutional structures of EUSRs;
(3) Engage in strategic learning; and
(4) Take 'learning by doing' as an organizing principle for further developing EU foreign policy.

First of all, the EU needs **more boundary spanners,** i.e. usually senior national diplomats with a career in multilateral organizations, including—evidently, but often neglected—in the European Union itself.

- For their mission to be successful, it is crucial that EUSRs have an in-depth understanding of the Brussels institutional machinery and of the respective positions of the member states (in addition to the conflict matter, of course). While fairly autonomous in the field with room for initiative, they must regularly exchange with the CFSP 'headquarters' in Brussels and seek consensus among member states. Other than for rare high-profile missions, the former politician-turned-EUSR should therefore be the exception.

- A standard EUSR profile thus exists (cf. section 4.8), and it would be advisable to make this known throughout member states and EU institutions, so that when the next call for applications is out the right candidates will be forthcoming. There is merit in making specific calls rather than choosing from a (future) pool of potential EUSRs, not least because the former involves member states directly.

- Moreover, because sending an envoy is part of a decision about the EU's mid- to long-term engagement, there is usually no need to rush in the beginning. In the past, most mandates witnessed at least half a year of preparation and consultation before being passed, leaving enough time for member states (and EU institutions) to select and present their candidates.

At the same time, in order to strengthen the EUSRs' boundary spanning function it is necessary to **build up the EUSRs as an institution.**

– This means to provide joint administrative support for their work, an idea that is not even novel but has not yet been implemented. In addition, EUSRs should be, even physically speaking, included in the Council structures in Brussels rather than to have them dispersed at two different locations outside the *Justus Lipsius* building.
– It should also imply that EU officials take seriously the 'lessons-learned' seminars that were introduced in 2005. They could provide a good opportunity for exchanges among EUSRs as well as between them and their colleagues from the Council Secretariat and, possibly, also from member states and the Commission. The seminars should be organized by a CFSP lessons-learned unit within the Secretariat that supervises the effectiveness of the EU's foreign policy operations (cf. Grevi 2007, 149).[397] If such work were done continuously and at the broad operational level, the seminar could also be held annually rather than every six months, as is presently the case and has proven to be under serious time constraints from all sides. This should help to instill a learning spirit in all personnel involved.

Learning should also be extended to the level of strategy in order to provide a coherent policy framework for the boundary spanning activities of EUSRs.

– The EU Security Strategy of 2003 as the first attempt to provide such a frame is in need of an overhaul. It was the product of the European fallout over Iraq rather than the deliberate attempt of strategizing the continent's role in world affairs. At the time, the EU had only just begun to deploy operations under its ESDP; now, these missions have become commonplace.
– A reassessment of the ESS in the light of the past five years should duly consider the role of EUSRs. Ideally, it would give way to a continuous review of both actions and strategies in order to improve the EU's foreign policy. Just as the revision clause of the Maastricht Treaty proved to be an "in-built mechanism for learning" (Reynolds 2005, 11), a regular review of the EU's fundamental strategy document would enhance European foreign policy culture and debate.

Finally, **the EUSRs' learning by doing experience,** born from their invention twelve years ago without any role model, is instructive in itself. Created as substitutes for policy, the EU Special Representatives soon became Solana's deputies in Brussels and his ambassadors abroad. Their trial-and-error approach is symptomatic for the overall advancement of EU foreign policy. Therefore, it is natural to look at their function also with a view to the establishment of the EEAS envisaged by the Treaty of Lisbon (cf. subsection 1.4.3).

---

397 A model to look at—and possibly improve on—is the briefing and debriefing programme run by the UN training institute UNITAR (see subsection 2.1.2; cf. Peck 2004, 325).

7.3.2   Implications for the EU foreign service

Due to the continuing political sensitivities of the Treaty's ratification in general, and among some member states with regard to the EEAS in particular, there has so far been no systematic preparatory work for the EU's diplomatic service. The few official publications that exist on the EEAS are generally very cautious in their approach, and they do not make any references to the role of the EU Special Representatives, neither as a model institution nor with regard to what they would become once the service is established. The 2005 Joint Progress Report by the High Representative and the Commission on the European External Action Service was the first document to be published on this matter (High Representative/Secretary-General/European Commission 2005), and the last before the two negative referenda in France and the Netherlands stalled the ratification process. It elaborated on the form and function of the new service, though without mentioning the EUSRs at all. Likewise, the Commission's 'Europe in the World' communication one year later was very unadventurous regarding the development of the EEAS (European Commission 2006). It explicitly aimed at practical steps for more coherence that could be taken without a Treaty change, and mentioned the EUSRs only as part of enhanced coordination in and joint reporting from the field.

This scarcity of official reference to the example of the EUSRs cannot deny the model function of the latter. Those who work with the EUSRs every day do reflect a great deal on this, confirming that, to some extent, the EUSRs are indeed seen as the predecessors of the EEAS. Be it when establishing reporting structures, when resorting to flexibility in responding to crises, or most visibly when introducing double-hatting: On more than one occasion, people involved in the process regarded the EUSRs as a useful experiment with a view to establishing an EU foreign service.[398]

Therefore, it appears apt to advance some recommendations on how the EEAS might benefit from the experiences of the EUSRs:

(1) EUSRs should continue to serve in the new EU foreign service;
(2) Their existing and reasonably successful coordination mechanisms with the Commission should be maintained;
(3) New envoys should be given a similarly broad portfolio of tasks, to be fulfilled in a proactive manner; and
(4) As boundary spanners to the outside world, they should by given a considerable policy input function.

These recommendations are now developed in a more detailed way with reference to each of the four levels introduced in this analysis: Structural, procedural, operational, and ideational.

---

398 In the language of OL, one could therefore speak of latent learning, as it would only take the consolidation of the existing reflection into organizational rules for organizational learning to materialize.

An immediate question is whether EUSRs will still be needed once the **structures of the new EU foreign service** have been established. The answer is a decisive 'yes and no.' Most probably, the EEAS would mean the end of country-specific EUSR mandates, as these could be taken over by the then-Heads of EU Delegation. This would terminate mandates for places like Macedonia, Moldova, and Afghanistan. Of course, one could do away completely with the EUSRs as special envoys outside the normal system and have directors from within the EEAS cover in the future what is now the EUSRs' work. However, regional representatives of the double-hatted foreign minister would still make sense. Whether based in Brussels or in the field, they could tackle crises requiring urgent intervention or help develop the EU's strategic approach to pivotal global regions. Moreover, EUSRs could be appointed within the new service with a view to addressing specific issues of a horizontal, functional nature: Overcoming the present distinction between EUSRs and the Personal Representatives of the High Representative, one could then conceive of Special Representatives for nuclear non-proliferation, new epidemics, terrorism, human rights, or energy and climate affairs.

In addition to these conceptual reflections of how the EEAS should be envisaged, the sheer difficulty of building a fully-fledged diplomatic service from scratch may make the EUSRs necessary for some time to come. Yet, herein also lies a danger: Though member states publicly support the idea of a coherent and integrated foreign policy, in practice they may be much more fearful to cede control over foreign policy, often regarded—and sometimes fiercely guarded—as a haven of national sovereignty. Having established a fair degree of control over the EUSRs via the PSC, they may not like country-specific EUSRs to be replaced by all-powerful Heads of Union Delegations that report only to the foreign minister.[399] It is therefore essential that PSC-bound EUSRs will not be used as an instrument of fragmentation in order to compete with the EEAS directors and Heads of Delegation alike, which will be tied into administrative structures. Realistically, however, such a development is not at all unlikely, thus involuntarily mirroring the often-strenuous relationship that U.S. presidential envoys have with the State Department in Washington and U.S. embassies abroad.[400]

In essence, the function of Special Representative—not necessarily the title—should therefore be retained in the future EEAS, and those fulfilling this function should be fully integrated into the new service's structures.

At the **procedural level,** the EUSRs' close cooperation, both in the field and at head-quarters, with ESDP missions, member states, and, increasingly, the Commission has prepared them well for the EEAS. Cross-pillar cooperation should, in theory, become

---

399 The new Article 33 TEU in the consolidated version of the Lisbon Treaty (ex Article 18 (5) TEU) adopts the original formulation on appointing EUSRs but additionally stipulates that "The special representative shall carry out his mandate under the authority of the High Representative" without any mention of the PSC. However, this does not necessarily imply that the PSC would no longer be involved in 'strategic guidance' as it is today.

400 Another parallel can be found earlier in history: Just like the young United States had envoys before it had permanent ambassadors, the EUSRs will precede an eventual EU foreign service.

less strenuous thanks to the foreign minister's two hats. Nonetheless, 'old habits die hard,' so the delicate balancing act between institutional interests that EUSRs have learned to perform will also be a central feature of foreign policy-making under the new EEAS. In addition, the recommendations made above about personnel selection and lessons-learned seminars are just as valid for the EEAS.

With regard to **operations,** the pragmatic and proactive style of EUSRs, interpreting and developing their mandates with a results-oriented approach could serve as an example for the EEAS. Pragmatism and political common sense in daily practice will be impor-tant, especially when the formal architecture of the new service will not only take time to be built but might also be if not contested then at least strained by institutional turf wars. The broad portfolio of tasks that EUSRs fulfill should also serve as a model for the new service, as it underscores the EU's comprehensive approach towards crisis management.

Finally, as far as the **ideational** level is concerned, the policy input function of the EEAS should be decisively strengthened. The EUSRs have demonstrated the effectiveness of bridging policy areas such as ESDP, the neighborhood policy, and enlargement policy. They provide valuable information, intelligence, and analysis for the benefit not only of those member states that do not have a diplomatic representation in a given country or region, but also of the EU as an international actor in its own right. This has also helped to combine the economic incentives provided under the Community pillar with the po-litical leverage exercised through CFSP. Most of all, the EUSRs have demonstrated the usefulness of a dynamic learning by doing approach. In this way, their example can help the EEAS to develop into an effective policy machinery.

7.4   Summary and outlook

Summing up the findings of this study, one can say that the EU Special Representatives provide useful learning experiences for the EU, and that OL theories provide a methodo-logical framework for their evaluation and thus for the explanation of EU foreign policy development.

On the theoretical-methodological side, a differentiation between organizational learning (phase 1) and organizational change (phase 2) as two elements of organizational develop-ment has demonstrated to be useful. For the first phase, a '4R' definition of organiza-tional learning as a 'rewriting of rules as a result of reflection' has proven particularly apt to capture the notion of learning so that it is applicable to a political organization. Four levels of rules (structures, procedures, operations, and ideas) further differentiated where learning could take place. For the second phase, change could be identified either at the institutional level (the shape of an organization) or the policy level (the behavior of an organization). The mechanisms of learning and change were displayed by filters (organi-zational culture and absorption capacity in phase 1) and barriers (change resistance and institutional design in phase 2). In addition to this modeling of the process of learning, the concept of boundary spanners usefully captured the mutually constituting relationship between the subject of learning and its (inner and outer) environment.

Evidence of learning and change could be found at all levels:

- At the institutional level (structures and procedures), the following instances could be detected: The invention of EUSRs as well as their increasing number, their integration into CFSP Structures and the establishment of (limited) structures of their own, their budgetary position, the EUSRs cooperation with Commission and Parliament, standardization of general mandate provisions, personnel selection, and lessons-learned seminars.
- At the policy level (operations and ideas), an expansion of the EUSRs' tasks, different bases of operation and positions in the ESDP chain of command, their role in EU internal coordination and external cooperation with partners, the EUSRs' important input for policy, the calculated use of envoys by the EU, including though double-hatting, and their contribution to fostering the EU's strategic role, all evidenced the EU's capacity for learning and change.

Beyond the mere ascertainment that learning does take place, this evidence has produced the following additional findings:

- The organizational culture works as the main filter of the EU's learning, shaped by four characteristics: A value of external coherence; an orientation at national role models; a broad set of instruments and a comprehensive approach; and a global ambition. This filter can be so strong that, just like any other organization, the EU only learns what it wants to learn.
- A certain focus on internal issues exists, though with little capacity for deutero learning. In this setting, the EUSRs provide important information as boundary spanners, while remaining institutionally weak themselves.
- Further research is needed on the detailed workings of cognitive filters as well as on the substance of the worldviews of EU officials. In addition, researchers might want to look at how OL interacts with socialization processes.

From this follows that organizational learning, if and when it occurs, needs to be factored into explanations of change, i.e. treated as an independent variable, not just as a conditioning factor. The main barrier to the implementation of learning, in turn, is change resistance from member states. It supersedes the institutional design that might prevent change from being put in place, as states ultimately have control over the latter. Moreover, the research highlights the importance of internal processes: Events and critical junctures enable, but do not produce change. All in all, the EU developed its envoys in a learning by doing fashion, copying rather from member states and the United States than from international organizations such as the United Nations.

The explanatory strength of OL notwithstanding, it should be seen as a contributing factor within a multidisciplinary approach rather than a mono-causal attempt to explain European foreign policy-making. Indeed, with its two-phase model that highlights the different dynamics of each phase, OL offers fertile ground for approaches such as constructivism and rationalism (that are oftentimes regarded as antagonistic) to join their explicative forces. This work's contribution is to establish OL as a significant approach next to the more mainstream explanations of IR and European foreign policy theory.

In this vein of promoting cross-disciplinary research, the question arises how exactly can OL be methodologically combined with the mainstream theoretical approaches? Furthermore, one might ask about other contributing factors or about how one can differentiate OL-based change from non-learning-based change?

So far the EUSRs have been treated as a case of organizational learning—beyond that, they have turned out to be an important instrument of the EU's foreign policy. Their mere presence is an important factor in obliging member states to devise a policy for a given country or region. Additionally important are their boundary spanning activities. Special Representatives help establish and consolidate a political position of the EU by internally straddling policy areas as well as institutions (not to mention that they provide valuable information too). This contributes to an externally coherent stance, which again eases the EUSRs' cooperation in multilateral settings. More than just representing the Union abroad and enhancing the EU's standing, they embody the Union's approach to comprehensive crisis management, which is regarded as one of the hallmarks of the EU's international identity as a 'distinct power'. Thus, the EUSRs have greatly contributed to building a more integrated EU foreign policy.

The significant internal role of EUSRs points to a general observation of the development of EU foreign policy: That the latter is not exclusively (maybe not even mainly) conceived towards the external world, but just as well to the EU's internal affairs. CFSP is rightly viewed as a driver of European integration, as much as political integration also furthers closer cooperation in foreign policy. Ultimately, the question of an EU foreign service—regardless of the potential example set by the EUSRs or the current limbo of the Lisbon Reform Treaty—will be answered with a view to its integration potential rather than to its problem-solving capacity.[401]

These policy-oriented considerations lead to the following questions: Beyond the comparison of three sets of envoys conducted at the outset of this study, what are the roles of other envoys, for example of regional organizations such as NATO or the AU? Is it possible to generalize about 'the envoy function'? How could an organization like the EU strengthen its learning capacities? And, with regard to international identity, how do third parties perceive the appearance and actions of the Union? Is this congruent with the EU's apparent self-image as a 'distinct power'?

---

401 More precisely, the latter is a function of the former: Only if it 'works' (in terms of problem solving capacity) can the EU foreign service deliver its integration potential.

Table 5: Summary of Main Findings and Conclusions

		Definition	Operationalization	Evidence of Learning and Change	Findings	Conclusions	Further Research
Organizational Development	Organizational learning (Phase 1)	Rewriting of Rules as a Result of Reflection	Differentiation between structural, procedural, operational, and ideational rules. Two filters: Organizational culture, absorption capacity	Invention of EUSRs; Increasing Number of EUSRs; Integration into CFSP Structures; EUSR Structures; Budgetary Issues. Cooperation with Commission and Parliament; Standardization of General Mandate Provisions; Selection of EUSRs; Lessons-learned Seminars. Tasks; Basis of Operation; EU Political Coordination; ESDP Chain of Command; External Cooperation. Policy Input; Calculated use of envoys; Double-hatting; The EU's Strategic Role	Learning does take place. Organizational culture as main filter with four characteristics: – external coherence, – national role models, – comprehensive approach, – global ambition. EUSRs provide information as boundary spanners, but remain institutionally weak. Internal focus of learning, though little capacity for deutero learning (learning to learn).	Two-phase model of learning and change with different dynamics promotes cross-disciplinary research (e.g. constructivist and rationalist approaches). OL as one explanatory factor alongside other (e.g. interest- or value-based) explanations. Events and critical junctures enable, but do not produce change	How do cognitive filters work in detail? What are the world-views of EU officials? How does OL interact with socialization processes?
	Organizational change (Phase 2)	Learning-based change	Differentiation between institutional change and policy change. Two barriers: Change resistance, institutional design		Organizational learning to be treated as independent variable. Main barrier to implementation of learning is change resistance from member states		What are other contributing factors? How to differentiate non-learning-based change? How can OL be combined with mainstream theoretical approaches?
EUSRs and EU foreign policy			Boundary spanners between the subject of learning and the learning environment	Eight different roles (internal and external as well as presence and actor-ness): obligation, analysis, proposals, and coordination, visibility, dissemination, activity, and cooperation	EU pursued learning-by-doing approach, copying rather than from in-(member) states than from international organizations	EUSRs have an important internal function, bridging institutions and policies. EUSRs embody EU's international identity. CFSP as driver of European integration, and vice versa	How can the EU's learning capacity be strengthened? Do other multilateral envoys (e.g. of NATO or the AU) have similar functions?

Table 5 (cf. above) summarizes both the findings of this study and the need for further research.

This study's political premise was the EU's claim to learn from its past external actions. Having analyzed an important, yet hitherto little regarded foreign policy instrument, one can say that the Union does indeed learn, though different from the way its leaders would like to have it. This study therefore concludes with an appeal to not only talk about learning but to take it seriously. The improvements possibly resulting from organizational learning should help the EU advance on its way to becoming a serious international actor—not least in conjunction with the other grand claim that it likes to make, i. e. of being a different kind of world power.

If the EU were to seriously learn from its actions—contrary to the Hegelian approach quoted at the beginning of this chapter, that is—it could truly claim to be such a distinct power. As Karl Deutsch famously argued, „to have power means not to have to give in, and to force the environment or the other person to do so. Power in this narrow sense is the priority of output over intake, the ability to talk instead of listen. In a sense, it is the ability to afford not to learn" (Deutsch 1966, 111). To be a global power and to learn, or even: being a global power because it is able to learn and improve its actions, would ultimately legitimize the EU's global ambition.

Annex:
List of Interviewees, List of Abbreviations,
Index of Figures, Index of Tables, and Bibliography

A. List of Interviewees

Note: All institutions are based in Brussels, except otherwise noted. Interviews took place at the seat of the institution, unless otherwise noted. Positions are given for the time of the interview, unless a specific time frame is given in brackets.

1. Current or former EU Special Representatives

Aldo Ajello, former EUSR for the Great Lakes (March 1996–February 2007)

Erwan Fouéré, EUSR for Macedonia, Skopje [interview in Brussels]

Pekka Haavisto, former EUSR for Sudan (July 2005–April 2007) [telephone interview]

Kalman Miszei, EUSR for Moldova [interview in Berlin]

Pierre Morel, EUSR for Central Asia

Marc Otte, EUSR for the Middle East Peace Process [interview in Berlin]

Christian Schwarz-Schilling, former EUSR for Bosnia and Herzegovina, Sarajevo (January 2006–June 2007) [interview in Berlin]

Peter Semneby, EUSR for the South Caucasus

Roeland van de Geer, EUSR for the Great Lakes

Francesc Vendrell, EUSR for Afghanistan, Kabul [interview in Berlin]

2. Current or former staff from the EUSRs, the Council Secretariat (including the Policy Unit), member states' permanent missions or foreign ministries

Gints Apals, Political Advisor, EUSR for Central Asia, and DG E (Central Asia), Council Secretariat

Alessandra Baldi, Task Force Central Asia, Policy Unit, Council Secretariat

Jens Beiküfner, Political Advisor, EUSR for Central Asia [interview in Berlin]

Jorge César das Neves, Task Force Africa, Policy Unit, Council Secretariat; in parallel: Political Advisor, EUSR for Sudan (June–December 2005), and Political Advisor, EUSR for the Great Lakes (June–September 2007).

Cesira D'Aniello, Head of Coordination Unit, Council Secretariat

Arndt Freytag von Loringhoven, European Correspondent, German Foreign Office, Berlin

Clara Ganslandt, Coordination Unit, Council Secretariat

Julie Godin, Political Advisor, EUSR for the Great Lakes

Carl Hallergard, Cabinet of the High Representative, Council Secretariat; former Head of Cabinet, EUSR for Macedonia (2001–2003)

Frank Hartmann, Deputy Head of Unit (Central Europe), German Foreign Office, Berlin; former Chef de cabinet, Office of the High Representative (OHR)/EUSR for Bosnia and Herzegovina (February 2006–June 2007)

Christoph Heusgen, Foreign Policy Advisor, German Federal Chancellery, Berlin; former Head of the Policy Unit, Council Secretariat (1998–2005)

Rolf Krause, Head of Unit (Sub-Saharan Africa), German Foreign Office, Berlin

Stefan Lehne, Head of Unit (Balkans & South Caucasus), Policy Unit, Council Secretariat [interview in Berlin]

Marie-Louise Lindorfer, Political Advisor, EUSR for the Great Lakes, and DG E, Council Secretariat

Rüdiger Lotz, Political Advisor, EUSR for Macedonia (October 2001–November 2002)

Jochen Möller, Political Advisor, EUSR for the Middle East Peace Process

Elena Maria Peresso, Assistant to the Director-General E (Robert Cooper), Council Secretariat

Viktor Richter, Political Advisor, EUSR for Central Asia (October 2005–August 2007) [interview in Berlin]

Thomas Schieb, Deputy European Correspondent, German Foreign Office, Berlin

Stefan Schneck, Political Advisor, EUSR for Moldova [interview in Berlin]

Pirkka Tapiola, Eastern Europe & Central Asia, Policy Unit, Council Secretariat

György Tatar, Horizontal Security Issues, Policy Unit, Council Secretariat

Stefan Tressing, Macedonia Desk, Policy Unit, Council Secretariat

Tobias Tunkel, Political Advisor, EUSR for the Middle East Peace Process

Rainer Uher, Coordination Unit, Council Secretariat

Clemens von Goetze, PSC Ambassador, Permanent Mission of Germany to the European Union

Tania von Uslar, Policy Unit, Council Secretariat

Annika Weidemann, Political Advisor, EUSR for Moldova

Andreas Wiedenhoff, Policy Unit, Council Secretariat

Alexandros Yannis, Political Advisor, EUSR for the South Caucasus, and Policy Unit, Council Secretariat

3. Staff from the European Commission and Members of the European Parliament

Juha Auvinen, Head of Unit, CFSP and RRM, DG Relex, European Commission

Christian Berger, Head of Unit, Crisis Management and conflict prevention, DG Relex, European Commission

Monika Dvorakova, Officer, CFSP and RRM, DG Relex, European Commission

Maria McLoughlin, DG Relex, European Commission; former Political Advisor, EUSR for the Great Lakes (1996–1997)

Doris Pack, Member of the European Parliament

Marc van Bellinghen, Deputy Head of Unit, Crisis management and conflict prevention, DG Relex, European Commission

4. Staff from European-policy think tanks

Ariane Berthoin Antal, Social Science Research Centre Berlin (WZB), Berlin

Kathrin Böhling, Social Science Research Centre Berlin (WZB), Berlin

Pierre-Antoine Braud, EU Institute for Security Studies, Paris

Giovanni Grevi, EU Institute for Security Studies, Paris

B. List of Abbreviations

AFET	Affaires Etrangères [EP foreign affairs committee]
AMIS	African Union Mission in Sudan
AU	African Union
BiH	Bosnia and Herzegovina
BST	Border Support Team [in Georgia]
CARDS	Community Assistance for Reconstruction, Development and Stabilisation
CAREC	Central Asia Regional Economic Cooperation Program
CARICC	Central Asian Regional Information and Coordination Centre
CFSP	Common Foreign and Security Policy
CICA	Conference on Interaction and Confidence-Building Measures in Asia
COPS	Comité de Politique et Sécurité [cf. PSC]
COPPS	Co-ordinating Office for Palestinian Police Support
Coreper	Comité des Représentants Permanents [Committee of Permanent Representatives]
COREU	Correspondance Européenne [EU telex communication network]
CPCC	Civilian Planning and Conduct Capability
CSTO	Collective Security Treaty Organisation
DG	Directorate-General
DPA	Department of Political Affairs [of the UN]
DPKO	Department of Peacekeeping Operations [of the UN]
DRC	Democratic Republic of Congo [formerly Zaire]
EC	European Community
EEAS	European External Action Service
ENP	European Neighbourhood Policy
EP	European Parliament
EPC	European Political Cooperation
ESDP	European Security and Defence Policy
EU	European Union
EUBAM	European Union Border Assistance Mission [for Moldova and Ukraine]
EUFOR	European Union Force
EUJUST	European Union Rule of Law Mission
EUMS	European Union Military Staff
EUPAT	European Union Police Advisory Team [in Macedonia]
EUPM	European Union Police Mission
EUPOL	European Union Police Mission
EURASEC	Eurasian Economic Community
EUSR	European Union Special Representatives
FYROM	Former Yugoslav Republic of Macedonia
HIV/AIDS	Human Immunodeficiency Virus/Acquired Immune Deficiency Syndrome
HR	High Representative
IGC	Intergovernmental Conference [of the EU]
IO	International Organisation
ISAF	International Security Assistance Force [in Afghanistan]

IR	International Relations [as an academic discipline]
JCMB	Joint Coordination and Monitoring Board [for Afghanistan]
JHA	Justice and Home Affairs
MEP	Member of the European Parliament
MEPP	Middle East Peace Process
NATO	North Atlantic Treaty Organization
OAU	Organization of African Unity
OHR	Office of the High Representative
OL	Organizational Learning
ONUC	Opération des Nations Unies au Congo [UN mission in the Congo]
OSCE	Organisation for Security and Cooperation in Europe
PCA	Partnership and Cooperation Agreement
PIN	Peace Implementation Network
PLO	Palestine Liberation Organization
PoCo	Political Committee
POLAD	Political Advisor
PSC	Political and Security Committee [cf. COPS]
Relex	Relations Extérieures [External Relations of the EC]
RRM	Rapid Reaction Mechanism
RT	Reform Treaty [amending TEU and TEC]
SAA	Stabilisation and Association Agreement
SAP	Stabilisation and Association Process
SCO	Shanghai Cooperation Organization
SG	Secretary-General
SFOR	Stabilisation Force [in Bosnia and Herzegovina]
SRSG	Special Representative of the [UN] Secretary-General
SSR	Security Sector Reform
TCE	Treaty establishing a new Constitution for Europe
TEC	Treaty establishing a European Community
TEU	Treaty on European Union
UK	United Kingdom
UN	United Nations
UNAMA	United Nations Assistance Mission in Afghanistan
UNCh	United Nations Charter
UNDP	United Nations Development Programme
UNHCR	United Nations High Commissioner for Refugees
UNICEF	United Nations Children's Fund
UNIFIL	United Nations Interim Force in Lebanon
UNITAR	United Nations Institute for Training and Research
UNMIK	United Nations Mission in Kosovo
UNSMA	United Nations Special Mission to Afghanistan
U.S.	United States [of America]
WEU	Western European Union

C. Index of Figures

D. Index of Tables

E. Deutschsprachige Zusammenfassung

Die vorliegende Arbeit untersucht anhand der Sonderbeauftragten der Europäischen Union (EU), ob sich Lernprozesse in der EU-Außenpolitik nachweisen lassen. Das Erkenntnisinteresse ist es, die Mechanismen und Bedingung von Organisationalem Lernen (OL) zu bestimmen und seine Auswirkungen auf organisationalen Wandel zu untersuchen. Auf diese Weise soll die Tragfähigkeit von OL als middle-range theory beleuchtet werden. Darüber hinaus schließt die Studie eine empirische Lücke, die mit Blick auf die Arbeit der EU-Sonderbeauftragten (EUSB) besteht.

Das Forschungsdesign ist aufgrund eines fehlenden einheitlichen theoretischen OL-Ansatzes explorativ. Im ersten Teil der Arbeit werden die EUSB in ihrer Entwicklung von dem ersten Mandat 1996 bis zum Jahr 2007 vorgestellt (Kapitel 1). Anschließend werden sie mit den Sonderbeauftragten des Generalsekretärs der Vereinten Nationen und den Sondergesandten des Präsidenten der Vereinigten Staaten verglichen (Kapitel 2). Diese Gegenüberstellung fördert bereits erste Rückschlüsse über die Funktionsweise von Sonderbeauftragten / -gesandten sowie mögliche Lernmomente zu Tage, welche für die theoretische Einbettung hilfreich sind.

Das dritte Kapitel setzt den theoretischen Rahmen der Arbeit. Nach Sichtung bestehender, jedoch unzulänglicher Ansätze wird ein analytisches Zweiphasenmodell entwickelt, das zwischen Lernen auf der einen und Wandel auf der anderen Seite unterscheidet. Lernen wird als »Regeländerung aufgrund von Reflexion« definiert; als Regelebenen werden Strukturen, Verfahren, Operationen und Ideen unterschieden. Wandel kann auf institutioneller oder politischer Ebene erfolgen. Für beide Phasen werden Filter (z. B. Organisationale Kultur) und Barrieren (z. B. Wandelresistenz) benannt, welche den Prozess beeinflussen können. Als Lernsubjekt werden die Entscheidungsgremien der Gemeinsamen Außen- und Sicherheitspolitik (GASP) der EU bestimmt; die EUSB agieren als Grenzgänger (boundary spanners) zwischen Subjekt und Umgebung.

Der empirische Teil (Kapitel 4 bis 6) untersucht mit diesem analytischen Modell 18 verschiedene Lernvorgänge, welche anhand des explorativen Ansatzes herausgearbeitet wurden. Zunächst werden Regelveränderungen auf den vier Ebenen (Strukturen, Verfahren, Operationen und Ideen) erörtert; anschließend wird analysiert, ob diese lernbasierten Regelveränderungen auch (institutionellen oder politischen) Wandel bewirkt haben. Im Einzelnen werden untersucht: Die Einrichtung von zwei EUSB 1996 sowie ihr deutlicher Anstieg auf neun Mandate bis zum Jahr 2007; ihre Einbeziehungen in die Strukturen der GASP, der (begrenzte) Aufbau eigener Strukturen sowie ihre budgetäre Verortung; ihre Zusammenarbeit mit Europäischer Kommission und Europäischem Parlament; die Vereinheitlichung von Mandaten, die Einführung eines Personalauswahlprozesses und das Abhalten von Lessons-learned-Seminaren; die stetige Ausweitung der Aufgaben der EUSB; ihre unterschiedlichen Standorte sowie ihre Position in der operativen Befehlskette; ihre Rolle in der internen Koordination und externen Zusammenarbeit; die Zulieferungen der EUSB für die Politikgestaltung, ihren zunehmend kalkulierten Einsatz durch die EU, u. a. durch die Konstruktion eines »Doppelhuts«, sowie ihren Beitrag zur Stärkung der strategischen Rolle der Union.

Zusammenfassend lässt sich sagen, dass Lernen in Organisationen tatsächlich stattfindet und Wandel verursachen kann. Die Sonderbeauftragten als Grenzgänger haben der EU diverse Lernvorgänge ermöglicht, und das entwickelte Modell stellt ein geeignetes methodisches Instrument dar, diese sowie ihren möglichen Einfluss auf Wandel in der Europäischen Außenpolitik zu untersuchen. Besondere Bedeutung kommt der Organisationalen Kultur zu, da diese als Ausdruck der (außenpolitischen) Identität der EU die Lernerfahrungen stark beeinflusst. Damit unterstützt die OL-Theorie solche Ansätze, die Wandel als langfristige Veränderungen begreifen, während einschneidende äußere Ereignisse (kritische Augenblicke oder junctures) letztere nicht bestimmen, sondern nur ermöglichen.

Insgesamt ist der OL-Ansatz als ein Beitrag zu multidisziplinärer Forschung zu verstehen, in der lernbasierte Erklärungen als unabhängige Variablen neben solchen stehen, die auf Interessen, Ideen oder externen Faktoren beruhen. Gerade das Zweiphasenmodell ist darüber hinaus geeignet, den Dialog zwischen konstruktivistischen und rationalistischen Ansätzen zu befördern, da diese für jeweils eine der beiden Phasen geeignetere Erklärungsmodelle liefern.

Die Sonderbeauftragten selber haben sich – über ihre Funktion als Fallobjekt hinaus – als wichtiges außenpolitisches Instrument der EU dargestellt. Bereits ihre Anwesenheit (presence) zwingt die Mitgliedstaaten, eine Politik für eine bestimmte Region zu entwickeln, da sie sonst führungslos wären. Über die Informationsbeschaffung und -bewertung hinaus agieren sie als multiple Grenzgänger: Innerhalb der GASP (d. h. zu den Mitgliedstaaten und auch EU-Operationen), säulenübergreifend (d. h. hauptsächlich zur Kommission) sowie zu Drittstaaten und Partnerorganisationen. Mehr als bloße Repräsentanten der EU verkörpern sie deren singulären Ansatz in Außenpolitik und Krisenmanagement. So haben sie wesentlich zum Aufbau einer integrierteren EU-Außenpolitik beigetragen.

Schließlich deutet die gewichtige interne Rolle der EUSB auf eine Besonderheit der Europäischen Außenpolitik insgesamt hin. Diese wird nicht nur (und teilweise sogar nicht primär) mit Blick auf die Welt konzipiert, sondern hat eine nicht zu unterschätzende Wirkung ins Innere der EU. Die (Weiter-)Entwicklung der GASP ist deshalb genauso sehr Ausdruck wie Antrieb der europäischen Integration. Auch die Frage nach dem Aufbau eines europäischen Auswärtigen Dienstes wird letztlich – unabhängig von der Modellfunktion der EUSB oder der gegenwärtigen Ratifizierungskrise des Lissabonner Vertrags – eher vor dem Hintergrund eines möglichen internen Nutzens einer solchen Einrichtung als allein aufgrund ihrer externen Notwendigkeit entschieden werden.

F. Bibliography

Note: All internet links are valid as of 30 March 2009.

1. Official publications and speeches

Council of the European Union (1999) Annual report from the Council to the European Parliament on the main aspects and basic choices of CFSP, including the financial implications for the general budget of the European Communities–1998. Doc. 7051/99. Brussels, 16 April 1999.

Council of the European Union (2000) EU Special Representatives: Guidelines on appointing procedure and administrative arrangements. Doc. 7089/00. Brussels, 20 March 2000.

Council of the European Union (2002a) Annual report from the Council to the European Parliament on the main aspects and basic choices of CFSP, including the financial implications for the general budget of the European Communities–2001. Doc. 7330/02. Brussels, 18 April 2002.

Council of the European Union (2002b) Draft Council Joint Actions extending and amending the mandates of the Special Representative of the European Union for the Great Lakes Region, Afghanistan, the Middle East Peace Process, FYROM and the Stability Pact. Doc. 14003/02. Brussels, 3 December 2002.

Council of the European Union (2003a) Annual report from the Council to the European Parliament on the main aspects and basic choices of CFSP, including the financial implications for the general budget of the European Communities–2002. Doc. 7038/03. Brussels, 7 April 2003.

Council of the European Union (2003b) EU Special Representatives: Guidelines on appointment, mandate and financing. Doc. 13833/03. Brussels, 17 November 2003.

Council of the European Union (2004a) Action Plan for ESDP support to Peace and Security in Africa. Doc. 10538/4/04. Brussels, 16 November 2004.

Council of the European Union (2004b) Annual report from the Council to the European Parliament on the main aspects and basic choices of CFSP, including the financial implications for the general budget of the European Communities–2003. Doc. 8412/04. Brussels, 22 April 2004.

Council of the European Union (2004c) Civilian Headline Goal 2008. Doc. 15836/04. Brussels, 7 December 2004.

Council of the European Union (2004d) EU Special Representatives–Review of the mandate of the EUSR in fYROM. Doc. 9898/04. Brussels, 27 May 2004.

Council of the European Union (2005a) 2684th meeting of the Council of the European Union (Environment), held in Luxemburg on 17 October 2005–Revised Draft Minutes. Doc. 13362/1/05 REV 1. Brussels, 14 February 2006.

Council of the European Union (2005b) EU Concept for ESDP support to Security Sector Reform (SSR). Doc. 12566/4/05. Brussels, 13 October 2005.

Council of the European Union (2005c) The EU and Africa: Towards a Strategic Partnership. Doc. 15961/05. Brussels, 19 December 2005.

Council of the European Union (2006a) Annual report from the Council to the European Parliament on the main aspects and basic choices of CFSP, including the financial implications for the general budget of the European Communities–2005. Doc. 10314/06. Brussels, 8 June 2006.

Council of the European Union (2006b) Draft Council Conclusions on a Policy Framework for Security Sector Reform. Doc. 9967/06. Brussels, 6 June 2006.

Council of the European Union (2006c) Guidelines on appointment, mandate and financing of EU Special Representatives. Doc. 7223/1/06. Brussels, 21 March 2006.

Council of the European Union (2007a) Annual report from the Council to the European Parliament on the main aspects and basic choices of CFSP, including the financial implications for the general budget of the European Communities–2006. Doc. 6992/1/07. Brussels, 30 April 2007.

Council of the European Union (2007b) Extract from the Official directory of the European Union. Brussels, January 2007.

Council of the European Union (2007c) Guidelines on appointment, mandate and financing of EU Special Representatives. Doc. 11328/1/07. Brussels, 24 July 2007.

Council of the European Union (2007d) Summary of the appearances by the Council in the European Parliament in the field of CFSP/ESDP in 2006. Doc. 7358/07. Brussels, 14 March 2007.

Council of the European Union and European Commission (2007) Creation of a Delegation of the European Union to the African Union in Addis Ababa. Publication of a vacancy for a function of Head of the EU Delegation (COM/2007/10051). Brussels, Official Journal n° C191A – 17/08/2007.

Court of Auditors (2001) Special Report No 13/2001 on the management of the common foreign and security policy (CFSP), in: Official Journal of the European Communities, 44, 2001/C 338/01

EU Council Secretariat (2005) EU Special Representatives (EUSRs). A voice and face of the EU in crucial areas. Factsheet. Brussels.

European Commission (1996) Communication from the Commission to the Council: The European Union and the Issue of Conflicts in Africa: Peace-Building, Conflict Prevention and beyond. SEC(96) 332 final. Brussels, 6 March 1996.

European Commission (2003) Communication from the Commission: Wider Europe—Neighbourhood: A New Framework for Relations with our Eastern and Southern Neighbours. COM(2003) 104 final. Brussels, 11 March 2003.

European Commission (2004a) Communication from the Commission: European Neighbourhood Policy Strategy Paper. COM(2004) 373 final. Brussels, 12 May 2004.

European Commission (2004b) Communication from the Commission: Specific Rules for Special Advisers of the Commission entrusted with the implementation of operational CFSP actions. Brussels.

European Commission (2004c) Taking Europe to the world: 50 years of the European Commission's External Service. Brussels: European Communities, External Relations.

European Commission (2005a) Communication from the Commission: EU-Palestinian cooperation beyond disengagement - towards a two-state solution. COM(2005) 458 final. Brussels, 5 October 2005.

European Commission (2005b) RRM financing decision on the establishment of EUBAM. COM(2005) 4231. Brussels, 28 October 2005

European Commission (2006a) Communication from the Commission to the Council and the European Parliament: A Concept for European Community Support for Security Sector Reform. COM(2006) 253 final. Brussels, 24 May 2006.

European Commission (2006b) Communication from the Commission to the European Council of June 2006: Europe in the World—Some Practical Proposals for Greater Coherence, Effectiveness and Visibility. COM(2006) 278 final. Brussels, 8 June 2006.

European Commission (2006c) European Neighbourhood and Partnership Instrument. Georgia: Country Strategy Paper 2007-2013. Brussels.

European Commission (2007) Eurobarometer 68, First Results. December 2007.

European Community (1973) Document on the European Identity published by the Nine foreign ministers. Bulletin of the European Communities (N° 12, December 1973, pp. 118–122). Copenhagen, 14 December 1973.

European Community (2006) Regional Strategy Paper for Assistance to Central Asia for the period 2007-2013. Brussels.

European Council (1993) Presidency Conclusions. Brussels, 10 and 11 December 1993.

European Council (1999) Presidency Conclusions. Berlin, 24 and 25 March 1999.

European Council (2001) Presidency Conclusions. Göteborg, 15 and 16 June 2001.

European Council (2003) European Security Strategy: A Secure Europe in a Better World. Brussels.

European Council (2004a) Action Plan for the Civilian Aspects of ESDP. Brussels, 17 and 18 June 2004.

European Council (2004b) European Security Strategy–Bosnia and Herzegovina–Comprehensive Policy. Brussels, 17 and 18 June 2004.

European Council (2005) Presidency Conclusions. Brussels, 15 and 16 December 2005.

European Council (2007) The EU and Central Asia: Strategy for a New Partnership. Doc. 10113/07. Brussels, 31 May 2007.

European Parliament (2003) Resolution adopted by the "European Parliament Forum on Tibet: EU Response to Sino-Tibetan Dialogue". Brussels, 12 November 2003.

European Parliament (2005) Report on the annual report from the Council to the European Parliament on the main aspects and basic choices of CFSP, including the financial implications for the general budget of the European Communities–2004 (2005/2134(INI)). Committee on Foreign Affairs; Rapporteur: Elmar Brok (A6-0389/2005). Brussels, 1 December 2005.

European Parliament (2007) Common Foreign and Security Policy 2005. European Parliament resolution of 23 May 2007 on the annual report from the Council to the European Parliament on the main aspects and basic choices of CFSP, including the financial implications for the general budget of the European Union – 2005 (2006/2217(INI)). Rapporteur: Elmar Brok Brussels, 23 May 2007.

Ferrero-Waldner, Benita (2007) The European Union and the World: A Hard Look at Soft Power. Speech by EU Commissioner Ferrero-Waldner (Ref: SP07–410EN). Columbia University, New York (24 September 2007).

High Representative/Secretary General and European Commission (1999) Improving the Coherence and Effectiveness of the European Union Action in the Field of Conflict Prevention. Report Presented to the Nice European Council. Nice, 7–8 and 9 December 2000.

High Representative/Secretary-General and European Commission (2005) Joint Progress Report on the European External Action Service (9956/05). Brussels, 9 June 2005.

House of Lords, European Union Committee (2006) Europe in the World. Report with Evidence. 48th Report of Session 2005–06. HL Paper 268. London: The Stationery Office Limited.

House of Lords, Foreign Affairs Committee (2008) Foreign Policy Aspects of the Lisbon Treaty. Third Report of Session 2007–08. London: The Stationary Office Limited.

New Zealand, Ministry of Foreign Affairs and Trade (1980) United Nations Handbook: an annual guide for those working with and within the United Nations. Wellington.

New Zealand, Ministry of Foreign Affairs and Trade (1996) United Nations Handbook: an annual guide for those working with and within the United Nations. Wellington.

New Zealand, Ministry of Foreign Affairs and Trade (2006) United Nations Handbook: an annual guide for those working with and within the United Nations. Wellington.

Solana, Javier (2005a) Dayton @ 10: drawing lessons from the past. Policy Dialogue (S382/05). Brussels, 25 November 2005.

Solana, Javier (2005b) Seminar with EU Special Representatives: Opening remarks (S239/05). Brussels, 29 June 2005.

Solana, Javier (2008) Europe in the World: The Next Steps. Address by Javier Solana, Cyril Foster Lecture (S087/08). Oxford, 28 February 2008.

Solana, Javier and Oliver Rehn (2006) Summary note on the joint report on a Reinforced EU Presence in Bosnia and Herzegovina (S286/06). Brussels, 17 October 2006.

The Europa World Year Book 2006 (2006) 47th Edition. London: Routledge.

United Nations, DPKO (2003) Handbook on United Nations Multidimensional Peacekeeping Operations. New York, NY: Department of Peacekeeping Operations (DPKO).

United Nations, General Assembly (1996) Special representatives, envoys and related positions. Report of the Secretary-General (A/C.5/50/72). New York, NY.

United Nations, Secretary-General (2001) Remarks of Secretary-General Kofi Annan. Seminar of Special and Personal Representatives and Envoys (SG/SM/7760). Vienna, 2 April 2001.

2. Press documents

African Times (2004) Ambassador Leahy on Hopes for A Peaceful Great Lakes region, in: African Times, 15 November 2004.

Astill, James and Richard Norton-Taylor (2003) News roundup: Africa: 100 British troops to go to Congo, in: The Guardian, London, 11 June 2003.

BBC (2002) Analysis: The Expired Mandate, in: Radio 4: Current Affairs, United Kingdom, 1 August 2002.

Beatty, Andrew (2003) Israel waters down tough stance in face of EU criticism, in: EUobserver.com, 17 November 2003.

Beeston, Richard (2001) EU wants new Nato force for Macedonia, in: The Times, London, 10 September 2001.

Bocev, Pierre (2002) La diplomatie des Quinze au bord de la faillite, in: Le Figaro, Paris, 18 June 2002.

Castle, Stephen and Justin Huggler (2001) European force to take over; Replacing NATO troops clear sign of EU's resolve, in: The Toronto Star, C06.

CNN (2000) Albright calls for end to "Africa's first world war". Congo's Kabila says cease-fire "deadlocked", in: CNN.com, 24 January 2000.

Cunningham, Francine (1996) EU appoints envoy to join negotiations, in: The Scotsman, 11, 29 October 1996.

Dempsey, Judy (2007) Afghan police program in turmoil; Commander quits over political fights, in: The International Herald Tribune, New York, 13 September 2007.

Doyle, Mark (1998) Africa's "First World War" to dominate summit in: BBC News, London, December 17, 1998.

Edmonton Journal (2001) Congo ceasefire sought by EU envoy, in: Edmonton Journal, Alberta, 29 January 2001.

Finn, Peter (2001) Peace Deal Signed in Macedonia; Pact Opens Way For NATO Troops, in: The Washington Post, Washington, D.C., 14 August 2001

George, Allan (2000) Peace Will Herald New Middle East Marshall Plan, in: Evening Standard (UK), London, 13 September 2000.

Graff, James (2002) Our Man in Afghanistan; His new mission for the E.U. looks like being the toughest assignment yet for Spanish diplomat Francesc Vendrell, in: Time Magazine, 29 July 2002.

Graff, James L., Barry Hillenbrand, Robert Kroon and Jan Stojaspal (1999) Peace Gets a Chance; Learning lessons from Bosnia, international bodies create collaborative mechanisms to rebuild Kosovo, in: Time Magazine, 5 July 1999.

Harrison, Selig S. (2002) The welcome is going sour; Afghanistan, in: The International Herald Tribune, New York, 10 July 2002.

Keinon, Herb, Gil Hoffman and Melissa Radler (2003) Seven days, in: The Jerusalem Post, 31 October 2003.

MacAskill, Ewen (2001) It's our turn to help: With Arafat warning of tragedy and Bush all but washing his hands of the Middle East, the EU must intervene, in: The Guardian, London, 3 August 2001.

Makovsky, David (1996) Netanyahu: Delay on Hebron agreement helps Oslo's right-wing opponents, in: The Jerusalem Post, 2, 31 October 1996.

Makovsky, David (1997) EU wrote letter of Hebron assurance to Arafat, in: The Jerusalem Post, Jerusalem, 10 February 1997.

Malu-Malu, Arthur (1998) Foreign troops to aid Congo drive, in: The Philadelphia Inquirer, Philadelphia, 2 October 1998.

Mideast Mirror (1998) Jerusalem "not keen" on EU peace-brokering role, in: Mideast Mirror (Vol. 12, N° 17), 27 January 1998.

Moratinos, Miguel Angel (2002) Account of the Taba talks of January 2001, in: Haaretz, Jerusalem, 14 February 2002.

Morrison, James (1997) No second fiddle, in: The Washington Times, A12, 11 February 1997.

Nolan, Stephanie (1997) Optimistic talk of progress on peace proved premature, in: The Independent, London, 31 July 1997.

Pelletreau, Robert H. (1998) The U.S., Britain and Europe: Prospects for a joint approach to the Middle East, in: Mideast Mirror, Vol. 12, N° 55.

Rettman, Andrew (2007) EU keen to bring international criminal court to Central Asia. EUobserver. com, 14 June 2007.

Schwarz-Schilling, Christian (2006) How to move Bosnia forward; Empowerment, in: The International Herald Tribune, New York, 2 February 2006.

Shaffer, Brenda (2003) A conflict that can be resolved in time; Nagorno-Karabakh, in: The International Herald Tribune, New York, 29 November 2003.

Smyth, Jamie (2005) Irish official appointed as head of EU commission delegation in Macedonia, in: The Irish Times, 18 October 2005.

The Economist (1997) Israel intransigent, in: The Economist, London, June 28, 1997.

The Economist (2009) Hillary Clinton at State: Not necessarily a team of rivals, in: The Economist, London, January 15, 2009.

Traynor, Ian (2007) German Bosnia chief 'fired' after just a year, in: The Guardian, London, 24 January 2007.

Wood, Nicholas and Richard Norton-Taylor (2001) Skopje sticks to deal by voting for reforms, in: The Guardian, London, 7 September 2001.

Zerkalo Nedeli (2007) Interview with EU Special Representative for the Republic of Moldova, Kálmán Mizsei, in: Zerkalo Nedeli, Kyiv, 23 November 2007.

3. Secondary sources

Aggestam, Lisbeth (2008) Introduction: ethical power Europe?, in: International Affairs, Vol. 84, N° 1, 1–11.

Ajello, Aldo (2000) Cavalier de la Paix. Quelle politique européenne commune pour l'Afrique? Entretiens avec le Représentant spécial de l'Union européenne pour la région des Grands Lacs. Propos recueillis par Pierre-Olivier Richard. Preface de Ahmedou Ould Abdallah. Postface de Michel Rocard. Bruxelles: Groupe de Recherche et d'Information sur la Paix et la Securite (GRIP).

Aldrich, Howard E. (1999) Organizations Evolving. London: Sage.

Allen, David and Michael E. Smith (1990) Western Europe's presence in the contemporary international arena, in: Review of International Studies, 16, 1, 19–37.

Allen, David and Michael E. Smith (1996) External Policy Developments. In: Nugent, Neill (Ed.), The European Union 1995: Annual Review of Activities. Journal of Common Market Studies, Vol. 34 (August 1996). Cambridge: Blackwell Publishers, 63–84.

Allen, David and Michael E. Smith (1998a) External Policy Developments. In: Edwards, Geoffrey and Georg Wiessala (Eds.), The European Union 1997: Annual Review of Activities. Journal of Common Market Studies, Vol. 36 (August 1998). Cambridge: Blackwell Publishers, 69–91.

Allen, David and Michael E. Smith (1998b) The European Union's Security Presence: Barrier, Facilitator, or Manager? In: Rhodes, Carolyn (Ed.), The European Union and the World Community. Oxford: Oxford University Press, 45–63.

Allen, David and Michael E. Smith (1999) External Policy Developments. In: Edwards, Geoffrey and Georg Wiessala (Eds.), The European Union: Annual Review 1998/1999. Journal of Common Market Studies, Vol. 37 (September 1999). Cambridge: Blackwell Publishers, 87–108.

Allen, David and Michael E. Smith (2000) External Policy Developments. In: Edwards, Geoffrey and Georg Wiessala (Eds.), The European Union: Annual Review of the EU 1999/2000. Journal of Common Market Studies, Vol. 38 (September 2000). Cambridge: Blackwell Publishers, 101–20.

Allison, Graham (1971) Essence of Decision: Explaining the Cuban Missile Crisis. New York, NY: HarperCollins.

Argyris, Chris (1992) On Organizational Learning. Oxford: Blackwell.

Argyris, Chris and Donald A. Schön (1978) Organizational Learning: A Theory of Action Perspective. Reading, MA: Addison-Wesley.

Asseburg, Muriel (2003a) From declarations to implementation? The three dimensions of European policy towards the conflict. In: Ortega, Martin (Ed.), The European Union and the Crisis in the Middle East (Chaillot Paper 62). Paris: European Union Institute for Security Studies, 11–26.

Asseburg, Muriel (2003b) The EU and the Middle East Conflict: Tackling the Main Obstacle to Euro-Mediterranean Partnership, in: Mediterranean Politics, 8, 2, 174–93.

Bachteler, Tobias (1997) Explaining the Democratic Peace: The Evidence from Ancient Greece Reviewed, in: Journal of Peace Research, 34, 3 (August 1997), 315–23.

Balthasar, Andreas and Stefan Rieder (2000) Learning from Evaluations: Effects of the Evaluation of the Swiss Energy 2000 Programme, in: Evaluation, 6, 3, 245–60.

Barnett, Michael N. and Liv Coleman (2005) Designing Police: Interpol and the Study of Change in International Organizations, in: International Studies Quarterly, 49, 593–619.

Barnett, Michael N. and Martha Finnemore (1999) The Politics, Power, and Pathologies of International Organizations, in: International Organization, 53, 4 (Autumn 1999), 699–732.

Barnett, Michael N. and Martha Finnemore (2004) Rules for the World: International Organizations in Global Politics. Ithaca, NY: Cornell University Press.

Barros-Garica, Xiana (2007) Effective Multilateralism and the EU as a Military Power: The Worldview of Javier Solana. EUI Working Papers RSCAS 2007/08. Fiesole, San Domenico (FI): European University Institute.

Bauer, Michael W. (2007) Introduction: Management Reforms in International Organizations. In: Bauer, Michael W. and Christoph Knill (Eds.), Management Reforms in International Organizations. Baden-Baden: Nomos, 11–23.

Bendiek, Annegret (2007) Komplexität und Kohärenz? – Die Geschichte des Stabilitätspaktes für Südosteuropa und die Rolle der Europäischen Union. In: Jopp, Matthias and Peter Schlotter (Eds.), Kollektive Außenpolitik – Die Europäische Union als internationaler Akteur. Baden-Baden: Nomos, 211–37.

Benner, Thorsten, Andrea Binder and Philipp Rotmann (2007) Learning to Build Peace? United Nations Peacebuilding and Organizational Learning: Developing a Research Framework, in: GPPi Research Paper Series, N° 7.

Bennett, Colin J. and Michael Howlett (1992) The lessons of learning: Reconciling theories of policy learning and policy change, in: Policy Sciences, 25, 3, 275–94.

Berenskoetter, Felix S. (2005) Mapping the Mind Gap: A Comparison of US and European Strategies, in: Security Dialogue, 36, 1, 71–92.

Berthoin Antal, Ariane, John Child, Meinolf Dierkes and Ikujiro Nonaka (2001a) Organizational Learning and Knowledge: Reflections on the Dynamics of the Field and Challenges for the Future. In: Dierkes, Meinolf, Ariane Berthoin Antal, John Child and Ikujiro Nonaka (Eds.), Handbook of Organizational Learning and Knowledge. Oxford: Oxford University Press, 921–39.

Berthoin Antal, Ariane, Uwe Lenhardt and Rolf Rosenbrock (2001b) Barriers to Organizational Learning. In: Dierkes, Meinolf, Ariane Berthoin Antal, John Child and Ikujiro Nonaka (Eds.), Handbook of Organizational Learning and Knowledge. Oxford: Oxford University Press, 865–85.

Beyers, Jan (2005) Multiple Embeddedness and Socialization in Europe: The Case of Council Officials, in: International Organization, 59, 4 (Autumn 2005), 899–936.

Bildt, Carl (1997) Hat Europa aus Bosnien gelernt? Schlußfolgerungen für die europäische Außenpolitik, in: Internationale Politik, 52, 7 (July 1997), 3–8.

Biscop, Sven (1999) The UK's Change of Course: a new Chance for the ESDI, in: European Foreign Affairs Review, 4, 253–68 .

Biscop, Sven (2007) The Ambigious Ambition. The Development of the EU Security Architecture, in: Studia Diplomatica, 60, 1, 265–78.

Böhling, Kathrin (2002) Learning from Environmental Actors about Environmental Developments: The Case of International Organizations. Schriftenreihe, Wissenschaftszentrum Berlin für Sozialforschung (FS II 02–110). Berlin.

Böhling, Kathrin (2007) Opening up the Black Box. Organizational Learning in the European Commission. Frankfurt am Main: Peter Lang.

Börzel, Tanja A. (2005) Mind the gap! European integration between level and scope, in: Journal of European Public Policy, 12, 2 (April 2005), 217–36.

Brandstrom, Annika, Fredrik Bynander and Paul t'Hart (2004) Governing by Looking Back: Historical Analogies and Crisis Management, in: Public Administration, 82, 1, 191–210.

Breslauer, George W. (1991) What Have We Learned about Learning? In: Breslauer, George B. and Philip E. Tetlock (Eds.), Learning in U.S. and Soviet Foreign Policy. Boulder, CO: Westview Press.

Breslauer, George W. and Philip E. Tetlock (1991a) Introduction. In: Breslauer, George B. and Philip E. Tetlock (Eds.), Learning in U.S. and Soviet Foreign Policy. Boulder, CO: Westview Press.

Breslauer, George W. and Philip E. Tetlock (Eds.) (1991b) Learning in U.S. and Soviet Foreign Policy. Boulder, CO: Westview Press.

Bretherton, Charlotte and John Vogler (1999) The European Union as a Global Actor. London: Routledge.

Bretherton, Charlotte and John Vogler (2006) The European Union as a Global Actor. London: Routledge (2nd edition).

Breul, Rainer (2005) Organizational Learning in International Organizations. The Case of the UN Department for Peacekeeping Operations. Diplomarbeit Fachbereich Politik- und Verwaltungswissenschaften. Konstanz: Universität Konstanz.

Brok, Elmar and Norbert Gresch (2004) Actors & witnesses. In: Gnesotto, Nicole (Ed.), EU Security and Defence Policy. The first five years (1999–2004). Paris: European Union Institute for Security Studies, 179–88.

Bull, Hedley (1982) Civilian Power Europe: A Contradiction in Terms, in: Journal of Common Market Studies, 21, 149–64.

Byman, Daniel L. and Kenneth M. Pollack (2001) Let Us Now Praise Great Men: Bringing the Statesman Back In, in: International Security, 25, 4 (Spring 2001), 107–46.

Calic, Marie-Janine (2003) The EU and the Balkans: From Association to Membership? SWP Comments 7. Berlin, May 2003.

Calic, Marie-Janine (2008) Das ewige Laboratorium. Die Politik der Europäischen Union auf dem Balkan: Eine Evaluierung, in: Internationale Politik, 63, 6 (June 2008), 26–31.

Cameron, Fraser (1999) The foreign and security policy of the European Union: past, present and future. Sheffield: Sheffield Academic Press.

Carlsnaes, Walter (2004) Introduction. In: Carlsnaes, Walter, Helene Sjursen and Brian White (Eds.), Contemporary European Foreign Policy. London: Sage, 1–7.

Carlsnaes, Walter, Helene Sjursen and Brian White (Eds.) (2004) Contemporary European Foreign Policy. London: Sage.

Carlsnaes, Walter and Steve Smith (1994) European Foreign Policy: The EC and Changing Perspectives in Europe. London: Sage.

Checkel, Jeffrey T. (2001) Why Comply? Social Learning and European Identity Change, in: International Organization, 55, 3 (Summer 2001), 553–88.

Checkel, Jeffrey T. (2005) International Institutions and Socialization in Europe: Introduction and Framework, in: International Organization, 59, 4 (Autumn 2005), 801–26.

Checkel, Jeffrey T. (2006) Constructivist approaches to European Integration, in: ARENA Working Paper N° 6, February 2006.

Christiansen, Thomas, Gerda Falkner and Knud Erik Jorgensen (2002) Theorizing EU treaty reform: beyond diplomacy and bargaining, in: Journal of European Public Policy, 9, 1 (February 2002), 12–32.

Coopey, John (1996) Crucial gaps in 'the learning organization': Power, politics and ideology. In: Starkey, Ken (Ed.), How organizations learn. London: International Thomson Business Press.

Coppieters, Bruno (2003) An EU Special Representative to a new periphery. In: Lynch, Dov (Ed.), The South Caucasus: a challenge for the EU (Chaillot Paper 65). Paris: European Union Institute for Security Studies, 159–70.

Coutto, Tatiana (2007) International Cooperation and Environmental Security: The Worldview of Joseph Borg. EUI Working Papers RSCAS 2007/12. Fiesole, San Domenico (FI): European University Institute.

Csigó, Monika (2006) Institutioneller Wandel durch Lernprozesse. Eine neo-institutionalistische Perspektive. Wiesbaden: VS Verlag.

Cyert, Richard and James G. March (1963) A Behavioral Theory of the Firm. Englewood Cliffs, NJ: Prentice-Hall.

Dannreuther, Roland (2002) Europe and the Middle East: Towards A Substantive Role in the Peace Process? Geneva Centre for Security Policy (GCSP) Occasional Paper Series 39 (August 2002), Geneva.

de Schoutheete de Tervarent, Philippe (1980) La Coopération Politique Européenne. Brussels: F. Nathan Editions Labor.

Deutsch, Karl W. (1966) The Nerves of Government: Models of Political Communication and Control; with a new introduction. New York, NY: Free Press (2nd edition).

Diedrichs, Udo (2004) The European Parliament in CFSP: More than a Marginal Player?, in: The International Spectator, 2/2004, 31–46.

Dierkes, Meinolf, Ariane Berthoin Antal, John Child and Ikujiro Nonaka (Eds.) (2001) Handbook of Organizational Learning and Knowledge. Oxford: Oxford University Press.

Dietl, Elisabeth (2005) Ausbau der Konfliktmanagementfähigkeiten der EU durch den Sonderbotschafter für den Nahen Osten. Frankfurt am Main: Peter Lang.

Dolowitz, David P. and David Marsh (2000) Learning from Abroad: The Role of Policy Transfer in Contemporary Policy-Making, in: Governance, 13, 1 (January 2000), 5–24.

Duchêne, François (1972) Europe's Role in World Peace. In: Mayne, Richard J. (Ed.), Europe Tomorrow: Sixteen Europeans Look Ahead. London: Fontana.

Duchêne, François (1973) The European Community and the Uncertainties of Interdependence. In:

Kohnstamm, Max and Wolfgang Hager (Eds.), A Nation Writ Large? Foreign-Policy Problems before the European Community. London: Macmillan.

Duffield, John (2007) What Are International Institutions?, in: International Studies Review, 9, 1–22.

Duke, Simon (2005) Linchpin COPS: Assessing the workings and institutional relations of the Political and Security Committee, EIPA Working Paper 2005/W/05. Maastricht: European Institute of Public Administration.

Duke, Simon (2006) The Commission and CFSP. EIPA Working Paper 2006/W/01. Maastricht: European Institute of Public Administration.

Eberwein, Wolf-Dieter, Matthias Ecker and Yasemin Topcu (1998) Lernen in der Außenpolitik. Das Auswärtige Amt und die Politik humanitärer Hilfe. In: Albach, Horst, Meinolf Dierkes, Ariane Berthoin Antal and Kristina Vaillant (Eds.), Organisationslernen – institutionelle und kulturelle Dimensionen. Berlin: Edition Sigma, 269–87.

Egeberg, Morten (1999) Transcending intergovernmentalism? Identity and role perceptions of national officials in EU decision-making, in: Journal of European Public Policy, 6, 3 (September 1999), 456–74.

Ehrhart, Hans-Georg and Albrecht Schnabel (1999) EU conflict prevention in the Balkans: The Royaumont process and beyond. In: Cross, Peter and Guenola Rasamoelina (Eds.), Conflict prevention policy of the European Union (CPN Yearbook 1998/99). Baden-Baden: Nomos, 55–69.

Elgström, Ole and Michael E. Smith (Eds.) (2006) The European Union's roles in international politics: concepts and analysis. London: Routledge.

Etheredge, Lloyd S. (1981) Government Learning: An Overview. In: Long, Samuel L. (Ed.), Handbook of Political Behavior. New York, NY: Plenum, 73–161.

Everts, Steven and Daniel Keohane (2003) The European Convention and EU Foreign Policy: Learning from Failure, in: Survival, 45, 3 (September 2003), 167–86.

Falkner, Gerda (2002) Introduction: EU treaty reform as a three-level process, in: Journal of European Public Policy, 9, 1 (February 2002), 1–11.

Faria, Fernanda (2004) La gestion des crises en Afrique subsaharienne – Le rôle de l'union européenne (Occasional Paper 55). Paris: European Union Institute for Security Studies.

Fiedler, Anja (2004) The Great Lakes Region: Testing Ground for a European Union Foreign Policy. In: Mahncke, Dieter, Alicia Ambos and Christopher Reynolds (Eds.), European Foreign Policy: From Rhetoric to Reality? Brussels: PIE–Peter Lang, 317–34.

Fiol, C. Marlene and Marjorie A. Lyles (1985) Organizational Learning, in: Academy of Management Review, 10, 4, 803–13.

Flanders, Henry (1894) Power of the President to Appoint Special Diplomatic Agents without the Advice and Consent of the Senate, in: The American Law Register and Review, 42, 3 [First Series] (33,1 [New Series]), 177–89.

Foley, Frank (2007) Between Force and Legitimacy: The Worldview of Robert Cooper. EUI Working Papers RSCAS 2007/09. Fiesole, San Domenico (FI): European University Institute.

Folke Bernadotte Academy (2003) Lessons Learned and Best Practices from the Western Balkans. Conference Proceedings N° 1. Stockholm, 8 and 9 October 2003.

Friedman, Victor J. (2001) The Individual as Agent of Organizational Learning. In: Dierkes, Meinolf, Ariane Berthoin Antal, John Child and Ikujiro Nonaka (Eds.), Handbook of Organizational Learning and Knowledge. Oxford: Oxford University Press, 398–414.

Fröhlich, Manuel (2006) The Peace-Makers – Zur Rolle der Special Representatives des UN-Generalsekretärs. Paper presented at the ÖGPW conference "Politics and Personality" in Vienna from 30 November to 2 December 2006.

Fröhlich, Manuel, Maria Bütof and Jan Lemanski (2006) Mapping UN Presence. A Follow-Up to the

Human Security Report, in: Die Friedens-Warte. Journal of International Peace and Organization, 81, 2, 13–23.

Fullilove, Michael (2005) All the President's Men: The Role of Special Envoys in U. S. Foreign Policy, in: Foreign Affairs, 84, 2 (March/April 2005), 13–18.

Galama, Anneke and Paul van Tongeren (Eds.) (2002) Towards Better Peacebuilding Practice: On Lessons Learned, Evaluation Practices and Aid & Conflict. Utrecht: European Centre for Conflict Prevention.

George, Alexander L. (1969) The 'Operational Code': A Neglected Approach to the Study of Political Leaders and Decision-Making, in: International Studies Quarterly, 13, 2 (June 1969), 190–222.

George, Alexander L. (1979) The Causal Nexus between Cognitive Beliefs and Decision Making Behavior: The 'Operational Code' Belief System. In: Falkowski, Lawrence S. (Ed.), Psychological Models in International Politics. Boulder, CO: Westview Press, 95–124.

George, Alexander L. (1994) The Two Cultures of Academia and Policy-Making: Bridging the Gap, in: Political Psychology, 15, 1, Special Issue: Political Psychology and the Work of Alexander L. George (March 1994), 143–72.

George, Alexander L. and Andrew Bennett (2004) Case Studies and Theory Development in the Social Sciences. Cambridge, MA: MIT Press.

Ginsberg, Roy H. (1999) Conceptualizing the European Union as an International Actor: Narrowing the Theoretical Capability-Expectations Gap, in: Journal of Common Market Studies, 37, 3, 429–54.

Ginsberg, Roy H. (2001) The European Union in International Politics. Baptism by Fire. Oxford: Rowman & Littlefield.

Ginsberg, Roy H. and Michael E. Smith (2007) Understanding the European Union as a Global Political Actor: Theory, Practice, and Impact. In: Meunier, Sophie and Mathleen R. McNamara (Eds.), Making History. European Integration and Institutional Change at Fifty. Oxford: Oxford University Press, 267–82.

Gnesotto, Nicole (Ed.) (2004a) EU Security and Defence Policy. The first five years (1999–2004). Paris: European Union Institute for Security Studies.

Gnesotto, Nicole (2004b) Introduction. In: Gnesotto, Nicole (Ed.), EU Security and Defence Policy. The first five years (1999–2004). Paris: European Union Institute for Security Studies.

Goertz, Gary and Jack S. Levy (2007) Causal explanation, necessary conditions, and case studies. In: Goertz, Gary and Jack S. Levy (Eds.), Explaining War and Peace: Case Studies and Necessary Condition Counterfactuals. New York, NY: Routledge, 9–45.

Goldstein, Julia and Robert O. Keohane (1993) Ideas and Foreign Policy: An Analytical Framework. In: Goldstein, Julia and Robert O. Keohane (Eds.), Ideas and Foreign Policy: Beliefs, Institutions, and Political Change. Ithaca, NY: Cornell University Press, 3–30.

Grevi, Giovanni (2007) Pioneering foreign policy: the EU Special Representatives (Chaillot Paper 106). Paris: European Union Institute for Security Studies.

Grevi, Giovanni and Fraser Cameron (2005) Towards an EU Foreign Service (EPC Issue Paper). Brussels: European Policy Centre.

Grieco, Joseph M. (1988) Anarchy and the Limits of Cooperation: A Realist Critique of the Newest Liberal Internationalism, in: International Organization, 42, 3 (Summer 1988), 485–507.

Gross, Tom (2001) New Prejudices for Old, in: National Review, Washington, D.C., 1 November 2001.

Haas, Ernst B. (1958) The Uniting of Europe: political, social and economical forces, 1950–1957. London: Stevens & Sons Ltd.

Haas, Ernst B. (1968) Beyond the Nation-state: Functionalism and International Organization. Stanford, CA: Stanford University Press.

Haas, Ernst B. (1990) When knowledge is power: three models of change in international organizations. Berkeley, CA: University of California Press.

Haas, Ernst B. (1991) Collective Learning: Some Theoretical Speculations. In: Breslauer, George and Philip E. Tetlock (Eds.), Learning in U.S. and Soviet Foreign Policy. Boulder, CO: Westview Press.

Haas, Ernst B. and Peter M. Haas (1995) Learning to Learn: Improving International Governance, in: Global Governance, 1, 3, 255–84.

Haas, Peter M. (1992) Introduction: epistemic communities and international policy coordination, in: International Organization, 46, 1 (Winter 1992) 'Knowledge, Power, and International Policy Co-ordination', 1–35.

Haine, Jean-Yves (2004) An historical perspective. In: Gnesotto, Nicole (Ed.), EU Security and Defence Policy. The first five years (1999–2004). Paris: European Union Institute for Security Studies, 35–53.

Hall, Peter A. (1993) Policy Paradigms, Social Learning, and the State: The Case of Economic Policymaking in Britain, in: Comparative Politics, 25, 3, 275–96.

Hansen, Annika S. (2006) Against all Odds – The Evolution of Planning for ESDP Operations. Civilian Crisis Management from EUPM onwards. ZIF Study 10/06. Berlin: Zentrum für Internationale Friedenseinsätze.

Hasenclever, Andreas and Peter Mayer (2007) Einleitung: Macht und Ohnmacht internationaler Institutionen. In: Hasenclever, Andreas, Klaus-Dieter Wolf and Michael Zürn (Eds.), Macht und Ohnmacht internationaler Institutionen: Festschrift für Volker Rittberger. Frankfurt/Main: Campus Verlag, 9–37.

Heclo, Hugh (1974) Modern Social Politics in Britain and Sweden. From Relief to Income Maintenance. New Haven, CT: Yale University Press.

Hedberg, Bo L. (1981) How organizations learn and unlearn. In: Nystrom, Paul C. and William H. Starbuck (Eds.), Handbook of Organizational Design: Vol. 1. Adapting Organizations to Their Environments. Oxford: Oxford University Press, 3–27.

Hedberg, Bo L. and Rolf Wolff (2001) Organizing, Learning, and Strategizing: From Construction to Discovery. In: Dierkes, Meinolf, Ariane Berthoin Antal, John Child and Ikujiro Nonaka (Eds.), Handbook of Organizational Learning and Knowledge. Oxford: Oxford University Press, 535–56.

Herrmann, Richard, Thomas Risse and Marilynn Brewer (Eds.) (2004) Transnational Identities: Becoming European in the EU. Boulder, CO: Rowman & Littlefield.

Hill, Christopher and Karen E. Smith (Eds.) (2000) European foreign policy: key documents. London: Routledge.

Hill, Christopher and Michael E. Smith (Eds.) (2005) International Relations and the European Union. Oxford: Oxford University Press.

Hocking, Brian (2004) Diplomacy. In: Carlsnaes, Walter, Helene Sjursen and Brian White (Eds.), Contemporary European Foreign Policy. London: Sage, 91–109.

Hoffmann, Stanley (2000) Towards a Common European Foreign and Security Policy?, in: Journal of Common Market Studies, 38, 2, 189–98.

Hofmann, Stephanie and Christopher Reynolds (2007) Die EU-Nato-Beziehungen. Zeit für »Tauwetter«, in: SWP-Aktuell, 37, Juli 2007.

Holbrooke, Richard (1998) To End a War. New York, NY: Random House.

Hooghe, Liesbet (2005) Several Roads Lead to International Norms, but Few Via International Socialization: A Case Study of the European Commission, in: International Organization, 59, 4 (Autumn 2005), 861–98.

Howkins, Darren G., David A. Lake, Daniel L. Nielson and Michael J. Tierney (2006) Delegation under anarchy: states, international organizations, and principal-agent theory. In: Howkins, Darren G., David A. Lake, Daniel L. Nielson and Michael J. Tierney (Eds.), Delegation and agency in International Organizations. Cambridge: Cambridge University Press, 3–38.

Howorth, Jolyon (2000) Britain, France and the European Defence Initiative, in: Survival, 42, 2 (January 2000), 33–55.

Howorth, Jolyon (2005a) From Security to Defence: the EU as International Actor. In: Hill, Christopher and Michael E. Smith (Eds.), The International Relations of the European Union. Oxford: Oxford University Press, 179–204.

Howorth, Jolyon (2005b) The Euro-Atlantic Security Dilemma: France, Britain, and the ESDP, in: Journal of Transatlantic Studies, 3, 1, 39–54.

Huber, George P. (1991) Organizational Learning: The Contributing Processes and the Literatures, in: Organization Science, 2, 1, 88–115.

Hunter, Robert E. (2002) The European Security and Defense Policy: NATO's Companion or Competitor? Santa Monica, CA: RAND Corporation.

International Crisis Group (2000) Scramble for the Congo: Anatomy of an Ugly War. Africa Report N° 26. Brussels, 20 December 2000.

International Crisis Group (2001) EU Crisis Response Capability: Institutions and Processes for Conflict Prevention and Management. ICG Issues Report N° 2. Brussels, 26 June 2001.

International Crisis Group (2002) EU Crisis Response Capabilities: An Update. ICG Issues Briefing Paper. Brussels, 29 April 2002.

International Crisis Group (2005a) EU Crisis Response Capability Revisited. Crisis Group Europe Report N° 160. Brussels, 17 January 2005.

International Crisis Group (2005b) Uzbekistan: The Andijon Uprising. Update Briefing. Asia Briefing N° 38. Bishkek/Brussels, 25 May 2005.

International Crisis Group (2006a) Central Asia: What Role for the European Union? Asia Report N° 113. Brussels, 10 April 2006.

International Crisis Group (2006b) Conflict Resolution in the South Caucasus: The EU's Role. Europe Report N° 173. Brussels, 20 March 2006.

International Crisis Group (2007) Breaking the Kosovo Stalemate: Europe's Responsibility. Europe Report N° 185. Brussels, 21 August 2007.

International Crisis Group (2008) Kosovo's First Month. Policy Briefing. Europe Briefing N° 47. Pristina/Belgrade/Brussels, 18 March 2008.

Internationale Politik (2008) Balkan-Blues. Europas ungelernte Lektionen. Berlin: Deutsche Gesellschaft für Auswärtige Politik.

Jaanson, Lucie (2008) Learning by doing. EU-Sonderbeauftragte in der Region des Westlichen Balkans. SWP-Diskussionspapier (04/2008). Berlin: Stiftung Wissenschaft und Politik.

Jachtenfuchs, Markus (1996) International policy making as a learning process? The European Union and the greenhouse effect. Aldershot: Ashgate.

Jachtenfuchs, Markus (1999) Ideen und Integration. Verfassungsideen in Deutschland, Frankreich und Großbritannien und die Entwicklung der EU. Habilitationsschrift. Mannheim: Universität Mannheim.

Jackson, Brian A., John C. Baker, Peter Chalk, Kim Cragin, John V. Parachini and Horacio R. Trujillo (2005a) Aptitude for destruction (Vol 1): organizational learning in terrorist groups and its implications for combating terrorism. Santa Monica, CA: RAND Corporation.

Jackson, Brian A., John C. Baker, Peter Chalk, Kim Cragin, John V. Parachini and Horacio R. Trujillo (2005b) Aptitude for destruction (Vol 2): case studies of organizational learning in five terrorist groups. Santa Monica, CA: RAND Corporation.

Jentleson, Bruce W. (2002) The Need for Praxis. Bringing Policy Relevance Back In, in: International Security, 26, 4 (Spring 2002), 169–83.

Jervis, Robert (1976) Perception and Misperception in International Politics. Princeton, NJ: Princeton University Press.

Jones, Bryan D. (1999) Bounded Rationality, in: Annual Review of Political Science, 2, 297–321.

Jopp, Matthias (2006) Europäische Sicherheits- und Verteidigungspolitik. In: Weidenfeld, Werner and Wolfgang Wessels (Eds.), Jahrbuch der Europäischen Integration 2005. Baden-Baden: Nomos, 231–40.

Jorgensen, Knud Erik (1993) EC External Relations as a Theoretical Challenge: Theories, Concepts, and Trends. In: Pfetsch, Frank R. (Ed.), International Relations and Pan-Europe. Theoretical Approaches and Empirical Findings. Münster: LIT Verlag, 211–34.

Juncos, Ana E. and Christopher Reynolds (2007) The Political and Security Committee: Governing in the Shadow, in: European Foreign Affairs Review, 12, 2, 127–47.

Kelley, Judith (2006) New Wine in Old Wineskins: Promoting Political Reforms through the New European Neighbourhood Policy, in: Journal of Common Market Studies, 44, 1 (March 2006), 29–55.

Kennan, George F. (1997) Diplomacy Without Diplomats?, in: Foreign Affairs, 76, 5, 198–213.

Keohane, Robert O. (1984) After Hegemony. Cooperation and Discord in the World Political Economy. Princeton, NJ: Princeton University Press.

Keohane, Robert O. (1989) Neoliberal Institutionalism: A Perspective on World Politics. In: Keohane, Robert O. (Ed.), International Institutions and State Power: Essays in International Relations Theory. Boulder, CO: Westview Press.

Kirkconnell, Laura J. (2002) How the Interagency Process Really Works: U.S. Response to the Albanian Insurgency in Macedonia. Research paper, National War College. Washington, DC.

Klaiber, Klaus-Peter (2007) The European Union in Afghanistan: Lessons Learned, in: European Foreign Affairs Review, 12, 1, 7–11.

Kleveman, Lutz C. (2003) The new great game: blood and oil in Central Asia. New York, NY: Atlantic Monthly Press.

Klimecki, Rüdiger G. and Hermann Lassleben (1998) What causes Organizations to learn? Discussion paper Nr. 22 (Management Forschung und Praxis). Konstanz: Universität Konstanz.

Klimecki, Rüdiger G., Hermann Lassleben and Markus Thomae (1999) Organisationales Lernen. Ein Ansatz zur Integration von Theorie, Empirie und Gestaltung. Discussion Paper Nr. 26 (Management Forschung und Praxis). Konstanz: Universität Konstanz.

Knight, W. Andy (2001) Learning in the United Nations. In: Knight, W. Andy (Ed.), Adapting the United Nations to a postmodern era: Lessons learned. Houndsmill: Palgrave, 28–38.

Knight, W. Andy and Joseph Masciulli (2001) Conclusion: Rethinking instead of Tinkering—an Ethical Consensus and General Lessons. In: Knight, W. Andy (Ed.), Adapting the United Nations to a postmodern era: Lessons learned. Houndsmill: Palgrave, 233–51.

Knill, Christoph and Michael W. Bauer (2007) Theorizing Management Reforms in International Organizations. In: Bauer, Michael W. and Christoph Knill (Eds.), Management Reforms in International Organizations. Baden-Baden: Nomos.

Knopf, Jeffrey W. (2003) The importance of international learning, in: Review of International Studies, 29, 185–207.

Koenig-Archibugi, Mathias (2004a) Explaining government preferences for institutional change in EU foreign and security policy, in: International Organization, 58, 1 (Winter 2004), 137–74.

Koenig-Archibugi, Mathias (2004b) International Governance as New Raison d'État? The Case of the EU Common Foreign and Security Policy, in: European Journal of International Relations, 10, 2, 147–88.

Krahmann, Elke (2003) Multilevel networks in European foreign policy. Aldershot: Ashgate.

Krasner, Stephen D. (1983) Structural causes and regime consequences: regimes as intervening variables. In: Krasner, Stephen D. (Ed.), International Regimes. Ithaca, NY: Cornell University Press, 1–21.

Krasner, Stephen D. (1993) Westphalia and All That. In: Goldstein, Julia and Robert O. Keohane (Eds.),

Ideas and Foreign Policy. Beliefs, Institutions, and Political Change. Ithaca, NY: Cornell University Press, 235–64.

Krause, Alexandra (2003) Die EU als friedenspolitischer Akteur in Afrikas Region der Großen Seen–eine Bilanz. In: Bonn International Center for Conversion [et al.] (Ed.), Friedensgutachten 2003. Münster: LIT Verlag, 166–69.

Krause, Alexandra and Peter Schlotter (2007) Die Kommission als »Politikunternehmer« – Die Europäische Union als außen- und sicherheitspolitischer Akteur im Kongo. In: Jopp, Matthias and Peter Schlotter (Eds.), Kollektive Außenpolitik – Die Europäische Union als internationaler Akteur. Baden-Baden: Nomos, 353–77.

Laffan, Brigid (2004) The European Union and its Institutions as ‚Identity Builders'. In: Herrmann, Richard, Thomas Risse and Marilynn Brewer (Eds.), Transnational Identities. Becoming European in the EU. Boulder, CO: Rowman & Littlefield, 75–96.

LaPalombara, Joseph (2001a) Power and Politics in Organizations: Public and Private Sector Comparisons. In: Dierkes, Meinolf, Ariane Berthoin Antal, John Child and Ikujiro Nonaka (Eds.), Handbook of Organizational Learning and Knowledge. Oxford: Oxford University Press, 557–81.

LaPalombara, Joseph (2001b) The Underestimated Contributions of Political Science to Organizational Learning. In: Dierkes, Meinolf, Ariane Berthoin Antal, John Child and Ikujiro Nonaka (Eds.), Handbook of Organizational Learning and Knowledge. Oxford: Oxford University Press, 137–61.

Lautze, Sue, Bruce D. Jones and Mark Duffield (1998) Strategic Humanitarian Coordination in the Great Lakes, 1996–1997: An Independent Assessment. United Nations, Office for the Coordination of Humanitarian Affairs. New York (March 1998).

Law, David M. (2007) Intergovernmental Organisations and Their Role in Security Sector Reform. In: Law, David M. (Ed.), Intergovernmental Organisations and Security Sector Reform. Zürich: LIT Verlag, 3–23.

Lebow, Richard Ned (2005) Contingency, Catalysts and Nonlinear Change: The Origins of World War I. In: Goertz, Gary and Jack S. Levy (Eds.), Explaining War and Peace: Case Studies and Necessary Condition Counterfactuals. New York, NY: Routledge, 85–112.

Legro, Jeffrey W. (2007) Rethinking the World: Great Power Strategies and International Order. Ithaca, NY: Cornell University Press.

Levitt, Barbara and James G. March (1988) Organizational Learning, in: Annual Review of Sociology, 14, August 1988, 319–38.

Levy, Jack S. (1994) Learning and foreign policy: sweeping a conceptual minefield, in: International Organization, 48, 2 (Spring 1994), 279–312.

Lewis, Jeffrey (2003) Institutional Environments and Everyday EU Decision-Making: Rationalist or Constructivist?, in: Comparative Political Studies, 36, 1/2, 97–124.

Lewis, Jeffrey (2005) The Janus Face of Brussels: Socialization and Everyday Decision Making in the European Union, in: International Organization, 59, 4 (Autumn 2005), 937–71.

Lucarelli, Sonia (2006) Introduction. In: Lucarelli, Sonia and Ian Manners (Eds.), Values and Principles of European Union Foreign Policy. London and New York: Routledge, 1–18.

Lucarelli, Sonia and Ian Manners (2006a) Conclusion: Valuing Principles in European Union Foreign Policy. In: Lucarelli, Sonia and Ian Manners (Eds.), Values and Principles in European Union Foreign Policy. London and New York: Routledge, 201–15.

Lucarelli, Sonia and Ian Manners (Eds.) (2006b) Values and Principles in European Union Foreign Policy. London and New York: Routledge.

Lynch, Dov (2003) The EU: towards a strategy. In: Lynch, Dov (Ed.), The South Caucasus: a challenge for the EU (Chaillot Paper 65). Paris: European Union Institute for Security Studies, 171–91.

Madsen, David W. and Malcolm F. McGregor (1979) Thucydides and Egesta, in: Phoenix, 33, 3 (Autumn 1979), 233–38.

Mahncke, Dieter, Alicia Ambos and Christopher Reynolds (2004) European foreign policy: from rhetoric to reality? Brussels: PIE–Peter Lang.

Malek, Tanja, Martin Koch and Alexandra Lindenthal (2002) Organizational responses to new environmental demands–Thinking about organizational learning. Paper presented for the Annual Conference of the International Studies Association, New Orleans, 24–27 March 2002, Panel on "IOs as Learning Organizations? IR Meets Organizational Sociology". New Orleans.

Manners, Ian (2002) Normative Power Europe: A Contradiction in Terms?, in: Journal of Common Market Studies, 40, 2, 235–58.

Manners, Ian and Richard G. Whitman (1998) Towards Identifying the International Identity of the European Union: A Framework for Analysis of the EU's Network of Relations, in: Journal of European Integration, 21, 231–49.

March, James G. and Johan P. Olsen (1976) Organizational learning and the ambiguity of the past. In: March, James G. and Johan P. Olsen (Eds.), Ambiguity and Choice in Organizations. Bergen: Universitetsforlaget, 54–68.

March, James G. and Johan P. Olsen (1998) The Institutional Dynamics of International Political Orders, in: International Organization, 52, 4 (Autumn 1998), 943–69.

Martens, Kerstin and Michael Brüggemann (2006) Kein Experte ist wie der andere. Vom Umgang mit Missionaren und Geschichtenerzählern (TranState Working Papers N° 39). Bremen: Sfb 597 »Staatlichkeit im Wandel«.

Martin, Lisa L. and Beth A. Simmons (2001) International Institutions: An International Organization Reader. Cambridge, MA: MIT Press.

Mattingly, Garrett (1937) The First Resident Embassies: Mediaeval Italian Origins of Modern Diplomacy, in: Speculum, 12, 4 (October 1937), 423–39.

Mattingly, Garrett (1955) Renaissance diplomacy. London: Cape.

Matveeva, Anna (2006) EU stakes in Central Asia (Chaillot Paper 91). Paris: European Union Institute for Security Studies.

Mayer, Sebastian (2004) Die EU als weltpolitischer Akteur. Anmerkungen zum Forschungsstand, in: WeltTrends, 12, 42 (Spring 2004), 65–77.

McLoughlin, Maria (1998) The role of a Special Envoy in the development of the CFSP: case of the Special Envoy for the Great Lakes region. Brussels: Working Document of the European Commission.

Mearsheimer, John (1995) The False Promise of Institutions, in: International Security, 19, 3, 5–49.

Metcalfe, Les (2005) Orientations to integration: the cultural dimension of EU institutional reform. In: Gravier, Magalie and Vassiliki Triga (Eds.), Organizational Culture in the institutions of the European Union (EUI working paper N° 2005/4). Fiesole, San Domenico (FI): European University Institute, 21–40.

Miner, Anne and Stephen Mezias (1996) Ugly duckling no more: Pasts and futures of organizational learning research, in: Organization Science, 7, 1, 88–99.

Missiroli, Antonio (2003) €uros for ESDP: financing EU operations (Occasional Paper 45). Paris: European Union Institute for Security Studies.

Missiroli, Antonio (2004) ESDP–How it works. In: Gnesotto, Nicole (Ed.), EU Security and Defence Policy. The first five years (1999–2004). Paris: European Union Institute for Security Studies, 55–72.

Moller, Bjorn (2002) Europe and the crises in the Great Lakes region, in: Strategic Review for Southern Africa (Pretoria), 24, 1 (June 2002), 27–62.

Moravcsik, Andrew (1993) Preferences and Power in the European Community: A Liberal Intergovernmentalist Approach, in: Journal of Common Market Studies, 31, 4, 473–524.

Moravcsik, Andrew (2002) In Defense of the 'Democratic Deficit': Reassessing Legitimacy in the European Union, in: Journal of Common Market Studies, 40, 4, 603–24.

Neugart, Felix (2001) Nahost- und Mittelmeerpolitik. In: Weidenfeld, Werner and Wolfgang Wessels (Eds.), Jahrbuch der Europäischen Integration 2000/2001. Bonn: Europa Union Verlag, 265–68.

Neugart, Felix (2003) Nahost- und Mittelmeerpolitik. In: Weidenfeld, Werner and Wolfgang Wessels (Eds.), Jahrbuch der Europäischen Integration 2002/2003. Bonn: Europa Union Verlag, 281–86.

Neugart, Felix (2006) Nahost- und Mittelmeerpolitik. In: Weidenfeld, Werner and Wolfgang Wessels (Eds.), Jahrbuch der Europäischen Integration 2006. Baden-Baden: Nomos, 279–82.

Nonneman, Gerd (2003) A European view of the US role in the Israeli-Palestinian conflict. In: Ortega, Martin (Ed.), The European Union and the Crisis in the Middle East (Chaillot Paper 62). Paris: European Union Institute for Security Studies, 33–46.

Nugent, Neill and Sabine Saurugger (2002) Organizational structuring: the case of the European Commission and its external policy responsibilities, in: Journal of European Public Policy, 9, 3 (June 2002), 345–64.

Nuttall, Simon J. (1992) European Political Cooperation. Oxford: Clarendon Press.

Nuttall, Simon J. (2000) European Foreign Policy. Oxford: Oxford University Press.

Nye, Joseph S. (1987) Nuclear learning and U.S.-Soviet security regimes, in: International Organization, 41, 3 (Summer 1987), 371–402.

Nye, Joseph S. (1990) Soft power, in: Foreign Policy, 80, Fall 1990, 153–71.

Nye, Joseph S. (2006) Soft Power and Smart Power, in: Internationale Politik–Transatlantic Edition, 7, 3 (Summer 2006), 10–13.

Olsen, Johan P. (1998) Political Science and Organization Theory. Parallel Agendas but Mutual Disregard. In: Czada, Roland, Adrienne Héritier and Hans Keman (Eds.), Institutions and Political Choice. On the Limits of Rationality. Amsterdam: VU University Press, 87–108.

Orbie, Jan (2006) Civilian Power Europe: Review of the Original and Current Debates, in: Cooperation and Conflict, 41, 1, 123–28.

Ortega, Martin (2003) Conclusion: peace lies in their hands. In: Ortega, Martin (Ed.), The European Union and the Crisis in the Middle East (Chaillot Paper 62). Paris: European Union Institute for Security Studies, 52–63.

Ortega, Martin (2004a) Conclusion: 'Region-building' in Europe and across the world. In: Ortega, Martin (Ed.), Global views on the European Union (Chaillot Paper 72). Paris: European Union Institute for Security Studies, 117–28.

Ortega, Martin (Ed.) (2004b) Global views on the European Union (Chaillot Paper 72). Paris: European Union Institute for Security Studies.

Ortega, Martin (2007) Building the future. The EU's contribution to global governance (Chaillot Paper 100). Paris: European Union Institute for Security Studies.

Ould-Abdallah, Ahmedou (2000) Burundi on the Brink (1993–95): A UN Special Envoy Reflects on Preventive Diplomacy. Washington, DC: Institute for Peace.

Parsons, Craig (2002) Showing Ideas as Causes: The Origins of the European Union, in: International Organization, 56, 1 (Winter 2002), 47–84.

Patokallio, Pasi (2004) European Union Policy on the Israeli-Palestinian Conflict: From Payer to Player? Cambridge, MA: Weatherhead Center for International Affairs, Harvard University.

Patton, Michael Quinn (2002) Qualitative Research and Evaluation Methods. Thousand Oaks, CA: Sage Publications.

Peck, Connie (2004) Special Representatives of the Secretary General. In: Malone, David M. (Ed.), The UN Security Council. From the Cold War to the 21st Century. Boulder, CO: Lynne Rienner, 325–39.

Peters, Joel (1998) The Arab-Israeli Multilateral Peace Talks and the Barcelona Process: Competition or Convergence?, in: The International Spectator, 33, 4 (October-December 1998), 63–76.

Petrov, Petar and Hylke Dijkstra (2007) Towards Maturity: The Recent Institutional Reform of the ESDP, in: CFSP Forum, 5, 5 (September 2007), 6–9.

Piana, Claire (2002) The EU's Decision-Making Process in the Common Foreign and Security Policy: The Case of the Former Yugoslav Republic of Macedonia, in: European Foreign Affairs Review, 7, 2, 209– 26.

Pierson, Paul (2000) Increasing Returns, Path Dependence, and the Study of Politics, in: The American Political Science Review, 94, 2, 251–67.

Pierson, Paul (2004) Politics in Time: history, institutions, and social analysis. Princeton, NJ: Princeton University Press.

PIN, Peace Implementation Network (1999) Command from the Saddle: Managing United Nations Peace-Building Missions (Fafo-report 266). Oslo: Fafo Institute for Applied Social Science.

Plischke, Elmer (1986) Diplomat in Chief. The President at the Summit. New York, NY: Praeger.

Pollack, Mark A. (2006) Delegation and discretion in the European Union. In: Howkins, Darren G., David A. Lake, Daniel L. Nielson and Michael J. Tierney (Eds.), Delegation and agency in International Organizations. Cambridge: Cambridge University Press, 165–96.

Portela, Clara (2007) Community Policies with a Security Agenda: The Worldview of Benita Ferrero-Waldner. EUI Working Papers RSCAS 2007/10. Fiesole, San Domenico (FI): European University Institute.

Puchala, Donald J. (1993) The Secretary-General and his Special Representatives. In: Gordenker, Leon and Benjamin Rivlin (Eds.), The Challenging Role of the UN Secretary-General. Making "The Most Impossible Job in the World" Possible. Westport, CT: Praeger, 81–97.

Putnam, Robert (1988) Diplomacy and Domestic Politics: The Logic of Two-Level Games, in: International Organization, 42, 3 (Summer 1988), 427–60.

Queller, Donald E. (1960) Thirteenth-Century Diplomatic Envoys: Nuncii and Procuratores, in: Speculum, 35, 2 (April 1960), 196–213.

Rashid, Ahmed (1997) The new great game: Battle for Central Asia's oil, in: Far Eastern Economic Review (Hongkong), 160, 15 (10 April 1997), 22–33.

Regelsberger, Elfriede (1996) Gemeinsame Außen- und Sicherheitspolitik. In: Weidenfeld, Werner and Wolfgang Wessels (Eds.), Jahrbuch der Europäischen Integration 1995/96. Bonn: Europa Union Verlag, 211–20.

Regelsberger, Elfriede (1997) Gemeinsame Außen- und Sicherheitspolitik. In: Weidenfeld, Werner and Wolfgang Wessels (Eds.), Jahrbuch der Europäischen Integration 1996/97. Bonn: Europa Union Verlag, 215–24.

Regelsberger, Elfriede (1999) Gemeinsame Außen- und Sicherheitspolitik. In: Weidenfeld, Werner and Wolfgang Wessels (Eds.), Jahrbuch der Europäischen Integration 1998/99. Bonn: Europa Union Verlag, 243–50.

Regelsberger, Elfriede (2000) Gemeinsame Außen- und Sicherheitspolitik. In: Weidenfeld, Werner and Wolfgang Wessels (Eds.), Jahrbuch der Europäischen Integration 1999/2000. Bonn: Europa Union Verlag, 233–42.

Regelsberger, Elfriede (2001) Gemeinsame Außen- und Sicherheitspolitik. In: Weidenfeld, Werner and Wolfgang Wessels (Eds.), Jahrbuch der Europäischen Integration 2000/2001. Bonn: Europa Union Verlag, 243–52.

Regelsberger, Elfriede (2002) Gemeinsame Außen- und Sicherheitspolitik. In: Weidenfeld, Werner and Wolfgang Wessels (Eds.), Jahrbuch der Europäischen Integration 2001/2002. Bonn: Europa Union Verlag, 233–42.

Regelsberger, Elfriede (2006) Gemeinsame Außen- und Sicherheitspolitik. In: Weidenfeld, Werner and Wolfgang Wessels (Eds.), Jahrbuch der Europäischen Integration 2005. Baden-Baden: Nomos, 241–48.

Reichwein, Alexander and Peter Schlotter (2007) Auf dem Weg zu einem kollektiven Akteur? Die EU-Politik gegenüber Mazedonien. In: Jopp, Matthias and Peter Schlotter (Eds.), Kollektive Außenpolitik – Die Europäische Union als internationaler Akteur. Baden-Baden: Nomos, 239–77.

Reynolds, Christopher (2005) Understanding the development of the ESDP: Perspectives and insights from historical institutionalism and theories of learning. In: Observatori de Política Exterior Europea, Working Paper n. 64 (June 2005). Barcelona: Universitat Autónoma de Barcelona

Rhodes, Carolyn (1998) The European Union and the World Community. Boulder, CO: Lynne Rienner.

Risse, Thomas (2004) European Institutions and Identity Change: What Have We Learned? In: Herrmann, Richard, Thomas Risse and Marilynn Brewer (Eds.), Transnational Identities: Becoming European in the EU. Boulder, CO: Rowman & Littlefield, 247–71.

Risse, Thomas (2005) Neo-Functionalism, European Identity, and the Puzzles of European Integration, in: Journal of European Public Policy, 12, 2 (April 2005), 291–309.

Rohloff, Christoph (1999) Krieg im Namen der Menschenrechte? Eine Bestandsaufnahme nach der Intervention im Kosovo. In: Rohloff, Christoph (Ed.), Krieg im Kosovo – Was nun? Friedens- und Sicherheitspolitik nach der NATO-Intervention. INEF-Report 38/1999. Duisburg: Institut für Entwicklung und Frieden, 1–45.

Rose, Richard (1991) What Is Lesson-Drawing?, in: Journal of Public Policy, 11, 1, 3–30.

Rose, Richard (1993) Lesson-Drawing in Public Policy: A Guide to Learning Across Time and Space. Chatham, NJ: Chatham House.

Rothman, Jay and Victor J. Friedman (2001) Identity, Conflict, and Organizational Learning. In: Dierkes, Meinolf, Ariane Berthoin Antal, John Child and Ikujiro Nonaka (Eds.), Handbook of Organizational Learning and Knowledge. Oxford: Oxford University Press, 582–97.

Sabatier, Paul A. and Hank C. Jenkins-Smith (1993) Policy Change and Learning: An Advocacy Coalition Approach. Boulder, CO: Westview Press.

Sandschneider, Eberhard (1996a) Die Europäische Union und die Transformation Mittel- und Osteuropas: Zum Problem exogener Stabilisierungsstrategien in Transformationsprozessen, in: Zeitschrift für Politikwissenschaft (Baden-Baden), 6, 1, 27–49.

Sandschneider, Eberhard (1996b) Systemtheoretische Perspektiven politikwissenschaftlicher Transformationsforschung. In: Merkel, Wolfgang, Eberhard Sandschneider and Dieter Segert (Eds.), Systemwechsel 2: Die Institutionalisierung der Demokratie. Opladen: Leske + Budrich.

Sandschneider, Eberhard (2005) Neue Welt, altes Denken, in: Internationale Politik, 60, 1 (January 2005), 5–14.

Schimmelfennig, Frank (2005) Strategic Calculation and International Socialization: Membership Incentives, Party Constellations, and Sustained Compliance in Central and Eastern Europe, in: International Organization, 59, 4 (Autumn 2005), 827–60.

Schmidt, Siegmar (1998) Die Afrikapolitik der Europäischen Union. In: Weidenfeld, Werner and Wolfgang Wessels (Eds.), Jahrbuch der Europäischen Integration 1997/98. Bonn: Europa Union Verlag, 265–72.

Schmitter, Philippe C. (1969) Three Neo-Functional Hypotheses about International Integration, in: International Organization, 23, 1 (Winter 1969), 161–66.

Schmitter, Philippe C. (2000) How to Democratize the European Union... and Why Bother? Lanham, MD: Rowman & Littlefield.

Schmitter, Philippe C. (2004) Neo-Neofunctionalism: Déjà vu, all over again? In: Wiener, Antje and Thomas Diez (Eds.), European Integration Theory. Oxford: Oxford University Press, 45–74.

Schneckener, Ulrich (2001) EU Crisis Management in Macedonia, in: Transatlantic Internationale Politik, 2, 3 (Autumn 2001), 90–94.

Schoen, Harald (2008) Identity, Instrumental Self-Interest and Institutional Evaluations. Explaining Public Opinion on Common European Policies in Foreign Affairs and Defence, in: European Union Politics, 9, 1, 5–29.

Schulze, Kirsten E. (2007) Mission Not So Impossible: The Aceh Monitoring Mission and Lessons learned for the EU. International Policy Analysis, July 2007. Berlin: Friedrich Ebert Stiftung.

Schwegmann, Christoph (2000) The Contact Group and its impact on the European institutional structure (Occasional Papers 16). Paris: Institute for Security Studies of the Western European Union.

Sedelmeier, Ulrich (2003) EU Enlargement, Identity and the Analysis of European Foreign Policy: Identity Formation through Policy Practice. EUI Working Paper RSC N° 2003/13. Fiesole, San Domenico (FI): European University Institute.

Senge, Peter M. (1990) The Fifth Discipline. The art and practice of the learning organization. London: Random House.

Sharkansky, Ira (1981) Intergovernmental Relations. In: Nystrom, Paul C. and William H. Starbuck (Eds.), Handbook of Organizational Design: Vol. 1. Adapting Organizations to Their Environments. Oxford: Oxford University Press, 456–70.

Shearer, David (1999) Africa's Great War, in: Survival, 41, 2 (Summer 1999), 89–106.

Sherriff, Andrew (2007) Security Sector Reform and EU Norm Implementation. In: Law, David M. (Ed.), Intergovernmental Organisations and Security Sector Reform. Münster: LIT Verlag, 85–102.

Simmons, Beth A. and Lisa L. Martin (2002) International Organisations and Institutions. In: Carlsnaes, Walter, Thomas Risse and Beth A. Simmons (Eds.), Handbook of International Relations. London: Sage, 192–211.

Simon, Herbert A. (1991) Bounded rationality and organisational learning, in: Organization Science, 2, 1, 125–34.

Sjursen, Helene (2006) What kind of power?, in: Journal of European Public Policy, 13, 2 (Special Issue March 2006), 169–81.

Smith, Hazel (2002) European Union Foreign Policy. What it is and what it does. Cambridge: Pluto Press.

Smith, Karen E. (2003) European Foreign Policy in a Changing World. Oxford: Polity.

Smith, Michael E. (2004) Europe's Foreign and Security Policy. The Institutionalization of Cooperation. Cambridge: Cambridge University Press.

Soetendorp, Ben (2002) The EU's Involvement in the Israeli-Palestinian Peace Process: The Building of a Visible International Identity, in: European Foreign Affairs Review, 7, 3, 283–95.

Spillmann, Kurt R. and Joachim Krause (Eds.) (2000) Kosovo: Lessons learned for international cooperative security. Bern: Peter Lang.

Starbuck, William H. and Bo L. Hedberg (2001) How Organizations Learn from Success and Failure. In: Dierkes, Meinolf, Ariane Berthoin Antal, John Child and Ikujiro Nonaka (Eds.), Handbook of Organizational Learning and Knowledge. Oxford: Oxford University Press, 327–50.

Stefanova, Radoslava (2003) New Security Challenges in the Balkans, in: Security Dialogue, 34, 2, 169–82.

Stein, Janice Gross (1994) Political Learning by Doing: Gorbachev as Uncommitted Thinker and Motivated Learner, in: International Organization, 48, 2 (Spring 1994), 155–84.

Steinmeier, Frank-Walter (2006) Politik als »lernendes System«. Reflexionen über Staatlichkeit in Zeiten der Globalisierung, in: Internationale Politik, 61, 8 (August 2006), 100–04.

Stern, Eric (1997) Crisis and Learning: A Conceptual Balance Sheet, in: Journal of Contingencies and Crisis Management, 5, 2, 69–86.

Stone, Diane (2001) Learning Lessons, Policy Transfer and the International Diffusion of Policy Ideas. CSGR Working Paper N° 69/01 (April 2001). Warwick: University of Warwick.

Suhrke, Astri (2000) From One Crisis to Another: Organisational Learning in UNHCR In: Carlsson, Jerker and Lennart Wohlgemuth (Eds.), Learning in Development Cooperation. Stockholm: Almqvist and Wiksell International, 69–87.

Tansey, Oisín (2007) Process Tracing and Elite Interviewing: A Case for Non-probability Sampling, in: PS: Political Science & Politics, 40, 4 (October 2007), 765–72.

Tetlock, Philip E. (1991) Learning in U.S. and Soviet Foreign Policy: In Search of an Elusive Concept. In: Breslauer, George and Philip E. Tetlock (Eds.), Learning in U.S. and Soviet foreign policy. Boulder, CO: Westview Press, 20–61.

Thelen, Kathleen (1999) Historical Institutionalism in Comparative Politics, in: Annual Review of Political Science, 2, 369–404.

Thorpe, Francis N. (1894) Is the President of the United States Vested with Authority under the Constitution to Appoint a Special Diplomatic Agent with Paramount Power without the Advice and Consent of the Senate?, in: The American Law Register and Review, 42, 4 [First Series] (33,1 [New Series]), 257–64.

Thucydides (1978) The History of the Peloponnesian War. Translated by Richard Livingstone. Oxford: Oxford University Press.

Tocci, Nathalie (2005) The Widening Gap between Rhetoric and Reality in EU Policy towards the Israeli-Palestinian Conflict (CEPS Working Document N° 217). Brussels: Centre for European Policy Studies.

Tocci, Nathalie (2006) Has the EU Promoted Democracy in Palestine…and Does it Still?, in: CFSP Forum, 4, 2 (March 2006), 7–10.

Tonra, Ben (2001) The Europeanisation of National Foreign Policy. Dutch, Danish and Irish Foreign Policy in the European Union. Aldershot: Ashgate.

Tonra, Ben (2003) Constructing the Common Foreign and Security Policy: The Utility of a Cognitive Approach, in: Journal of Common Market Studies, 41, 4, 731–56.

Tonra, Ben and Thomas Christiansen (Eds.) (2004) Rethinking European Union foreign policy. Manchester: Manchester University Press.

Triscritti, Fiorella (2007) Free Trade and New Economic Powers: The Worldview of Peter Mandelson. EUI Working Papers RSCAS 2007/11. Fiesole, San Domenico (FI): European University Institute.

Van Evera, Stephen (1997) Guide to Methods for Students of Political Science. Ithaca, NY: Cornell University Press.

Vance, Cyrus R. and David A. Hamburger (1997) Pathfinders for Peace. A Report to the UN Secretary-General on the Role of Special Representatives and Personal Envoys. New York, NY: Carnegie Commission on Preventing Deadly Conflict.

Vennesson, Pascal (2007) European Worldviews: Ideas and the European Union in World Politics. EUI Working Papers RSCAS 2007/07. Fiesole, San Domenico (FI): European University Institute.

Wallace, William (2005) Foreign and Security Policy: The Painful Path from Shadow to Substance. In: Wallace, Helen, William Wallace and Mark A. Pollack (Eds.), Policy-Making in the European Union. Oxford: Oxford University Press, 429–56.

Waltz, Kenneth N. (1979) Theory of International Politics. Reading, MA: Addison-Wesley.

Waters, Maurice (1956) Special Diplomatic Agents of the President, in: Annals of the American Academy of Political and Social Science, 307 (The Office of the American Presidency, September 1956), 124–33.

Weick, Karl E. and Frances Westley (1996) Organizational learning: Affirming an oxymoron. In: Clegg, Stewart R., Cynthia Hardy and Walter R. Nord (Eds.), Handbook of Organization Studies. London: Sage, 440–58.

Weidenfeld, Werner (2006) The EU's role in the world: efficiency and relevance in times of crisis. In: Zaborowski, Marcin (Ed.), Friends again? EU-US relations after the crisis. Paris: European Union Institute for Security Studies, 111–22.

Wendt, Alexander E. (1987) The Agent-Structure Problem in International Relations Theory, in: International Organization, 41, 3 (Summer 1987), 335–70.

White, Brian (2001) Understanding European foreign policy. Houndmills: Palgrave.

Whitman, Richard G. (1998) From Civilian Power to Superpower? The International Identity of The European Union. London: Macmillan.

Wiethoff, William E. (1981) A Machiavellian paradigm for diplomatic communication, in: Journal of Politics, 43, 4 (November 1981), 1090–104.

Wittgenstein, Ludwig (1958) Philosophical Investigations. Oxford: Blackwell.

Woods, Ngaire (2006) The Globalizers: The IMF, the World Bank and their Borrowers. Ithaca, NY: Cornell University Press.

Wright, Nancy E. (2003) Organizational Learning Curves, Angles, and Lines: Recognizing Diverse Types of Learning in the United Nations' Humanitarian Operations, in: Journal of Humanitarian Assistance (online), October 2003.

Wriston, Henry M. (1956) The Foreign Service and Representation Abroad, in: Proceedings of the American Philosophical Society, 100, 2, 105–13.

Wriston, Henry M. (1960) The Special Envoy, in: Foreign Affairs. An American Quarterly Review, 38, 2 (January 1960), 219–37.

Yee, Albert S. (1996) The Causal Effects of Ideas on Policies, in: International Organization, 50, 1 (Winter 1996), 69–108.

Yesson, Erik (2003) Sending Credible Signals: NATO's Role in Stabilizing Balkan Conflicts. NATO-EAPC Fellowship Final Report. Brussels, June 2003.

Zielonka, Jan (Ed.) (1998) Paradoxes of European foreign policy. The Hague: Kluwer Law International.

Zürn, Michael and Jeffrey T. Checkel (2005) Getting Socialized to Build Bridges: Constructivism and Rationalism, Europe and the Nation-State, in: International Organization, 59, 4 (Autumn 2005), 1045–79.